KAWAII DINOSAURS

LEARN TO DRAW 85 ADORABLE DINOS IN ALL THEIR GLORY

OLIVE YONG, CREATOR OF BICHI MAO

ROCK POINT

First published in 2026 by Rock Point,
an imprint of The Quarto Group,
135 West 36th Street, 13th Floor,
New York, NY 10018, USA
(212) 779-4972 www.Quarto.com

EEA Representation, WTS Tax d.o.o.,
Žanova ulica 3, 4000 Kranj, Slovenia.
www.wts-tax.si

10 9 8 7 6 5 4 3 2 1

ISBN: 978-1-57715-919-3

Digital edition published in 2026
eISBN: 978-1-57715-920-9

Library of Congress Cataloging-in-Publication Data

Names: Yong, Olive author
Title: Kawaii dinosaurs : learn to draw 85 adorable dinos in all their glory / Olive Yong, creator of Bichi Mao.
Description: New York, NY, USA : Rock Point, an imprint of The Quarto Group, 2026. | Summary: "Kawaii Dinosaurs is your easy-to-follow, step-by-step guide to drawing 85 adorable dinosaurs"-- Provided by publisher.
Identifiers: LCCN 2026000895 (print) | LCCN 2026000896 (ebook) | ISBN 9781577159193 paperback | ISBN 9781577159209 ebook
Subjects: LCSH: Dinosaurs in art--Juvenile literature | Drawing--Technique--Juvenile literature
Classification: LCC NC780.5 .Y66 2026 (print) | LCC NC780.5 (ebook)
LC record available at https://lccn.loc.gov/2026000895
LC ebook record available at https://lccn.loc.gov/2026000896

Group Publisher: Rage Kindelsperger
Editorial Director: Erin Canning
Creative Director: Laura Drew
Managing Editor: Cara Donaldson
Editor: Katelynn Abraham
Cover Design: Kim Winscher
Interior Design: Kim Winscher and Rebecca Pagel
Assistant Illustrators: Zee Qing and Wee Lim

Printed in Huizhou City, Guangdong, China TT052026

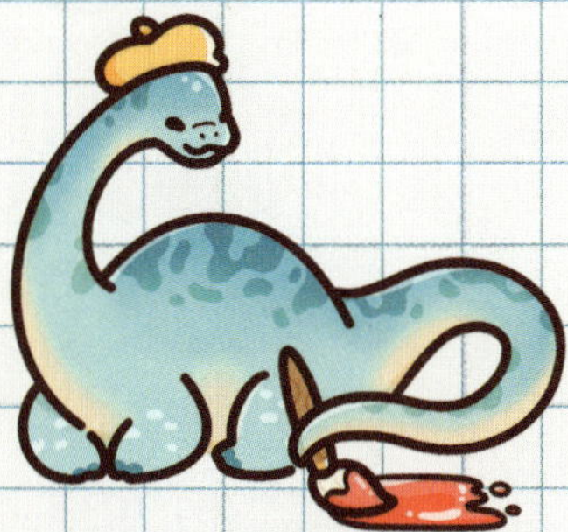

I am deeply grateful to Quarto Publishing Group for trusting me once again with this meaningful opportunity. Their continuous support has played a huge part in shaping this book.

This work is dedicated to my Niko Studio team whose commitment allows me to focus wholeheartedly on creating.

To my family and friends, thank you for believing in my passion and cheering me on through every step.

A special thanks to my editor, Erin, and to Katey, for your guidance, clarity, and kindness throughout this process. You've helped me grow with every book, and I'm truly thankful.

To all Bichi Mao readers around the world, your support and sharing breathe life into my work and inspire me to keep creating.

This year, I've learned the value of this principle: "Just do your best, time will do the rest." As W. Clement Stone once said, "Aim for the moon. If you miss, you may hit a star."

CONTENTS

HI!

My name is Olive Yong, and I'm a self-taught artist from Malaysia. Drawing has always been a passion of mine, but it was in June 2019 that I first ventured into digital art. I began sharing my creations across social media platforms under the brand name Bichi Mao, never expecting that humble start to lead to such incredible opportunities. It's been a whirlwind journey, and I'm truly grateful for the blessings that have come my way. Holding my eighth published book now feels like a dream come true.

My publications with Quarto Publishing Group began with *Kawaii Kitties: Learn How to Draw 75 Cats in All Their Glory*. I hope that this book inspires you to not only learn how to draw these adorable dinosaurs, but also to create your own characters, whether they are reptiles or something entirely different.

What Is Kawaii?

You might have heard the word. You have probably seen the hashtag. You definitely know the style. But what, exactly, does Kawaii mean?

Kawaii is a Japanese concept or idea, dating back to the 1970s, that translates closely to "cuteness" in English. In Japan, the usage of the word is quite broad and can be used to describe anything cute, from clothing and accessories to handwriting and art. So, if you are a fan of emoji art or the style of beloved characters such as Hello Kitty, Pokémon, or Pusheen the Cat, then you already know and love the kawaii style of art!

While there are many interpretations as to what constitutes the kawaii art aesthetic, most people can agree that kawaii art is usually composed of very simple black outlines, pastel colors, and characters or objects with a rounded, youthful appearance. Facial expressions in kawaii art are minimal and characters are frequently drawn with oversized hands and smaller bodies.

How to Use This Book

After some helpful information here in the beginning of the book about tools and techniques, there are eighty-five step-by-step tutorials divided into five sections: Mighty Friends, Moods, Daily Activities, Baby Dinos, and Dino Dress-Up. At the end of the book are coloring pages with lots of kawaii dinos for you to color and decorate.

Tools

Feel free to draw your kawaii dinosaurs with what you have available to you, but here are some suggestions of materials I like to use.

TRADITIONAL TOOLS

If you're drawing your dinos with traditional tools, use a pencil, such as a 2B/HB (a.k.a. a #2 pencil), for the initial sketch, and then use a black ink pen to finish your drawing once your sketch is final. You may want to invest in a high-quality eraser to easily get rid of any unwanted lines and marks. A ruler also may be helpful for when you're working with straight lines.

For coloring your dinosaurs, I recommend using colored pencils, crayons, or watercolors. Have fun experimenting with what works best for you. The coloring pages on page 142 are a great place to practice!

DIGITAL TOOLS

There are a number of software programs and apps for drawing digitally, whether you prefer drawing on a desktop, laptop, or iPad. I prefer using Procreate on an iPad, but see what works best for your artwork, equipment, and budget.

Regarding the brushes included with these programs, I like the Monoline brush in Procreate, but again, have fun experimenting.

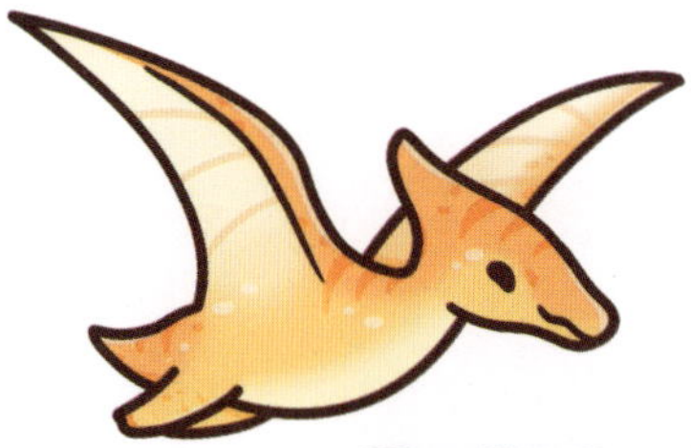

FUN FACT!

Plesiosaurs (marine reptiles), including *Elasmosaurus* and *Kronosaurus*, and pterosaurs (flying reptiles), including *Pterodactylus* and *Quetzalcoatlus*, are both prehistoric reptiles, but they are distinct from dinosaurs. Since they're not dinosaurs, they won't be featured in this book.

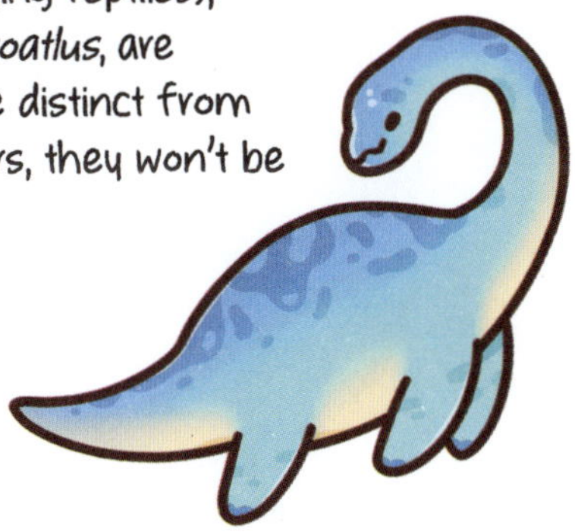

DRAWING YOUR DINO WORLD

I like to use a lot of curved lines and patterns in my drawings. That's what makes them cute and special! Here are some of the basic shapes you will see throughout the tutorials in this book.

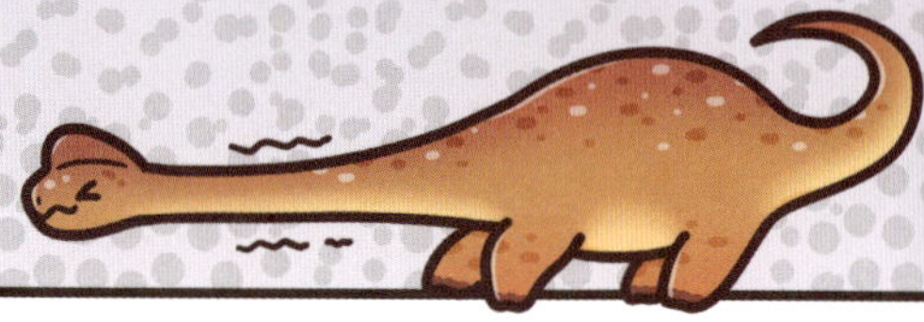

Leg Shapes

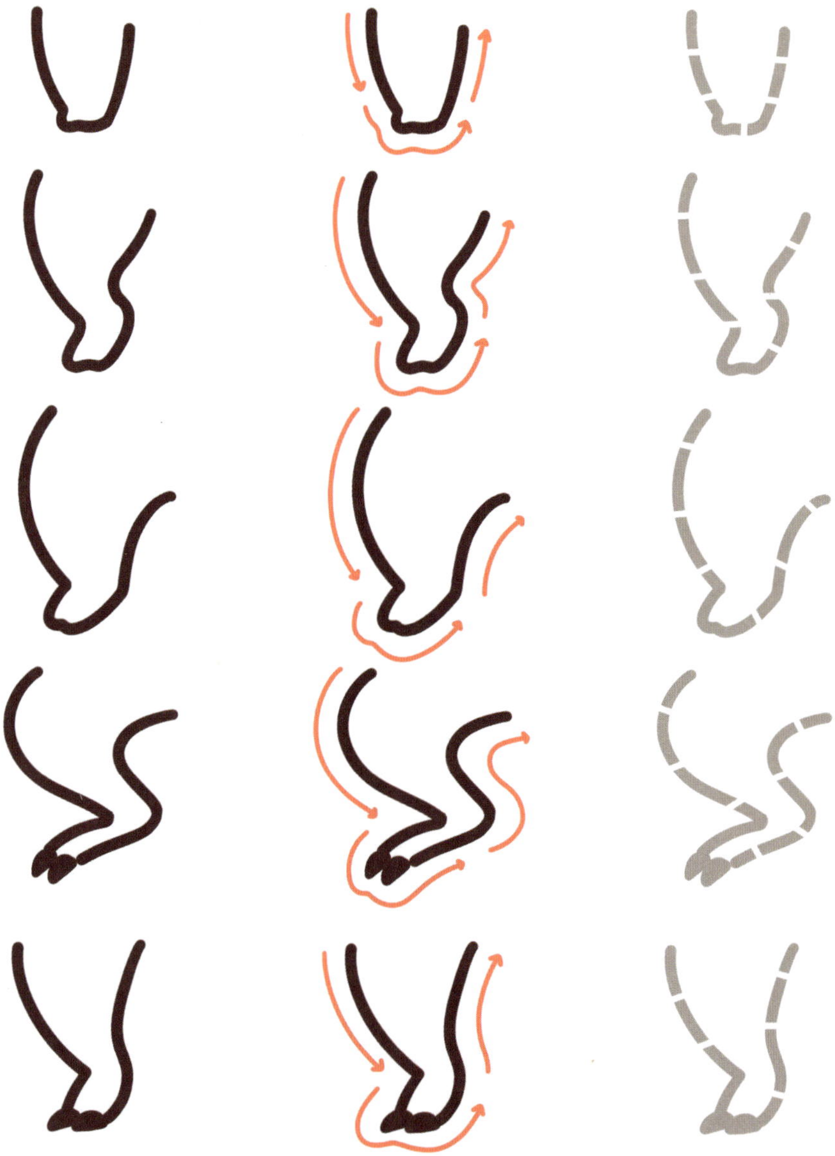

Try it out!

Try it out!

Try it out!

Try it out!

Try it out!

Arm Shapes

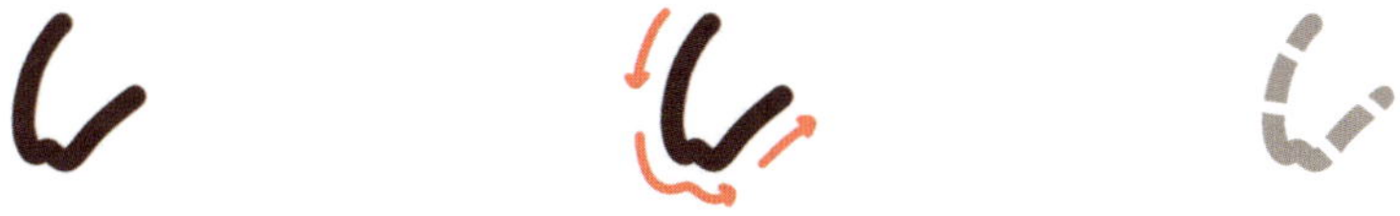

Try it out!

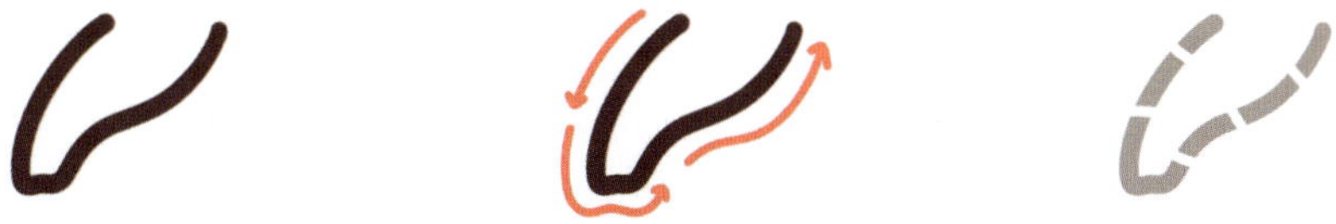

Try it out!

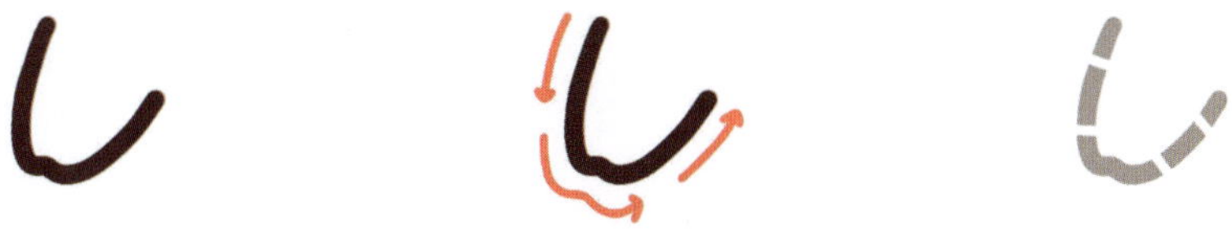

Try it out!

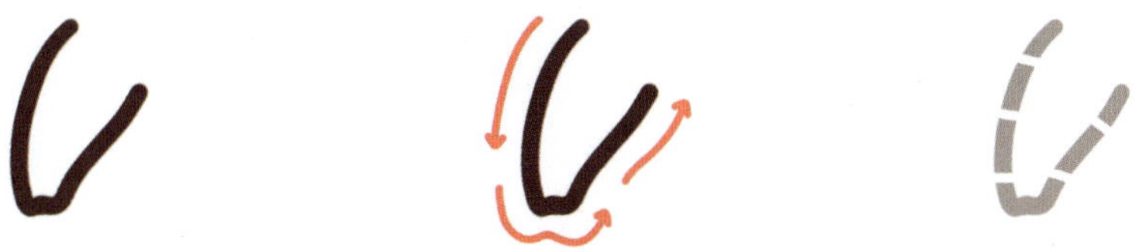

Try it out!

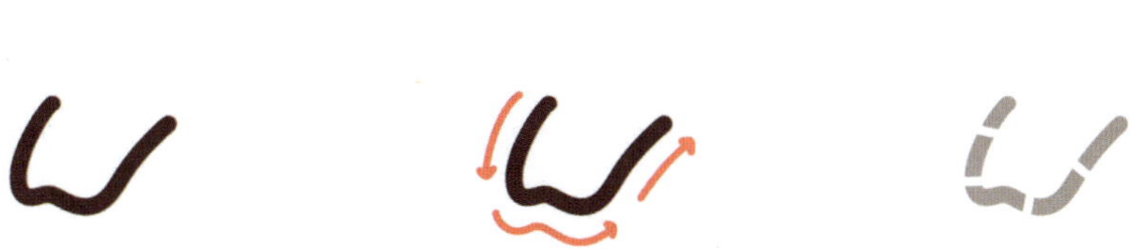

Try it out!

DRAWING YOUR DINO WORLD (CONTINUED)

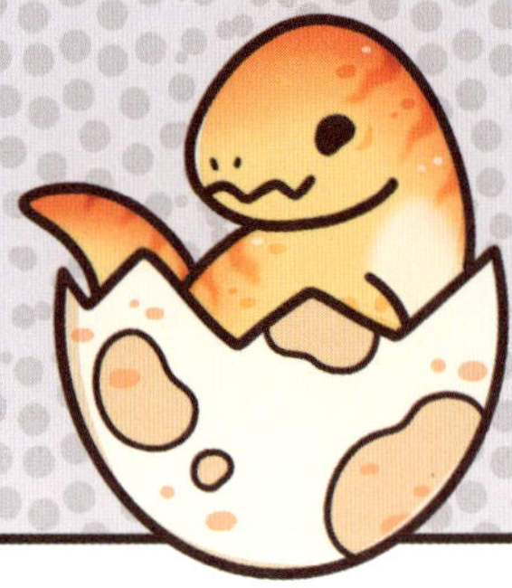

Patterns

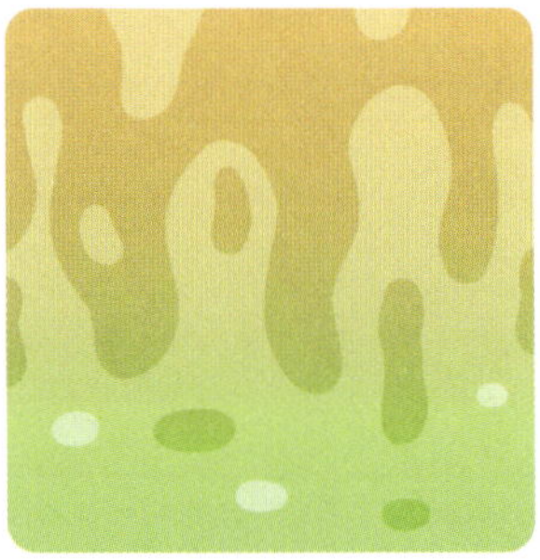

Drips

Stripes

Gradient

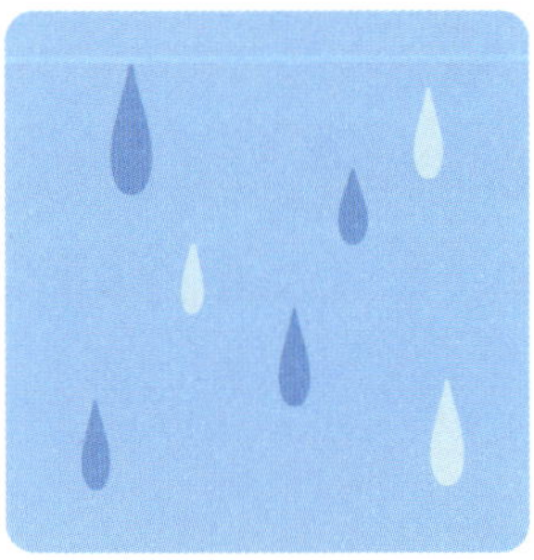

Teardrops

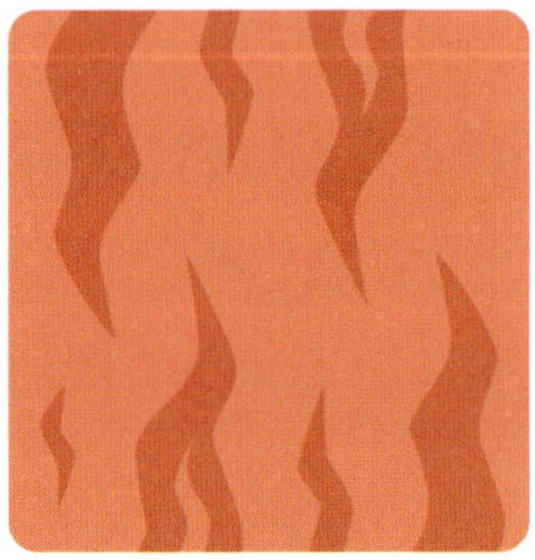

Zigzags

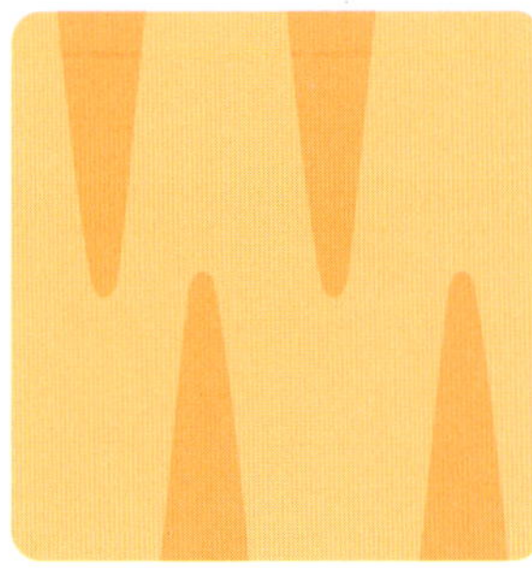

Spikes

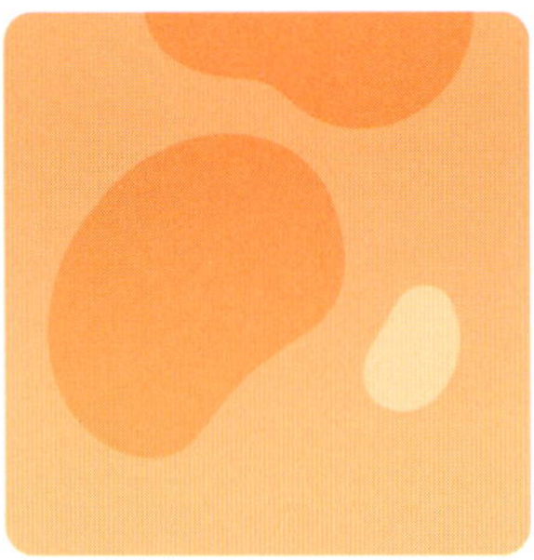

Blobs

Waves

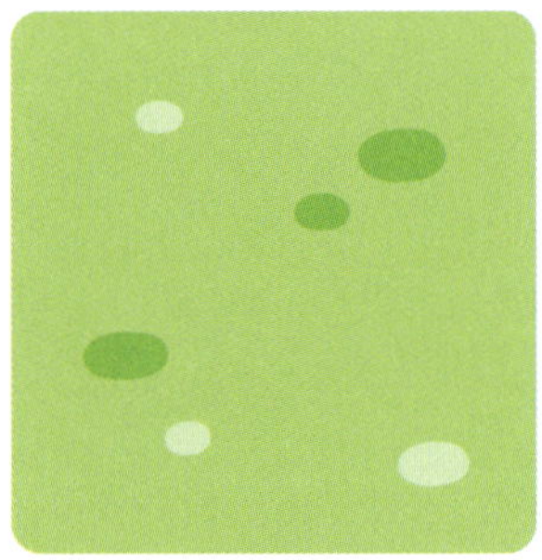

Ovals

FACIAL EXPRESSION DIRECTORY

Facial expressions are what give these dinosaurs their kawaii factor. Here, I will show you some of my favorite facial expressions.

Adult

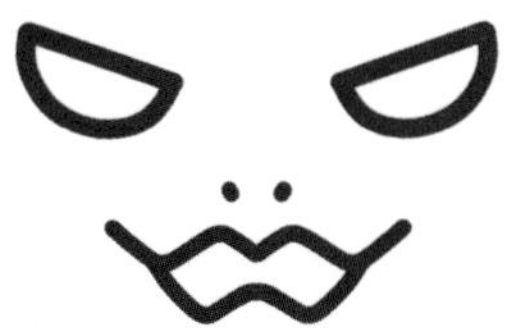

Angry

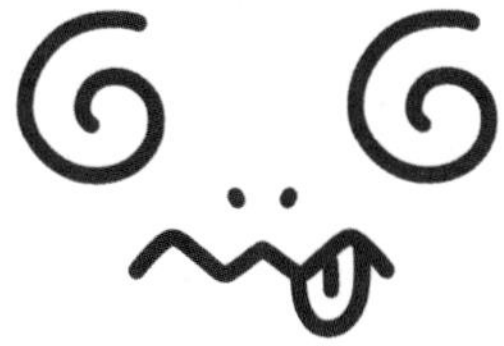

Dizzy

Happy

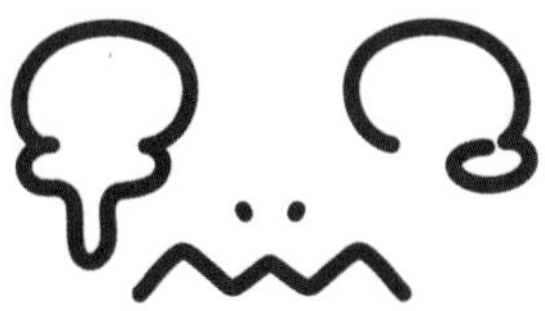

Sad

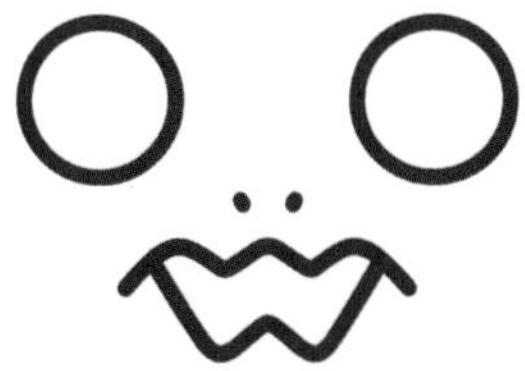

Shocked

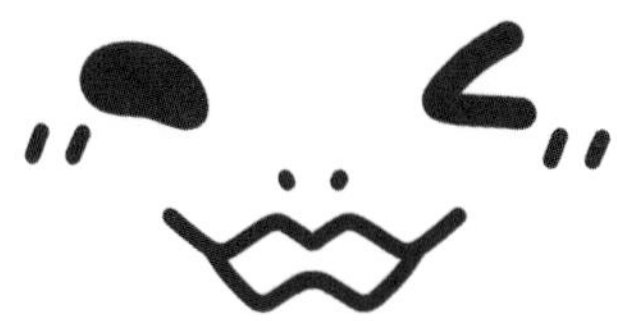

Winky

Baby

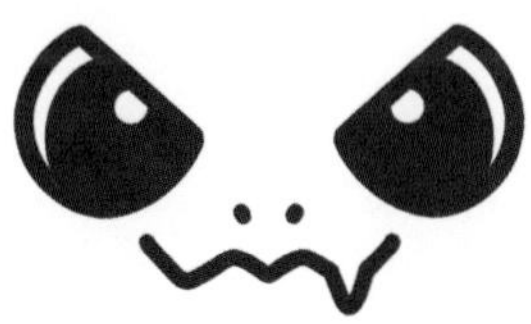

Angry

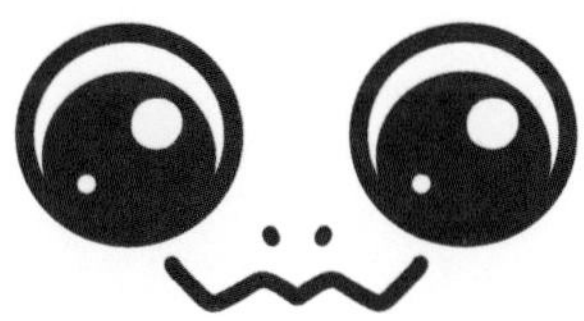

Happy

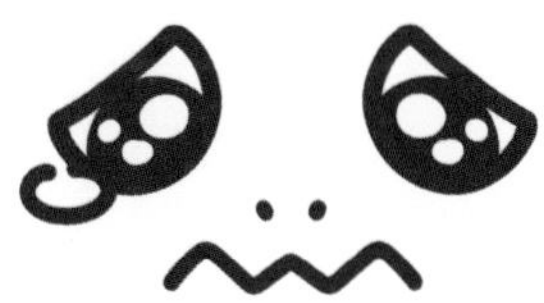

Sad

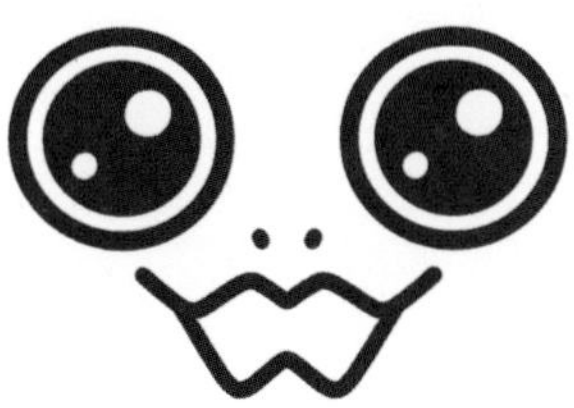

Shocked

Shy

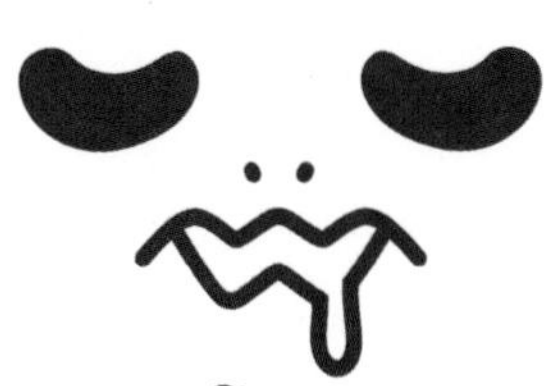

Sleepy

COLORING YOUR DINO WORLD

I love to color my dinosaurs with these combinations, but your creatures can be any color you like. Who's to say a Triceratops can't be purple? Don't forget to practice with the coloring pages on page 142!

Blue/Cream

Brown/Orange

Red/White

Green/Yellow

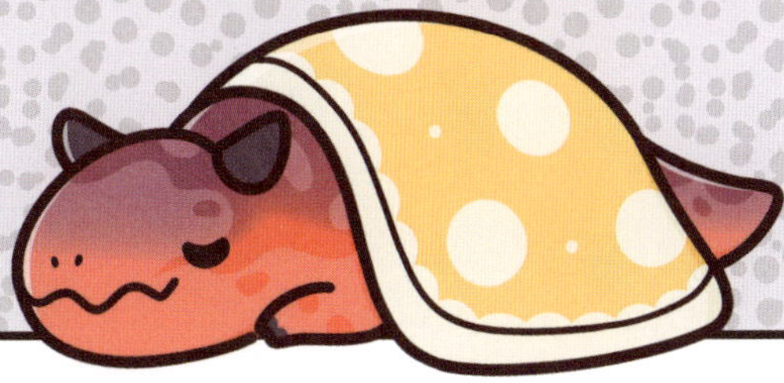

Burgundy/Gray

Pink/Yellow

Orange/Cream

Teal/Orange

MIGHTY FRIENDS

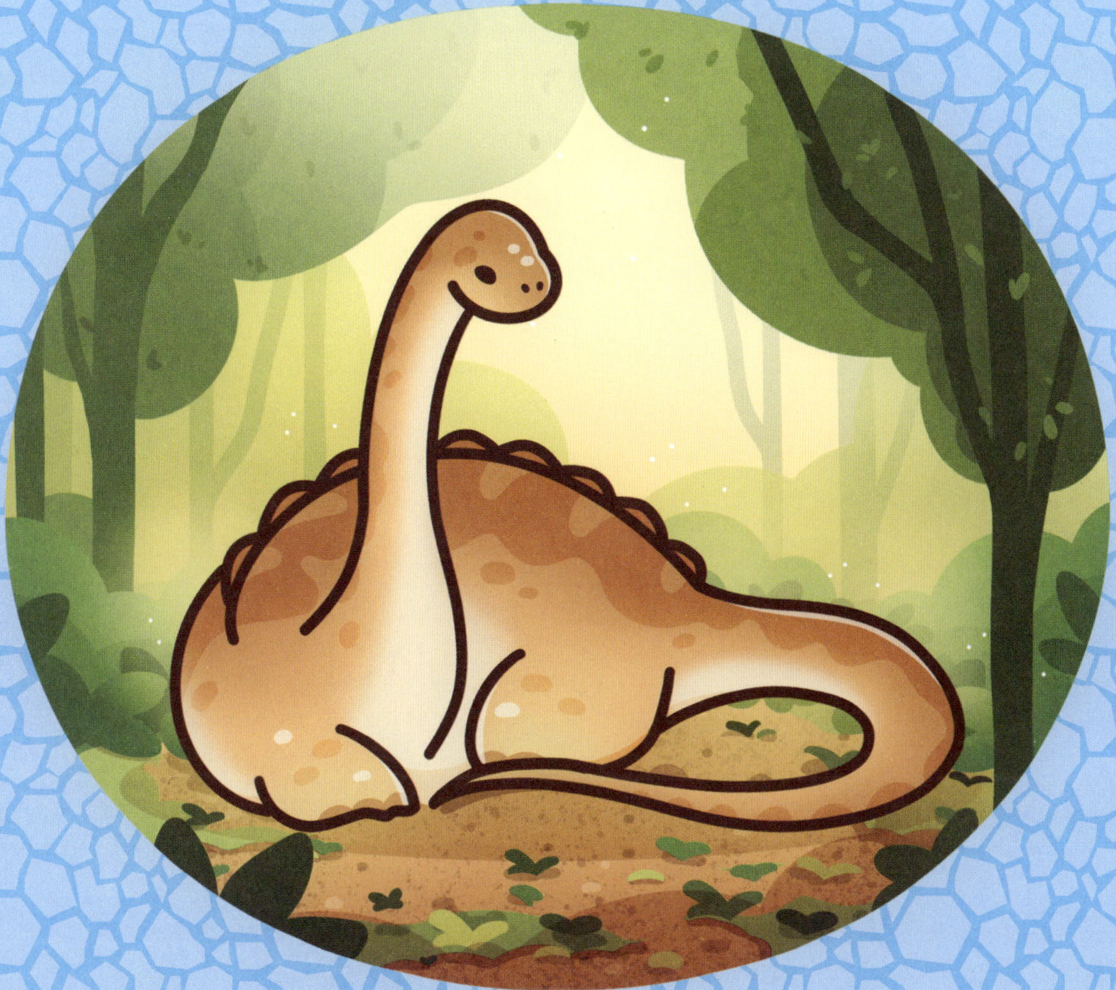

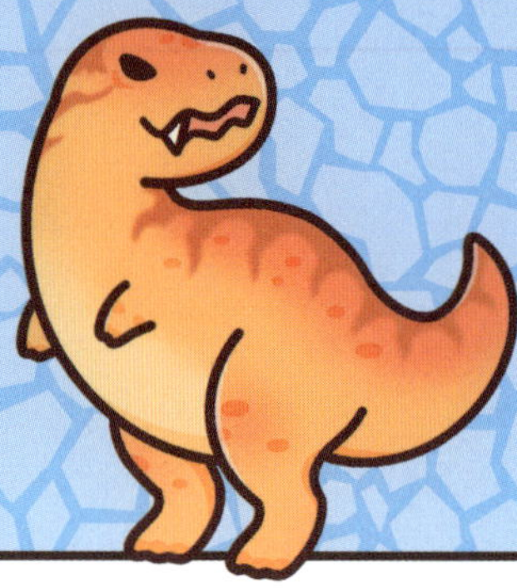

TYRANNOSAURUS

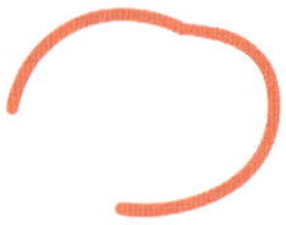

1. Draw a curved line with a bump for the snout.

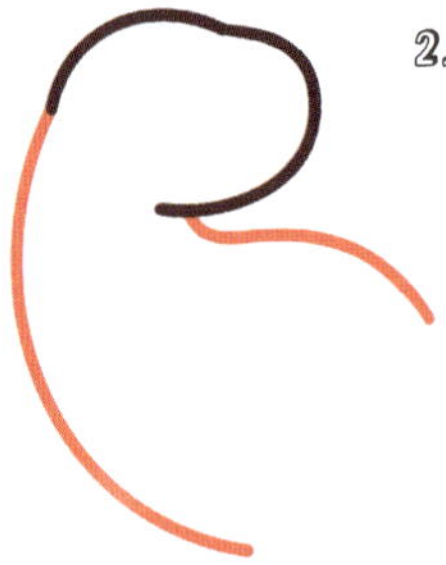

2. Add two curved lines for the neck and body.

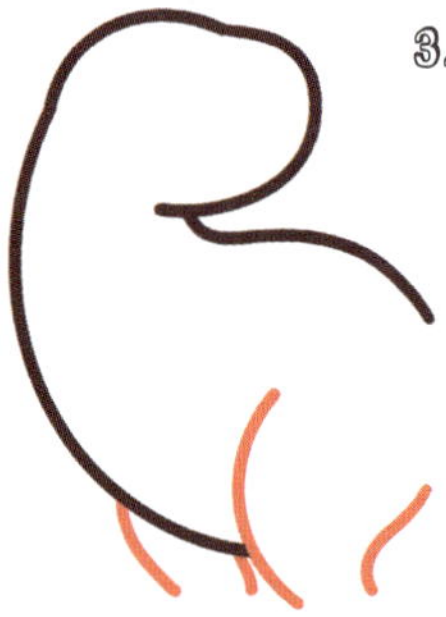

3. Add four curved lines for the legs.

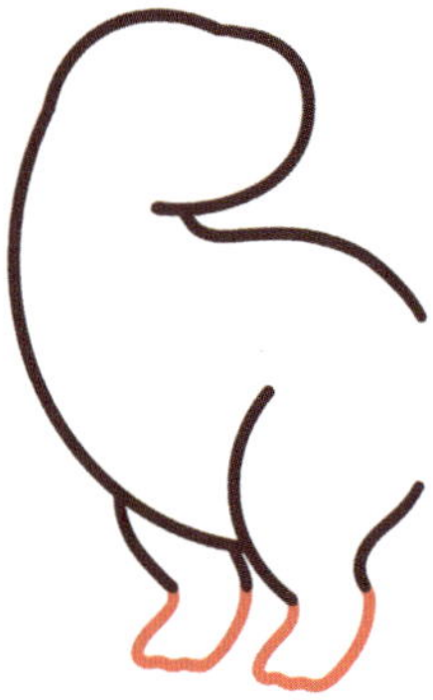

4. Draw two U-shaped feet with three toes each.

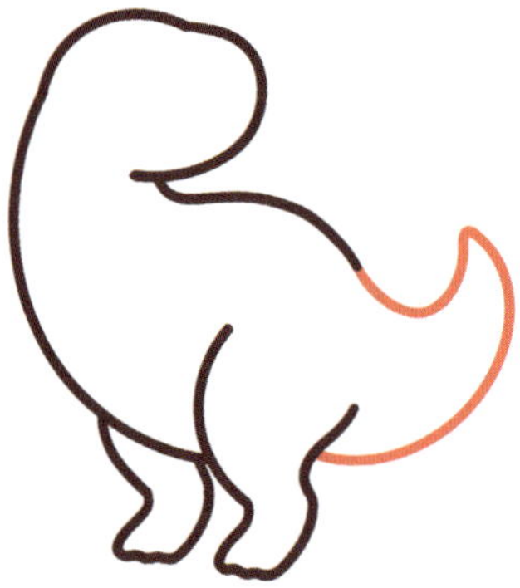

5. Add a short, curved tail.

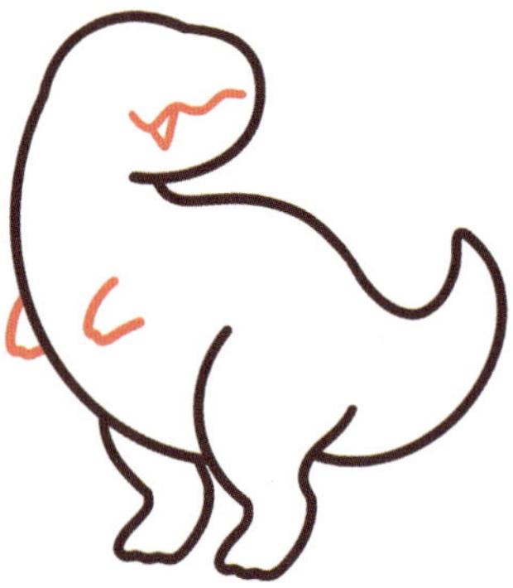

6. Draw two U-shaped arms with two fingers each. For the mouth, add a jagged line with a triangle tooth.

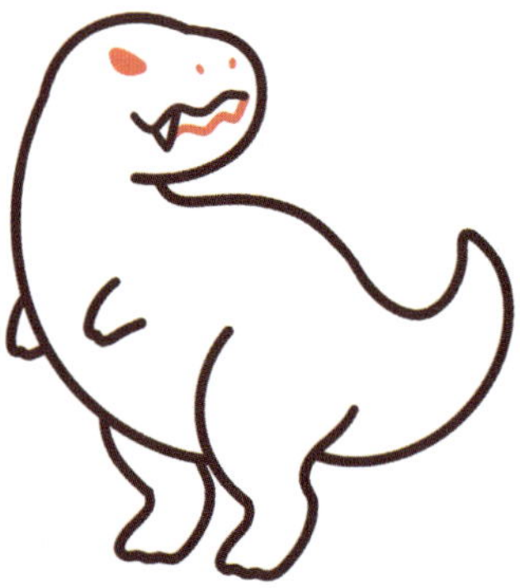

7. Add an oval eye and two dashes for the nostrils.

TRICERATOPS

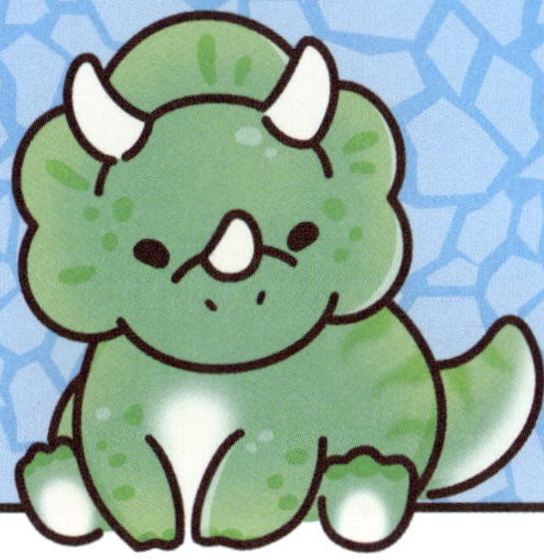

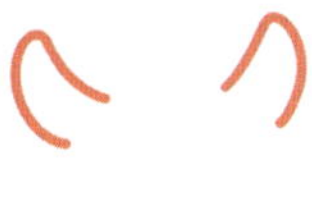

1. Draw two curved horns with incomplete bottoms.

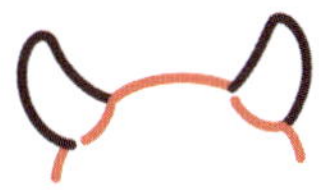

2. Add curved lines around the horns for the top of the head.

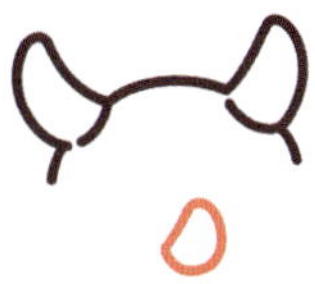

3. Add a round horned nose.

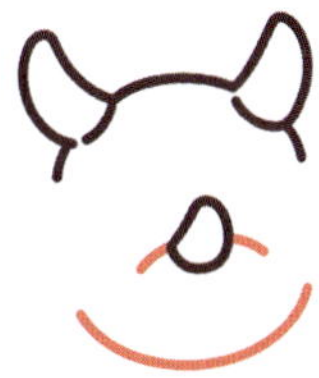

4. Draw two curved lines around the nose and for the chin.

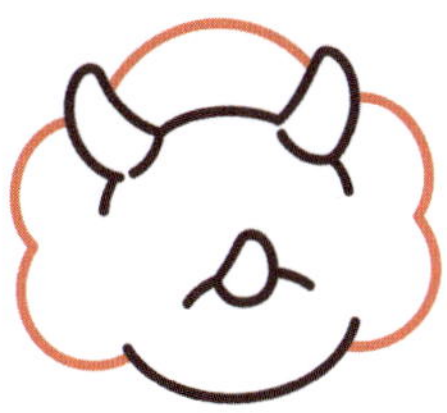

5. Draw five scallops around the head.

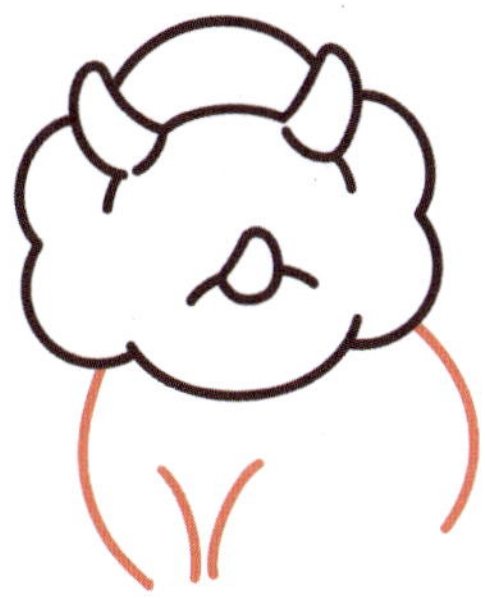

6. Add curved lines for the arms and the back of the body.

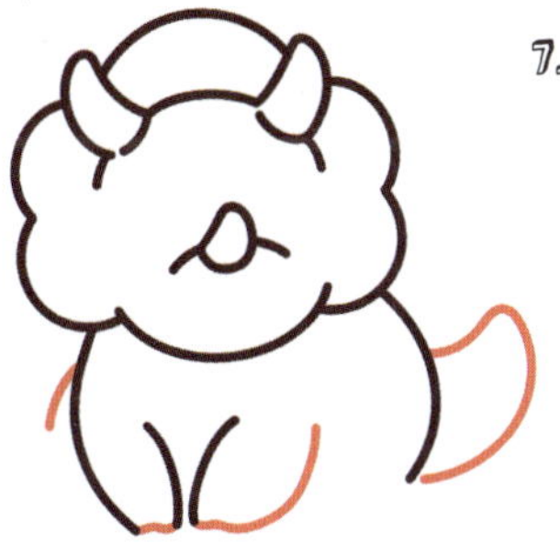

7. Add two fingers to each arm and the side of the right arm. Draw a short curve on the left and a triangle tail on the right.

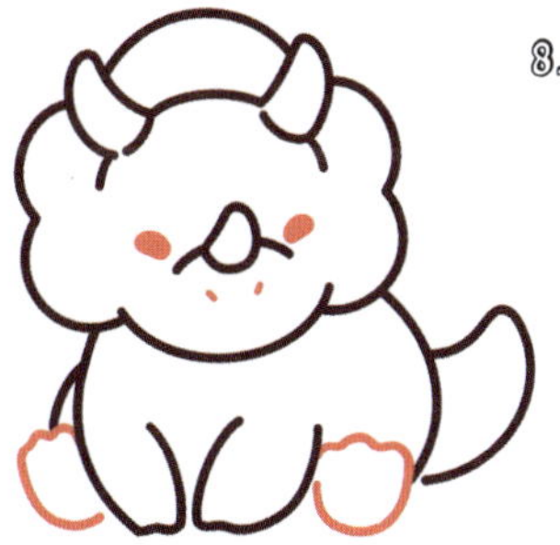

8. Add two oval eyes and two dashes for the nostrils. Draw round feet with three toes each.

ENIGMACURSOR

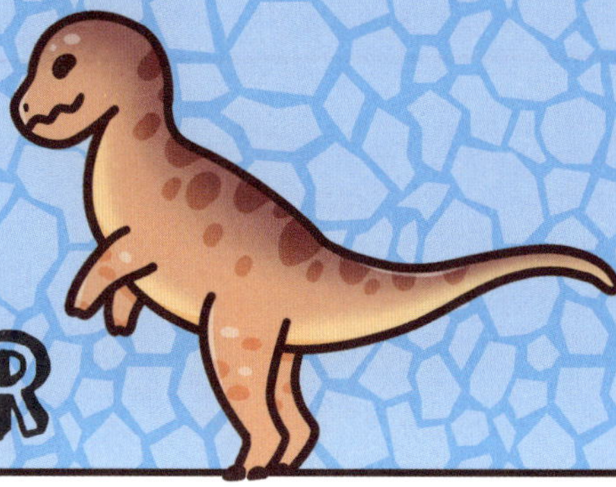

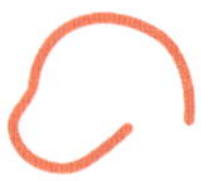

1. Draw a curved head with a square snout.

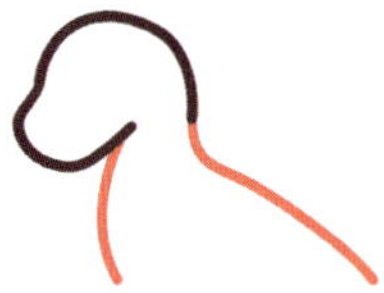

2. Add two curved lines for the neck and top of the body.

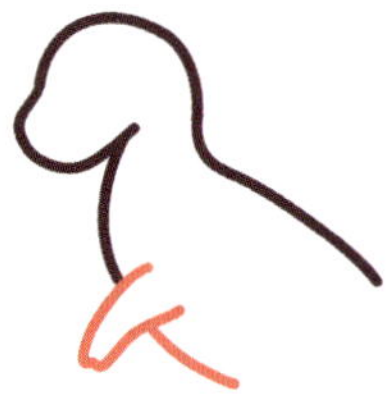

3. Add a thin arm with two fingers and a curve for the stomach.

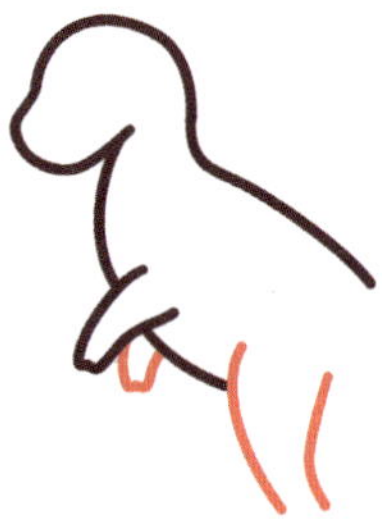

4. Add the second arm and two curved lines for the leg.

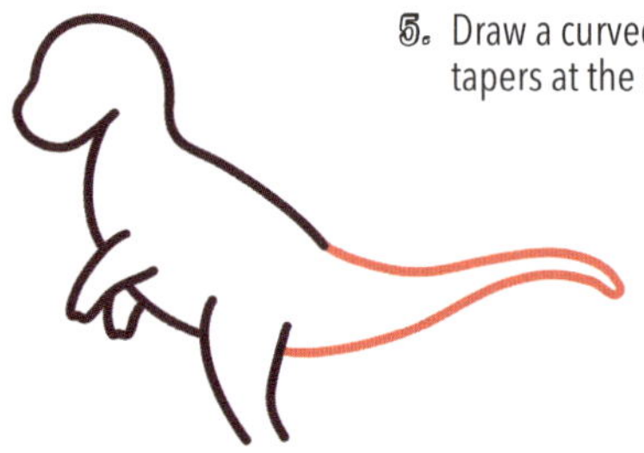

5. Draw a curved tail that tapers at the end.

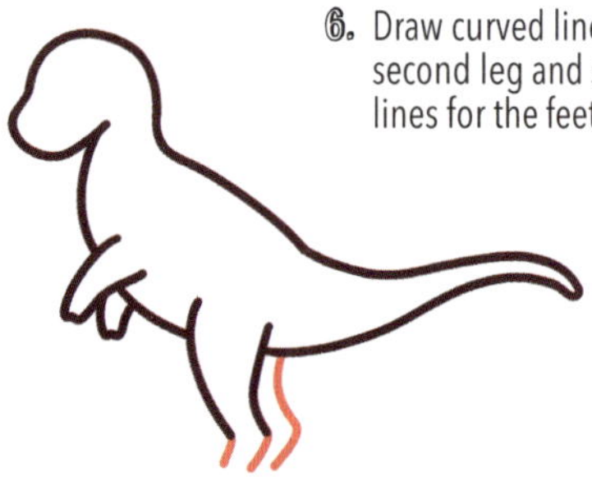

6. Draw curved lines for the second leg and straight lines for the feet.

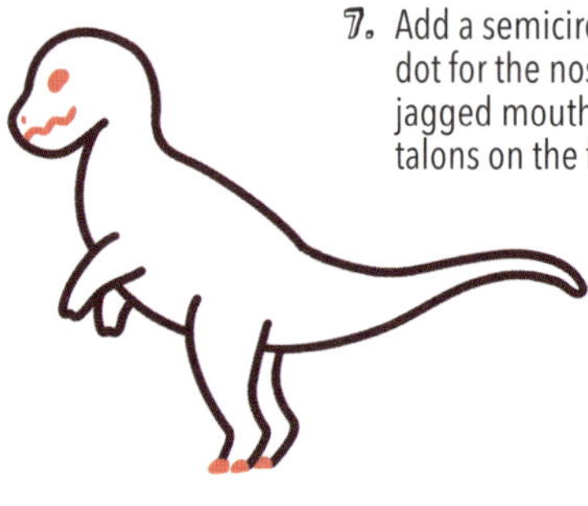

7. Add a semicircle eye, a dot for the nostril, and a jagged mouth. Draw three talons on the feet.

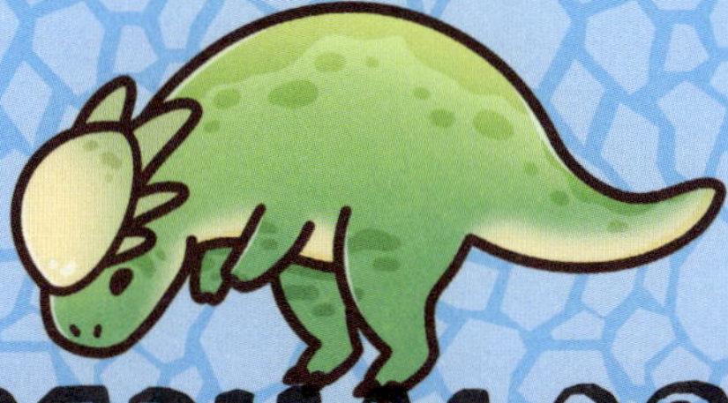

PACHYCEPHALOSAURUS

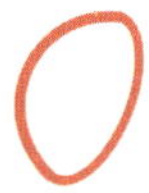

1. Draw an oval with pointed ends for the dome.

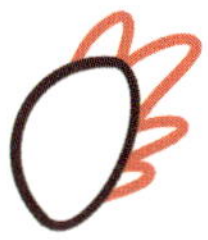

2. Add four spikes around the oval, with the top two as the largest.

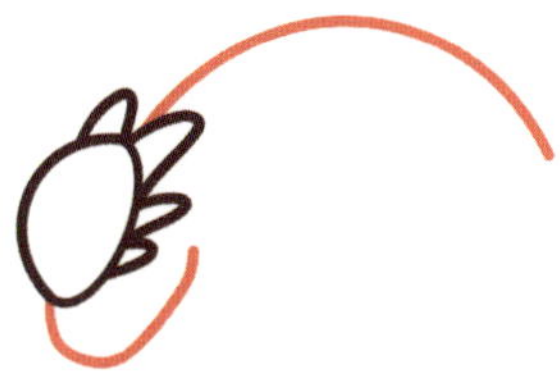

3. Draw a U shape for the head. Add a curved line for the top of the body.

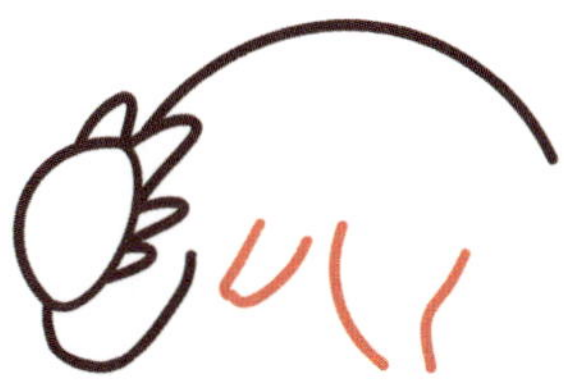

4. Draw a short arm with two fingers. Add two curved lines for the leg.

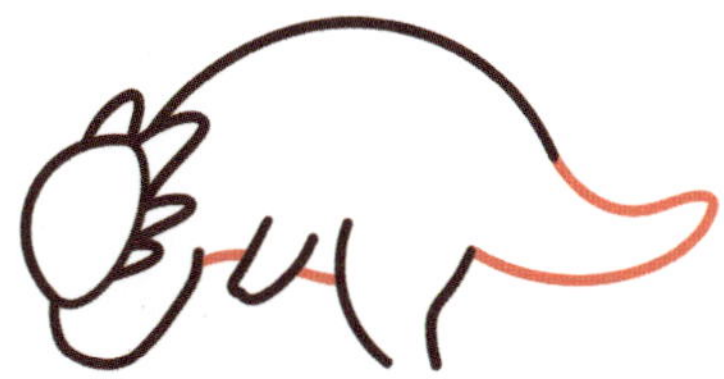

5. Add a curved line for the stomach and a curved tail.

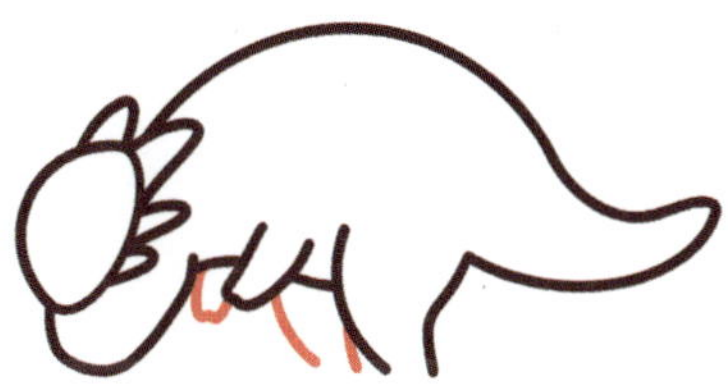

6. Add the second arm and curved lines for the second leg.

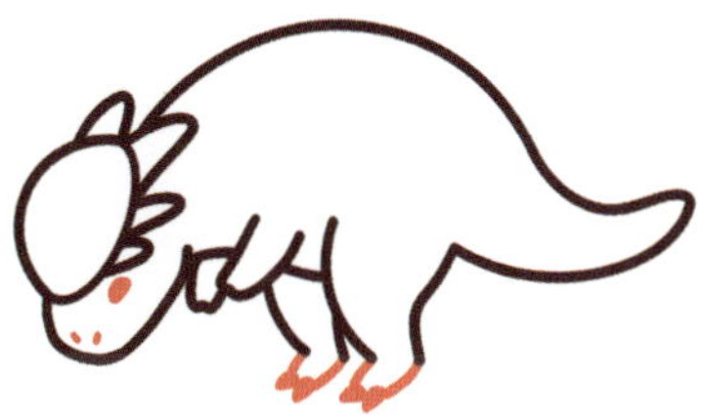

7. Add an oval eye and two dashes for the nostrils. Draw U-shaped feet with two talons each.

DEINOCHEIRUS

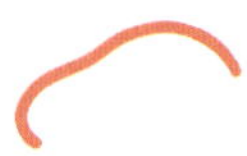

1. Draw a curved line with a bump for the head.

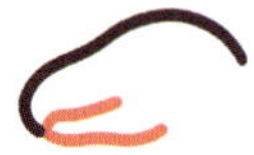

2. Add a line for the mouth and a wavy line for the chin.

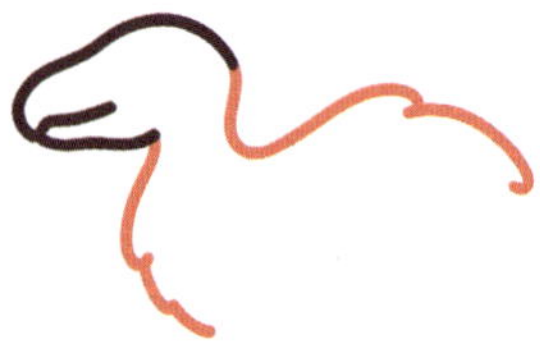

3. Make a U curve for the neck. Add two curved lines with feather details for the body.

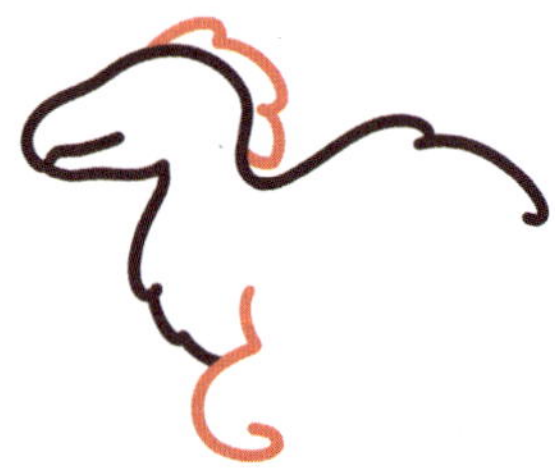

4. Add three feathers on top of the head. Add a V-line that curls into a feather for the wing.

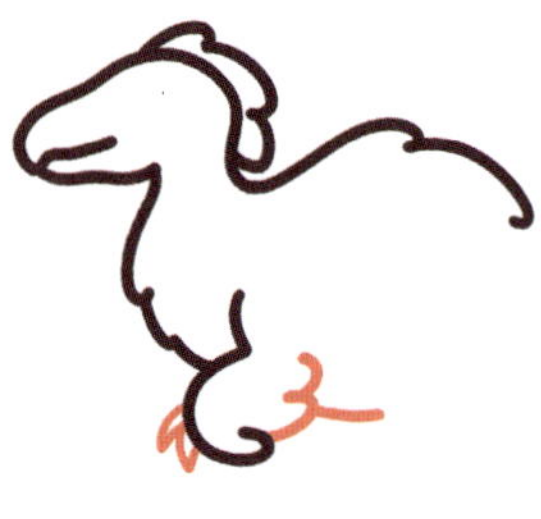

5. Add two U-shaped feathers to the wing and two pointed talons. Draw a curved line for the stomach.

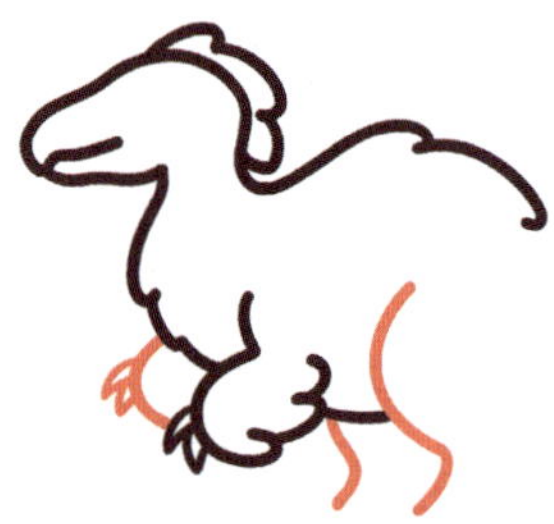

6. Add curved lines for the second wing and the legs. Draw two pointed talons on the wing.

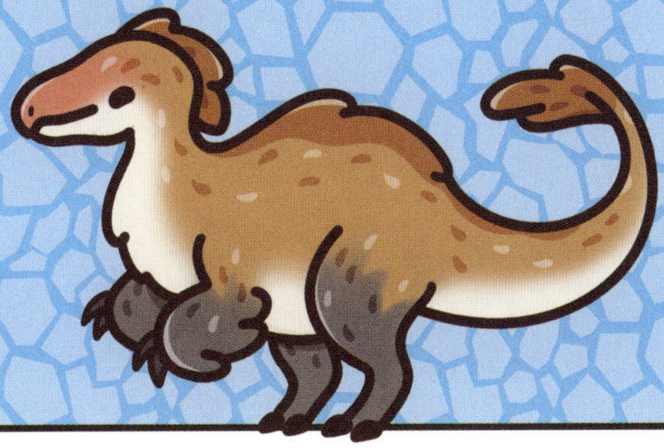

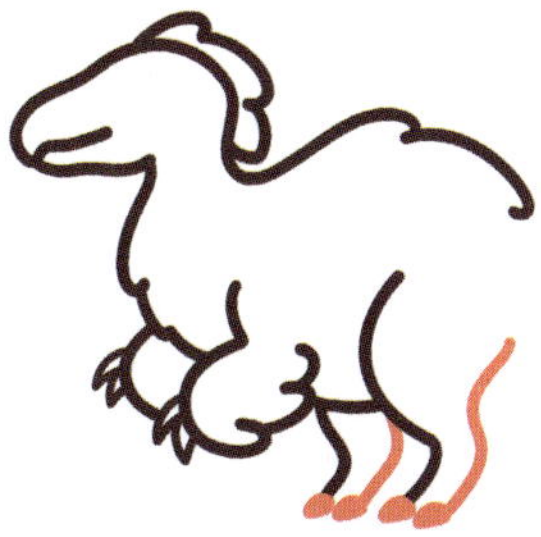

7. Draw a wavy line and two talons to each leg.

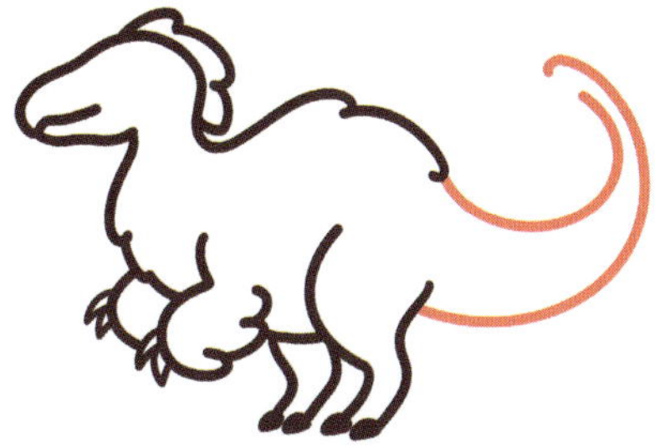

8. Add a curved tail that tapers at the end. Leave the end open.

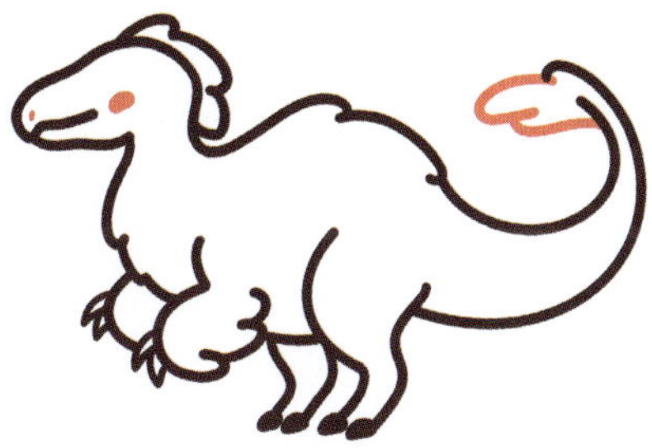

9. Draw two U-shaped feathers at the end of the tail. For the face, add an oval eye and a dash for the nostril.

PACHYRHINOSAURUS

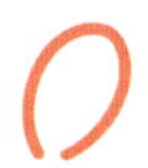

1. Draw an incomplete oval.

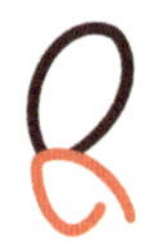

2. Add a triangle beak underneath in the shape of a pointed number nine.

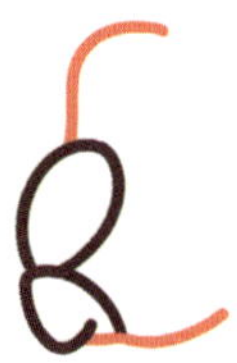

3. Add a rounded right angle on top of the oval. Draw a curved line with two bumps under the beak.

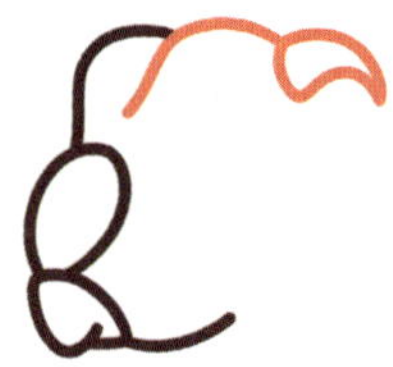

4. Add a curved line next to the right angle. Draw a curved, triangle horn.

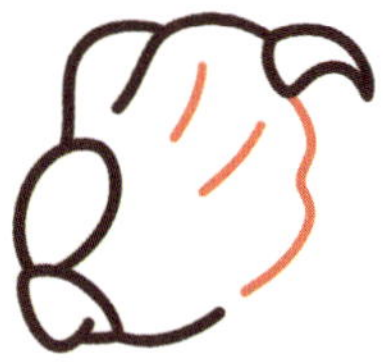

5. Draw a wavy line to complete the head. Add two lines for details.

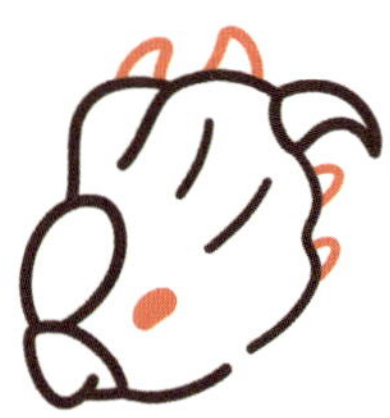

6. Add an oval eye and four triangles around the head.

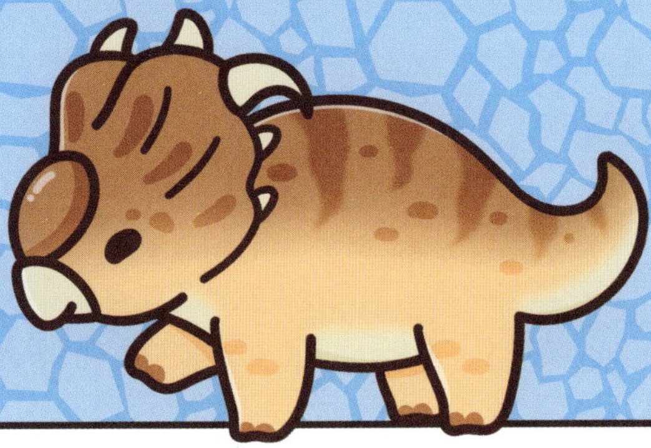

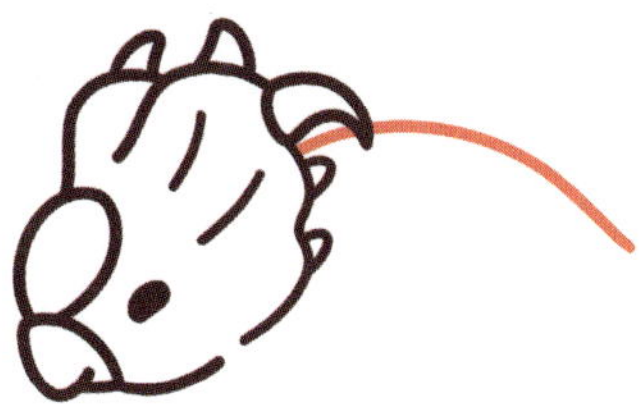

7. Draw a curve for the top of the body.

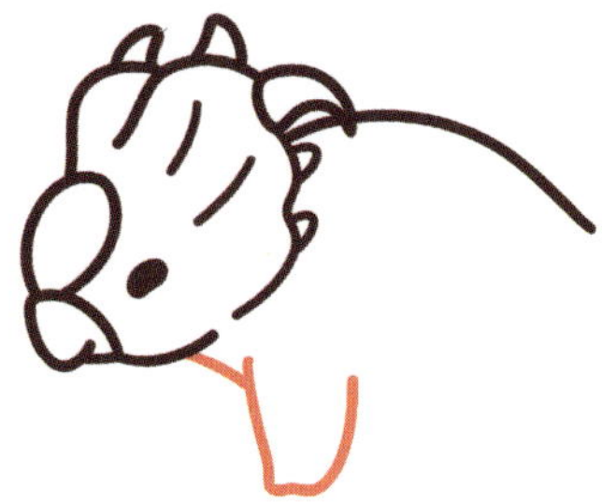

8. Draw a line for the neck. Add a U-shaped leg with two toes.

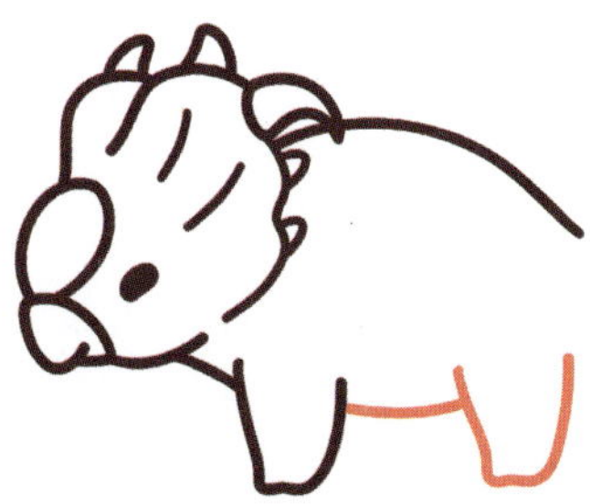

9. Add a curved line for the stomach and another U-shaped leg.

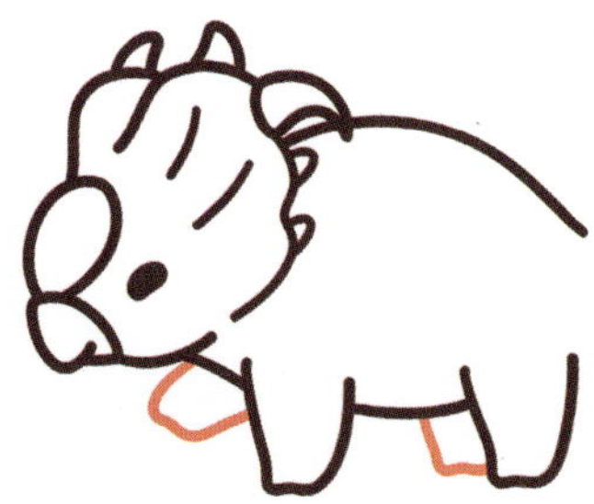

10. Add two more legs.

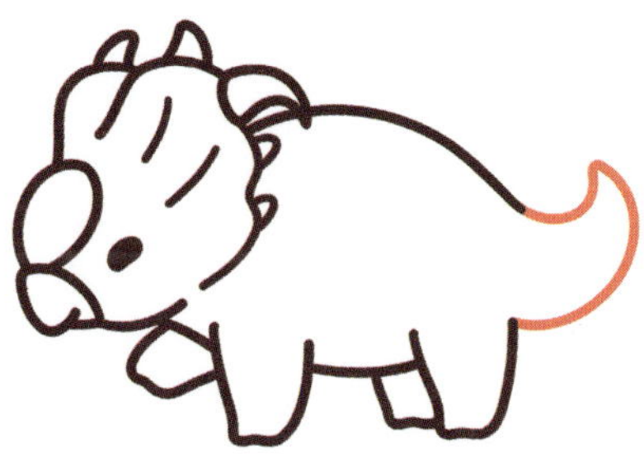

11. Draw a short, curved tail that tapers at the end.

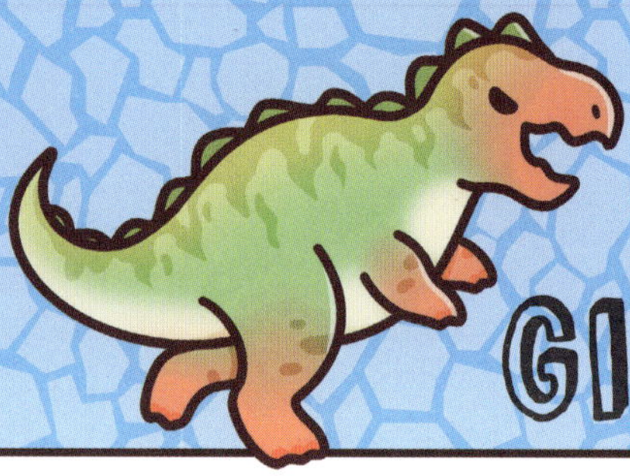

GIGANOTOSAURUS

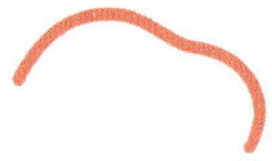

1. Draw a curved line with a bump for the snout.

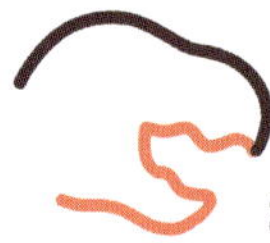

2. Add the mouth with a jagged V-line and a wavy line for the chin.

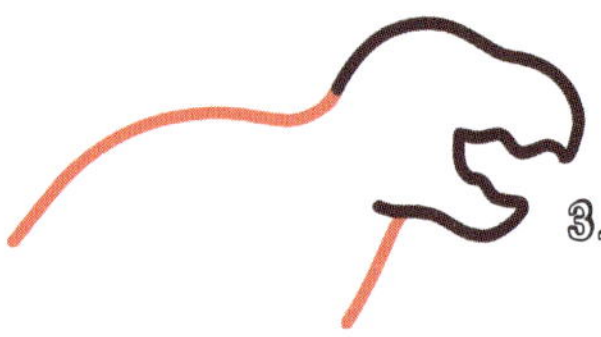

3. Draw a curved line for the top of the body and a straight line for the neck.

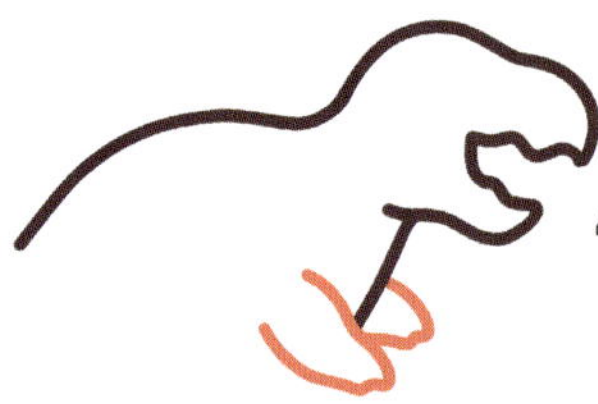

4. Add two U-shaped arms with two fingers each.

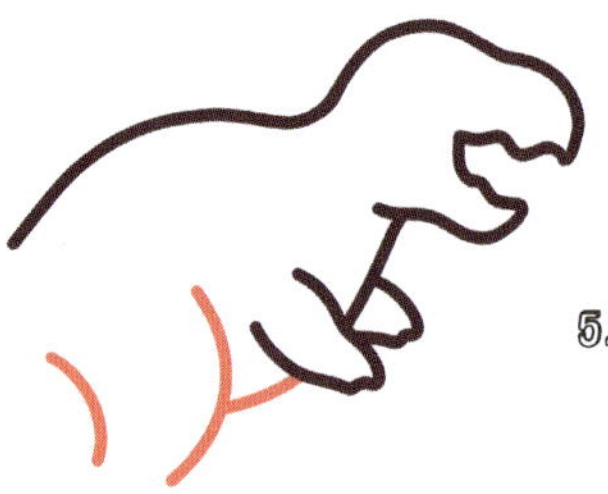

5. Add three curved lines for the stomach and the leg.

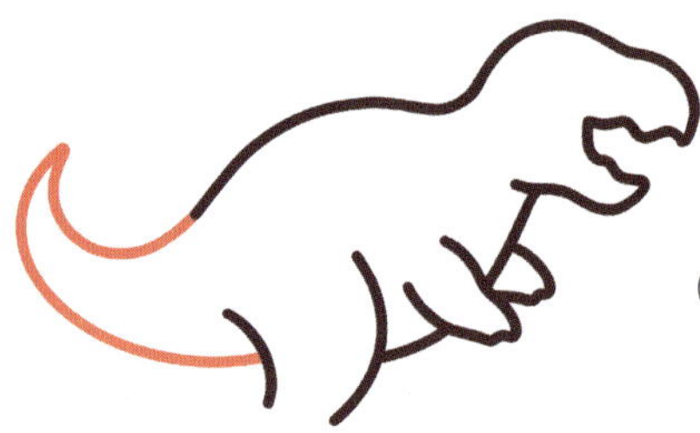

6. Add a curved tail that tapers at the end.

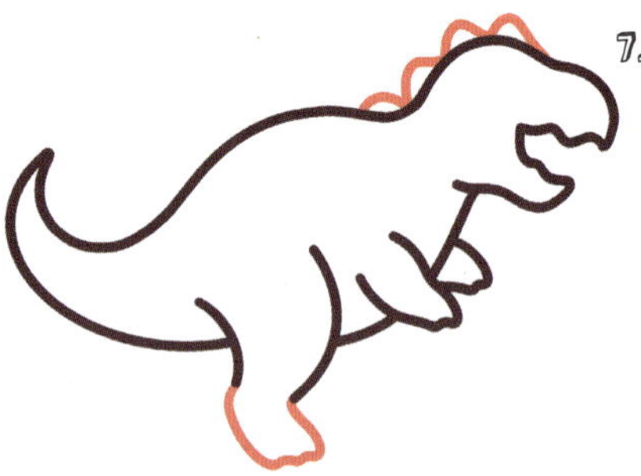

7. Draw a U-shaped foot with three toes. Add semicircle spikes on top of the head and neck.

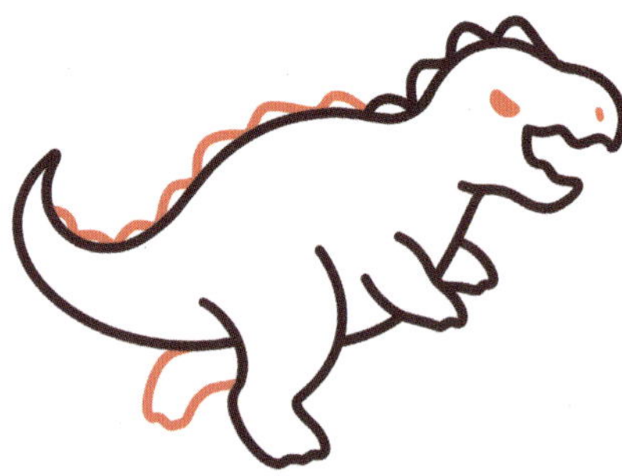

8. Add more spikes down to the tail. For the face, add a semicircle eye and a dash for a nostril. Finish with a curved leg with two toes.

TROODON

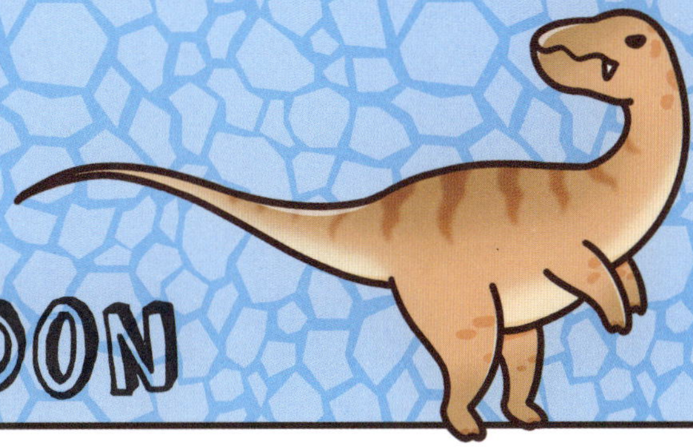

1. Draw an incomplete oval head with bumpy lines to define the snout.

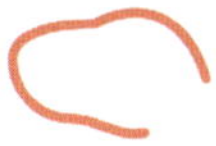

2. Add two curved lines for the neck.

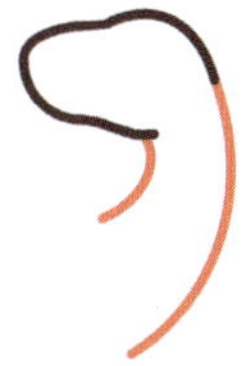

3. Draw a curved line for the top of the body.

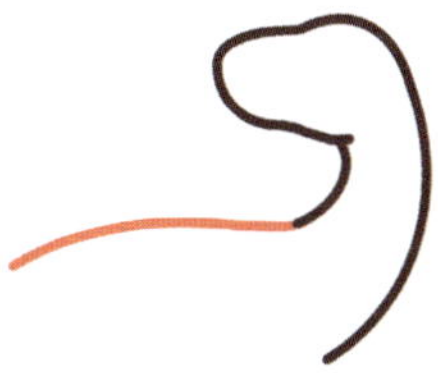

4. Add a thin arm with two fingers and a curve for the stomach.

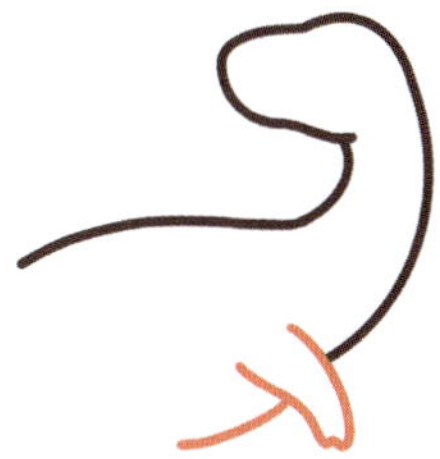

5. Draw four curved lines for the legs.

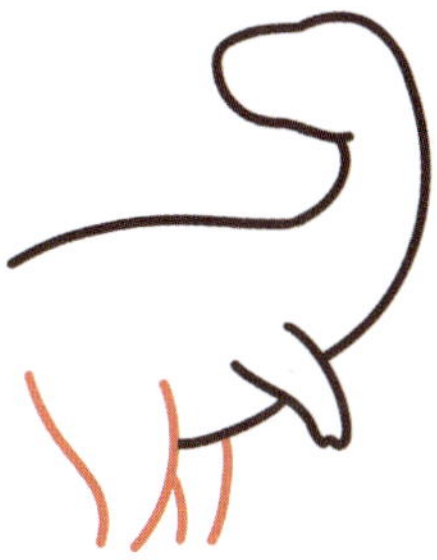

6. Add a second arm. Complete the legs with U-shaped feet with two toes each.

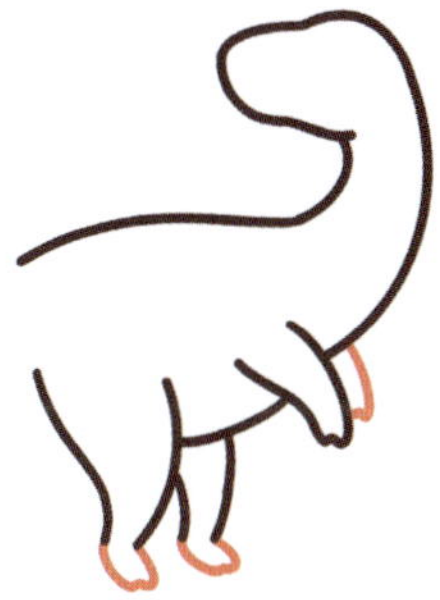

7. Draw a long, curving tail that ends in a point.

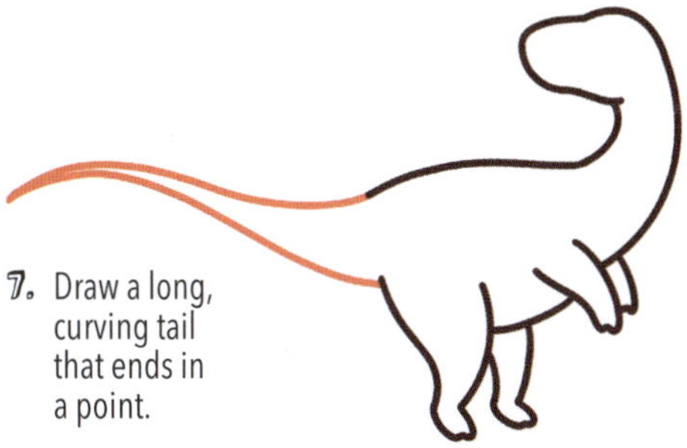

8. Draw an oval eye and a jagged mouth with a triangle tooth.

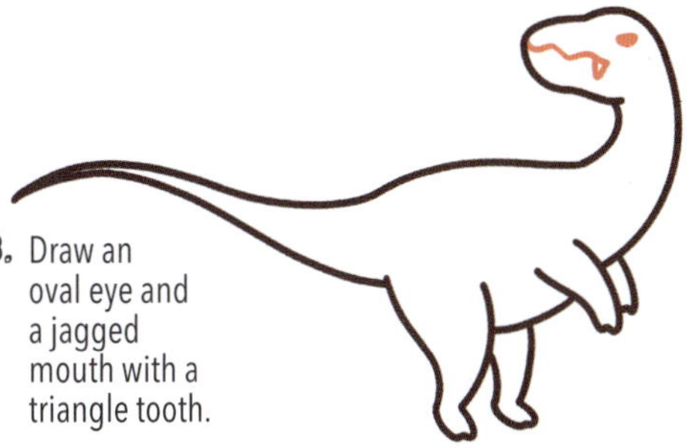

GIGANTORAPTOR

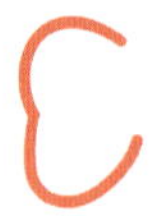

1. Draw an E-shaped head.

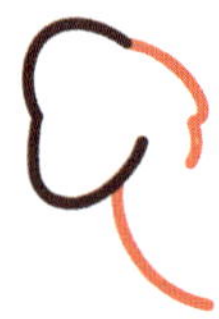

2. Add some feathers to the back of the head and a curved line for the neck.

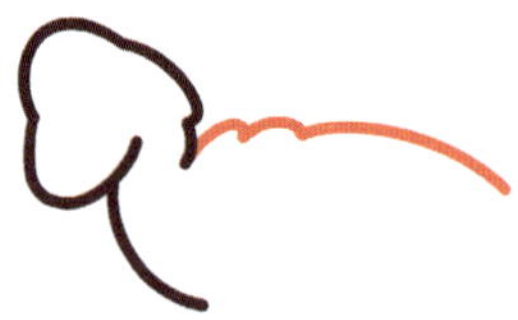

3. Draw a curved line for the top of the body with more feathers.

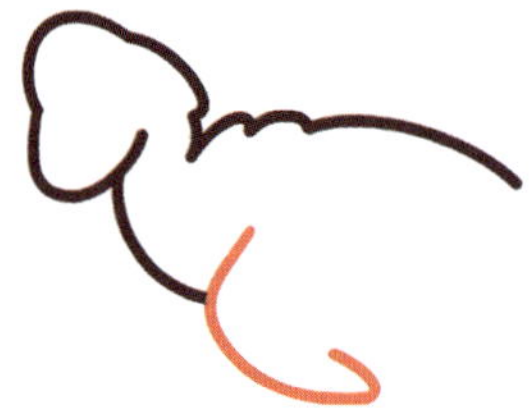

4. Draw a curved arm with a triangle tip.

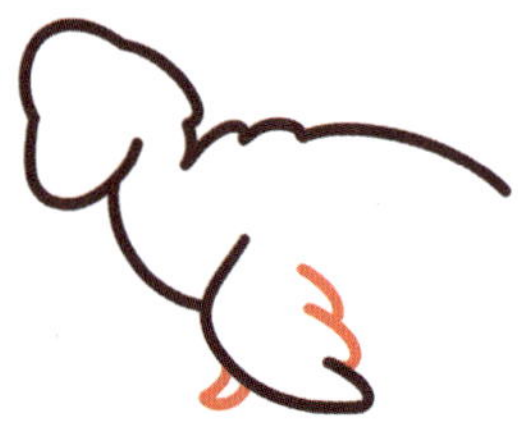

5. Add two U-shaped lines for feathers on the wing. Draw a pointed talon.

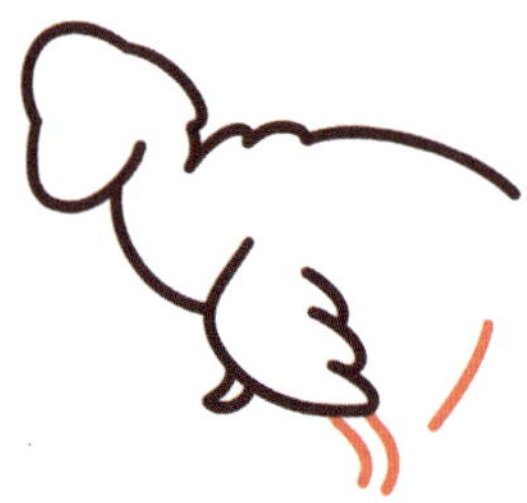

6. Add two curved lines and a straight line for the legs.

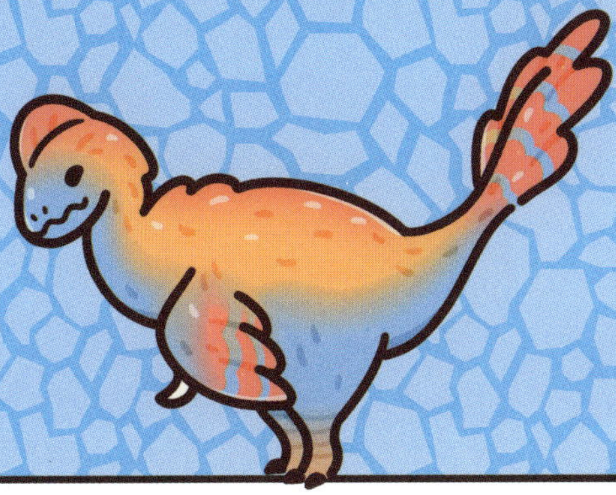

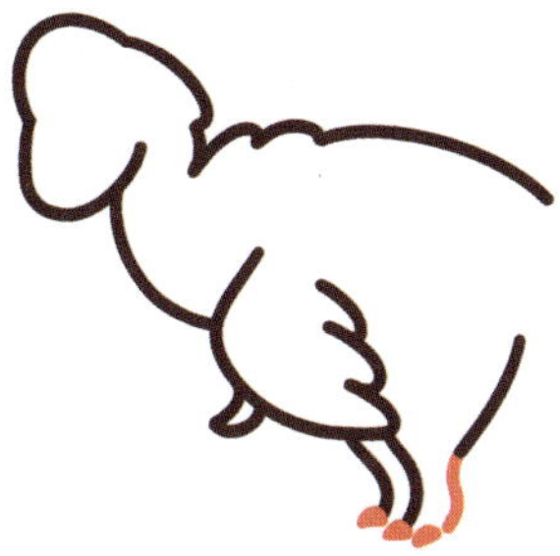

7. Draw another curved line to complete the back leg. Add three triangle talons.

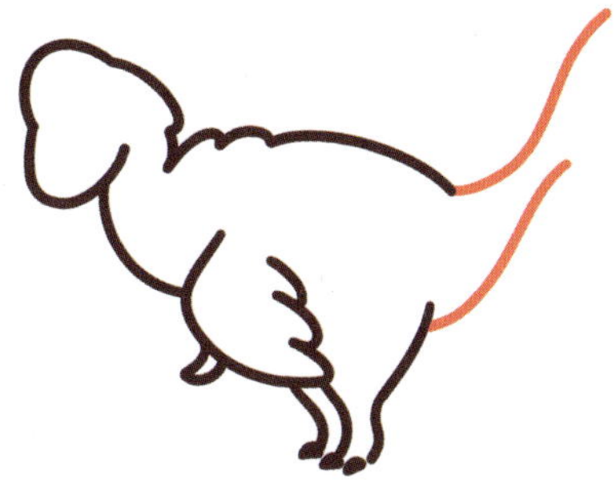

8. Add two wavy lines for the tail.

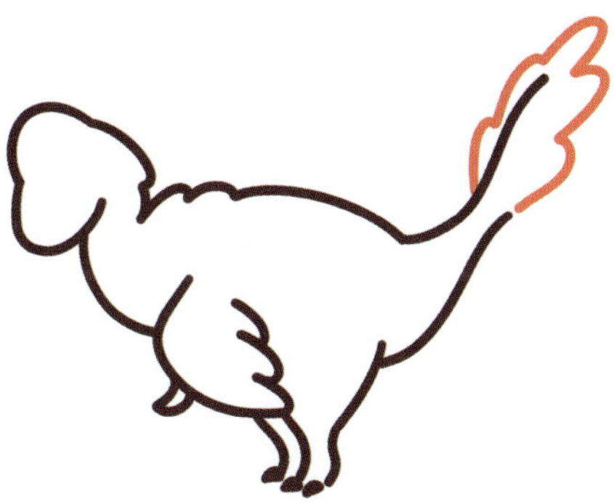

9. Draw a feathered tail with five rounded ends.

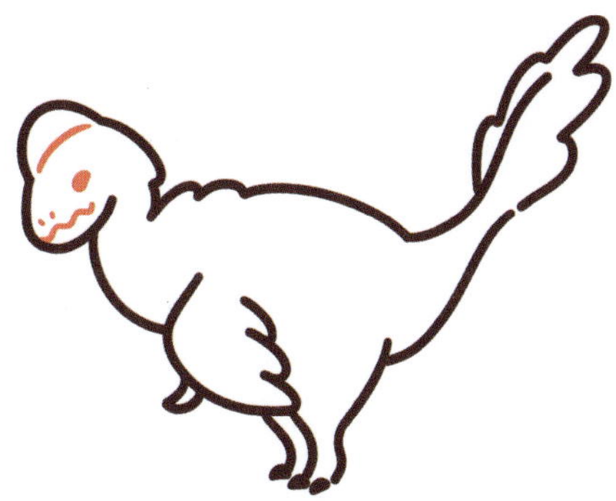

10. Add a curved line inside the head. For the face, add an oval eye, two dashes for the nostrils, and a jagged mouth.

ANCHIORNIS

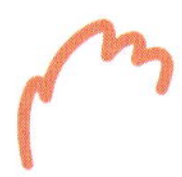

1. Draw the feathered top of the head.

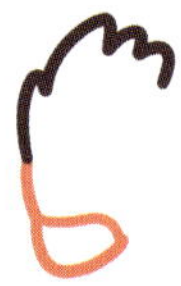

2. Add a curved line and a triangle beak.

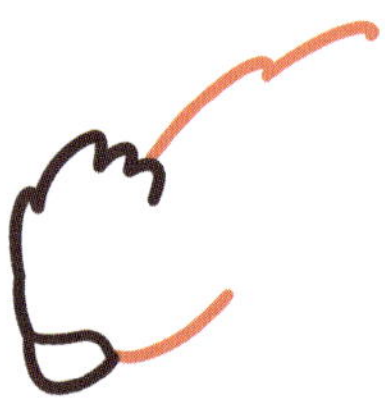

3. Draw a curved line for the neck. Add the top of the body with a feathered line.

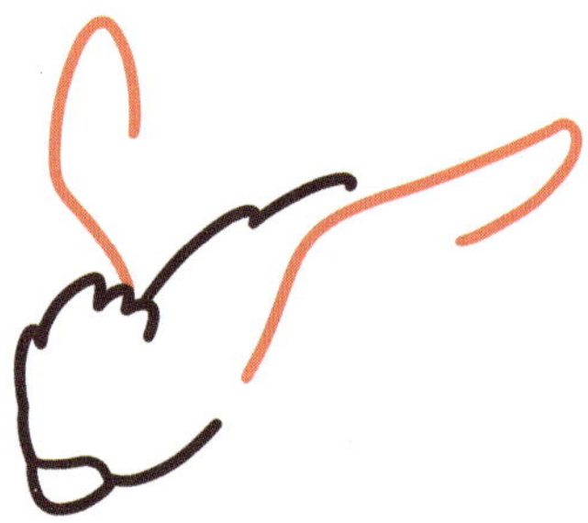

4. Draw two wings with angled lines with triangle tips.

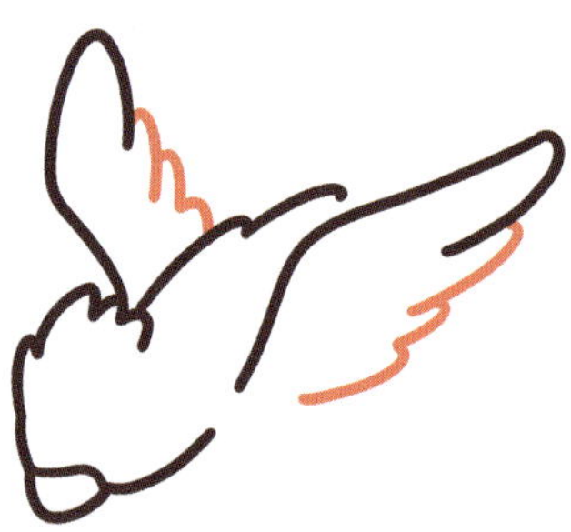

5. Add rounded feathers to the wings.

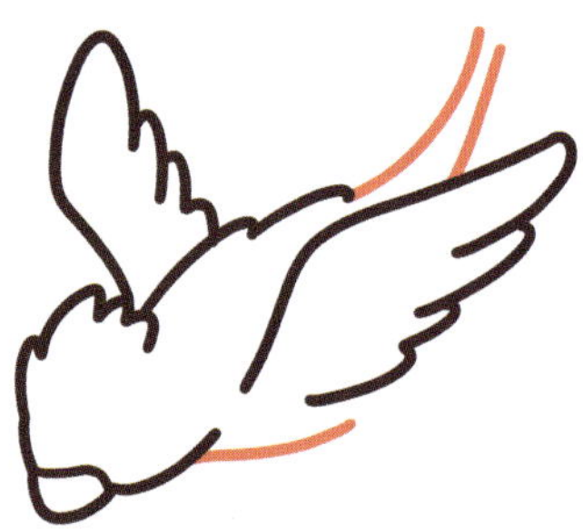

6. Draw a curved line for the stomach and two for the tail.

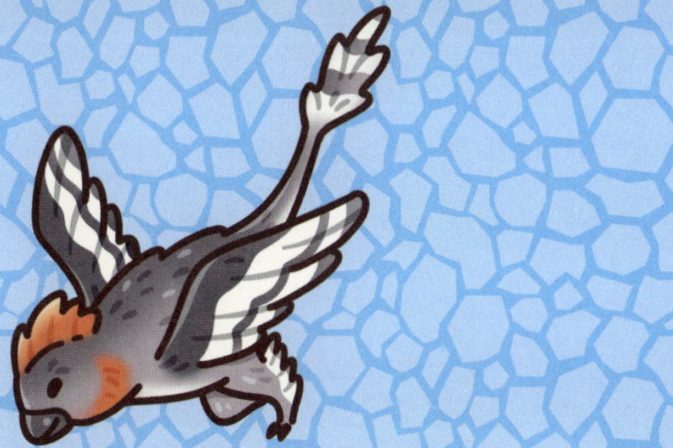

7. Add a feathered tail with five spikes.

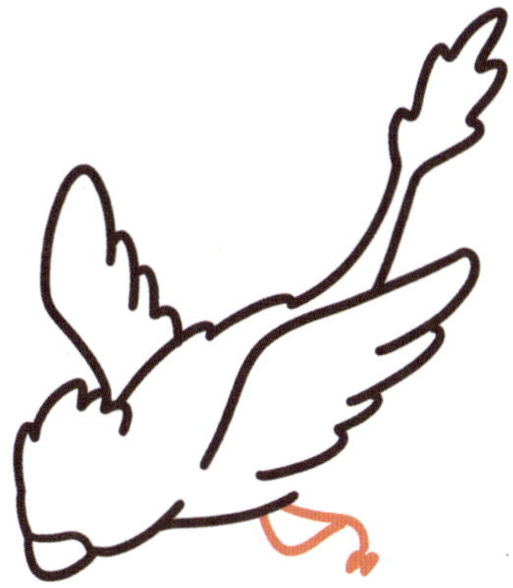

8. Draw a triangle, a curved line, and two talons for a leg.

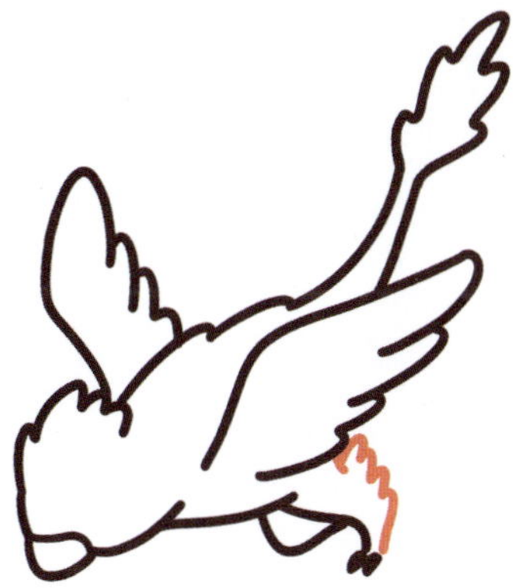

9. Complete the leg with a feathered line.

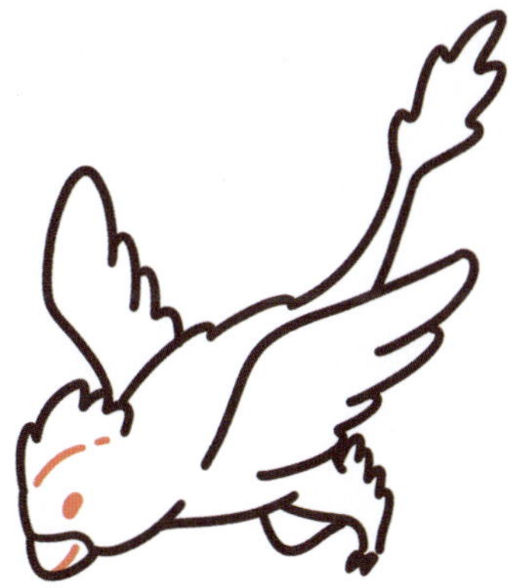

10. Add a curve inside the head. For the face, add an oval eye and a curved mouth.

DIPLODOCUS

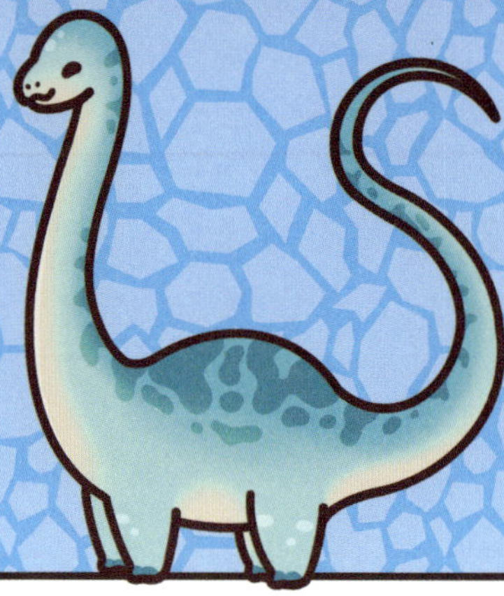

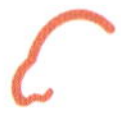

1. Draw a round head turned to the side with a bump for the snout and a W for the mouth.

2. Draw an oval eye, two dashes for the nostrils, and a curved line for the lower jaw.

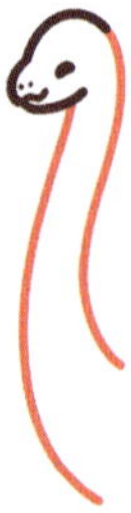

3. Draw two curved lines for the long neck.

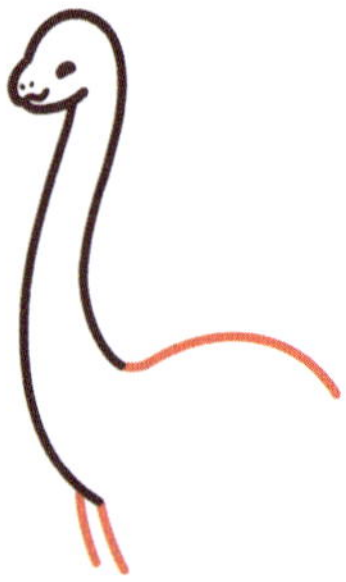

4. Add a curved line for the top of the body and two lines for the short legs.

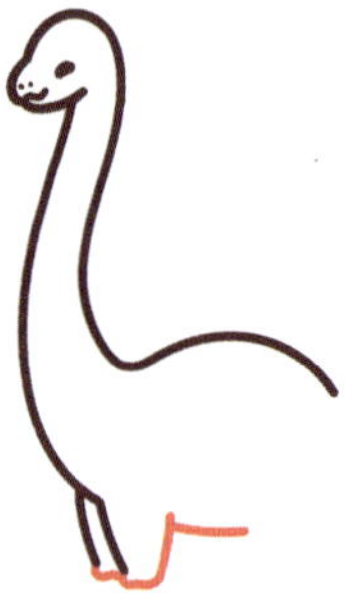

5. Draw the front toes with bumpy lines. Add a line for the back of the leg and a curve for the stomach.

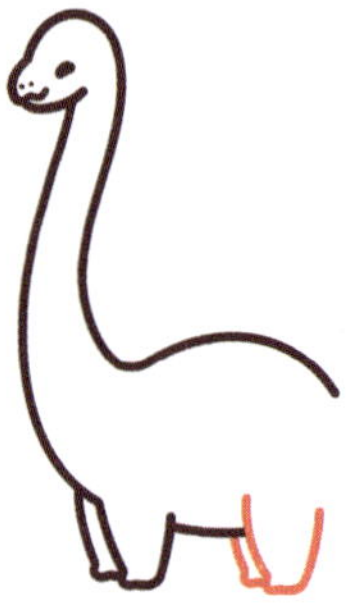

6. Add three lines for the back legs and draw the toes with bumpy lines.

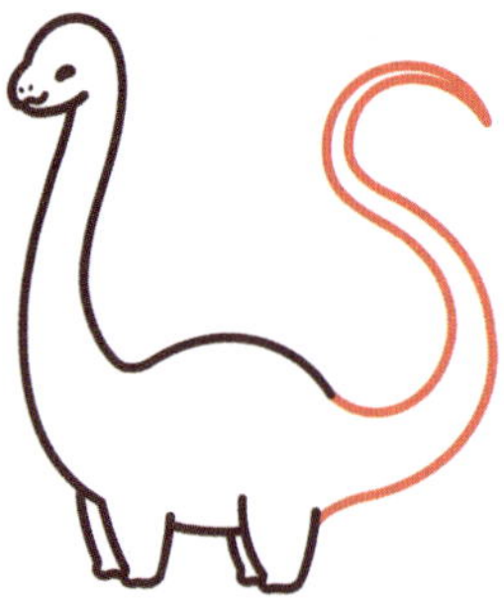

7. Add a long, curving tail that tapers at the end.

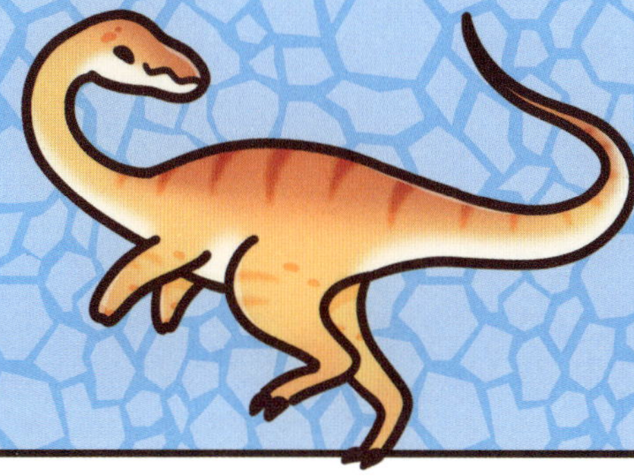

COELOPHYSIS

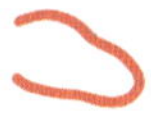

1. Draw an incomplete oval for the head with bumps on the top and bottom.

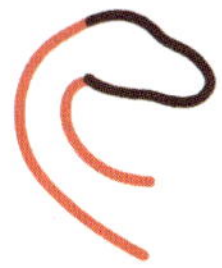

2. Add two curved lines for the slim neck.

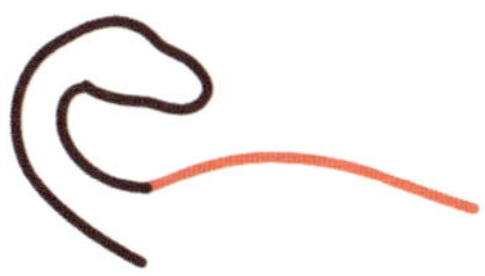

3. Draw a curved line for the top of the body.

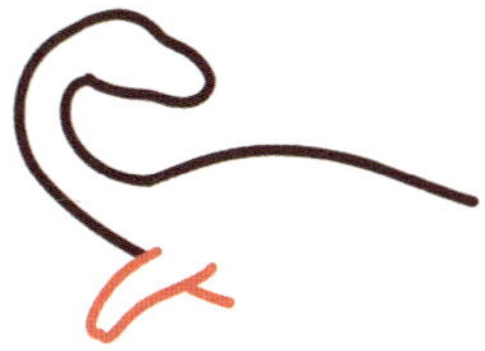

4. Add a rectangular arm with two fingers and a line for the stomach.

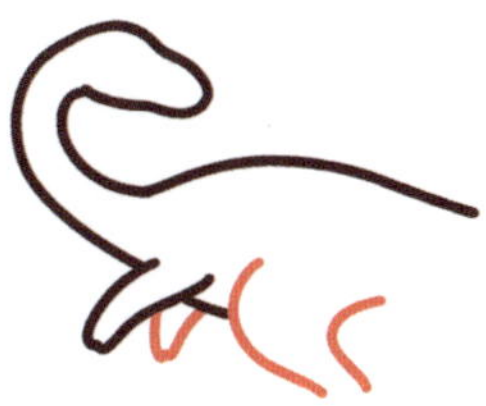

5. Add a triangular arm with two fingers. Draw two curved lines for the back leg.

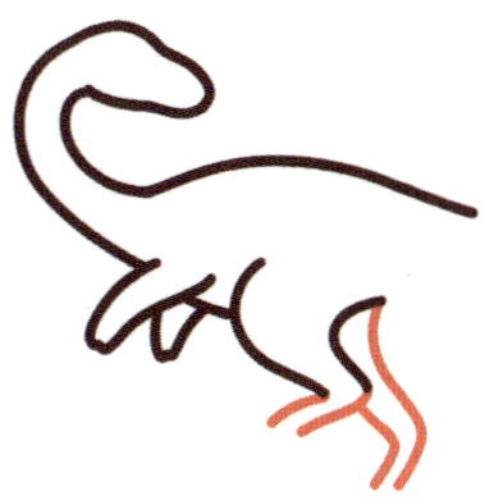

6. Add two lines to the back leg. Draw the second back leg with curved lines.

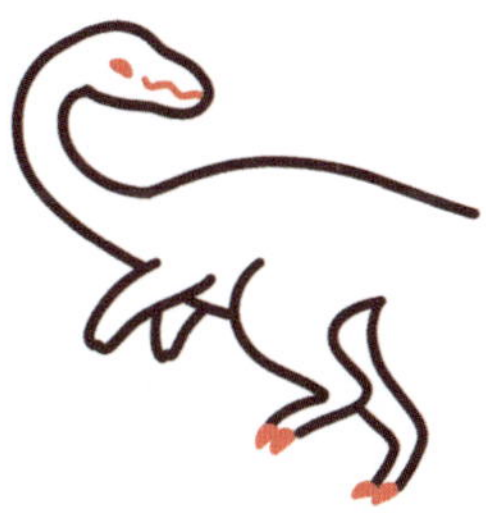

7. Draw a semicircle eye and a jagged mouth. Add two triangle talons to each foot.

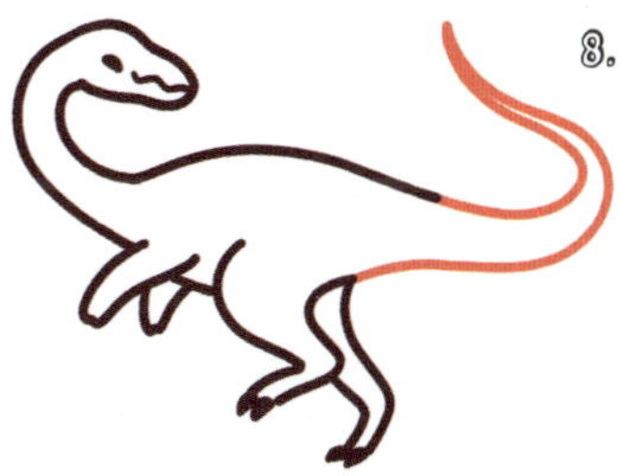

8. Draw a long, curved tail that ends in a point.

CORYTHOSAURUS

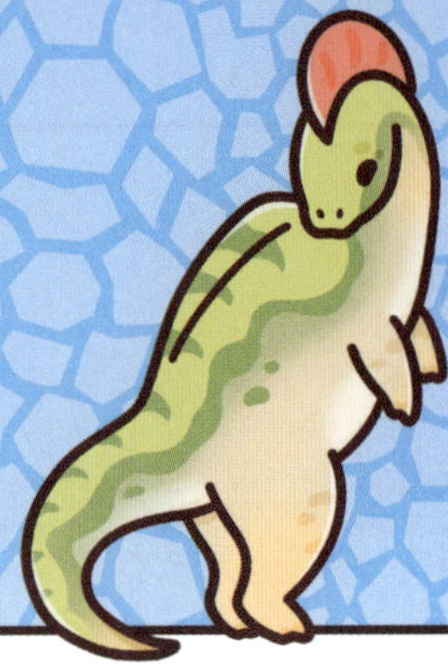

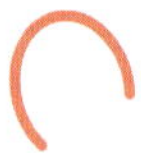

1. Draw an arch for the helmet on top of the head.

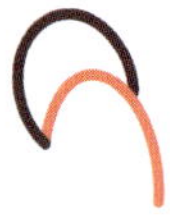

2. Add a curved line for the neck.

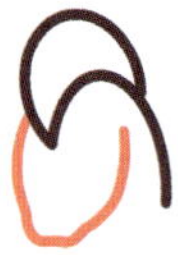

3. Draw an oval for the head with two bumps for the snout.

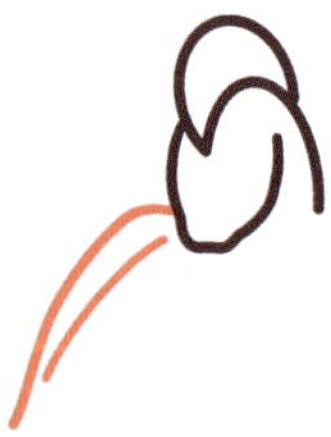

4. Add two curved lines on the left side of the head for the body.

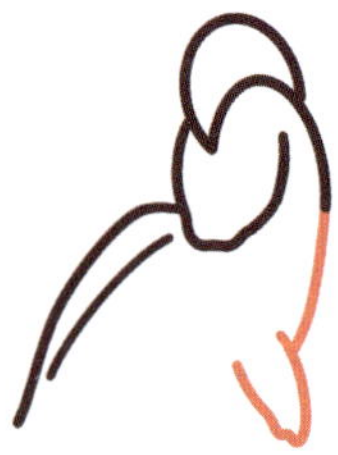

5. Draw a line for the right side of the body. Add a short arm with two fingers.

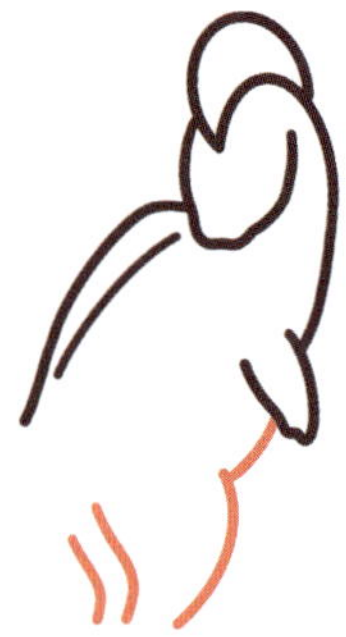

6. Add curved lines for the stomach and the legs.

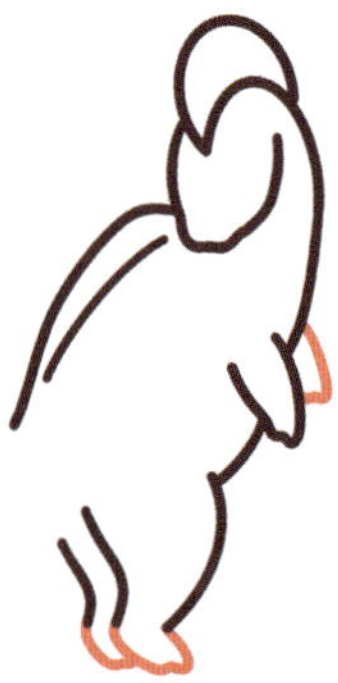

7. Add a second arm and the U-shaped feet with two toes each.

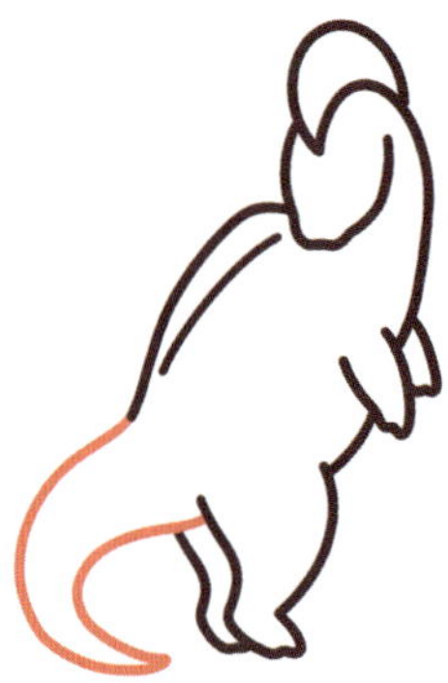

8. Draw a curved tail that tapers at the end.

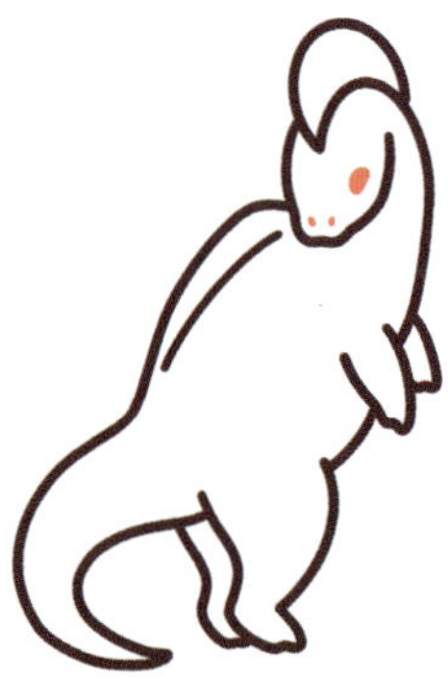

9. Add an oval eye and two dots for the nostrils.

VELOCIRAPTOR

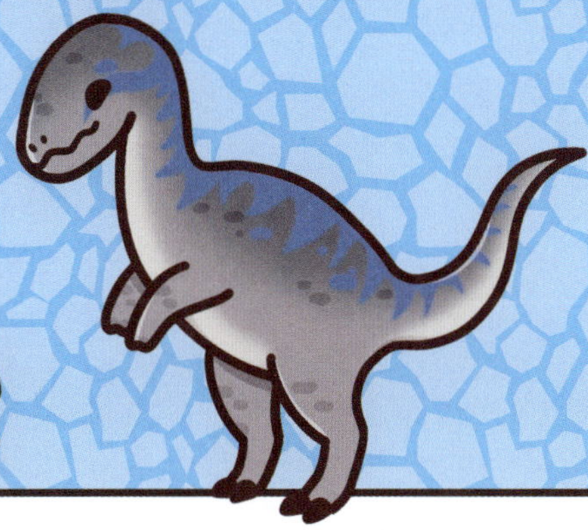

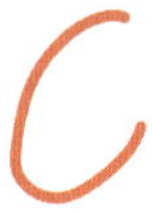

1. Draw a U-shaped head with a flat snout.

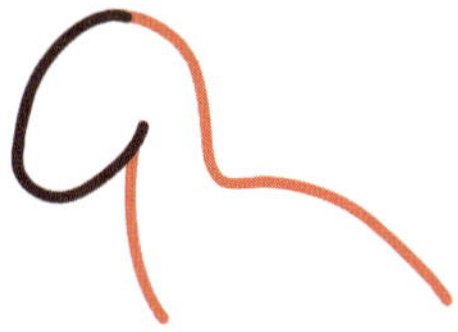

2. Add two curved lines for the back of the head, the neck, and the top of the body.

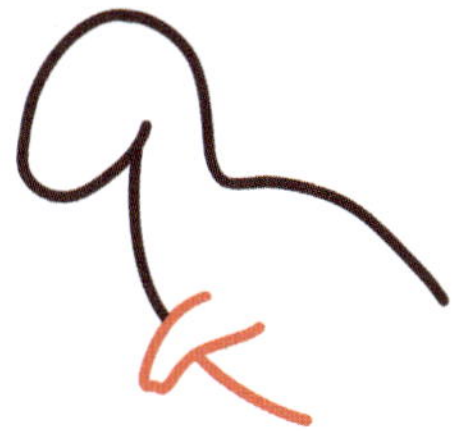

3. Add a short, thin arm with two fingers and a curve for the stomach.

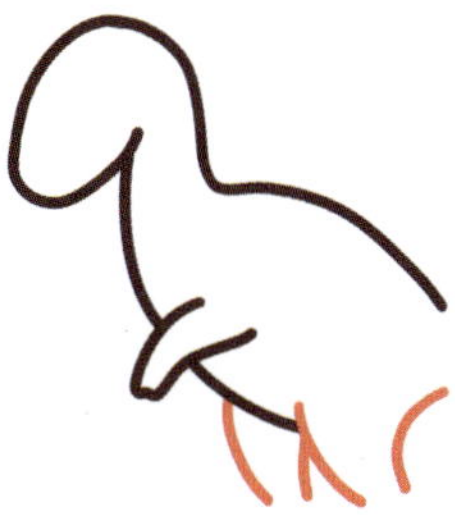

4. Draw four curved lines for the legs.

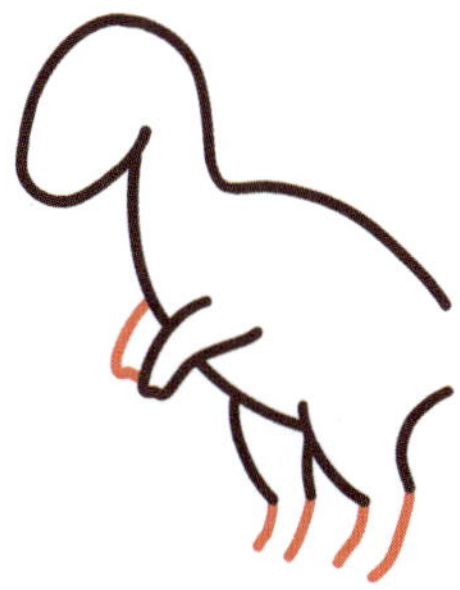

5. Add four more lines to the legs. Draw a second arm.

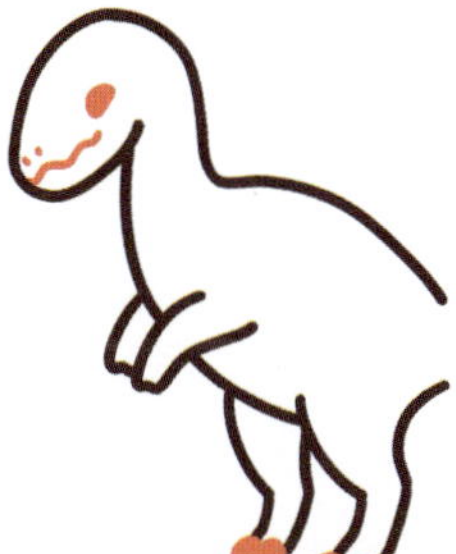

6. Add a semicircle eye, two dots for the nostrils, and a jagged mouth. Draw two triangle talons on each foot.

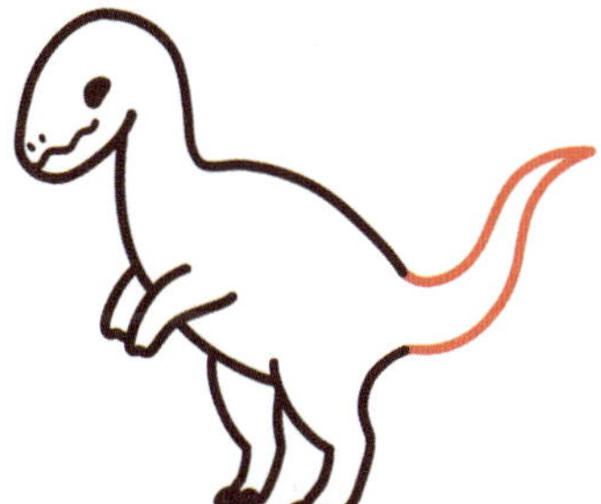

7. Draw a curved tail that ends in a point.

SPINOSAURUS

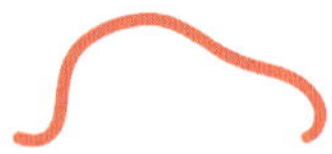

1. Draw a wavy line with a curve for the neck, the top of the head, and the snout.

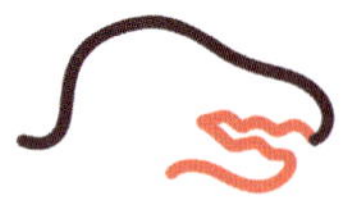

2. Add two jagged lines in a V for the mouth and a curved line for the chin.

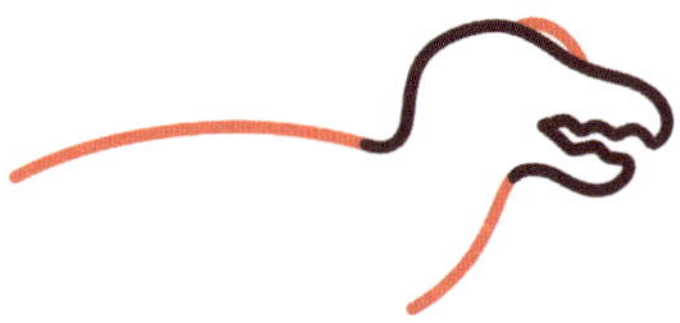

3. Add a curve above the head for the eye. Draw two curved lines for the top of the body and the neck.

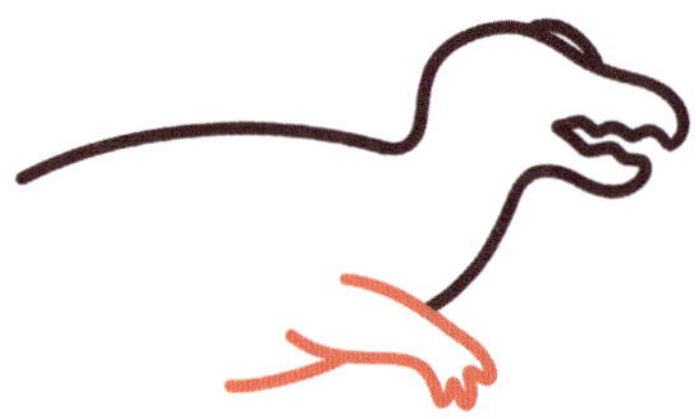

4. Add a curved arm with three fingers and a curved line for the stomach.

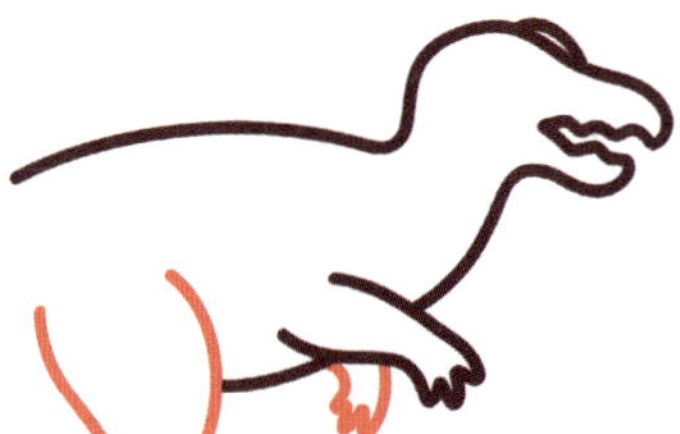

5. Add the second hand. Draw two curved lines for the leg.

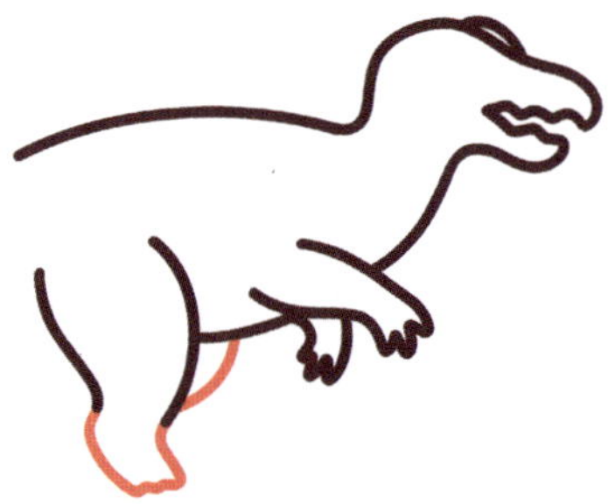

6. Add a curved line for the second leg. Draw a U-shaped foot with three toes.

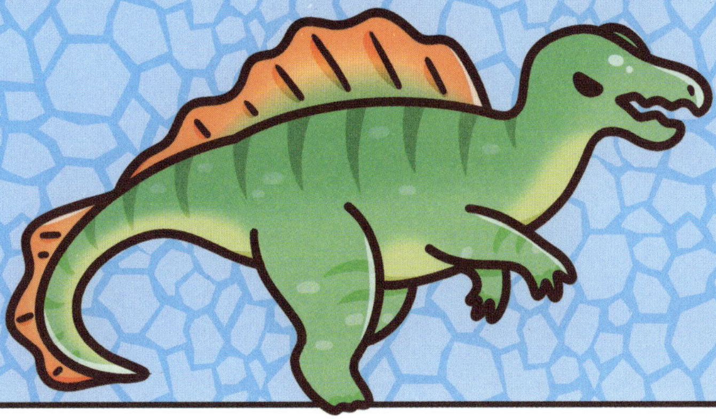

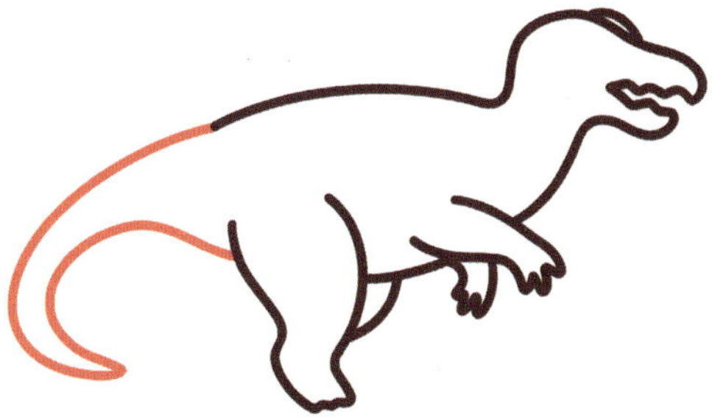

7. Draw a curved tail that tapers at the end.

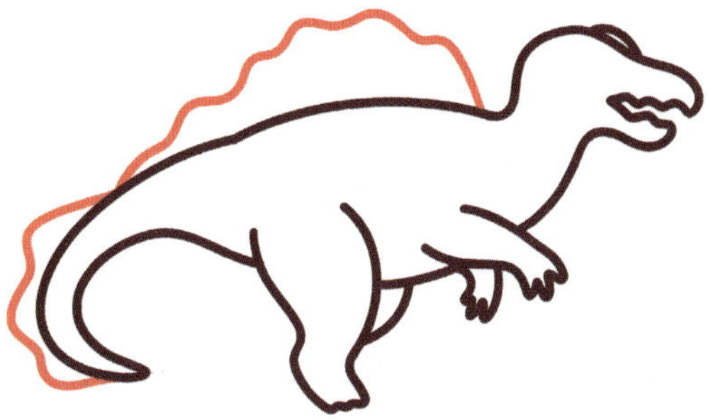

8. Draw a wavy sail from the back to the tail.

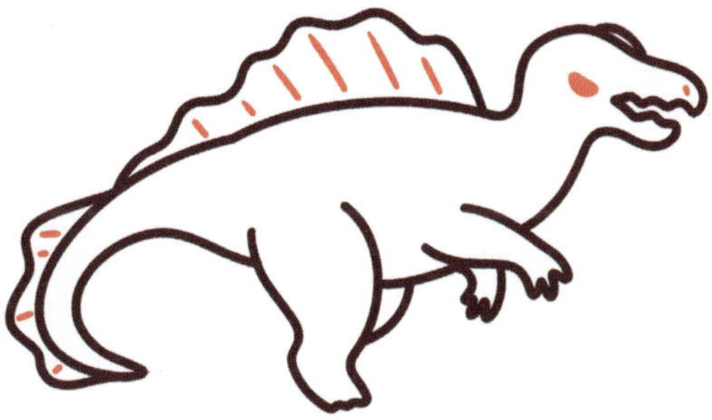

9. Add a semicircle eye and a dash for the nostril. Draw lines in the sail.

ALLOSAURUS

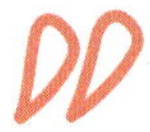

1. Draw two triangle horns.

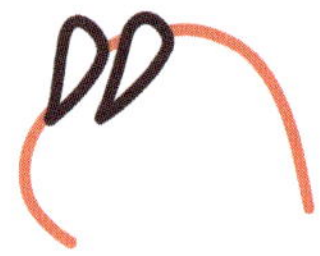

2. Add curved lines for the head.

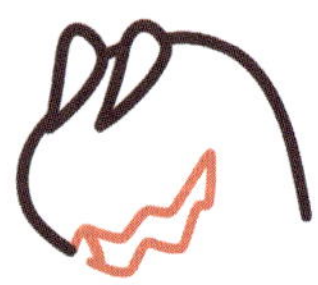

3. Draw an open jagged mouth.

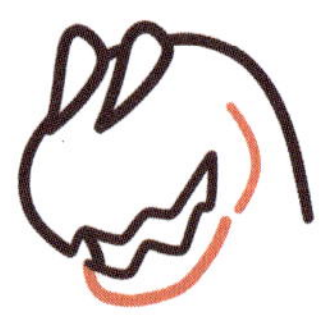

4. Add curved lines for the jaw.

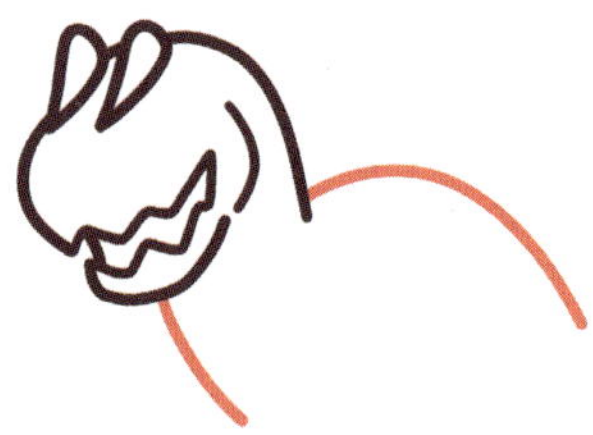

5. Add two curved lines for the neck and the top of the body.

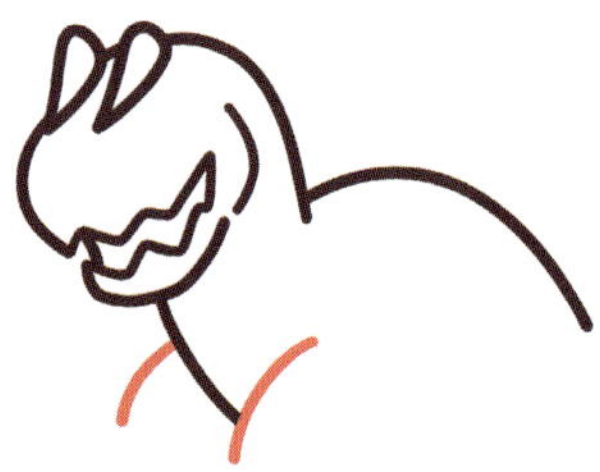

6. Draw two curved lines for the arms.

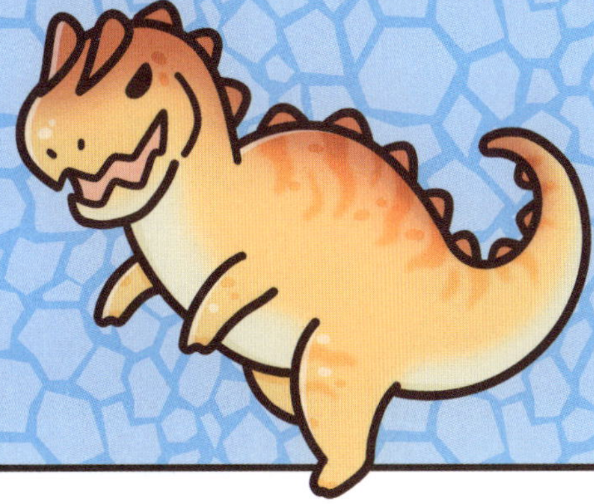

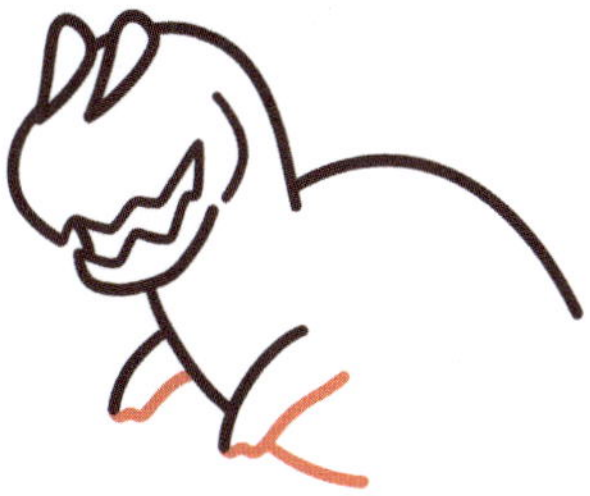

7. Finish the arms with a curved line and two fingers each. Add a curve for the stomach.

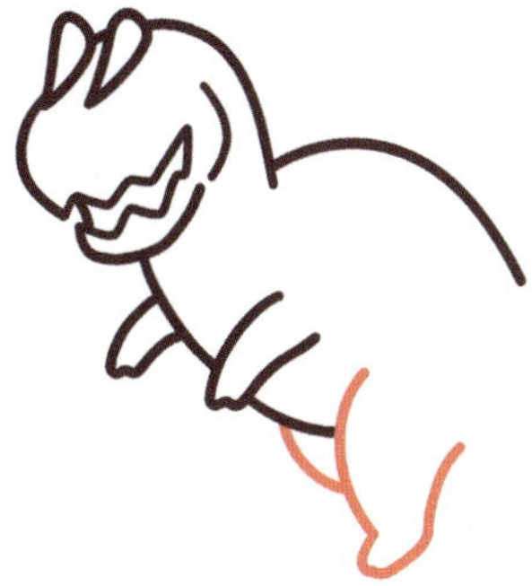

8. Add curved lines for the legs and a U-shaped foot with two toes.

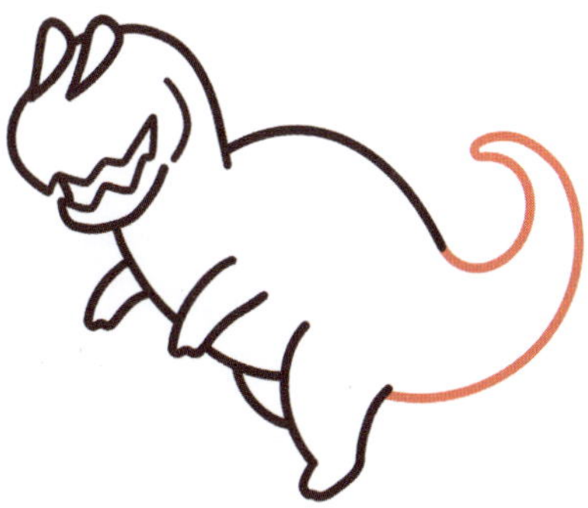

9. Draw a curved tail.

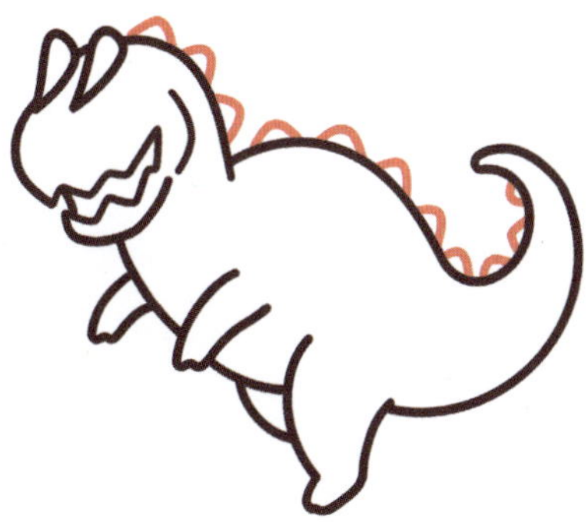

10. Add triangle spikes along the body from the head to the tail.

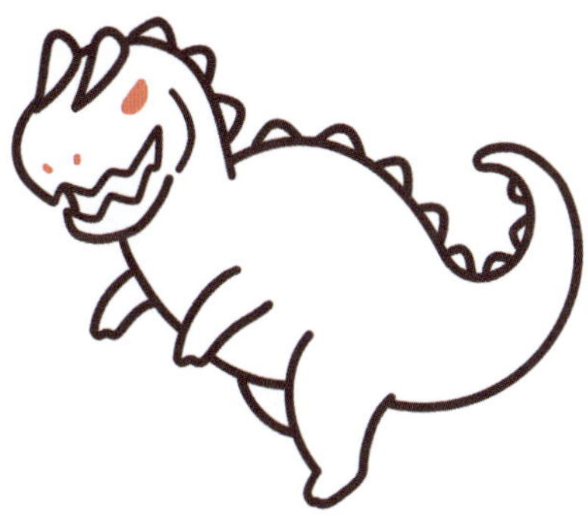

11. Draw a teardrop-shaped eye and two dots for the nostrils.

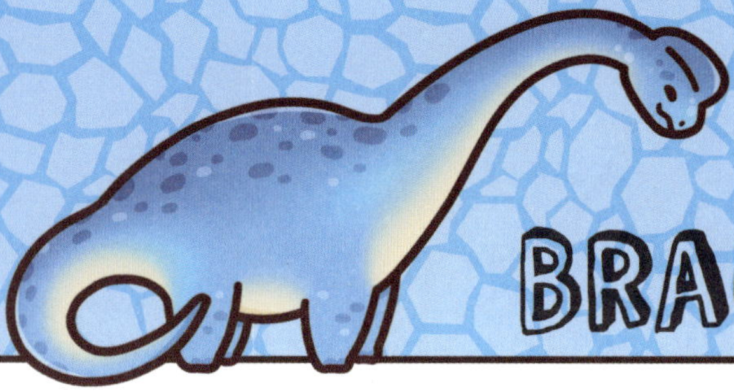

BRACHIOSAURUS

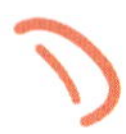

1. Draw a D shape for the nares.

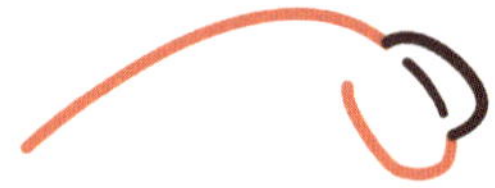

2. Add a round head under the nares and a curved line for the neck.

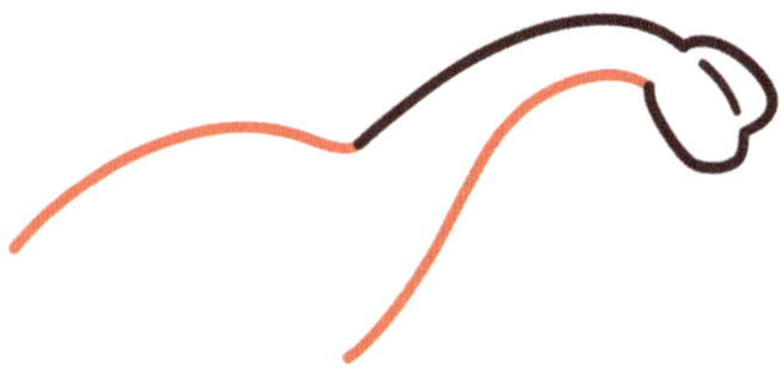

3. Draw two curved lines for the neck and the top of the body.

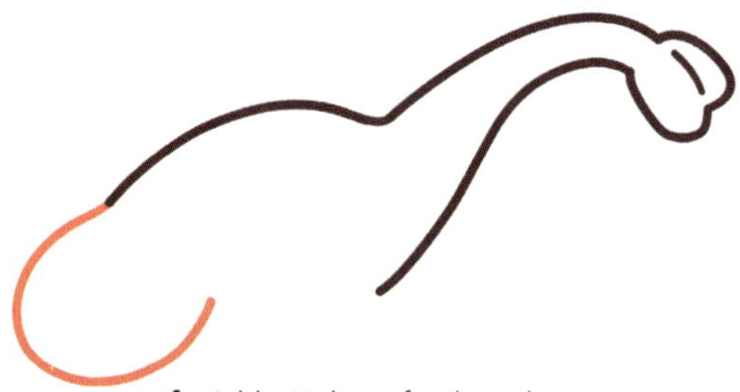

4. Add a U shape for the tail.

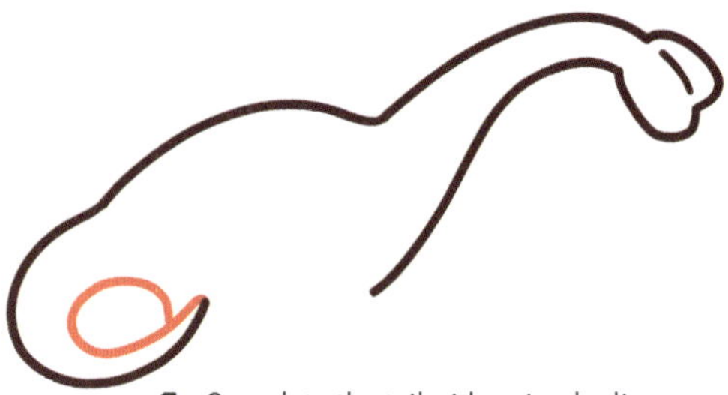

5. Complete the tail with a circular line.

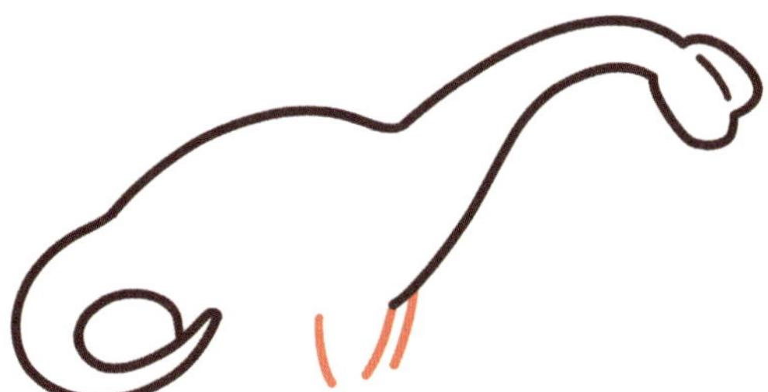

6. Draw three lines for the legs.

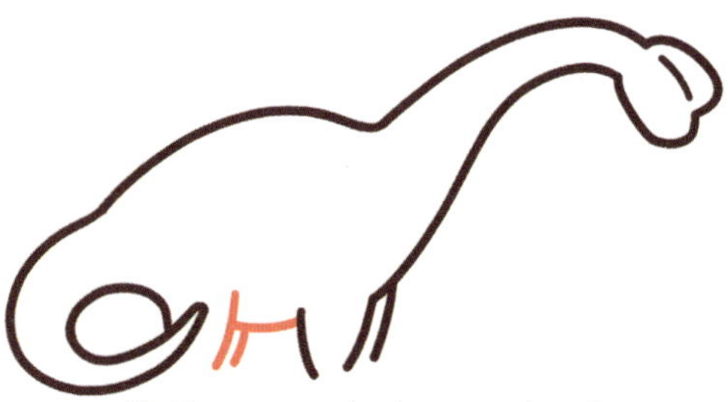

7. Draw a curve for the stomach and two more lines for the back legs.

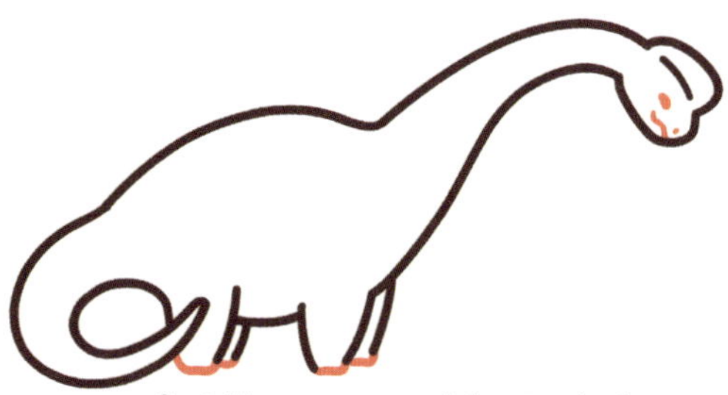

8. Add two toes to each leg. For the face, add an oval eye, a dot for the nostril, and a wavy mouth.

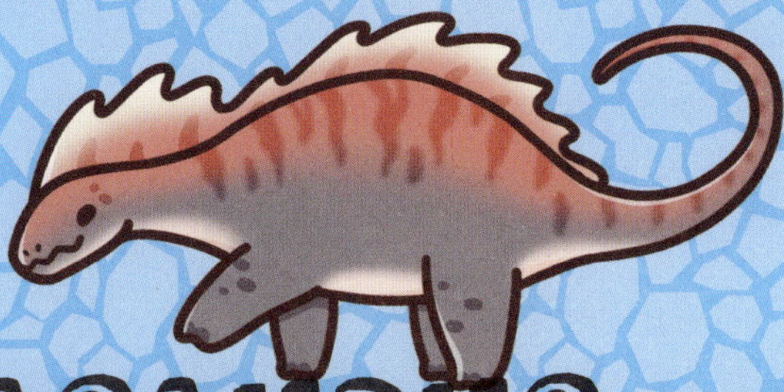

AMARGASAURUS

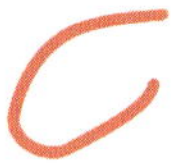

1. Draw a U-shaped head with a flat snout.

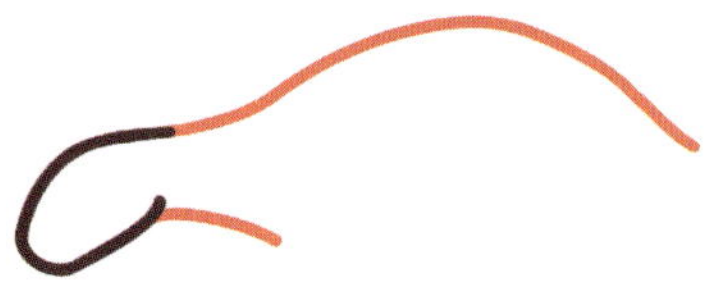

2. Add two curved lines for the top of the body and the neck.

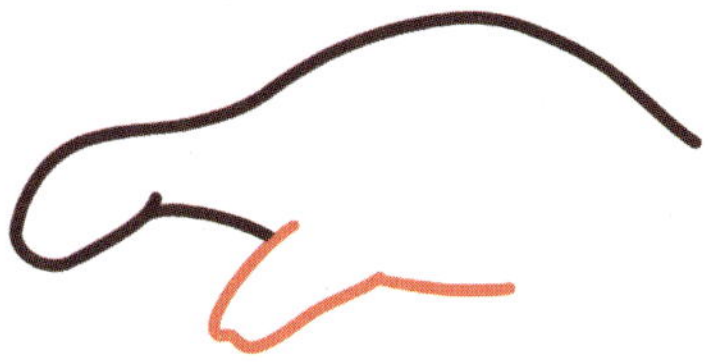

3. Draw a U-shaped leg with two toes. Add a curve for the stomach.

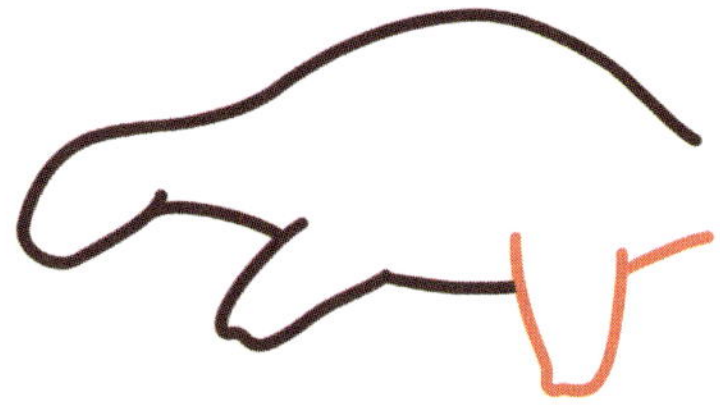

4. Add another leg and a line on the right.

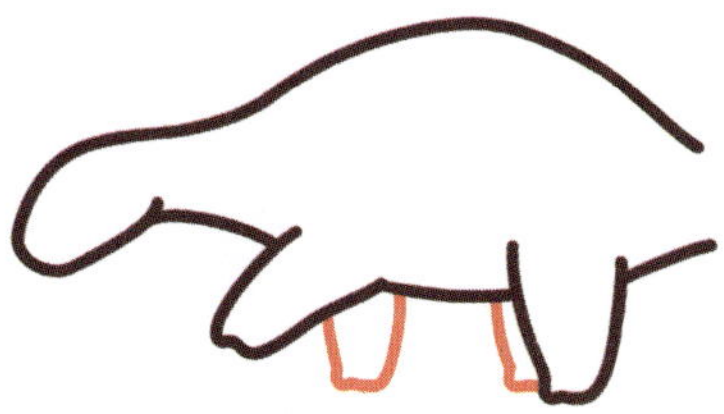

5. Add two more legs.

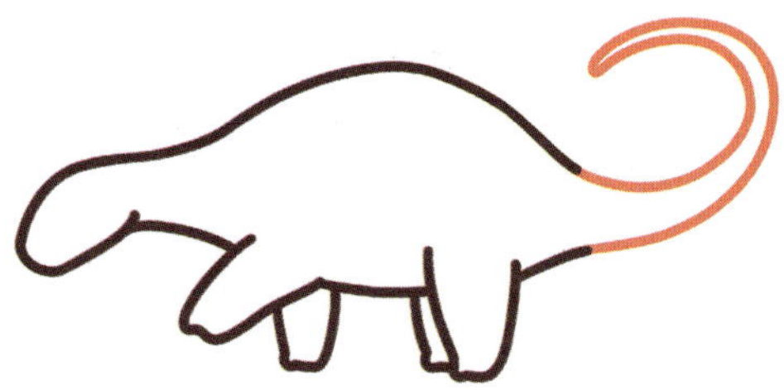

6. Draw a thin, curving tail that tapers at the end.

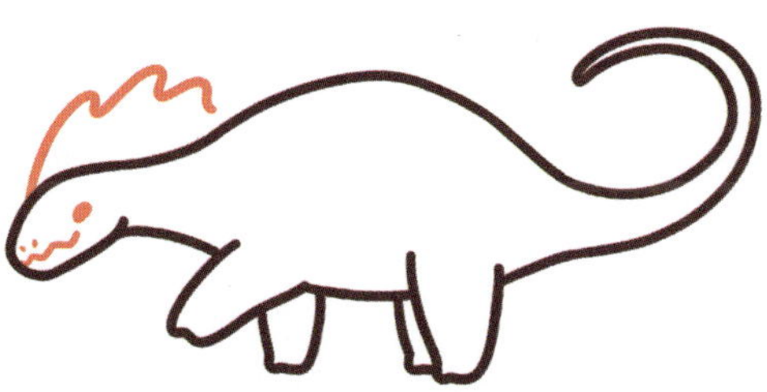

7. Draw three spikes on top of the head and neck. For the face, add an oval eye, two dots for the nostrils, and a jagged mouth.

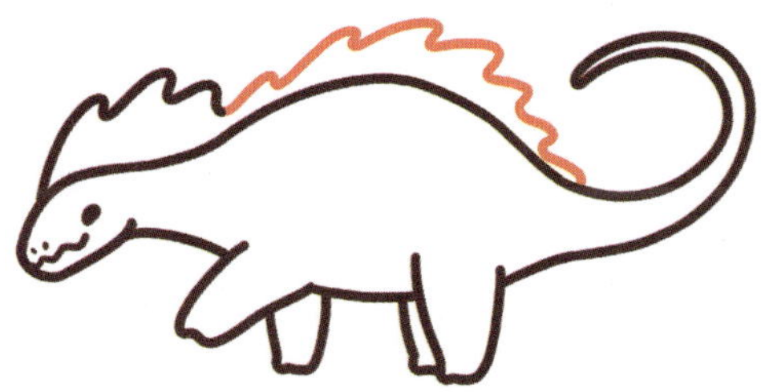

8. Continue the spikes down the body.

CARNOTAURUS

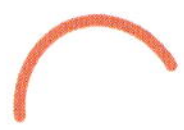

1. Draw an arch for the nose.

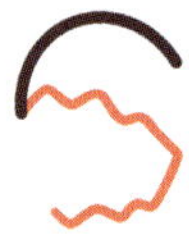

2. Draw jagged lines for an open mouth.

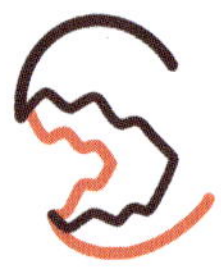

3. Add another jagged line for the other side of the mouth. Add a curved line for the chin.

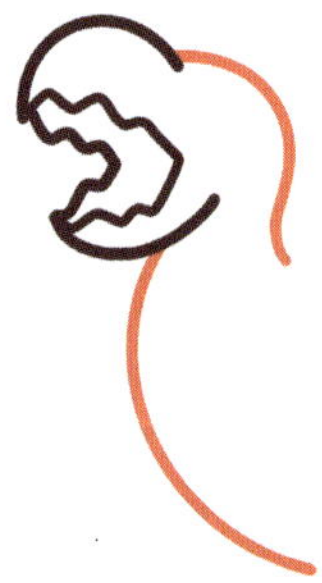

4. Add two curved lines for the top of the head and the neck.

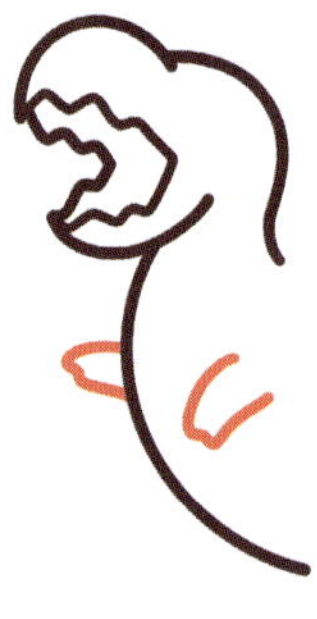

5. Draw two short arms with two fingers.

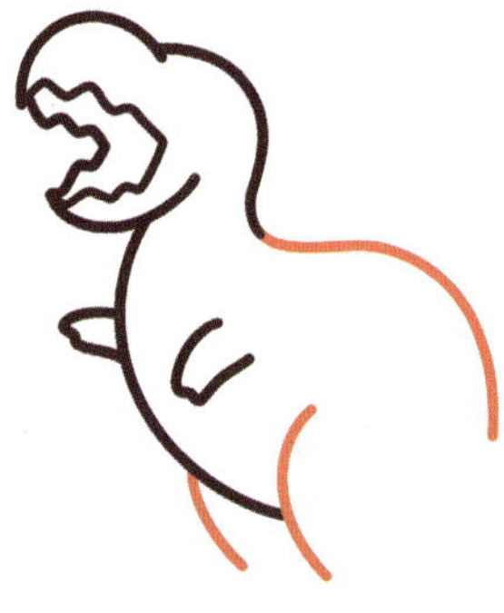

6. Draw three curved lines for the back of the body and the legs.

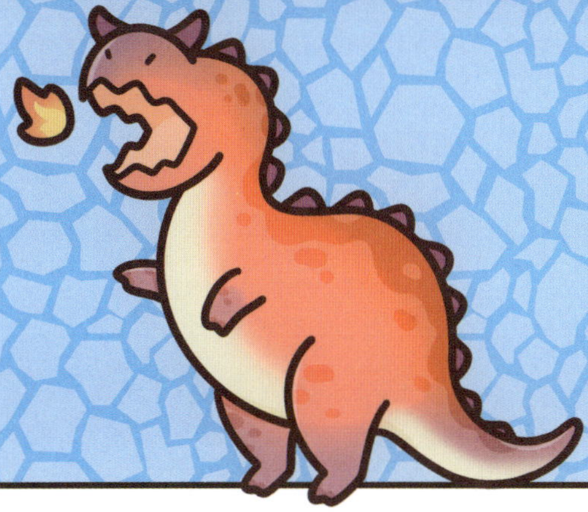

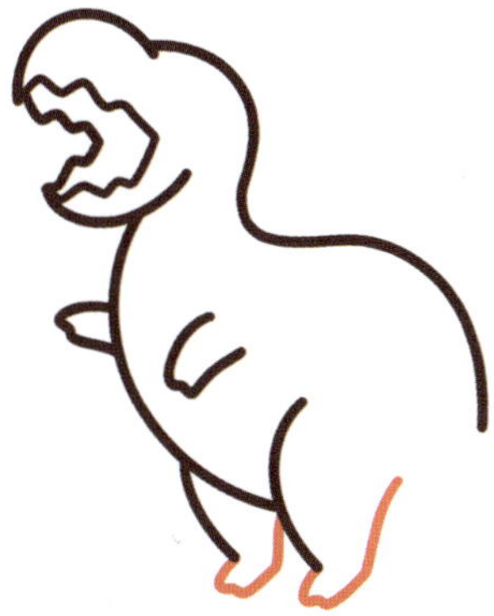

7. Complete the legs with curved lines and U-shaped feet, with two toes each.

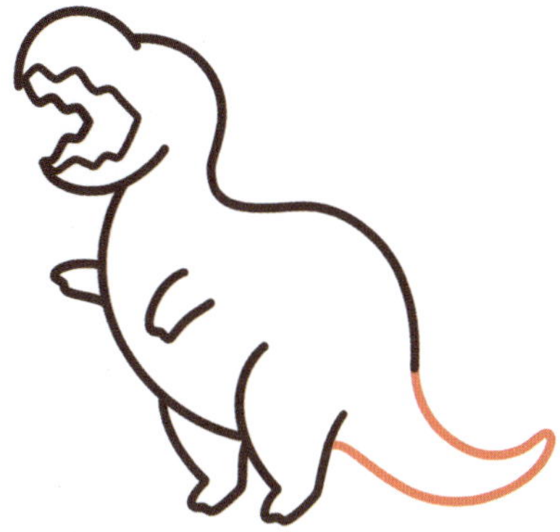

8. Add a curved tail.

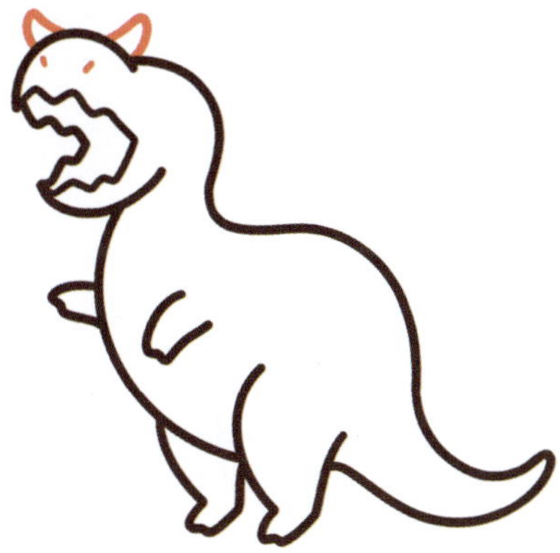

9. Draw two triangle horns on top of the nose and two dashes for the nostrils.

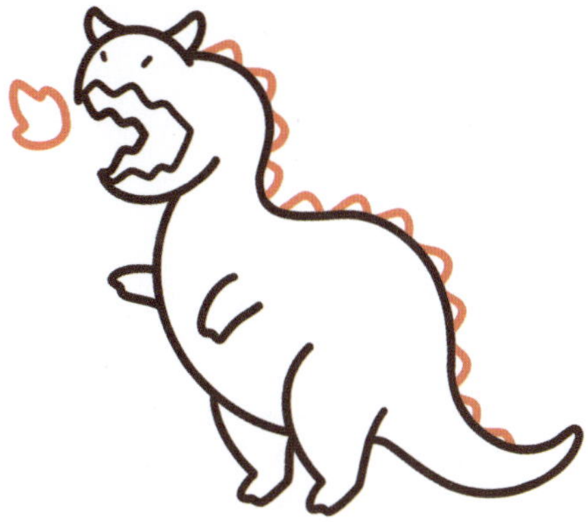

10. Add triangle spikes along the body from the head to the tail. Draw a flame in front of the mouth.

ANKYLOSAURUS

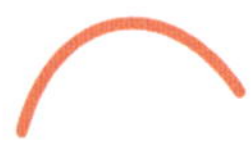

1. Draw an arch for the head.

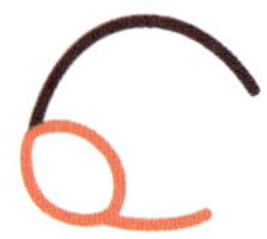

2. Add an oval nose and a curved line for the chin.

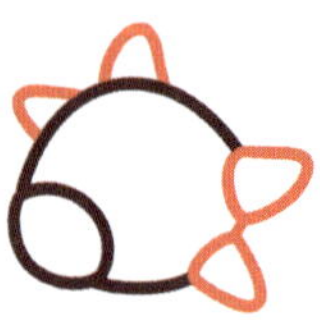

3. Add four triangle horns around the head.

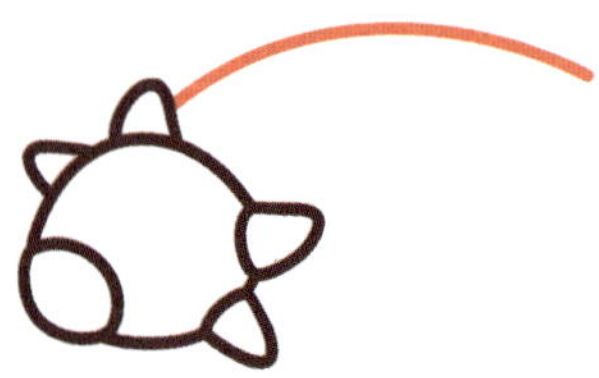

4. Draw a curved line for the top of the body.

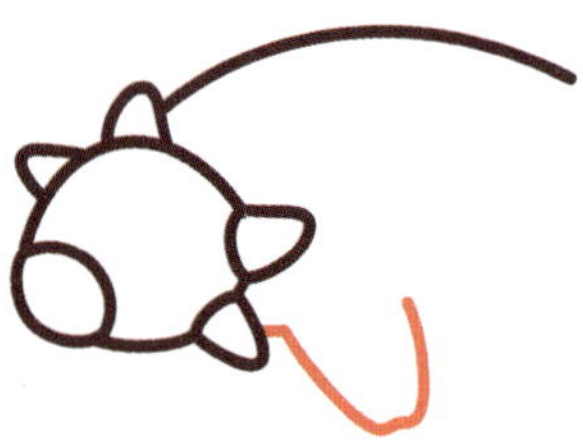

5. Add a short line and a U-shaped leg with two toes.

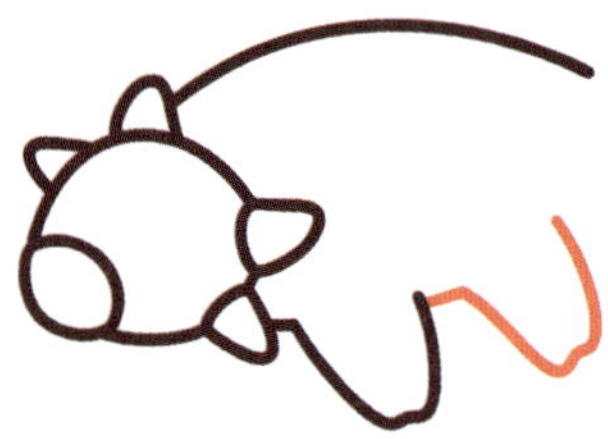

6. Add another short line for the stomach and a second leg.

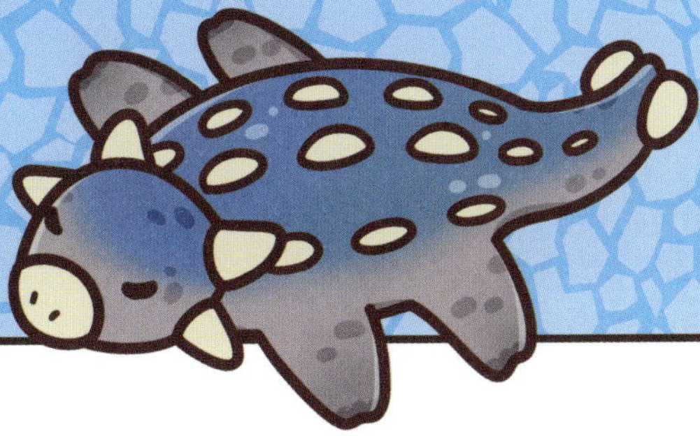

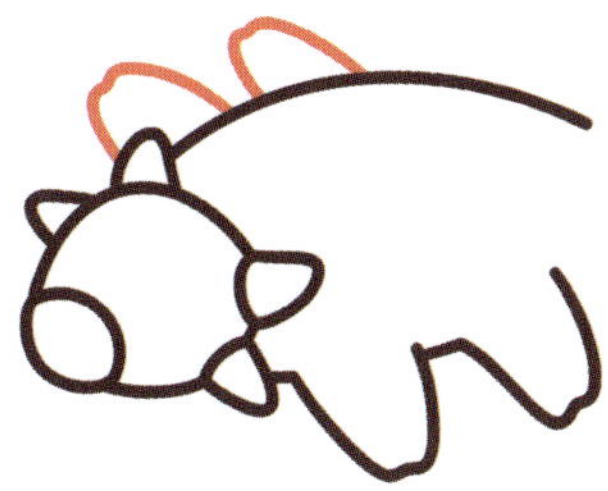

7. Add two more legs.

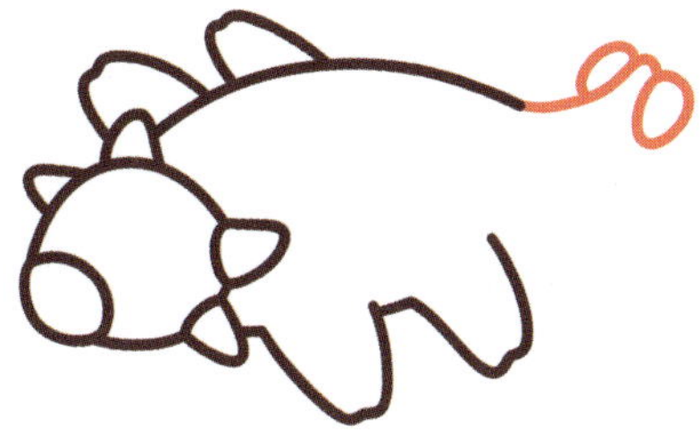

8. Draw a curved line that ends in a triangle. Add two ovals on each side of the end of the tail.

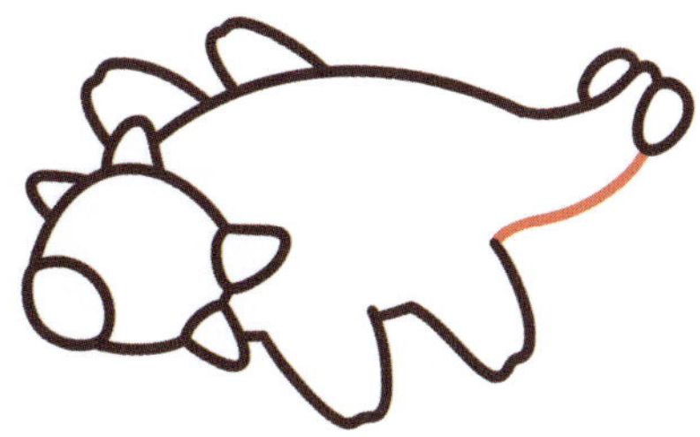

9. Complete the tail with a curved line.

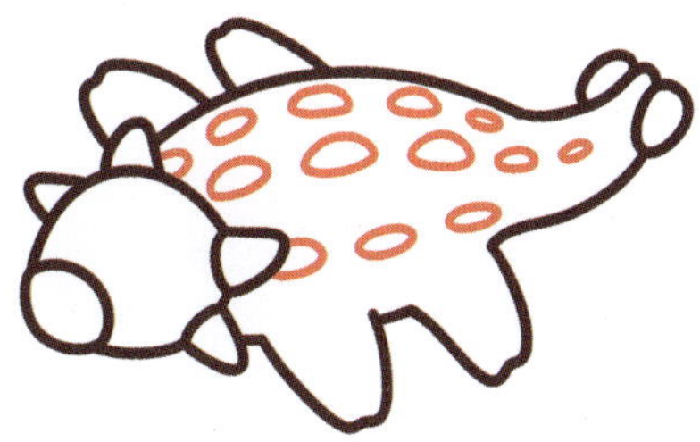

10. Draw ovals along the body for the armor.

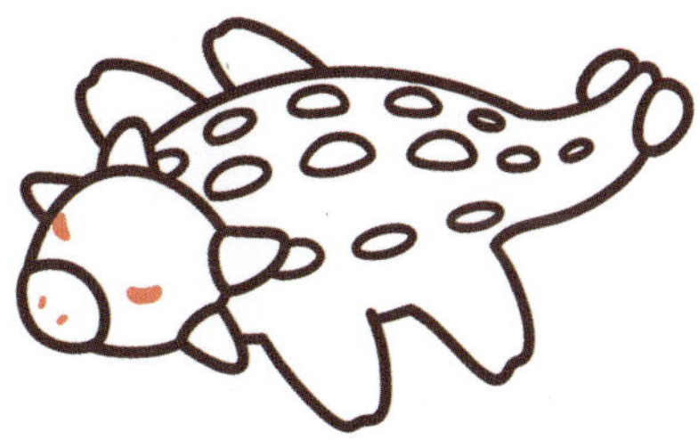

11. Add two oval eyes and two dashes for the nostrils.

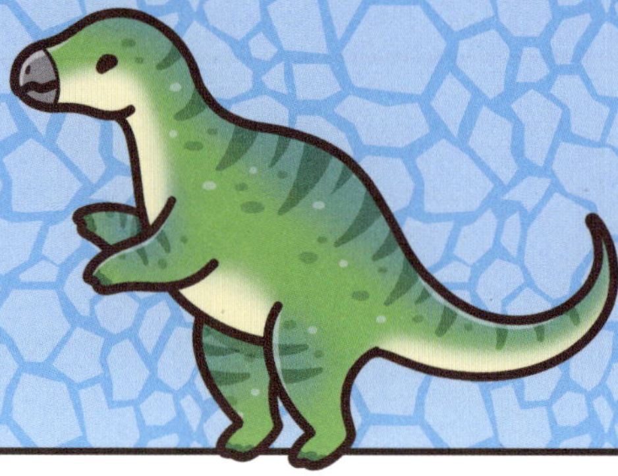

IGUANODON

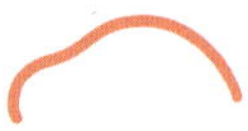

1. Draw a curved line with a bump for the snout.

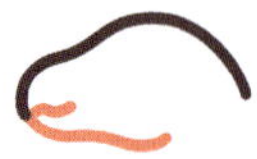

2. Add a wavy line for the mouth and the chin.

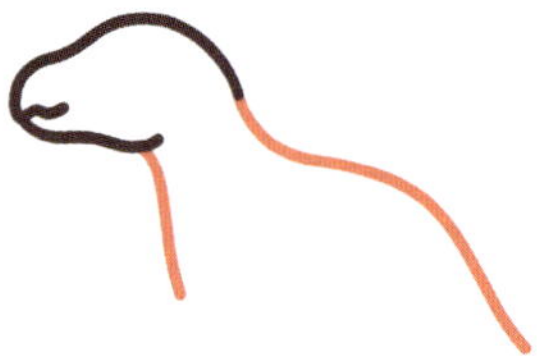

3. Draw two curved lines for the body and the neck.

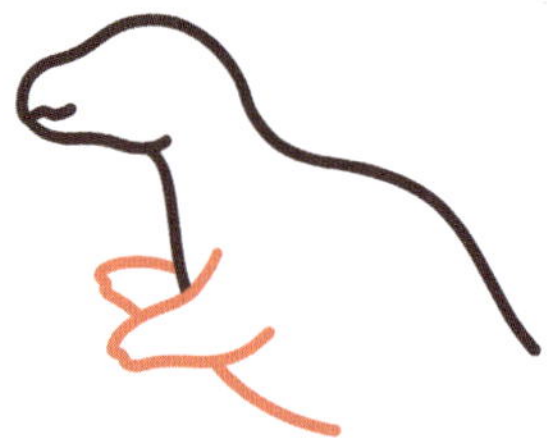

4. Add two U-shaped arms with two fingers each. Draw a curved line for the stomach.

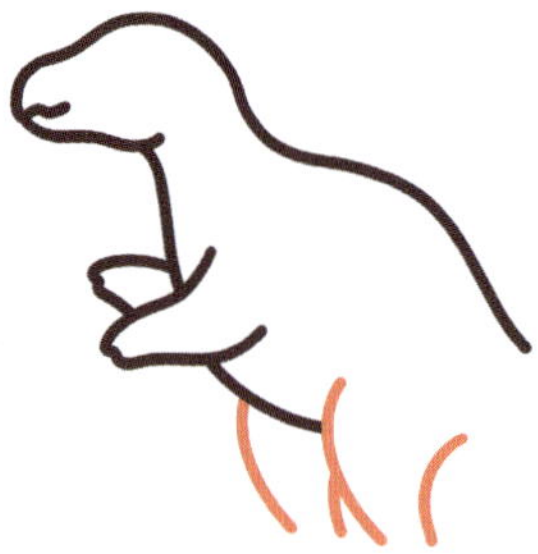

5. Draw four curved lines for the legs.

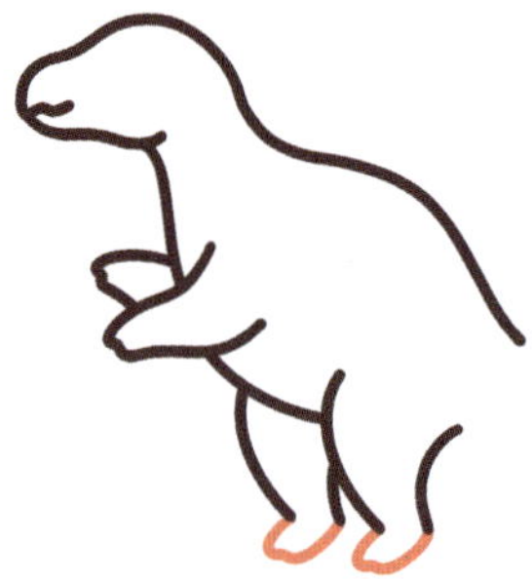

6. Add two U-shaped feet with two toes each.

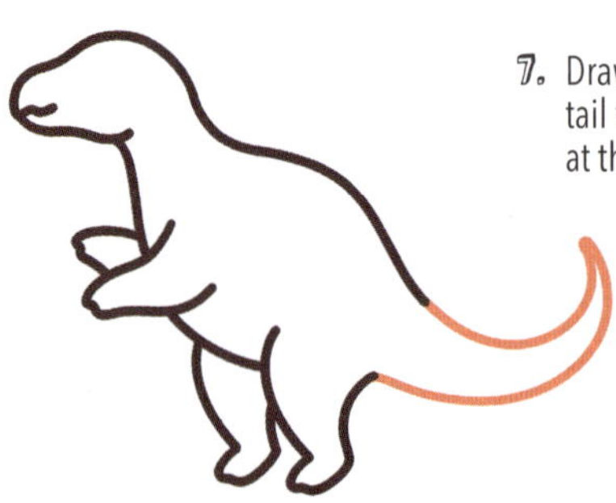

7. Draw a curved tail that tapers at the end.

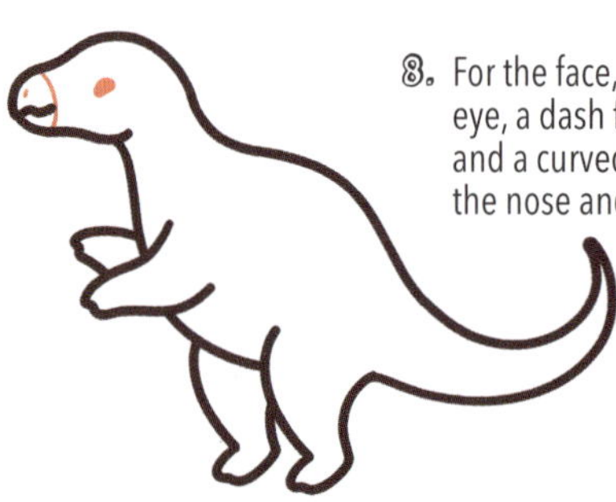

8. For the face, add an oval eye, a dash for the nostril, and a curved line around the nose and mouth.

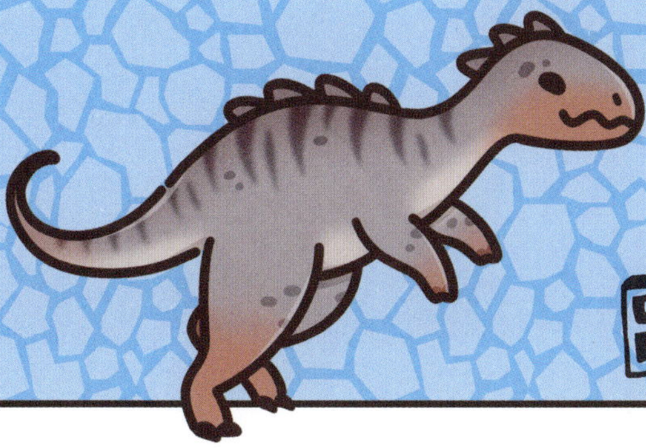

EORAPTOR

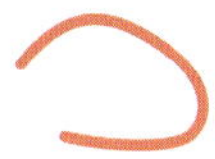

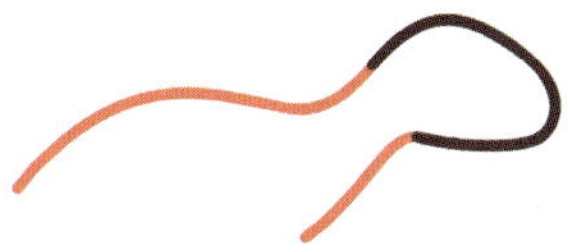

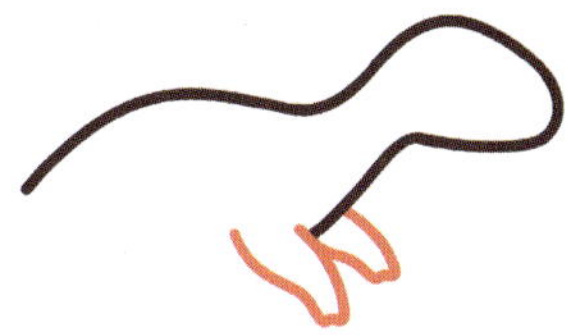

1. Draw an incomplete oval head.

2. Add two curved lines for the neck and the top of the body.

3. Draw two thin arms with two fingers each.

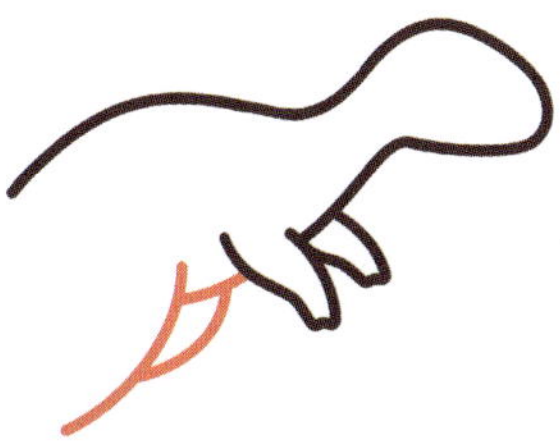

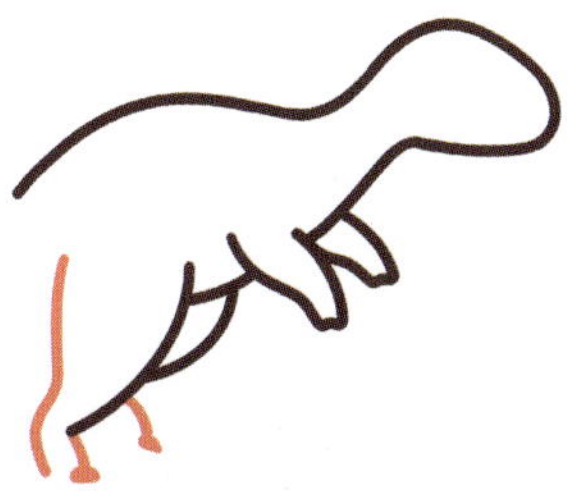

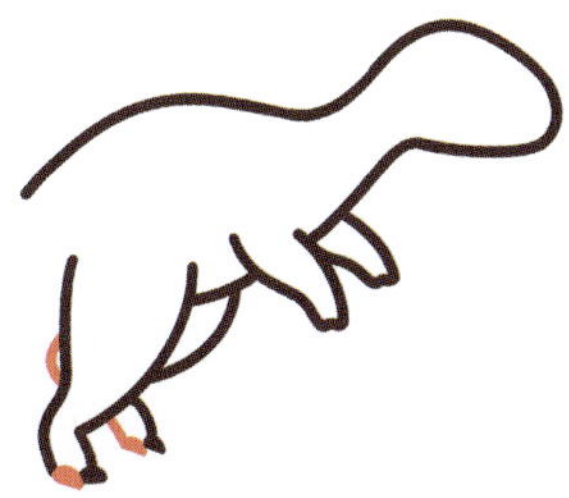

4. Add a curve for the stomach and two curves for the legs.

5. Complete the back leg with a curve and add an oval toe. Add a second foot.

6. Complete the feet with lines and a second toe. Add a curve for the second leg.

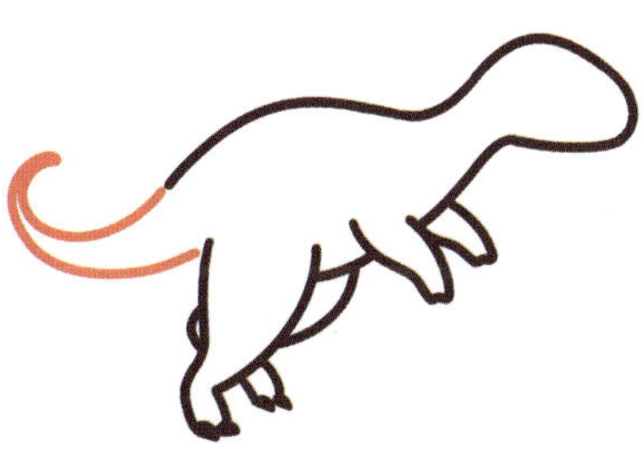

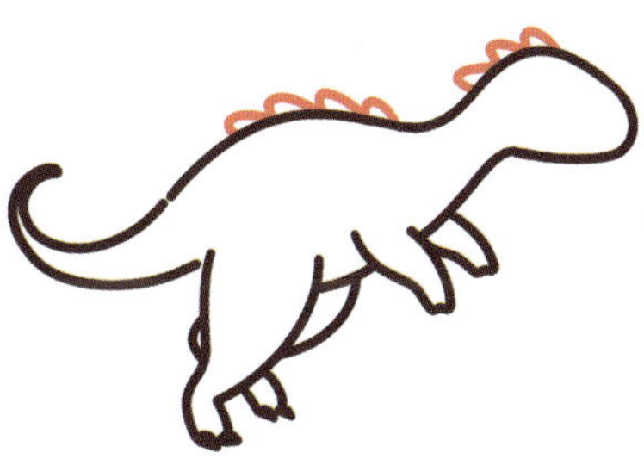

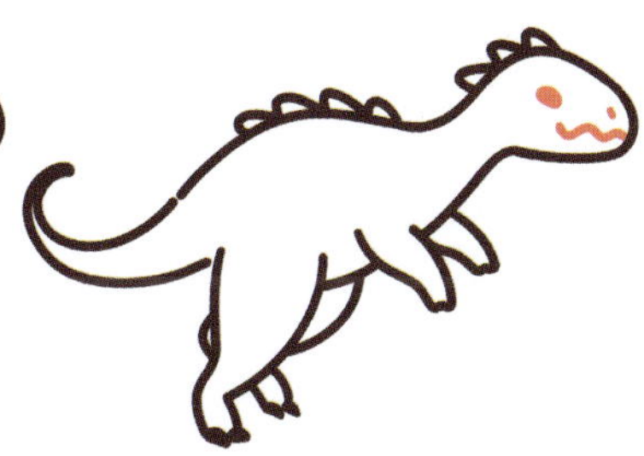

7. Draw a curved tail that ends in a point.

8. Add spikes on top of the head and the back.

9. Add an oval eye, a dash for the nostril, and a jagged mouth.

PARASAUROLOPHUS

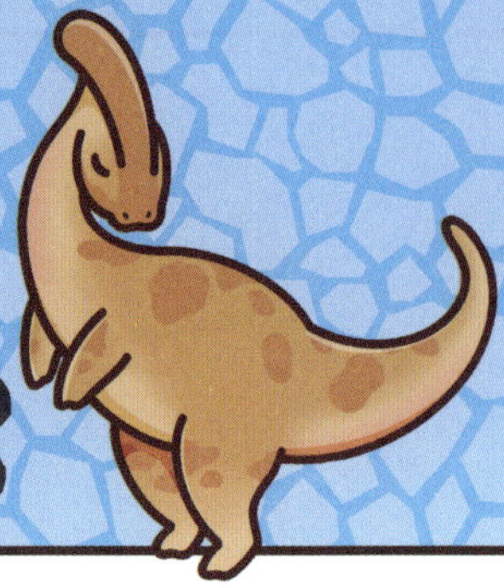

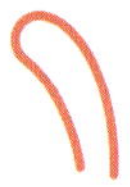

1. Draw an incomplete long, narrow oval.

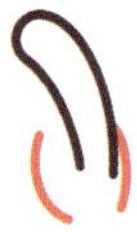

2. Add two curved lines on the sides of the oval for the head.

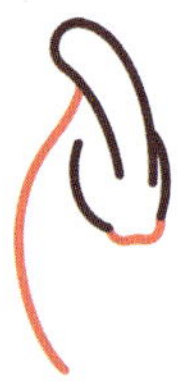

3. Add a curved line for the neck. Draw a bumpy line on the head for the snout.

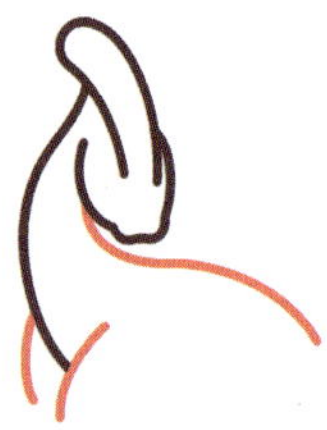

4. Draw three curved lines for the top of the body and the arms.

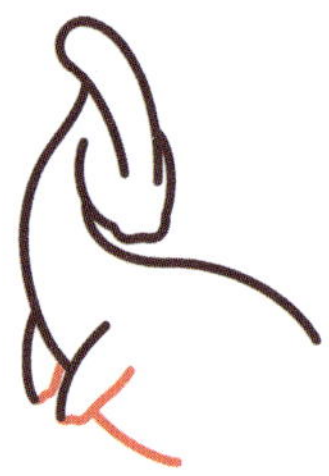

5. Complete the U-shaped arms with two fingers each. Add a curved line for the stomach.

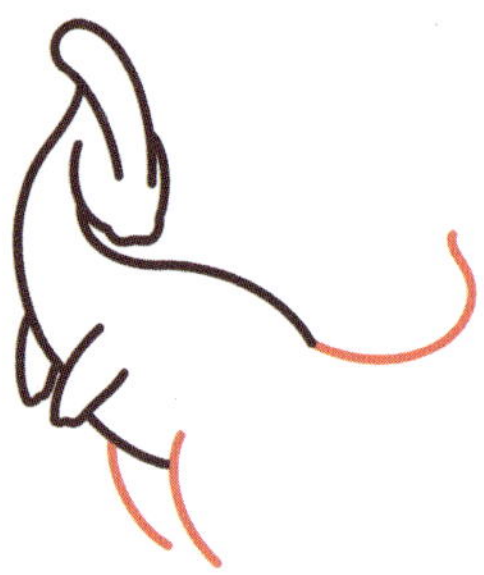

6. Add two curved lines for the legs and one for the tail.

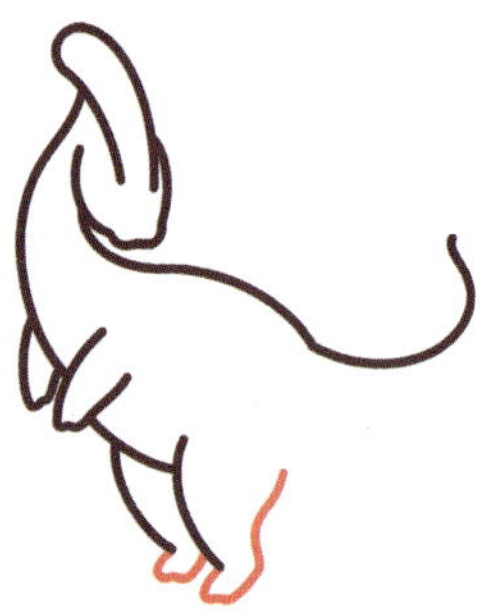

7. Complete the legs with a curved line and U-shaped feet with two toes each.

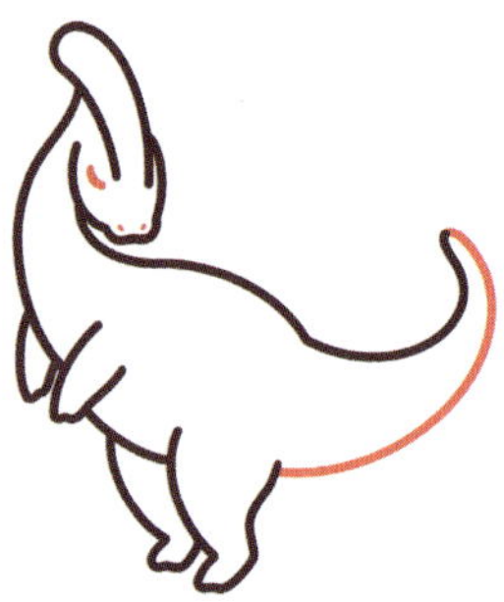

8. Add a U-shaped eye and two dots for the nostrils. Draw a curved line to finish the tail.

FUKUISAURUS

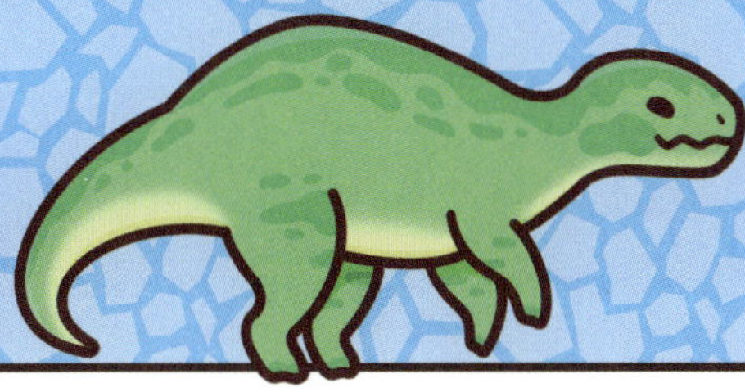

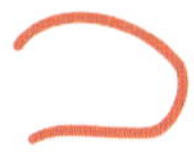

1. Draw a U-shaped head with a flat snout on the right.

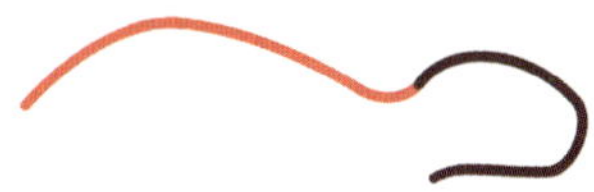

2. Add a curved line for the top of the body.

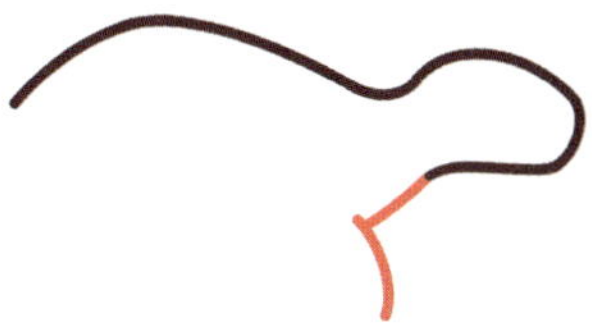

3. Add two curved lines for the neck and the arm.

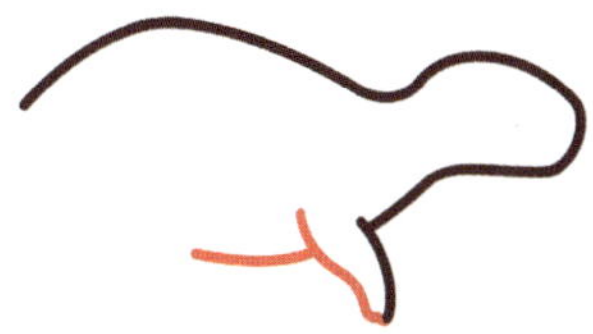

4. Complete the arm with a curved line. Add a curved line for the stomach.

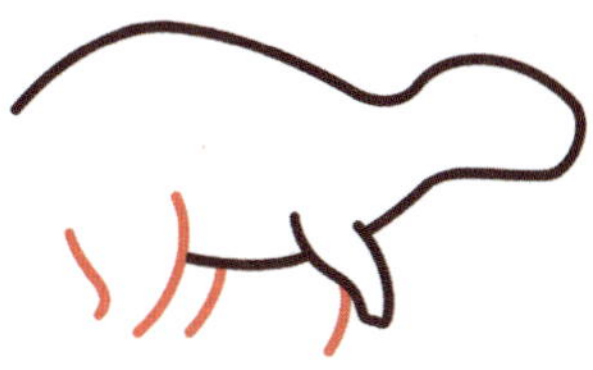

5. Draw four curved lines for the front arm and back legs.

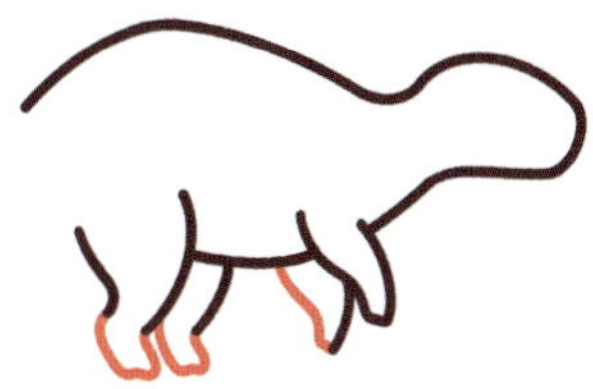

6. Complete the front arm and draw U-shaped feet for the back legs, with two toes each.

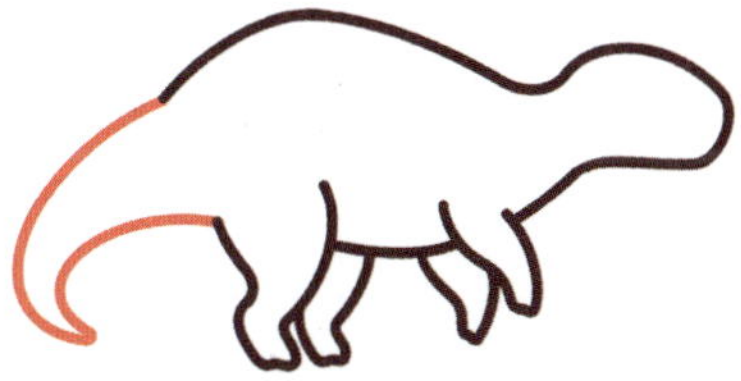

7. Draw a curved tail that tapers at the end.

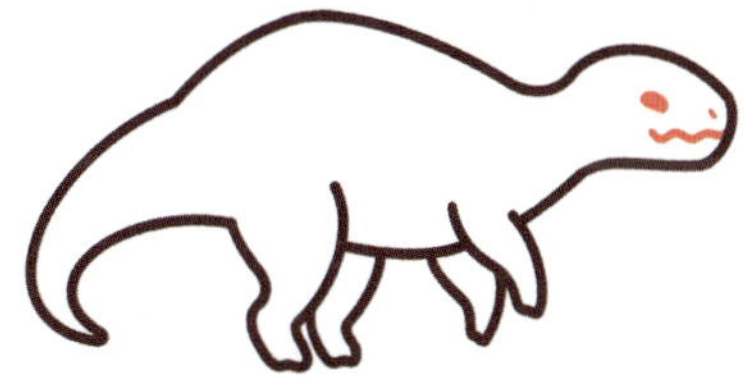

8. Add an oval eye, a dash for the nostril, and a jagged mouth.

MEGALOSAURUS

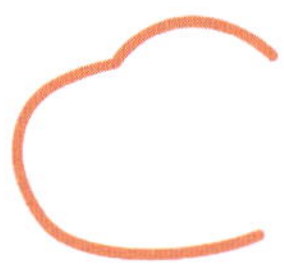

1. Draw a C shape with a bump for the eye.

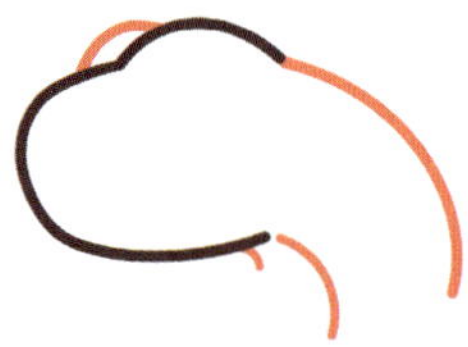

2. Draw a bump for the second eye. Add three curved lines for the neck.

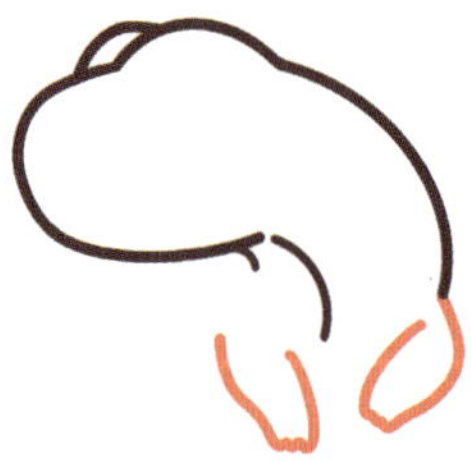

3. Add two U-shaped arms with three fingers each. Connect the right arm to the neck.

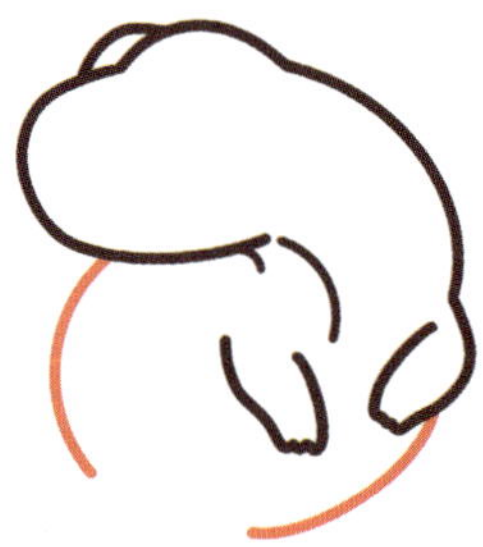

4. Add two curved lines for the body.

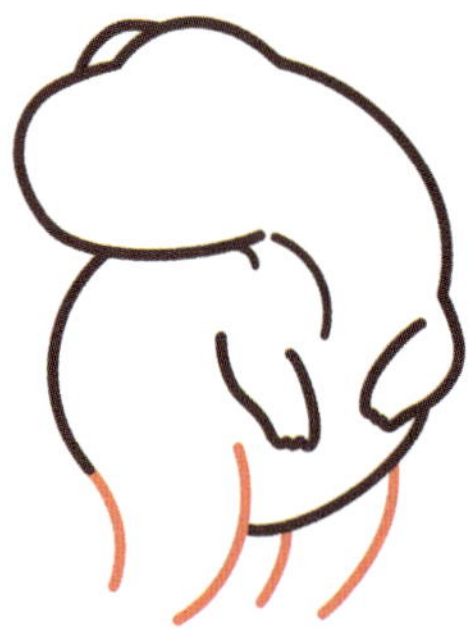

5. Add four curved lines for the legs.

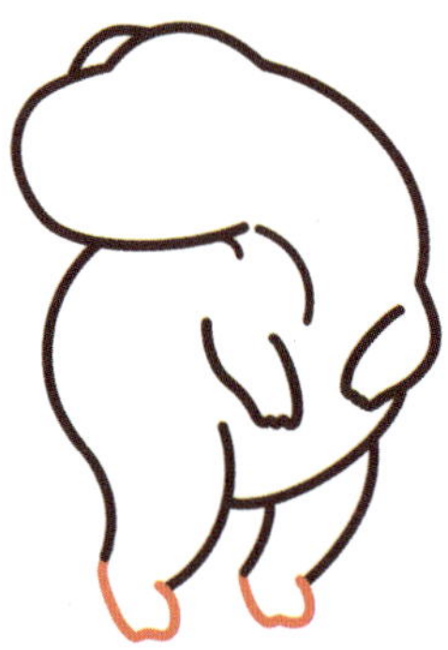

6. Add two U-shaped feet with two toes each.

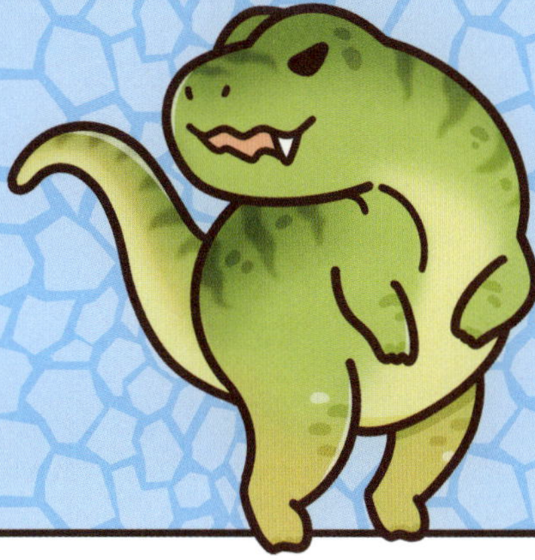

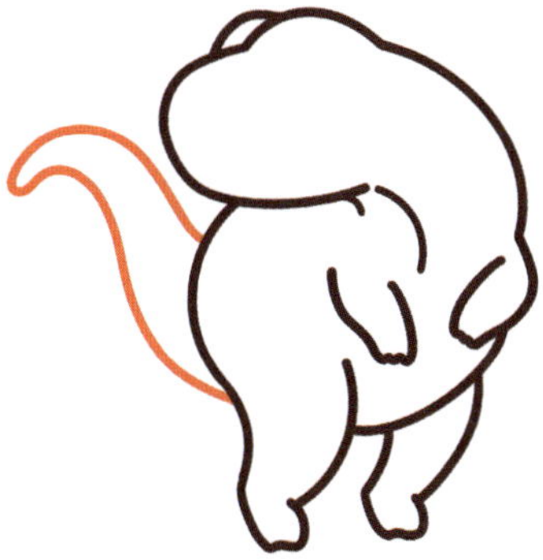

7. Draw a curved tail.

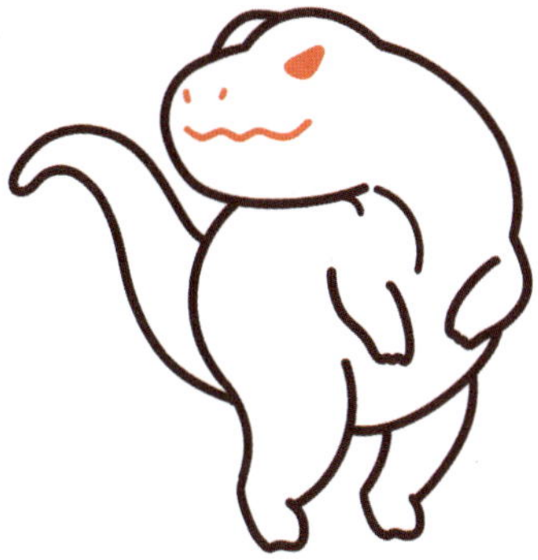

8. Add a triangle eye, two dashes for the nostrils, and a jagged mouth.

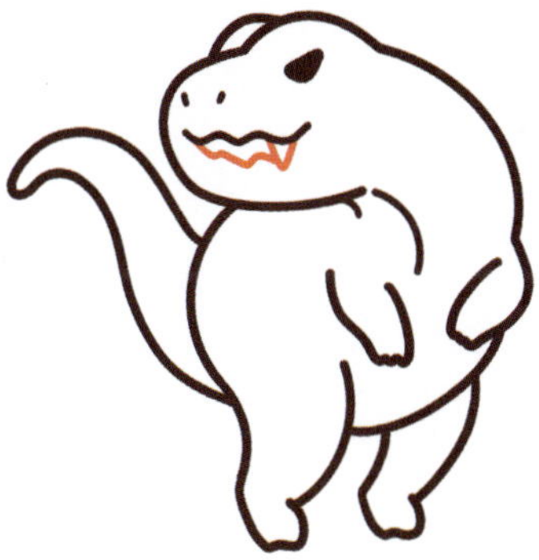

9. Add another jagged line to the mouth with a pointed tooth.

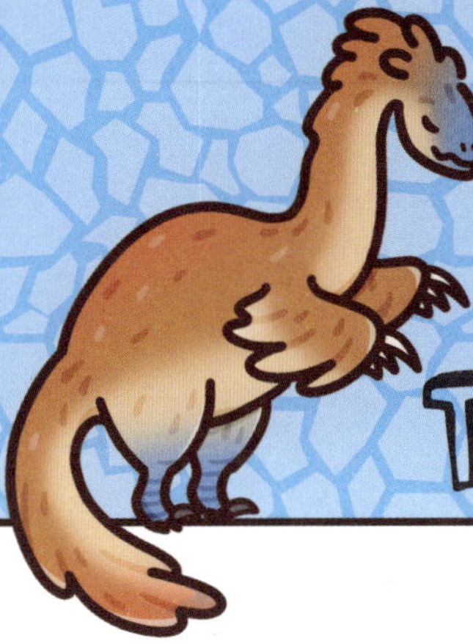

THERIZINOSAURUS

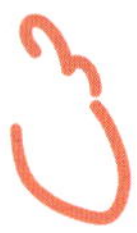

1. Draw a V-shaped head with an M-line on top.

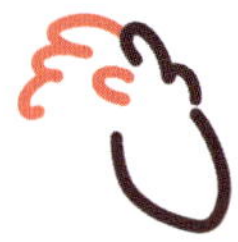

2. Add a U-shaped feather on top of the head and add more feathers behind it.

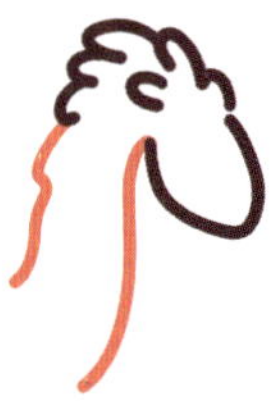

3. Draw two curved lines for the neck, with feathers along the back.

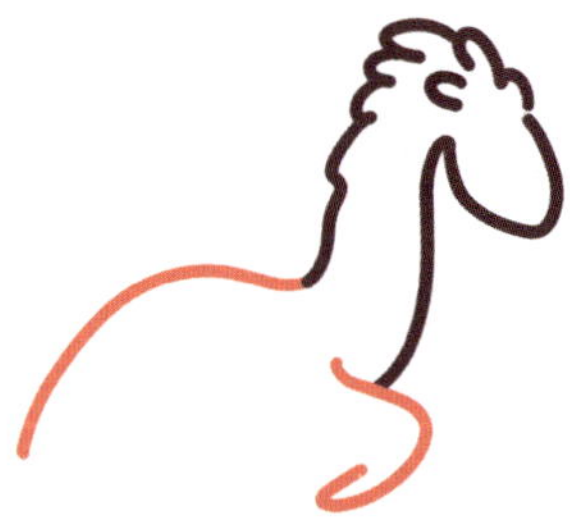

4. Add a curved line for the top of the body. Draw a V-shaped line for the arm that curves inward at the end.

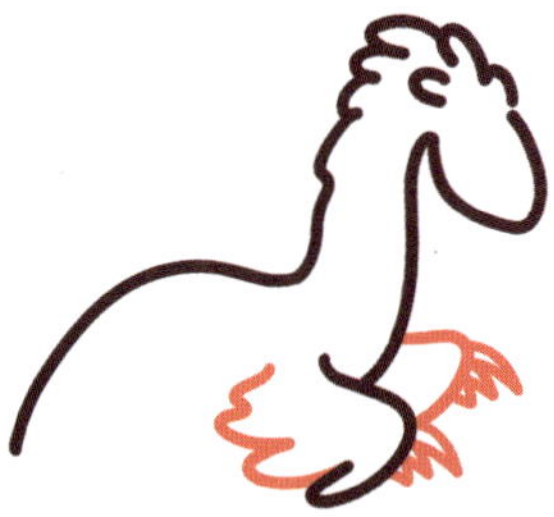

5. Add feathers and three talons to the wing. Draw a second wing with a triangle and three talons.

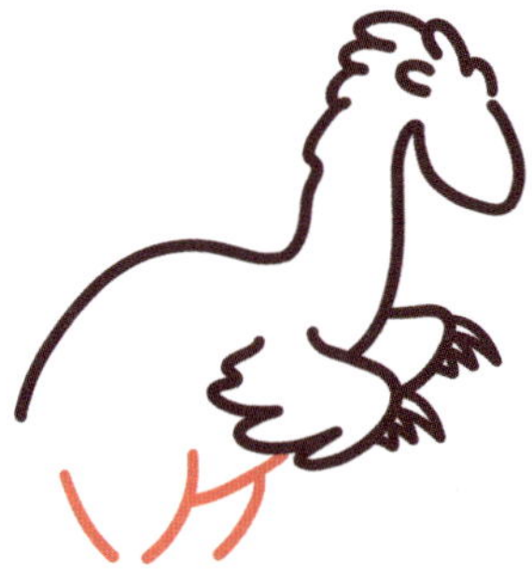

6. Draw curved lines for the stomach and legs.

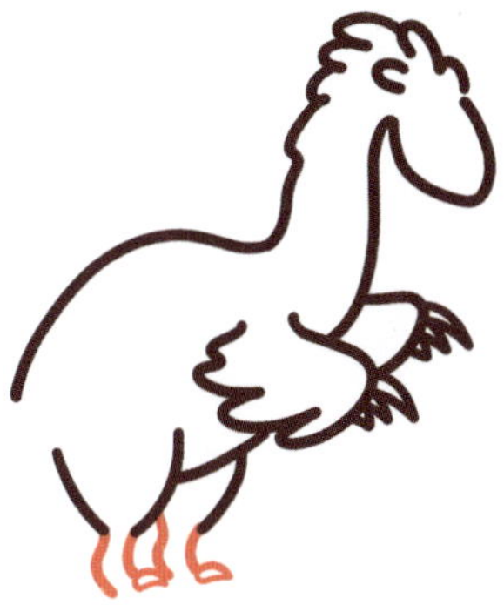

7. Add four curved lines for the legs and two triangle talons.

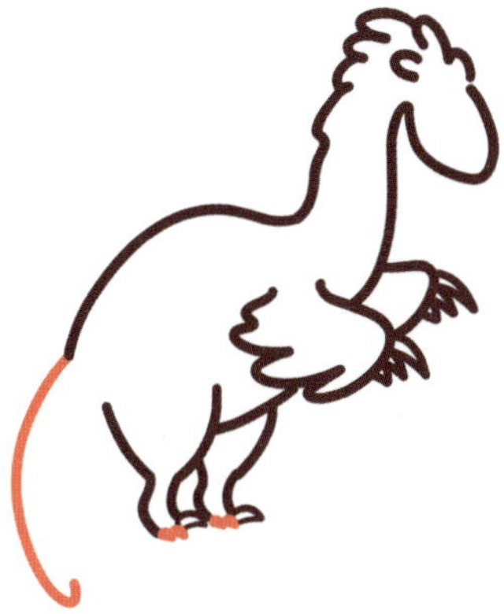

8. Draw two more talons to each foot. Add a curved line for the tail.

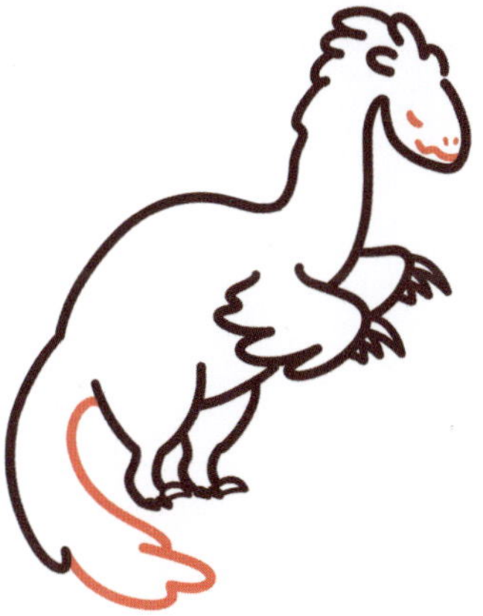

9. Complete the tail with a curved line and feathers at the end. Add a U-shaped eye, two dots for the nostrils, and a jagged mouth.

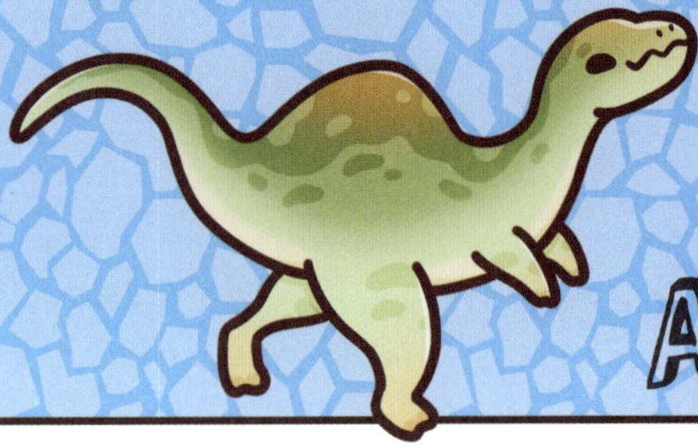

ALTISPINAX

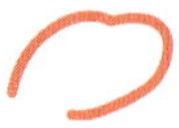

1. Draw an incomplete oval head with a bump for the snout.

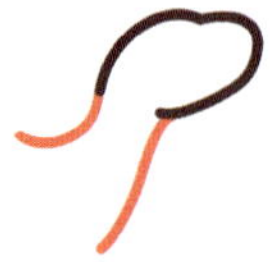

2. Add two curved lines for the neck.

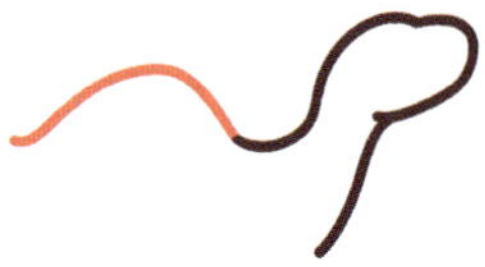

3. Add an arched line for the top of the body.

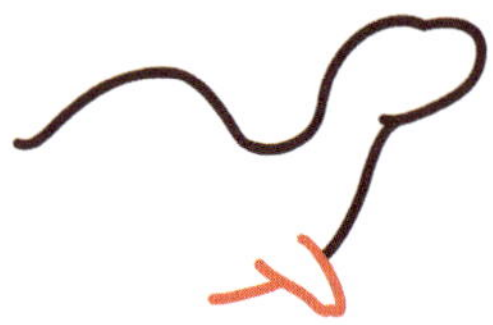

4. Draw a short arm with two fingers and a curved line for the stomach.

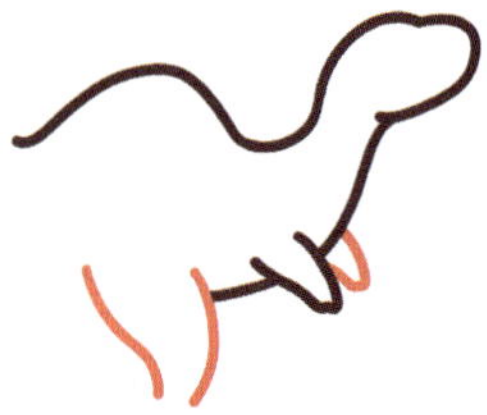

5. Add a second arm and two curved lines for the leg.

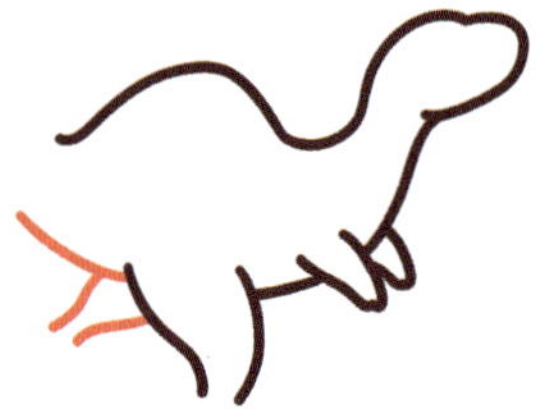

6. Add a curved line for the body and two wavy lines for the second leg.

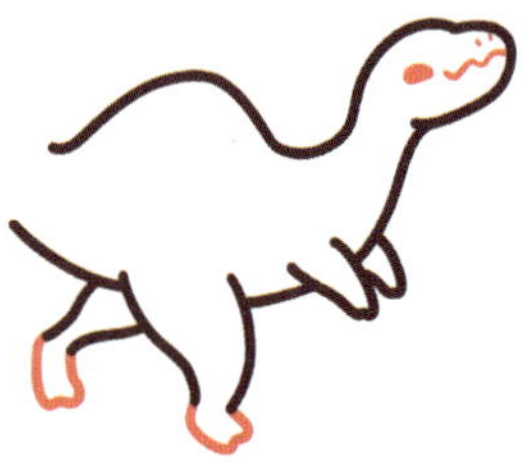

7. Add U-shaped feet with two toes each. For the face, add an oval eye, two dots for the nostrils, and a jagged mouth.

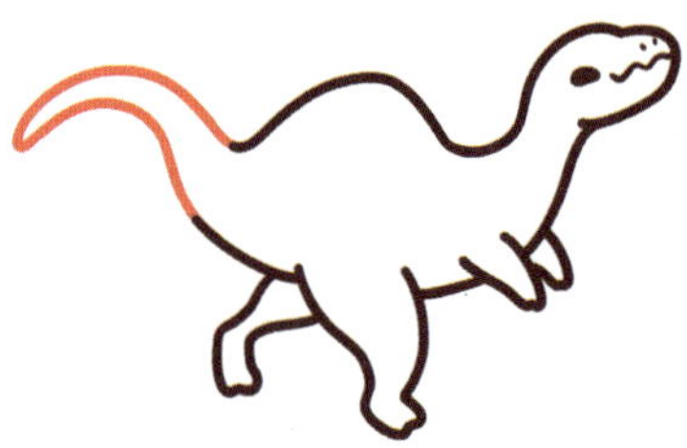

8. Draw a curved tail that tapers at the end.

STEGOSAURUS

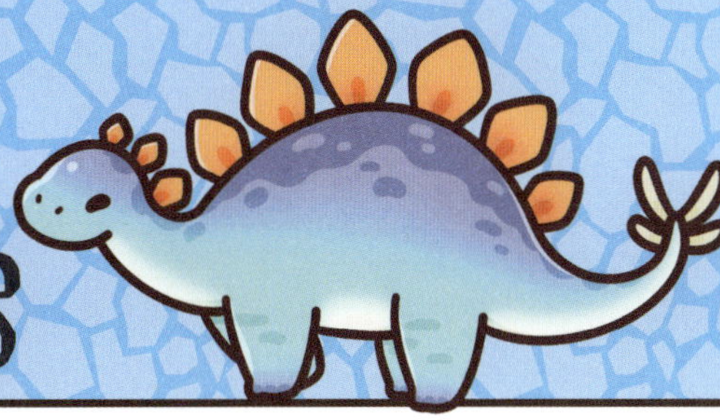

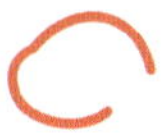

1. Draw a round head turned to the side with a bump for the snout.

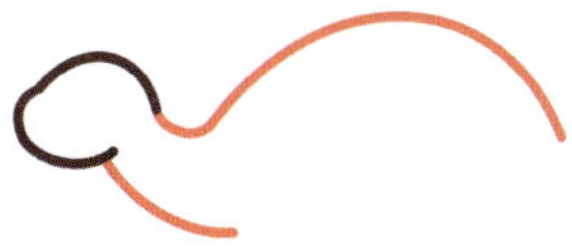

2. Draw curved lines for the humped back and the long neck.

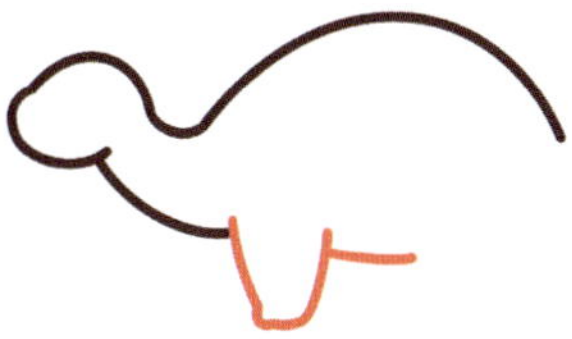

3. Add a U-shaped leg with a rounded toe. Draw a curve for the stomach.

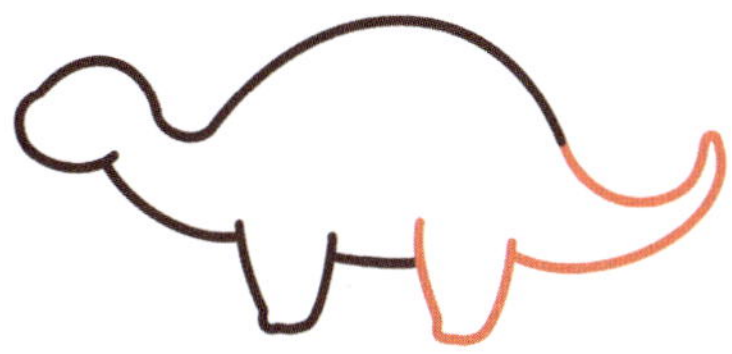

4. Add a second leg and a curved tail.

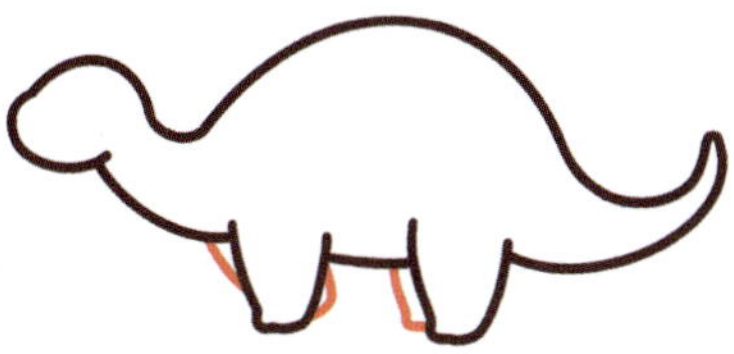

5. Draw two more legs so they are visible behind the first two legs.

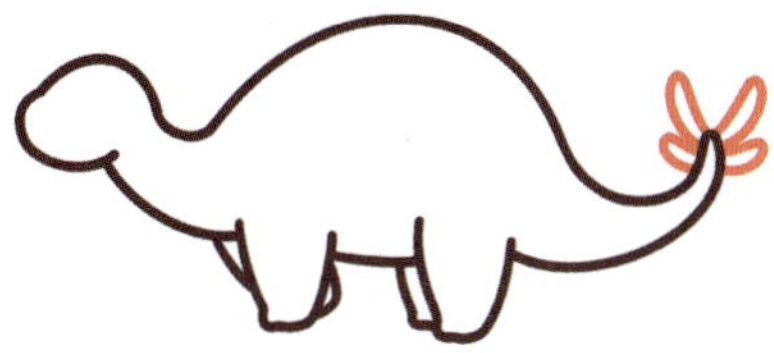

6. Add four ovals around the tip of the tail.

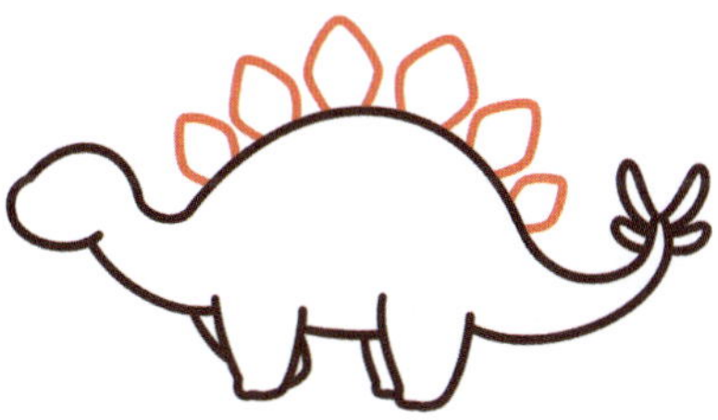

7. Add six diamonds along the back.

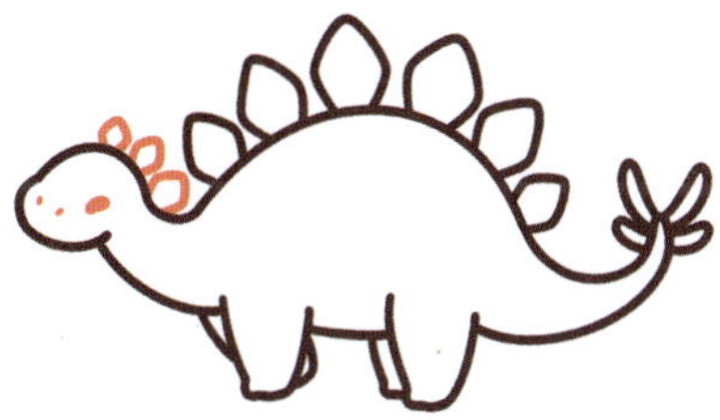

8. Add three more diamonds on top of the head. For the face, add an oval eye and two dashes for the nostrils.

ATROCIRAPTOR

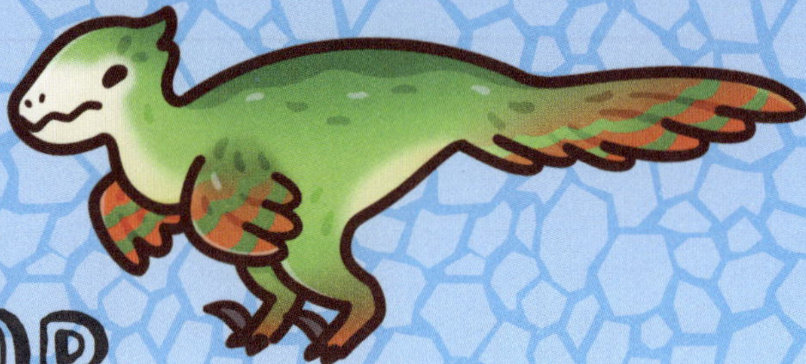

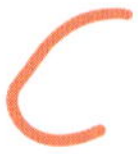

1. Draw a C shape with a pointed nose.

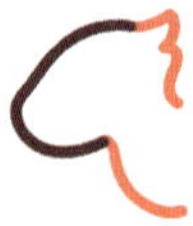

2. Add feathers on the back of the head and a curved line for the neck.

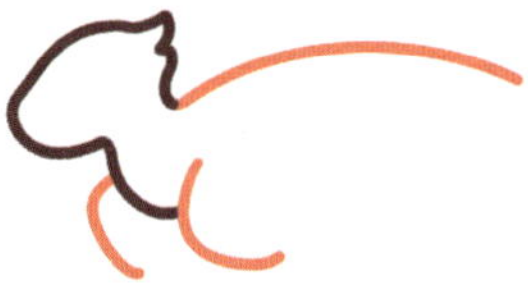

3. Draw three curved lines for the top of the body and the wings.

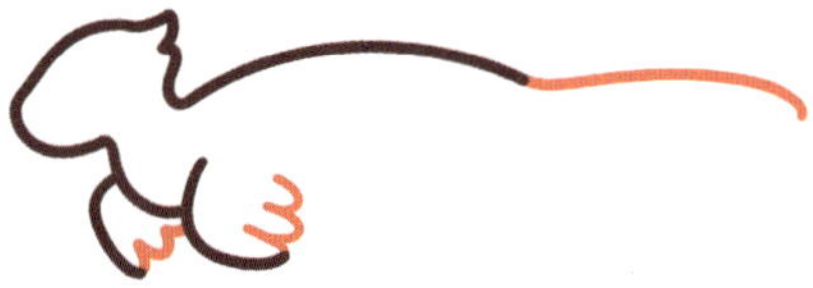

4. Add U-shaped feathers to the wings. Extend the body with a curved line for the tail.

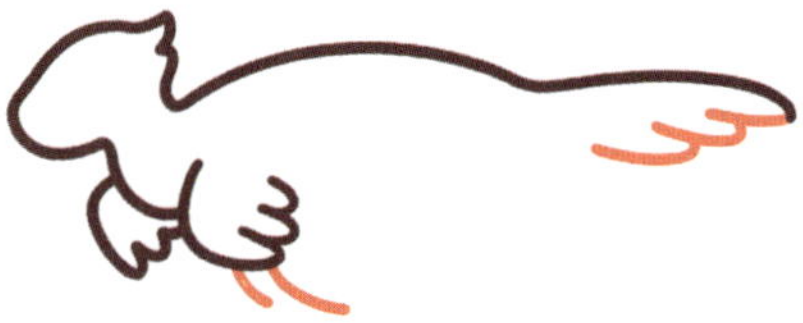

5. Add two curved lines for the legs. Draw three U-shaped feathers on the tail.

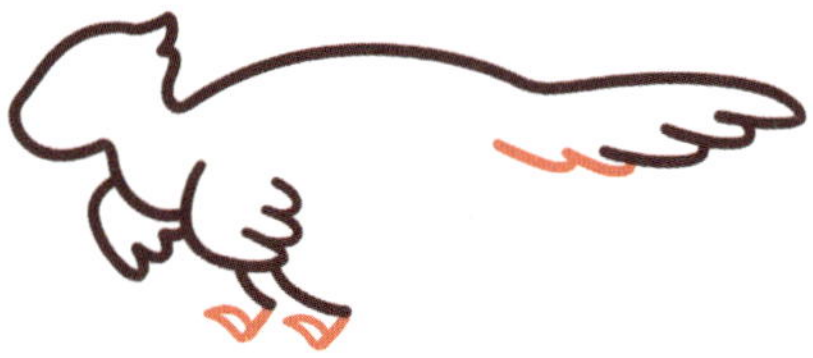

6. Add two more tail feathers. For each leg, add a line and a pointed talon.

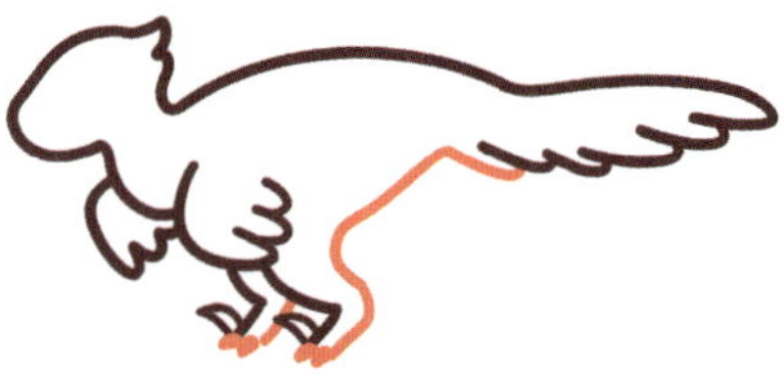

7. Draw a straight line and two talons for each foot. Add a curved line to complete the body and a final tail feather.

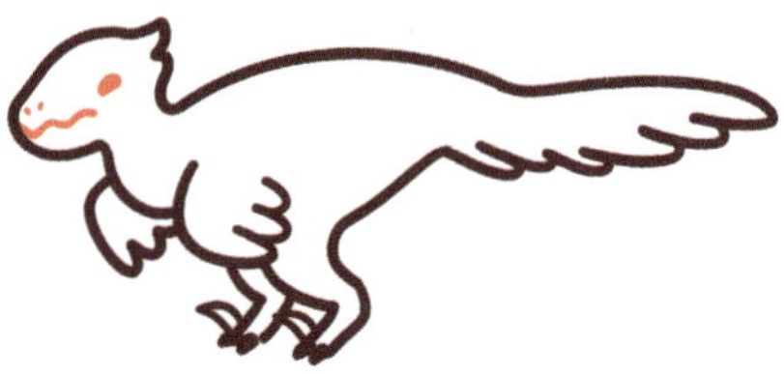

8. Add an oval eye, two dashes for the nostrils, and a jagged line for the mouth.

DILOPHOSAURUS

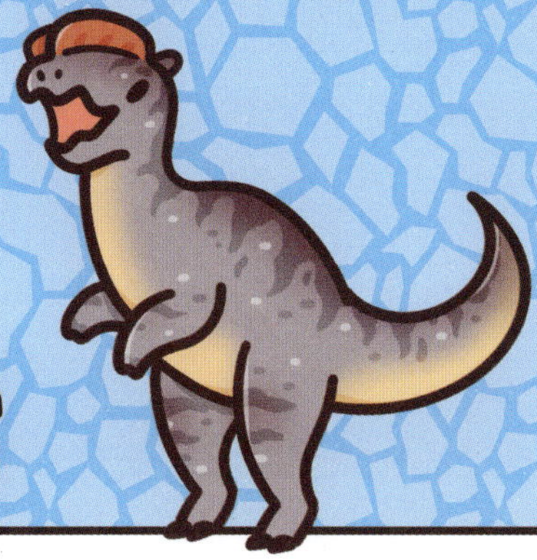

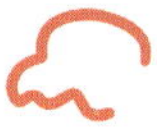

1. Draw an arch for the crest of the head with a pointed beak and a jagged line for the mouth.

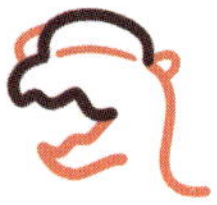

2. Add another jagged line and complete the chin. Draw curved lines under the crest and on the back of the head. Add two semicircles on each side of the crest.

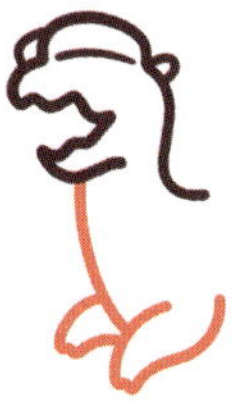

3. Draw a curved line for the body. Add two curved arms with two fingers each.

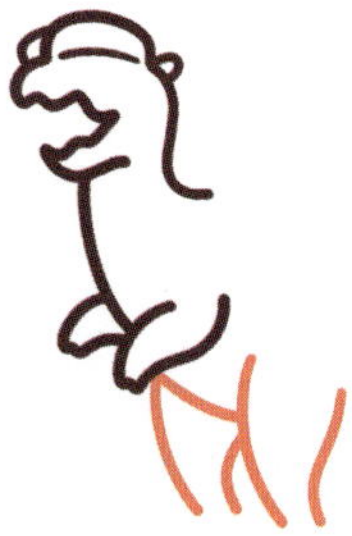

4. Add a curve for the stomach and four curved lines for the legs.

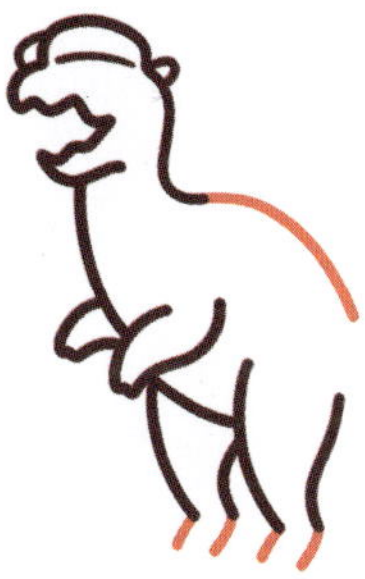

5. Add a curve for the top of the body and four straight lines for the feet.

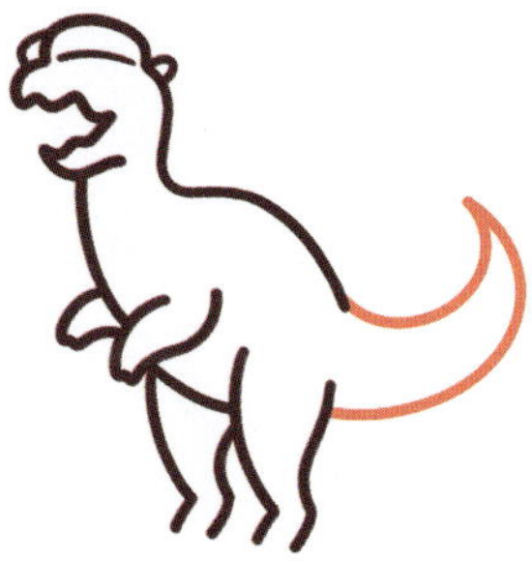

6. Draw a curved tail that tapers into a point.

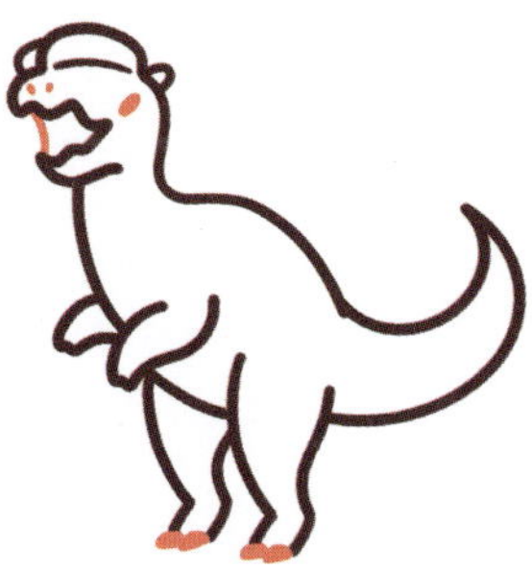

7. Add two talons to each foot. For the face, add an oval eye, two dashes for the nostrils, and a curved line for the mouth.

MOODS

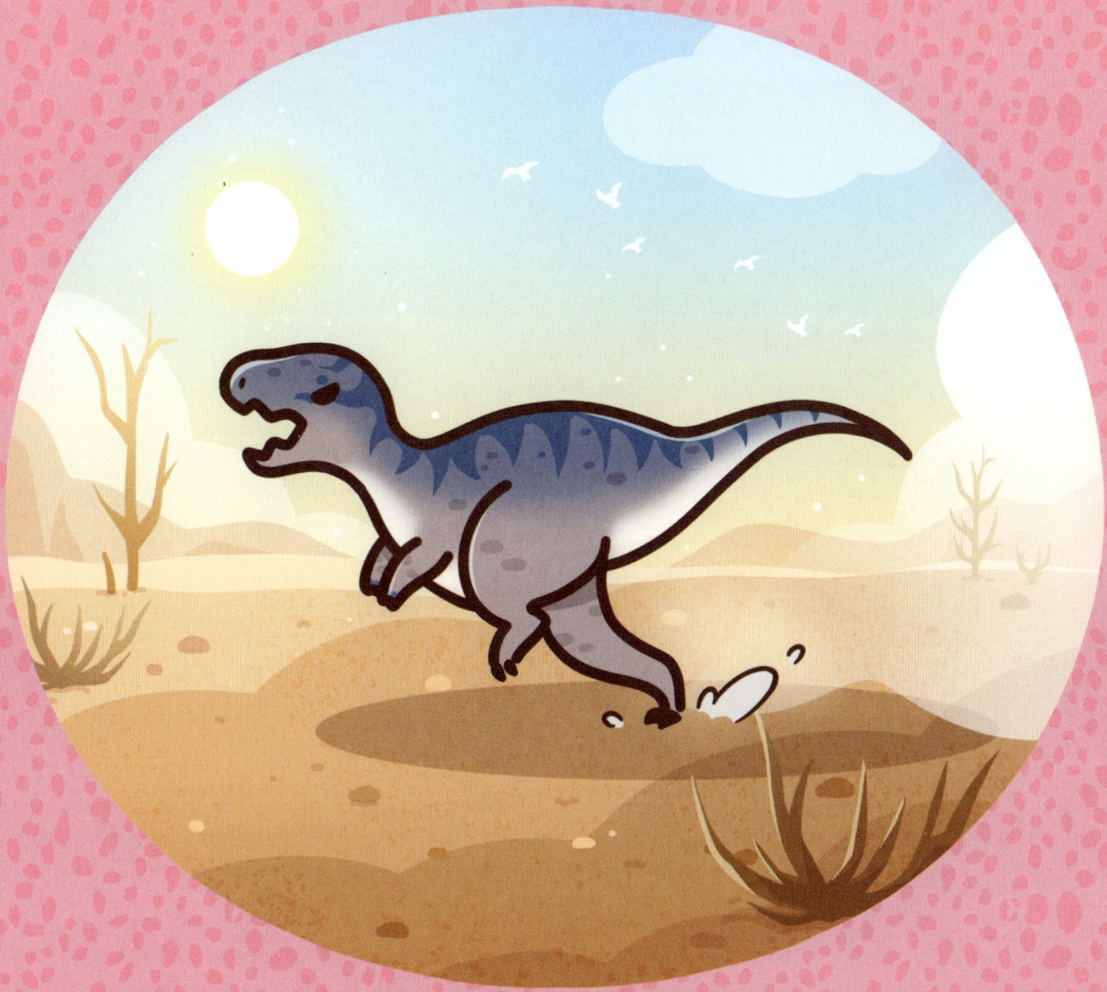

NAPTIME TRICERATOPS

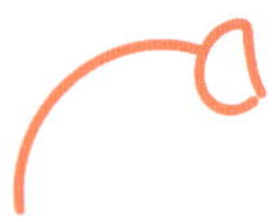

1. Draw a curved line attached to a semicircle ear.

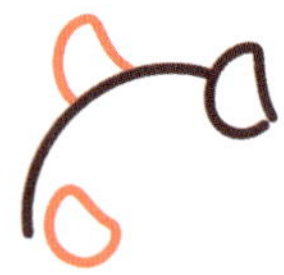

2. Add another ear and a semicircle horn for the nose.

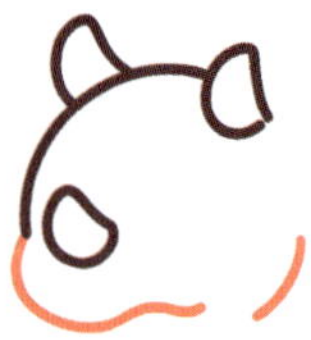

3. Draw the mouth and cheek with two curved lines.

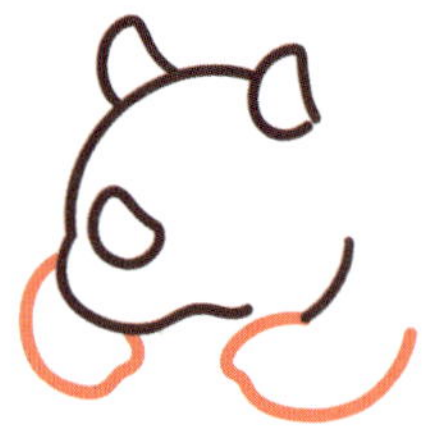

4. Add two oval arms under the head with two points for the fingers. Keep the right arm lines open.

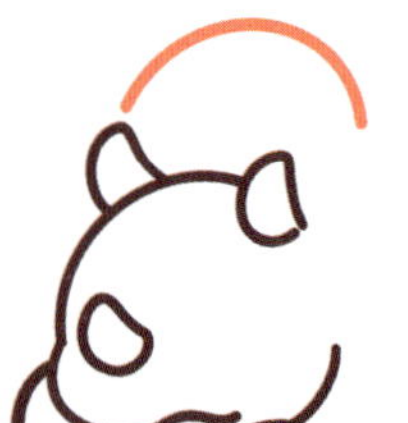

5. Add a curved line above the head and under the mouth.

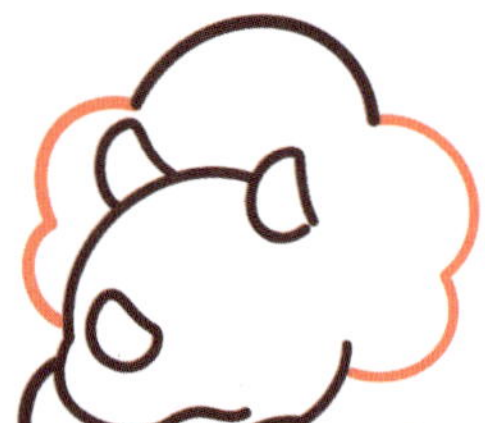

6. Draw two scallops around each side of the head.

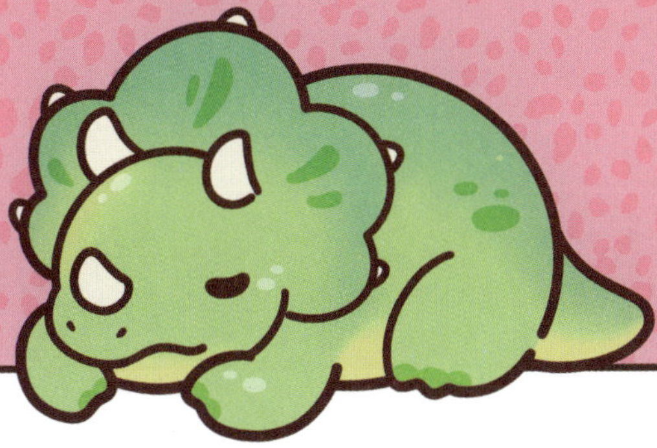

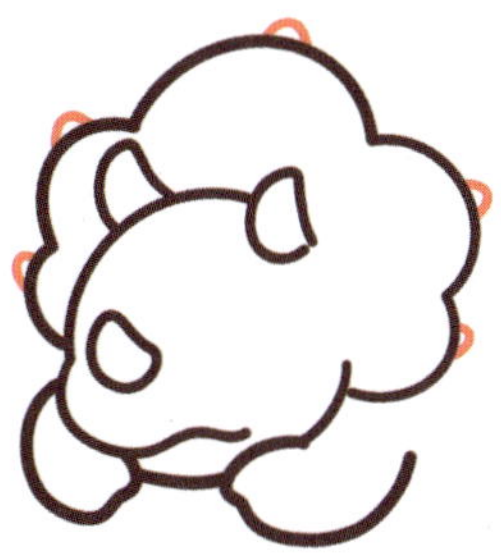

7. Add small triangular spikes on top of each scallop.

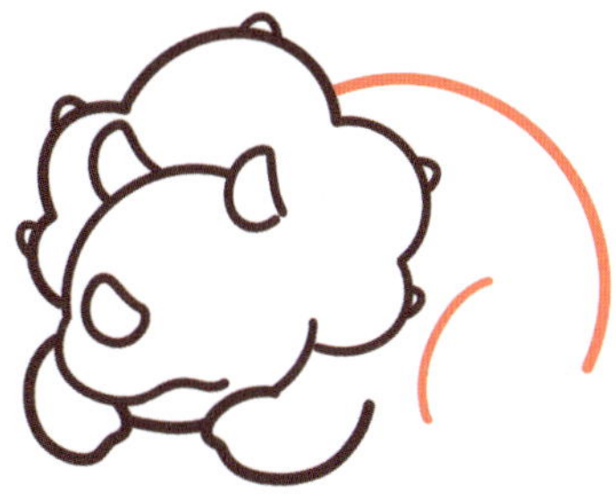

8. Draw the body and the back leg with curved lines.

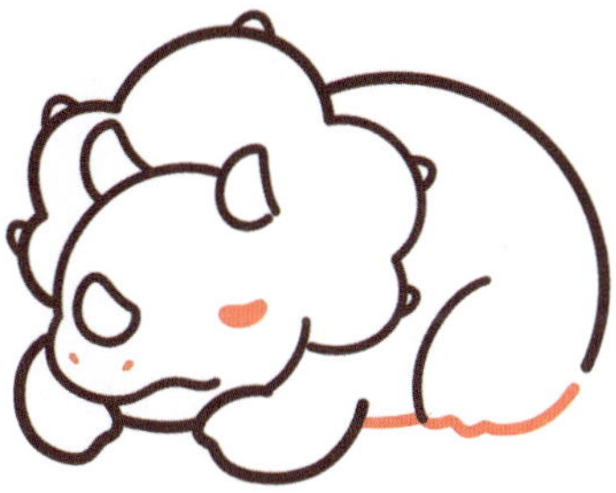

9. Add three toes to the foot and draw a line connecting the foot to the arm. For the face, add a closed bean-shaped eye and two dots for the nostrils.

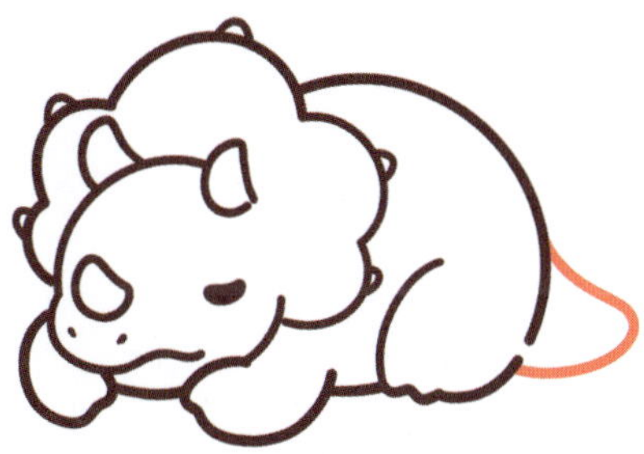

10. On the back of the body, add a short triangle tail.

SOARING MICROraptor

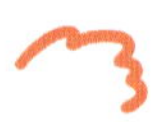

1. Draw the top of some spiky feathers.

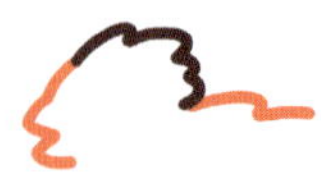

2. Add a curved line and W for the open beak. Add more feathers on the back.

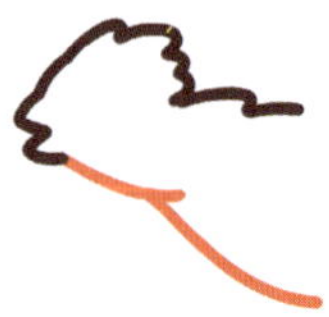

3. Draw two curved lines for the neck and the stomach.

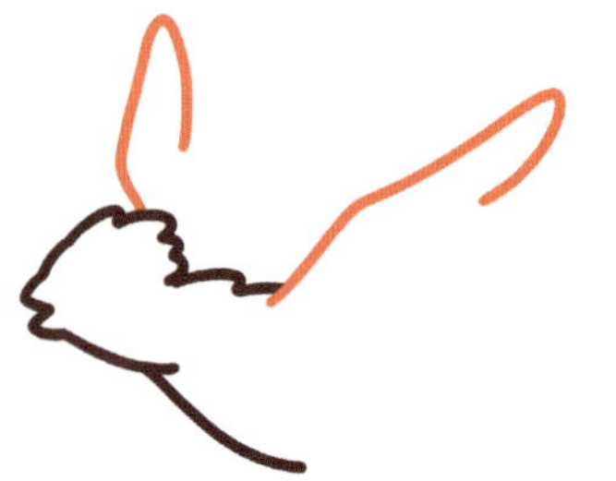

4. Add two wings with angled lines that curve inward at the tips.

5. Add rounded feathers to the wings.

6. Draw two curved lines for the tail.

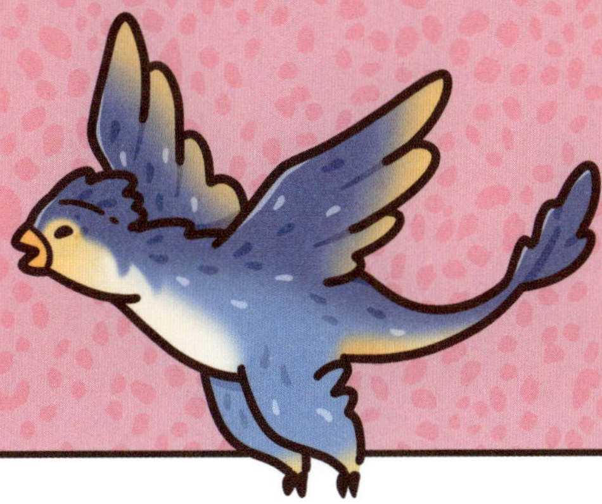

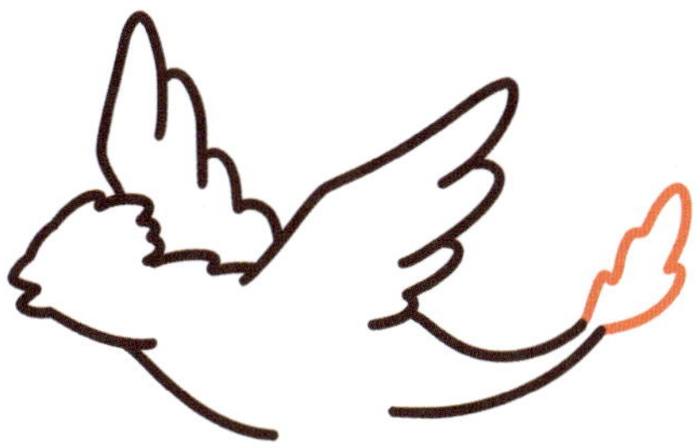

7. Add a feathered end to the tail in the shape of a leaf.

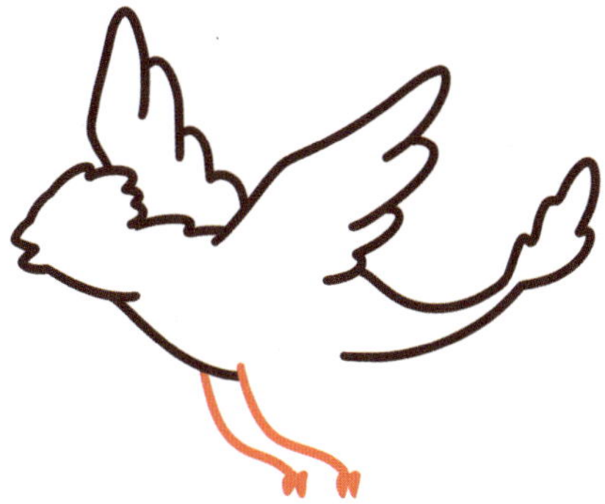

8. Add two wavy lines for the legs with two talons each.

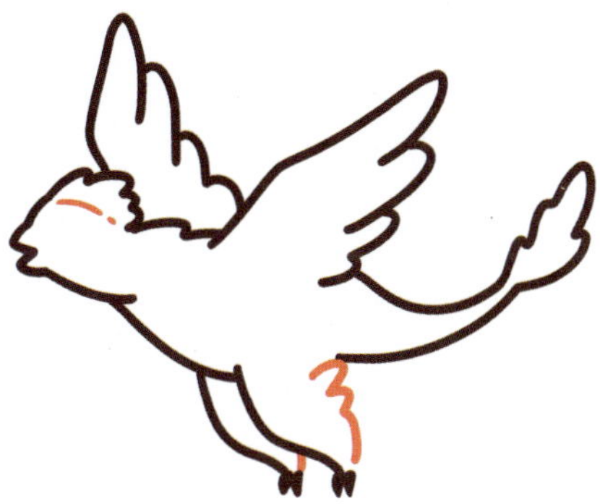

9. Draw curved lines on the head and feathers on the legs.

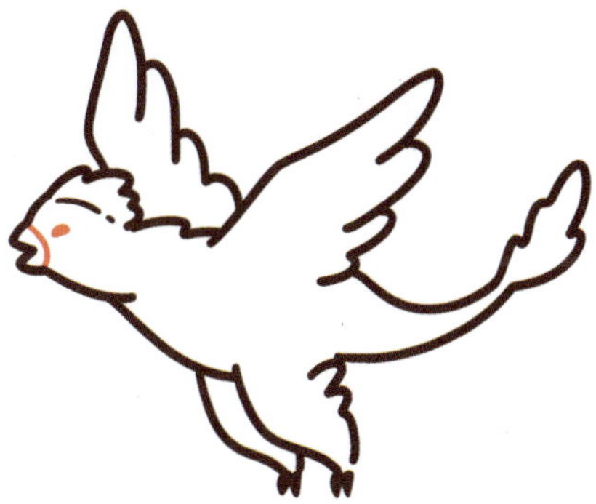

10. Draw a semicircle eye and a curve around the beak.

CURIOUS EORAPTOR

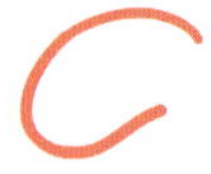

1. Draw an incomplete oval for the head.

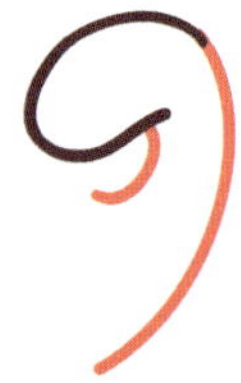

2. Add two curved lines for the neck.

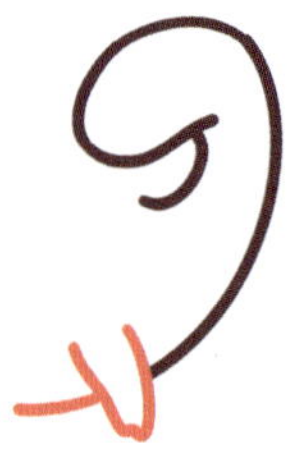

3. Add a short arm with two fingers and a curved line for the stomach.

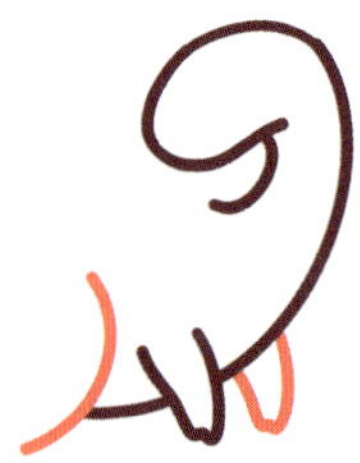

4. Draw the second arm. Add a curved line for the leg.

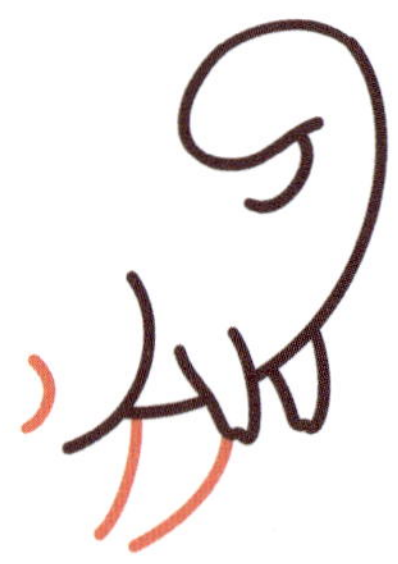

5. Add three curved lines for the legs.

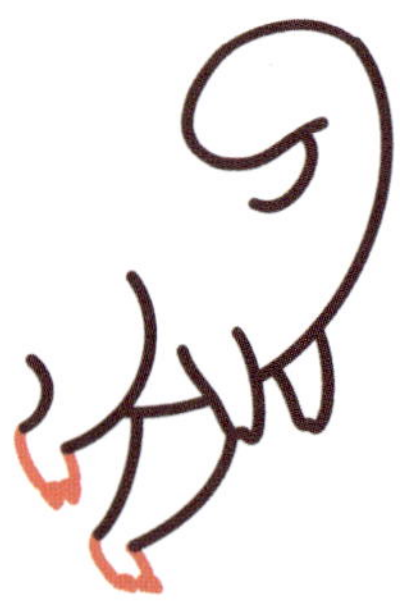

6. Draw U-shaped feet with two talons each.

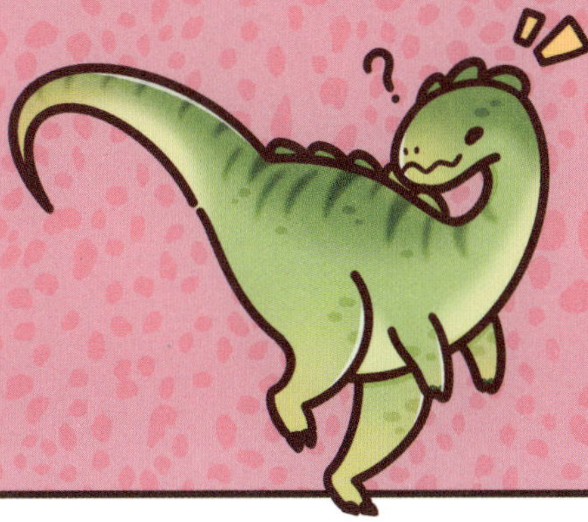

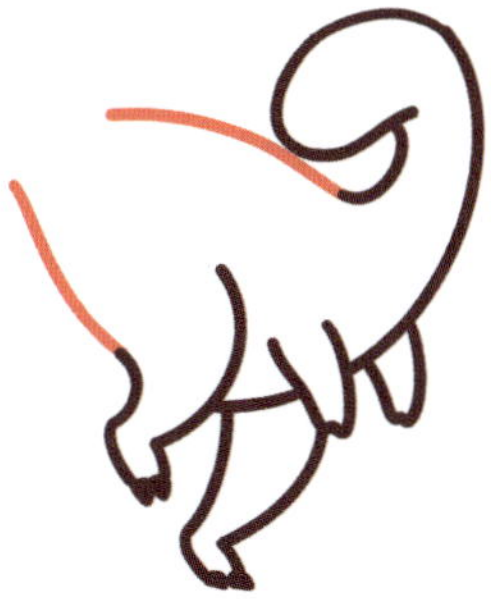

7. Add two curved lines for the body.

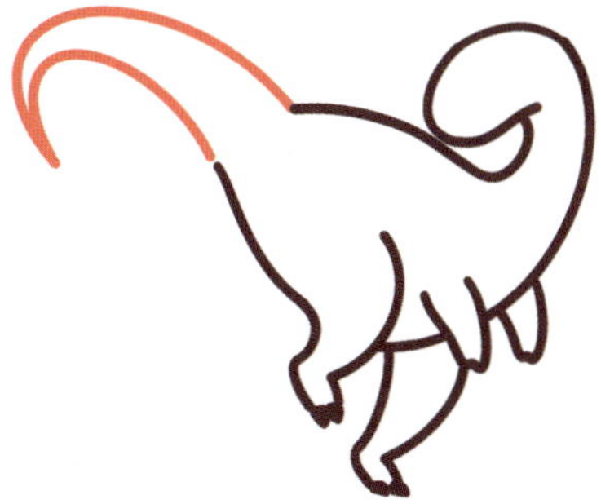

8. Add a curved tail that tapers to a point.

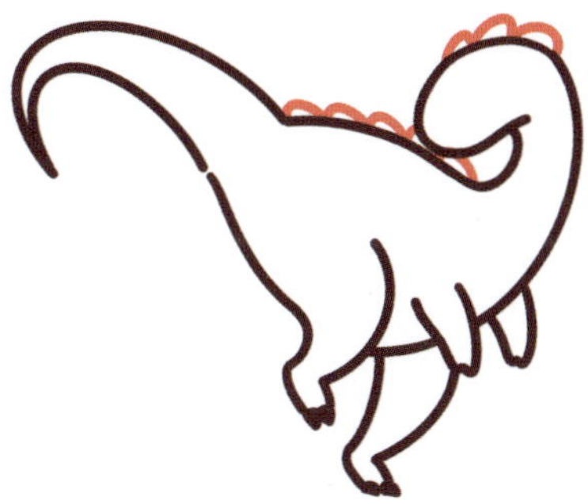

9. Add spikes on top of the head and the body.

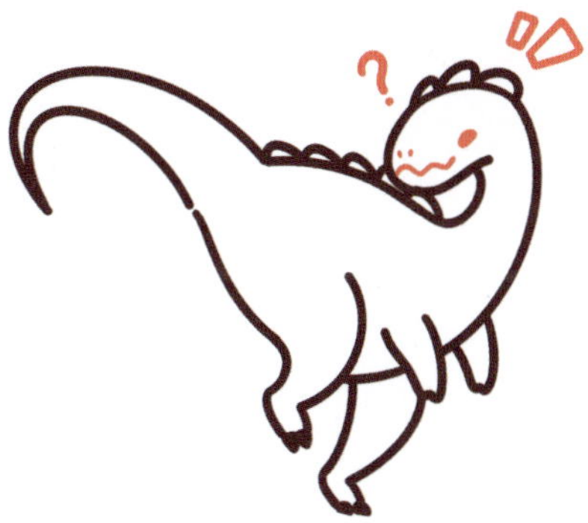

10. Add an oval eye, two dots for the nostrils, and a jagged mouth. Draw a question mark and shocked shapes around the head.

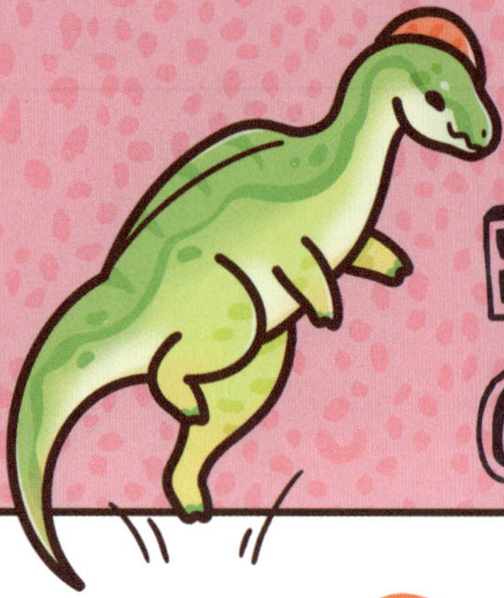

EXCITED CORYTHOSAURUS

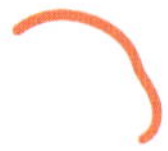

1. Draw a curved line for the head.

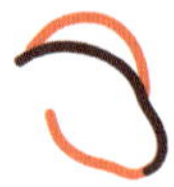

2. Add an arch above the head and a curved line for the chin.

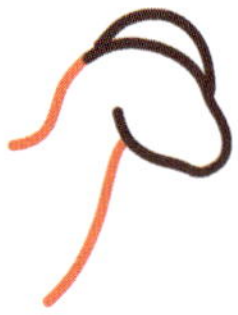

3. Add two curved lines for the neck.

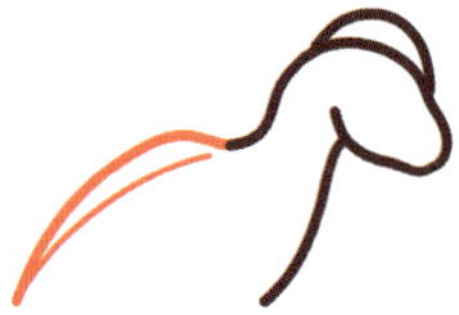

4. Add two curved lines for the top of the body.

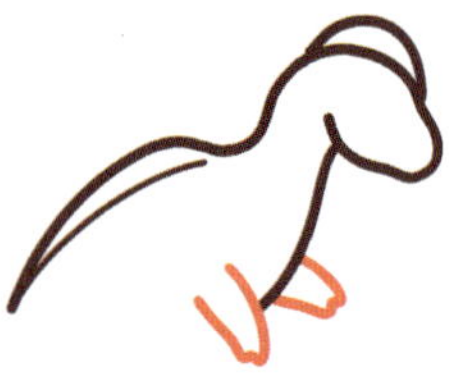

5. Draw two short arms with two fingers each.

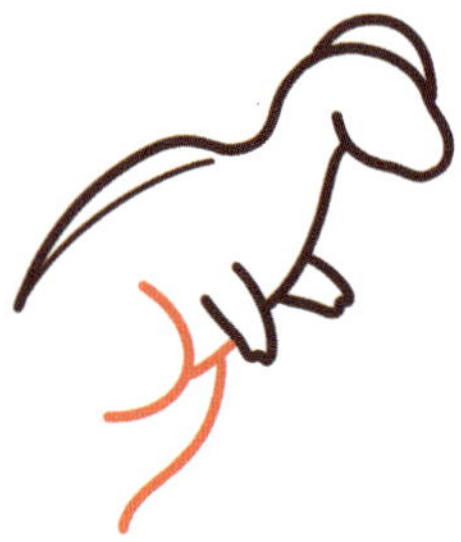

6. Add curved lines for the stomach and the legs.

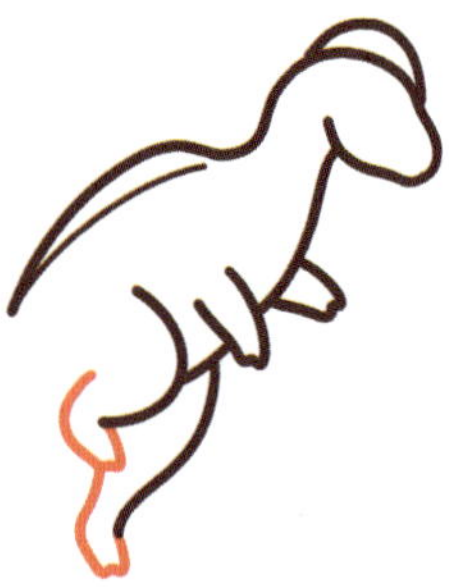

7. Complete the legs with curved lines and U-shaped feet with two toes each.

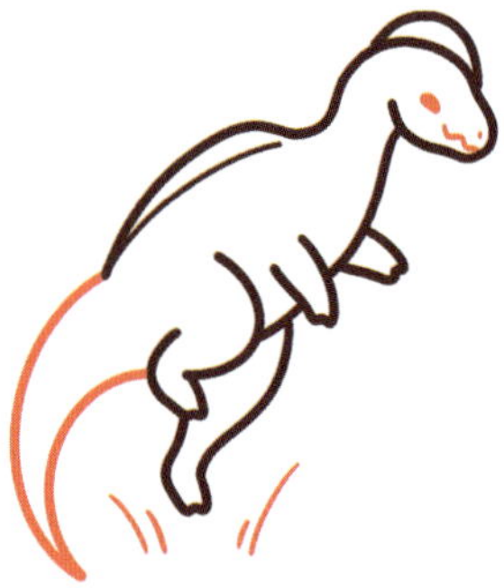

8. Draw a curved tail that tapers into a point. For the face, add an oval eye, a dot for the nostril, and a jagged mouth. Draw some action lines around the feet.

BASHFUL ANKYLOSAURUS

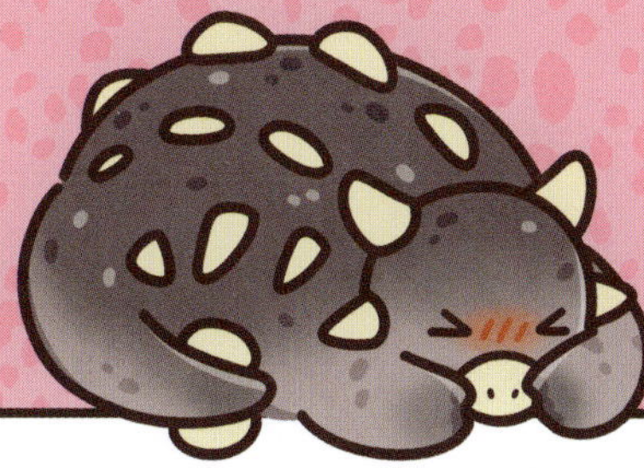

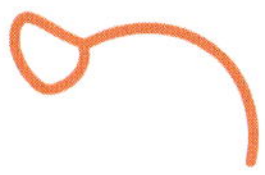

1. Draw an arch and a triangle horn.

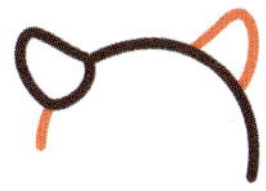

2. Add a curved line and a second horn.

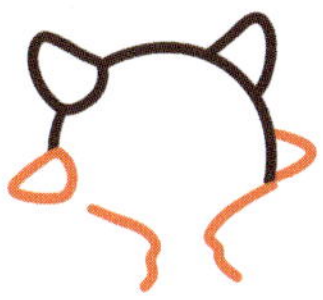

3. Add two more horns on the sides of the face. Start the hands under the head with a curved line and two bumps for the fingers.

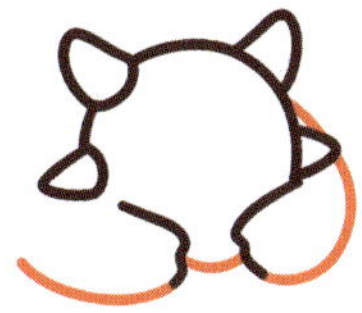

4. Draw curved lines for the arms and the nose.

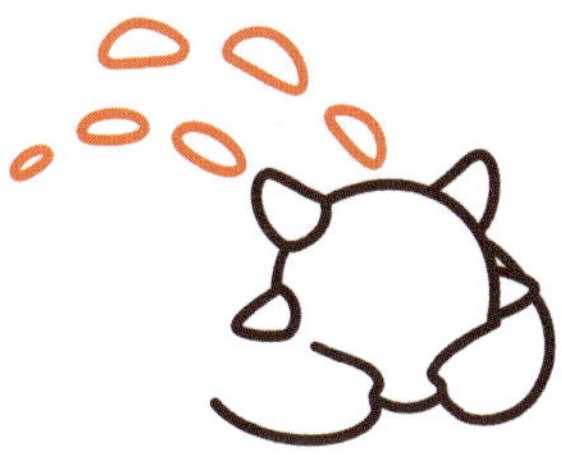

5. Add two lines of three ovals for the armor on top of the body.

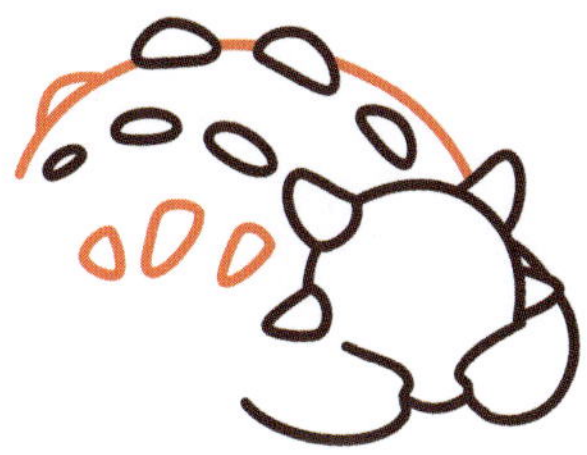

6. Draw a curved line for the body. Add more armor with semicircles and triangles.

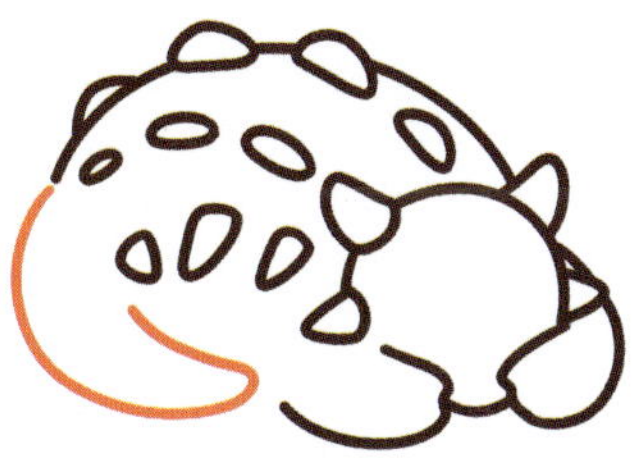

7. Add a curved tail that wraps around the body.

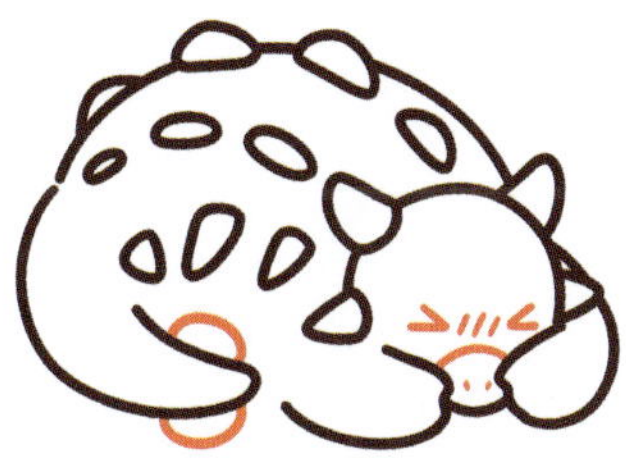

8. Draw two ovals at the tip of the tail. For the face, add two V eyes, three dashes for blush, and a curve and two dots for the nose.

HUNGRY BRACHIOSAURUS

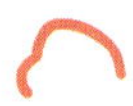

1. Draw an arch with two bumps.

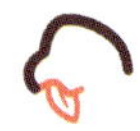

2. Draw a jagged line for the mouth with a teardrop-shaped leaf.

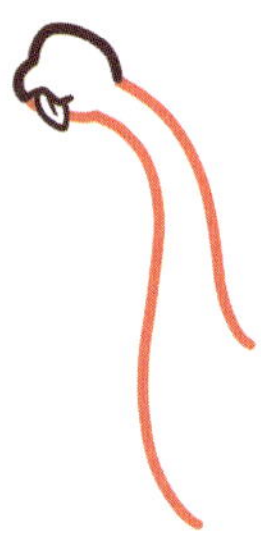

3. Add two curved lines for the long neck.

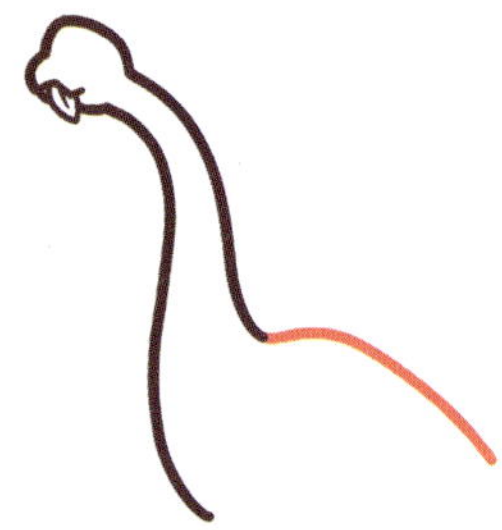

4. Add a curved line for the top of the body.

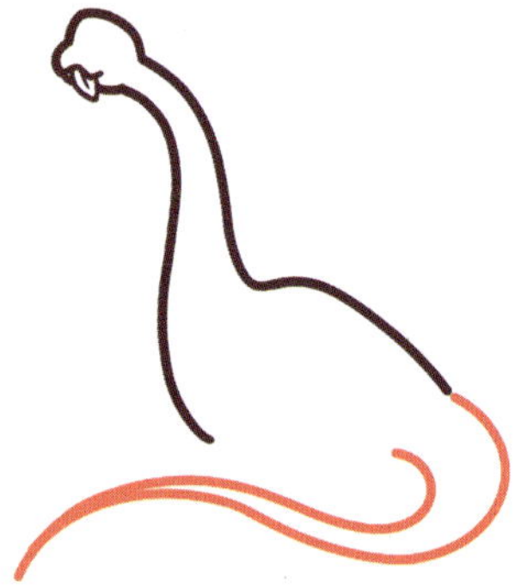

5. Draw a long, curved tail that tapers to a point.

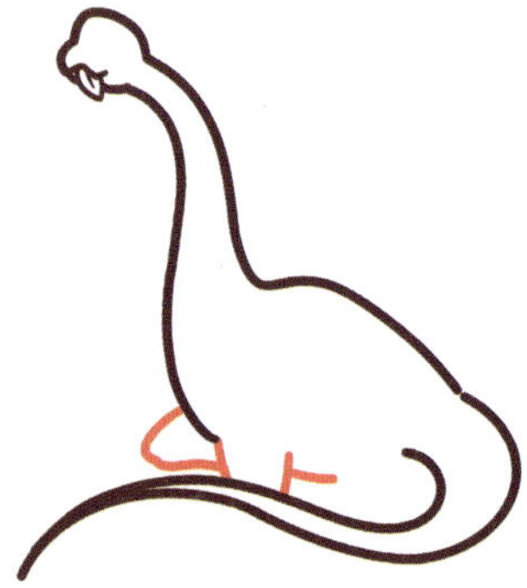

6. Add a U-shaped foot with two toes and curved lines for the second leg and stomach.

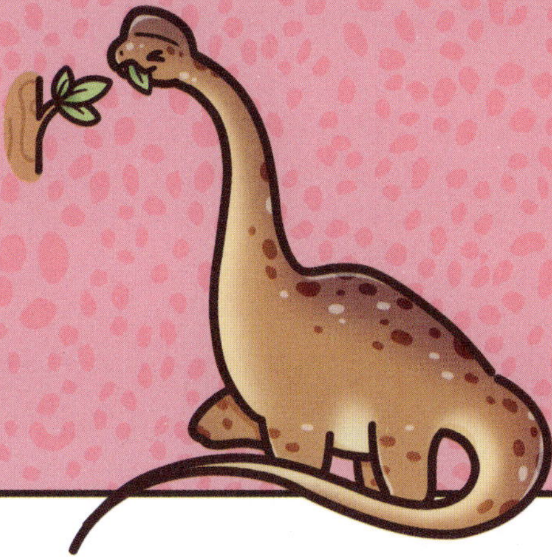

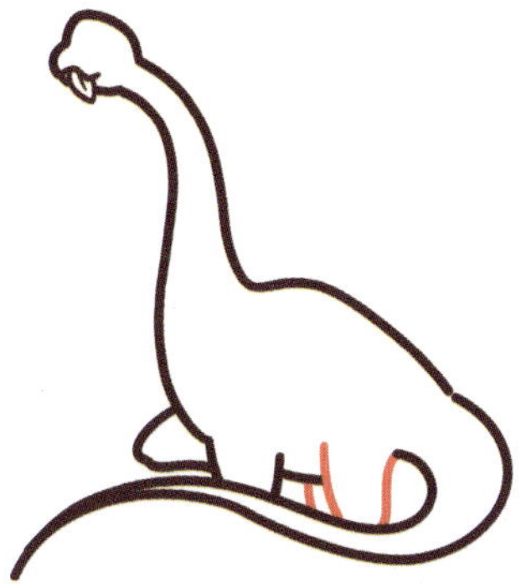

7. Add two more legs with three lines.

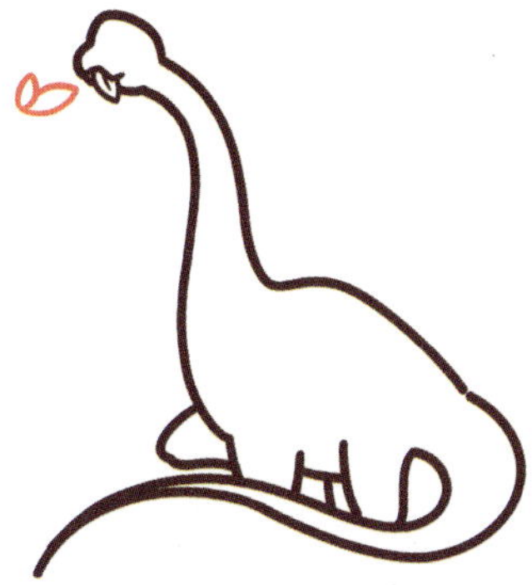

8. Draw two more leaves in front of the mouth.

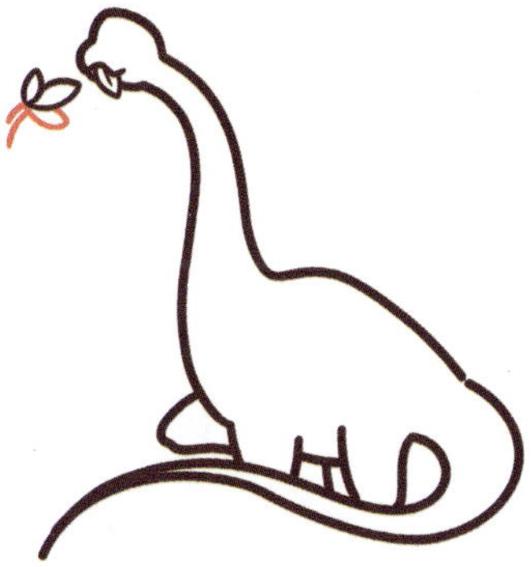

9. Add a third leaf and start the branch with two curved lines.

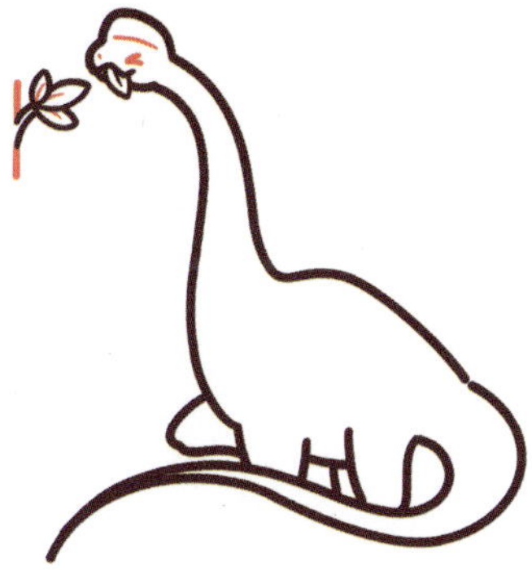

10. Complete the branch with lines. For the face, add a curved line, a V-shaped eye, and a dot for the nostril.

STOMPING CARNOTAURUS

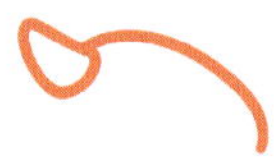

1. Draw a curved line and a triangle horn.

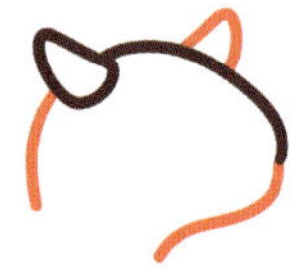

2. Add a second horn and two curved lines for the head.

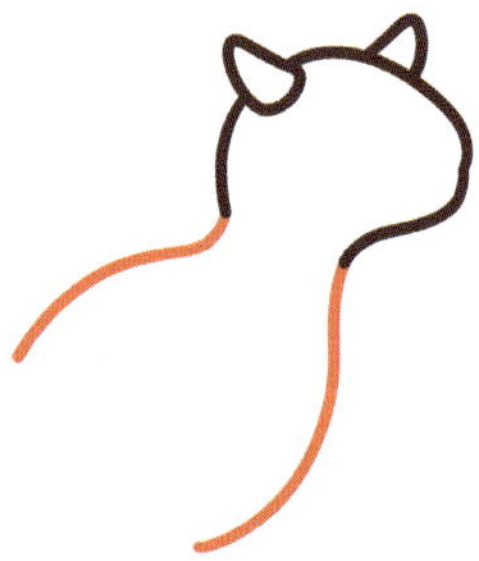

3. Draw two curved lines for the neck and the body.

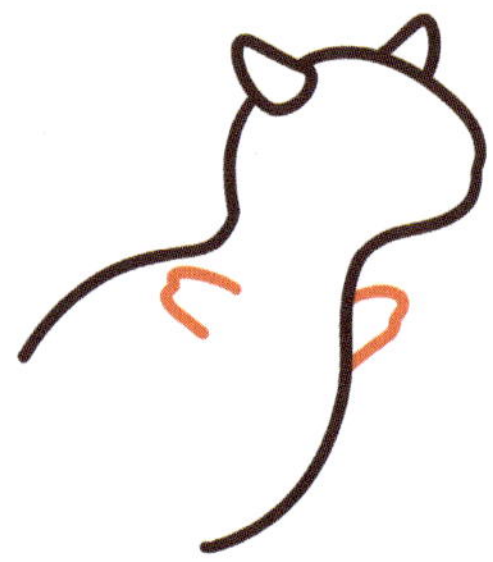

4. Add two U-shaped arms with two fingers each.

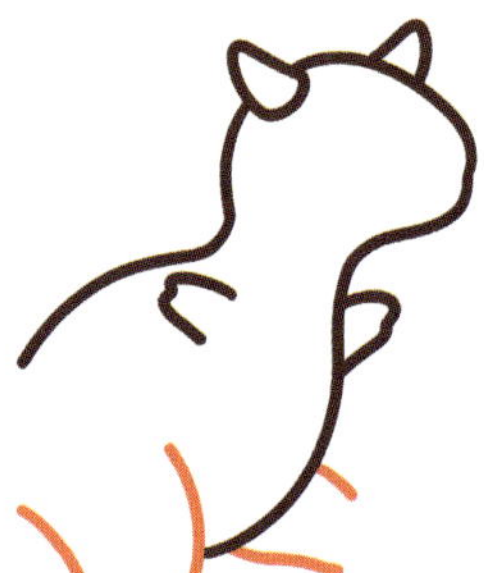

5. Add four curved lines for the legs.

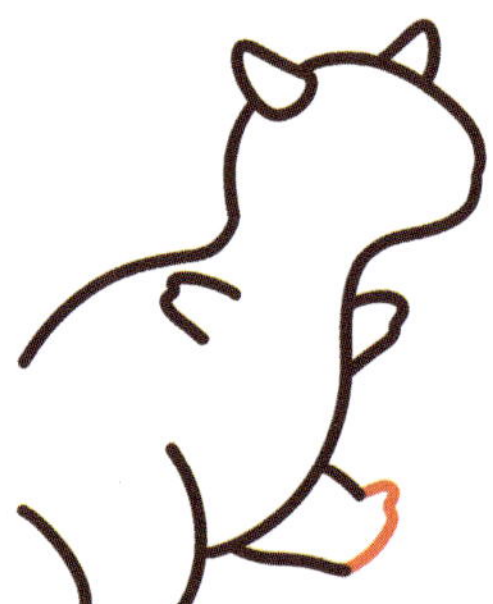

6. Add U-shaped feet with two toes each.

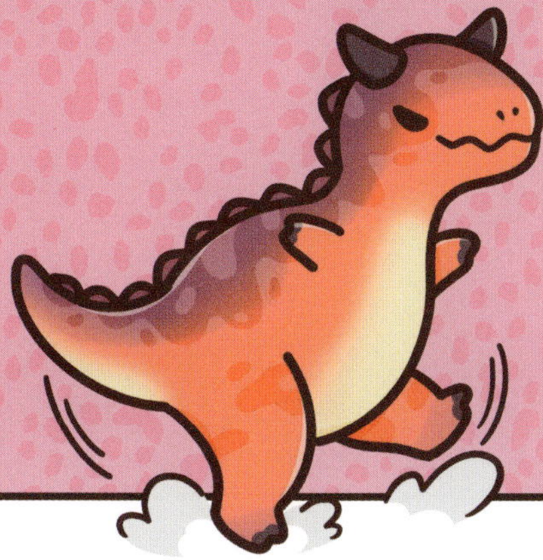

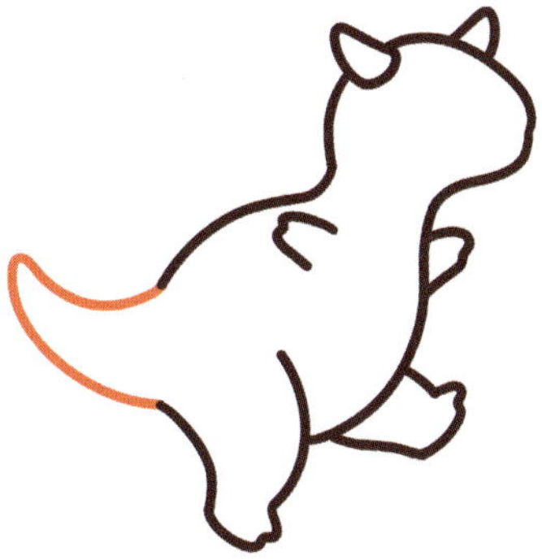

7. Draw a curved tail.

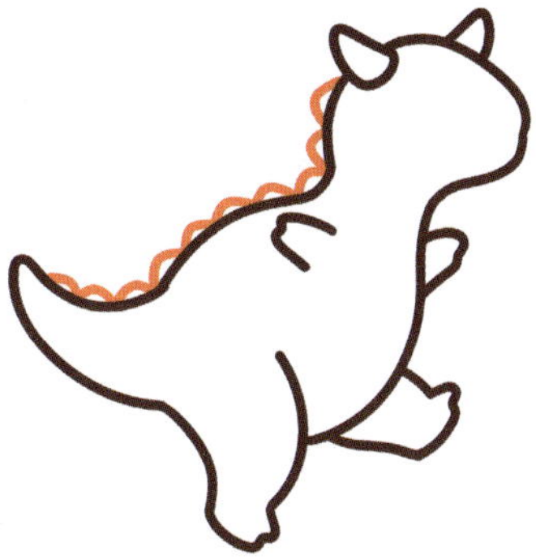

8. Add semicircle spikes from the back of the head to the tail.

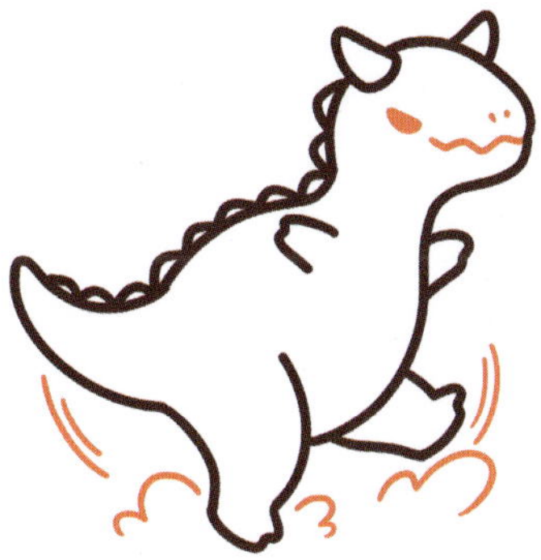

9. Add an oval eye, two dashes for the nostrils, and a jagged mouth. Draw action lines and clouds of dust around the feet.

CONFUSED THERIZINOSAURUS

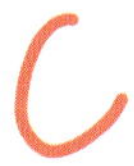

1. Draw a C for the head.

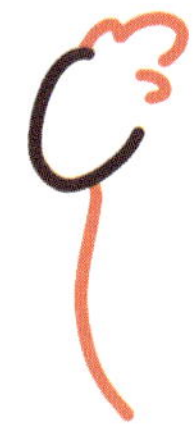

2. Add round feathers on the head and a curved line for the neck.

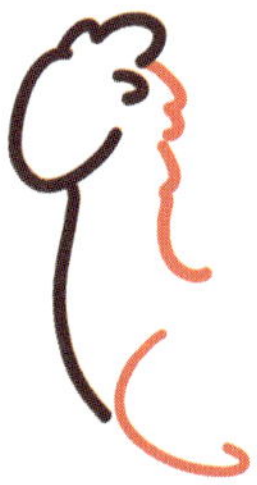

3. Draw a curved line for the top of the neck with more feathers. Add a curved line for the wing with a triangle end.

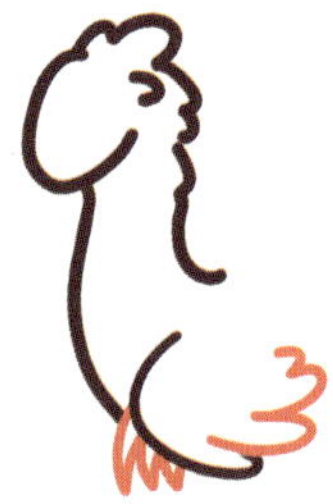

4. Add feathers and three spikes to the wing.

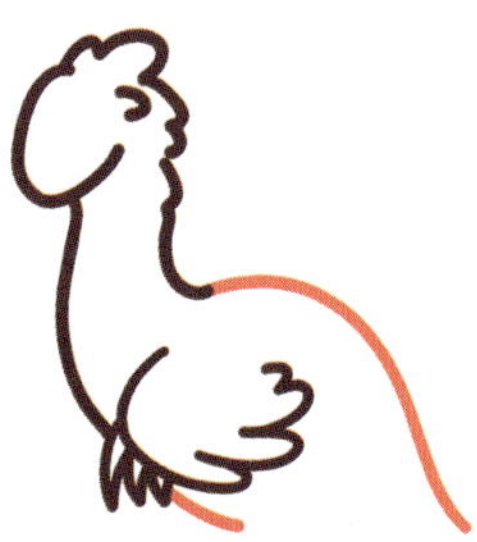

5. Draw a curved top of the body and stomach.

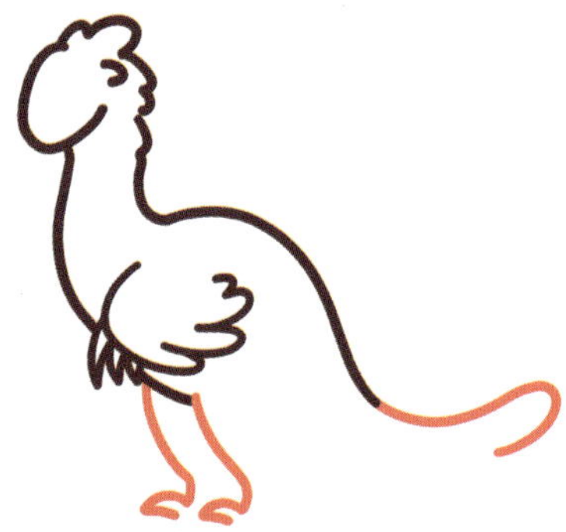

6. Add curved lines for the legs and the tail. Add a triangle talon to each foot.

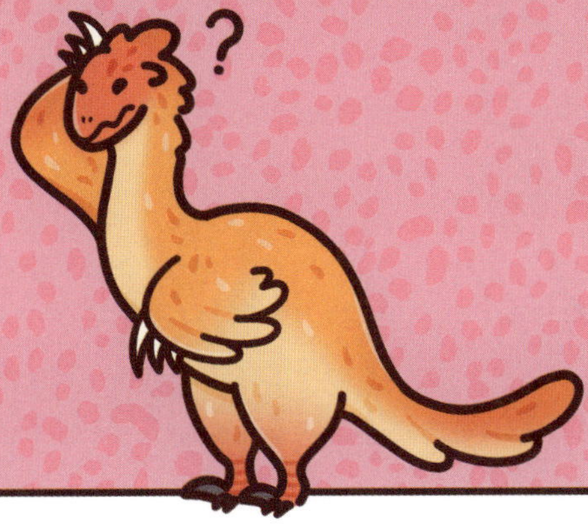

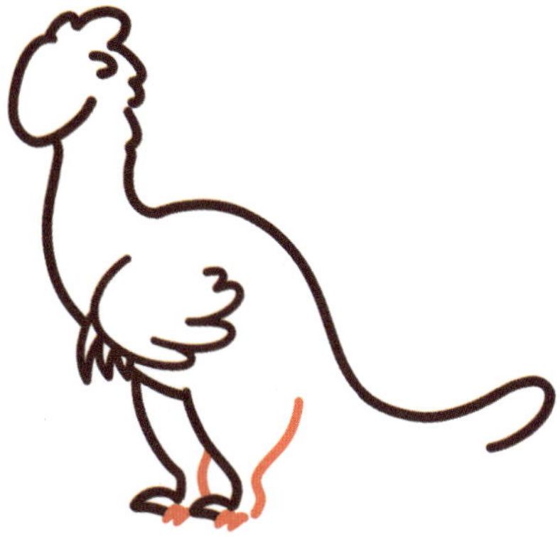

7. Complete the legs with curved lines and two more talons each.

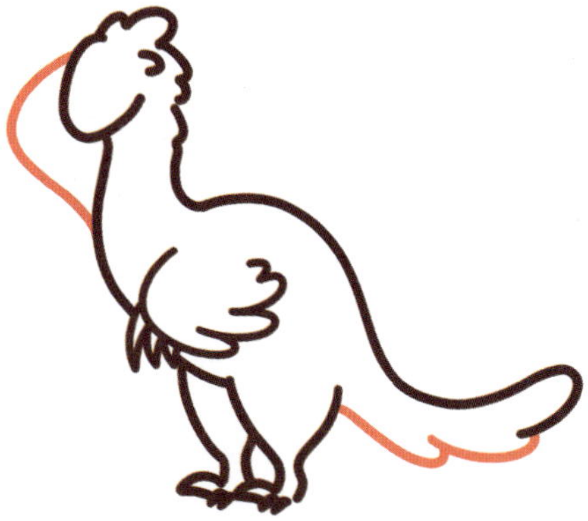

8. Add a curved line near the head for the second wing. Complete the tail with a feathered line.

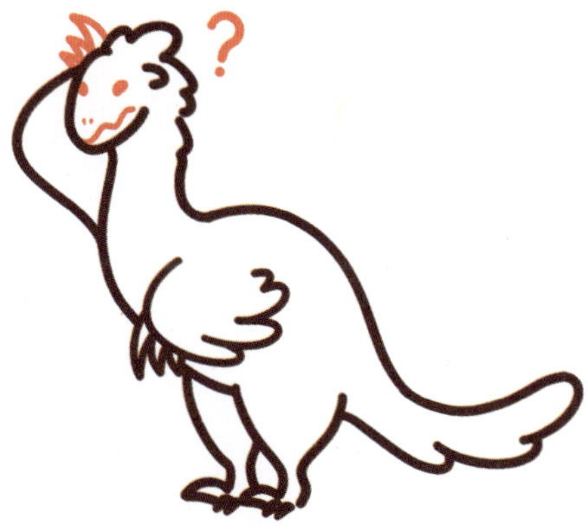

9. Add three spikes to the second wing and a question mark near the head. For the face, add two oval eyes, two dots for the nostrils, and a jagged mouth.

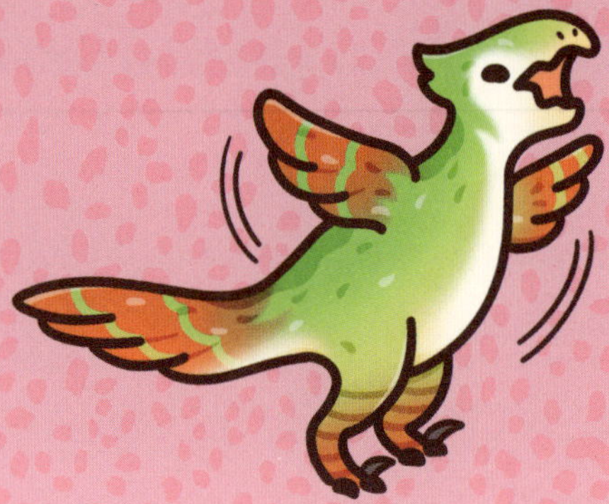

HAPPY ATROCIRAPTOR

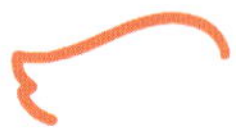

1. Draw a curved line with two pointed feathers.

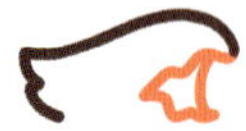

2. Add two jagged lines and a curved line for the mouth.

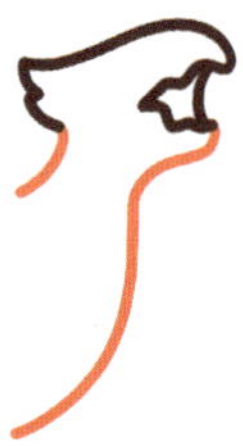

3. Draw two curved lines for the neck and the body.

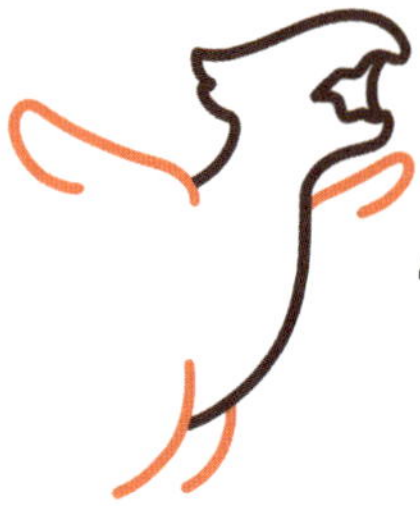

4. Add a line for each wing that curls in at the end. Draw two curved lines for the legs.

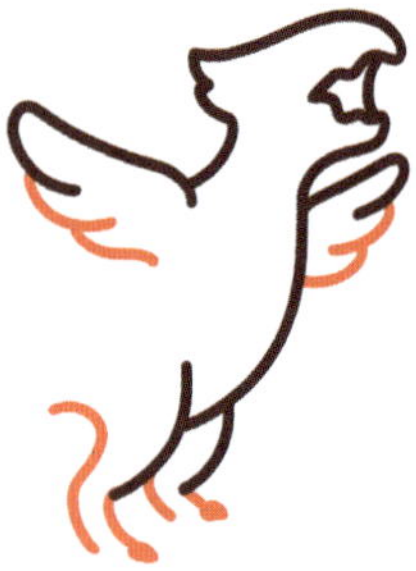

5. Draw two U-shaped feathers to each wing. Add curved lines and a talon for each foot and a curved line for the body.

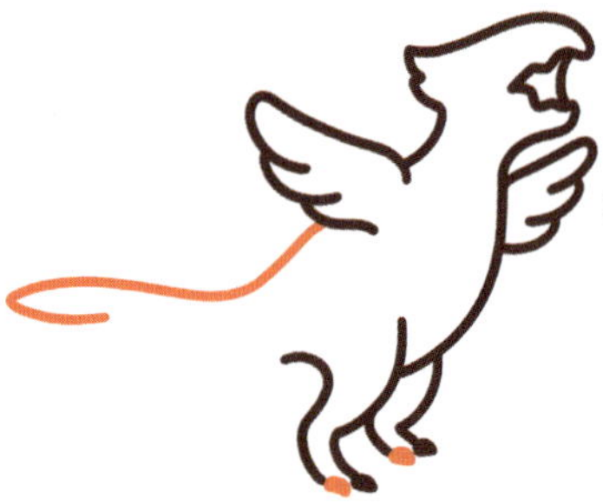

6. Draw the tail with a long wavy line that curls in for a pointed feather. Add another talon to each foot.

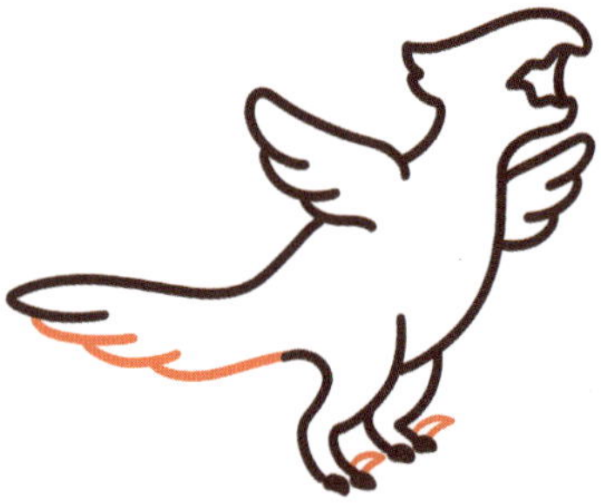

7. Add three U-shaped feathers to the tail. Add a pointed talon to each foot.

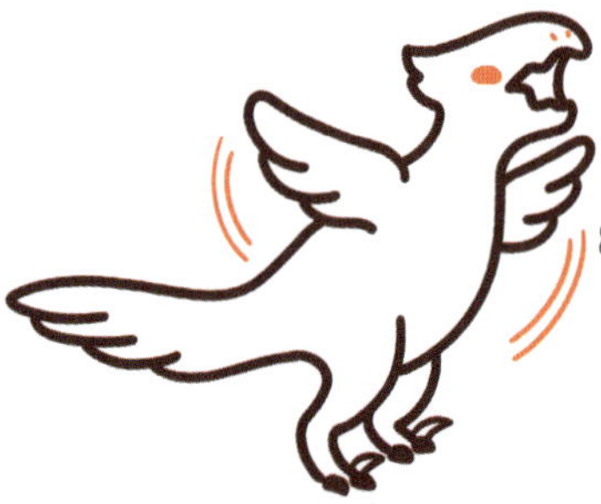

8. Draw an oval eye and two dashes for the nostrils. Add action lines under each wing.

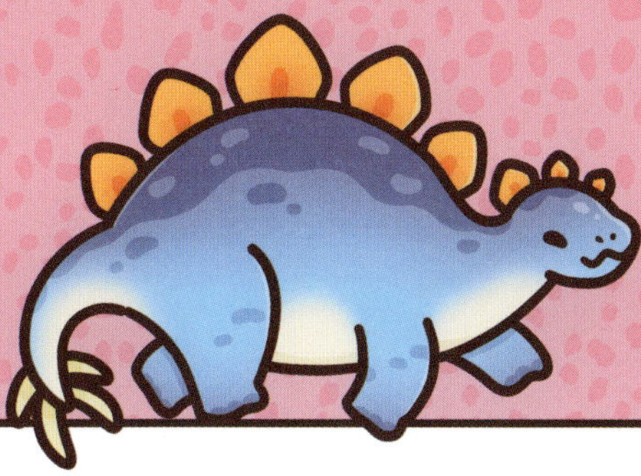

CONFIDENT STEGOSAURUS

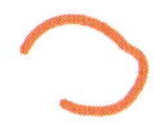

1. Draw a round head with a bump for the snout.

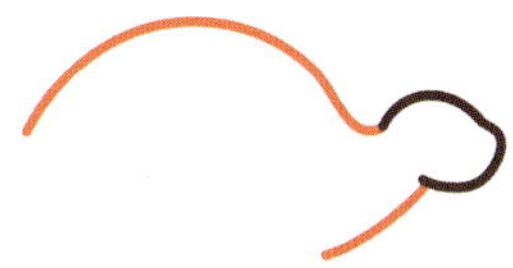

2. Add two curved lines for the neck and the top of the body.

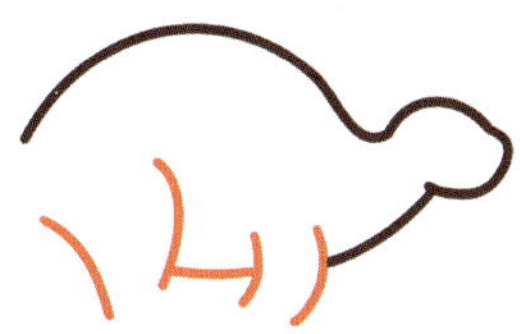

3. Add curved lines for the stomach and the legs.

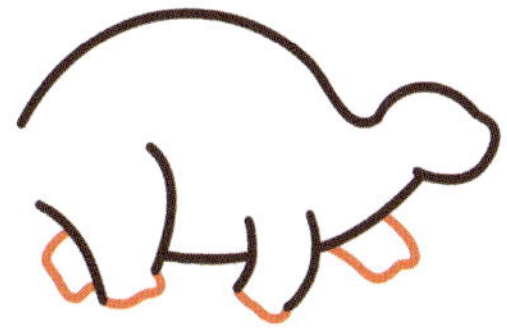

4. Draw a U-shaped front and back leg and add two toes to each foot.

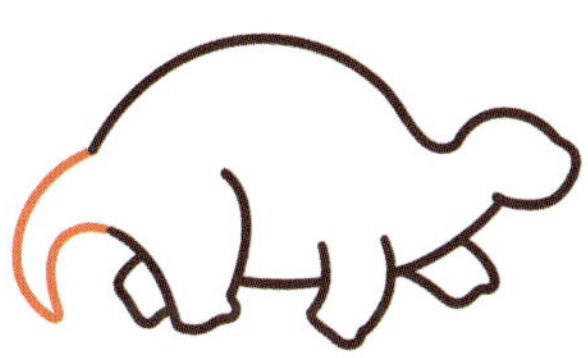

5. Add a curved tail with a pointed end.

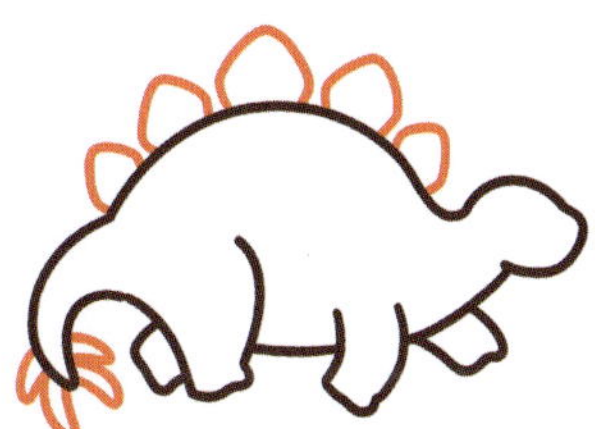

6. Add five diamond-shaped spikes on top of the body. Draw four spikes on the tip of the tail.

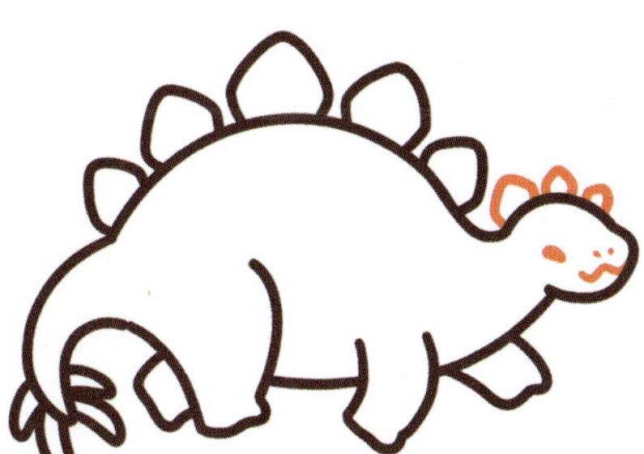

7. Add three diamonds on the head. For the face, add an oval eye, two dots for the nostrils, and a W mouth.

ANGRY PACHYCEPHALOSAURUS

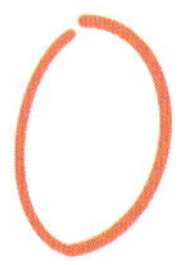

1. Draw an oval for the dome.

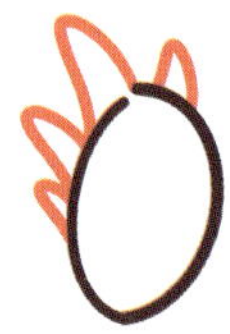

2. Add four triangle spikes around the dome.

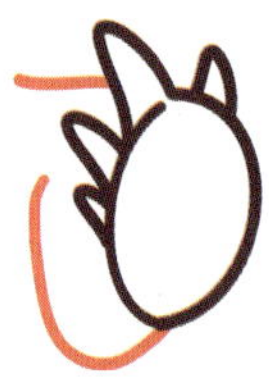

3. Draw two curved lines for the head and the neck.

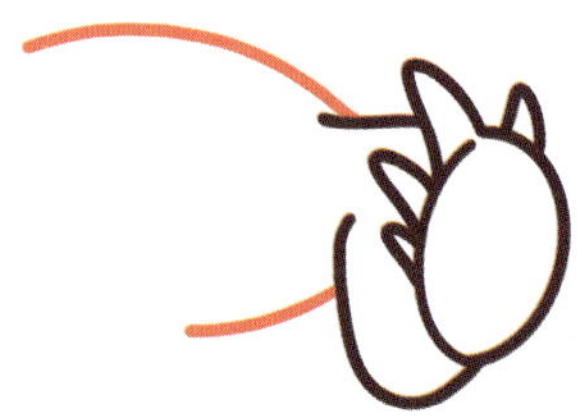

4. Add two more curved lines for the body.

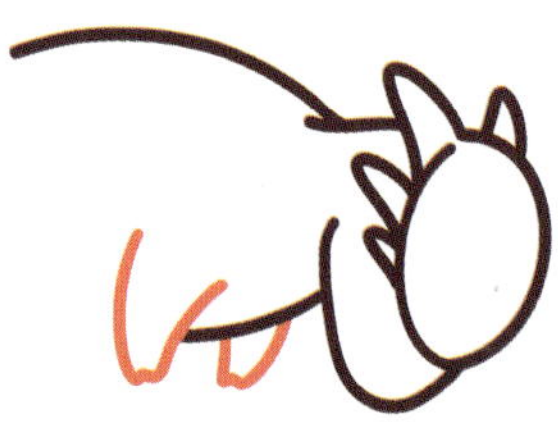

5. Add two U-shaped arms with two fingers each.

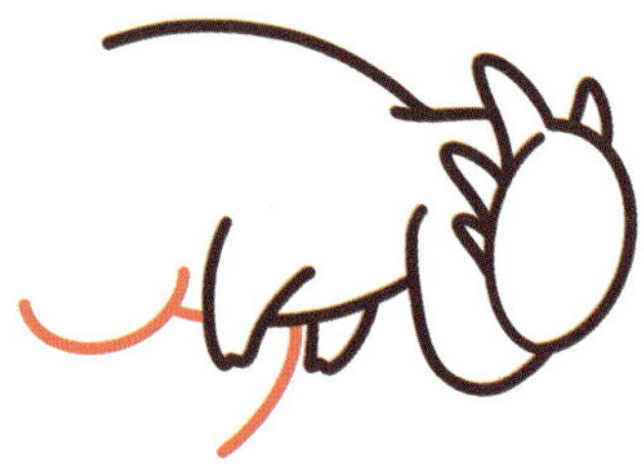

6. Draw three curved lines for the stomach and the legs.

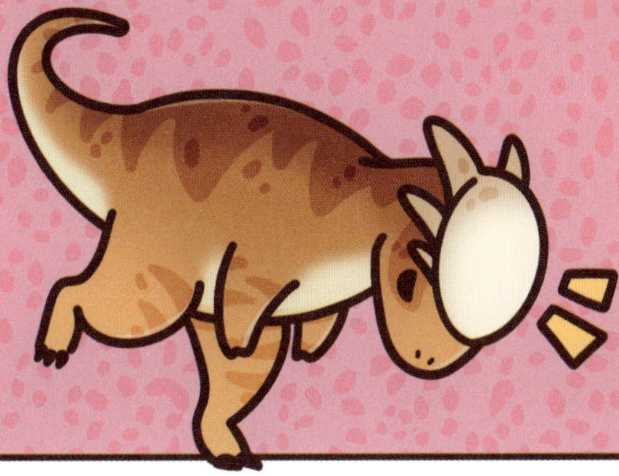

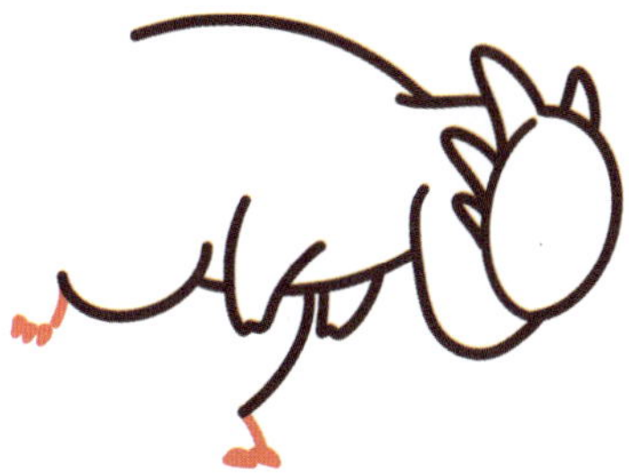

7. Draw small curved lines and talons for the feet.

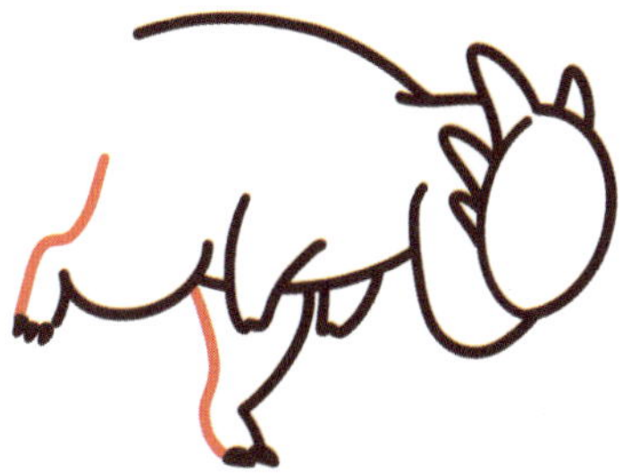

8. Complete the feet with curved lines.

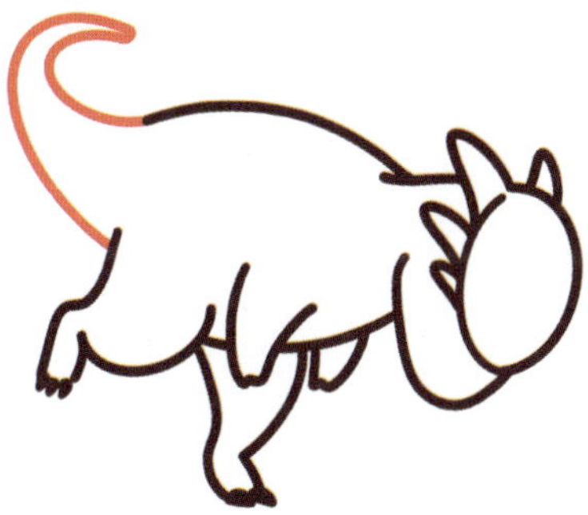

9. Add a curved tail that tapers at the end.

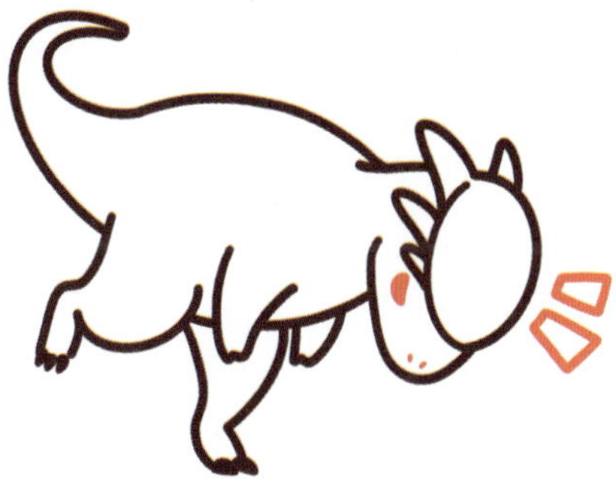

10. Add a semicircle eye and two dashes for the nostrils. Draw action shapes above the dome.

ZOOMIES VELOCIRAPTOR

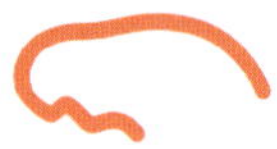

1. Draw a curved head with a jagged line for the mouth.

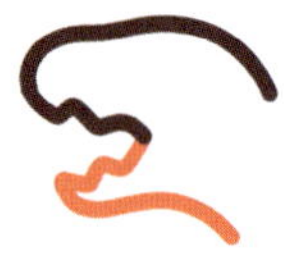

2. Add the bottom jaw with a jagged line and a curved line.

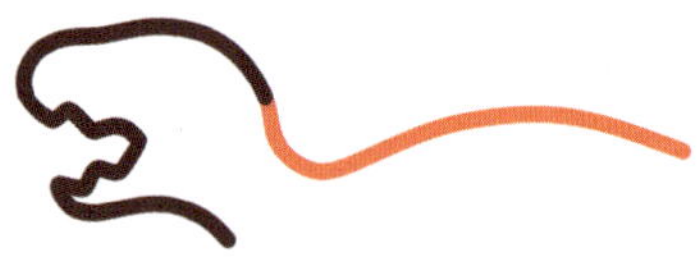

3. Add a curved line for the top of the body.

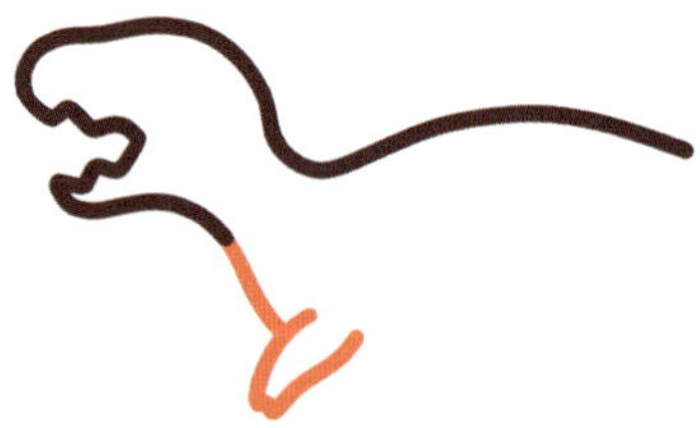

4. Add a curved line and a thin arm with two fingers.

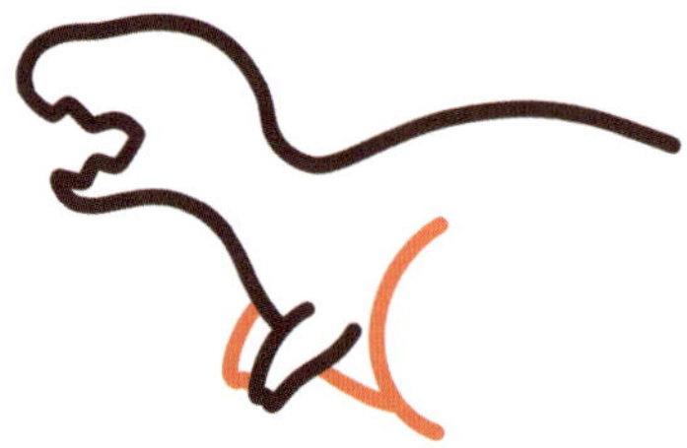

5. Draw a second arm. Add two curved lines for the stomach and the leg.

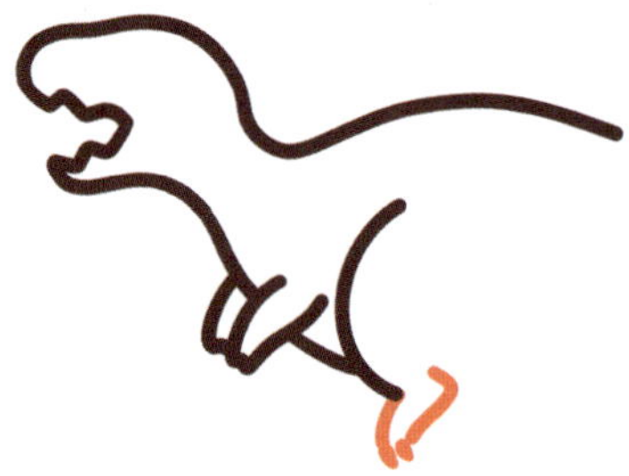

6. Add a curved line and an L-shaped line for the foot, with two talons.

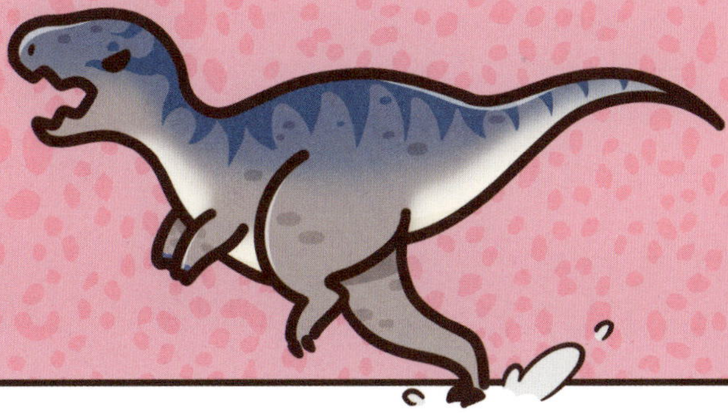

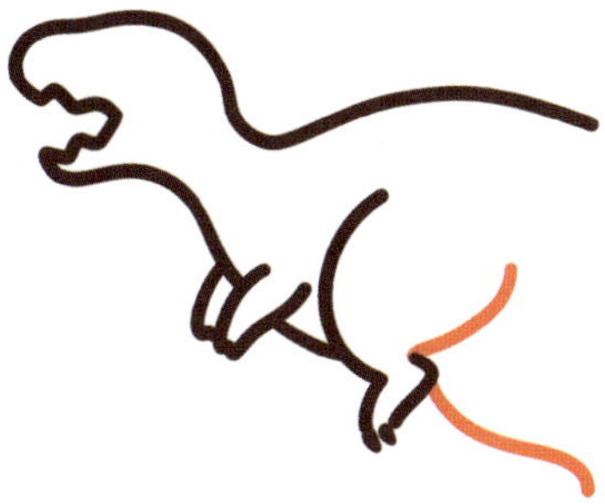

7. Add two curved lines for the back of the leg and the second leg.

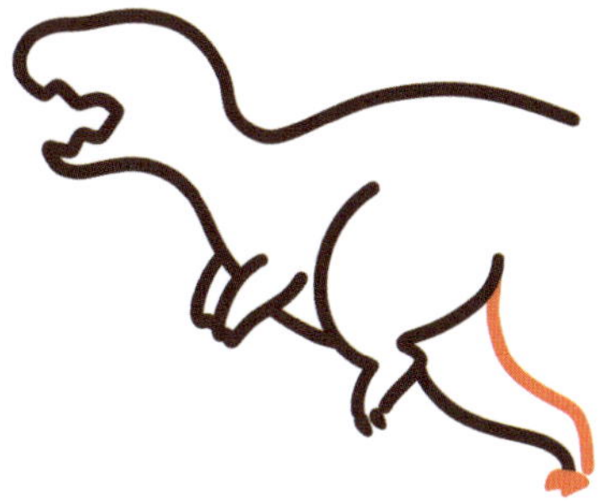

8. Add a curved line and two talons to the second leg.

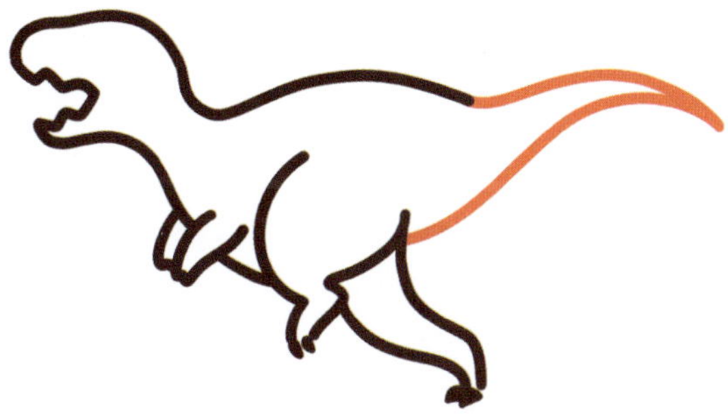

9. Draw a curved tail that tapers to a point.

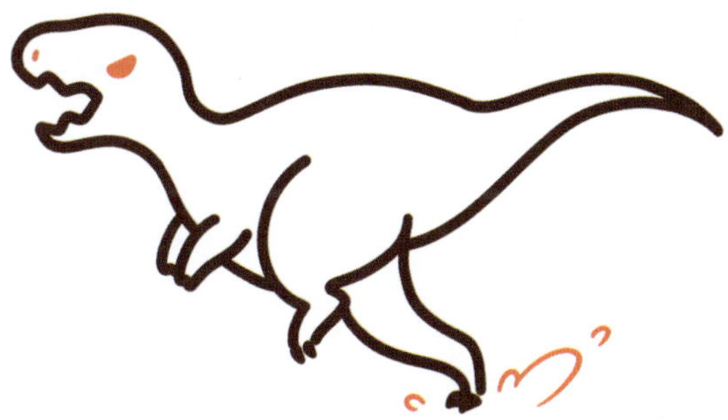

10. Add a semicircle eye and a dash for the nostril. Draw U and M shapes around the foot.

TIRED PARASAUROLOPHUS

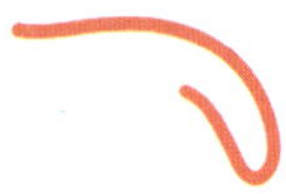

1. Draw a curved line that rounds at the end for the crest.

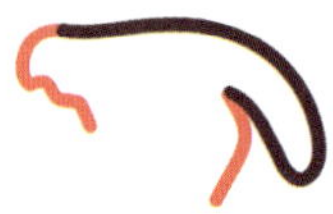

2. Add a curved and pointed nose and a jagged line for the mouth. Draw a curved line for the back of the head.

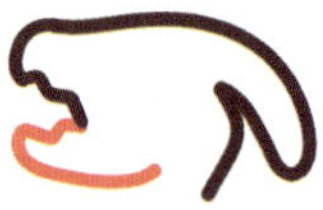

3. Add the bottom jaw with another jagged line and a curved line.

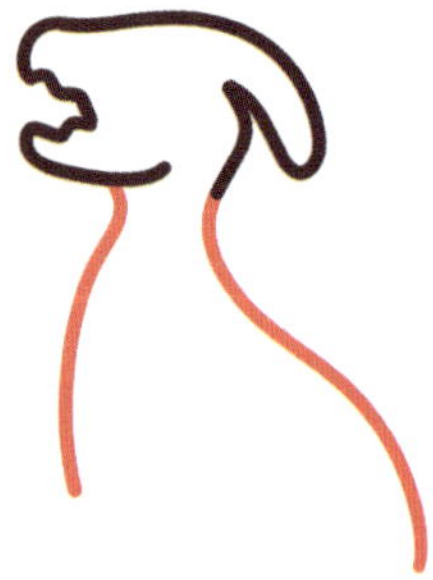

4. Add two curved lines for the body.

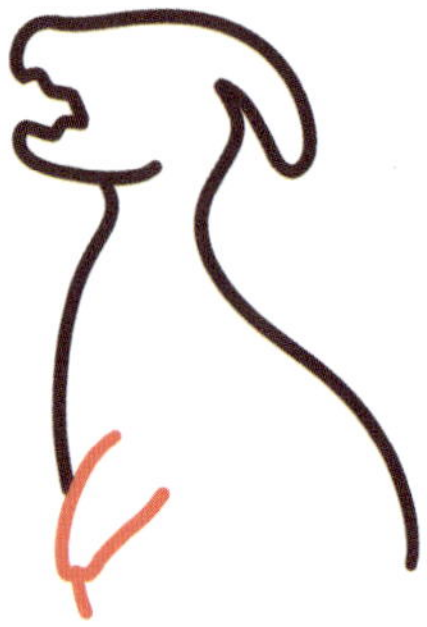

5. Draw a rectangular arm with two fingers and a curved line underneath.

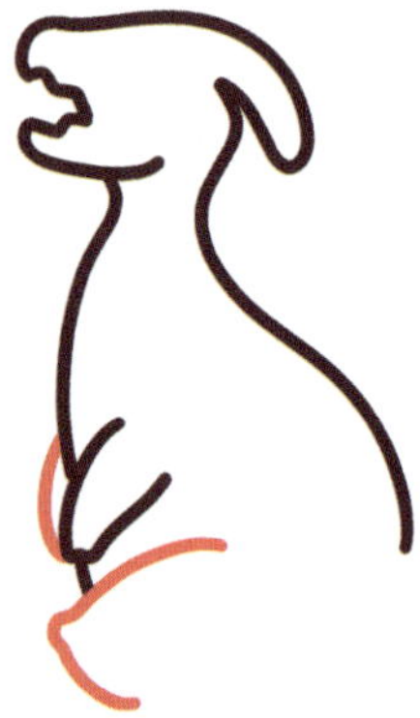

6. Add a curved line for the second arm. Draw the leg with an L shape, with a point for the toe.

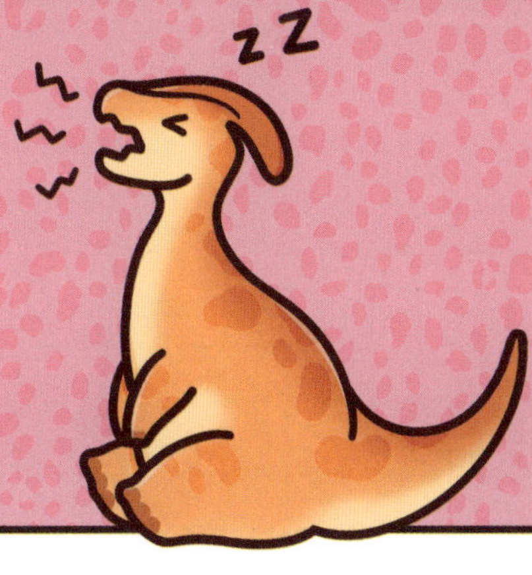

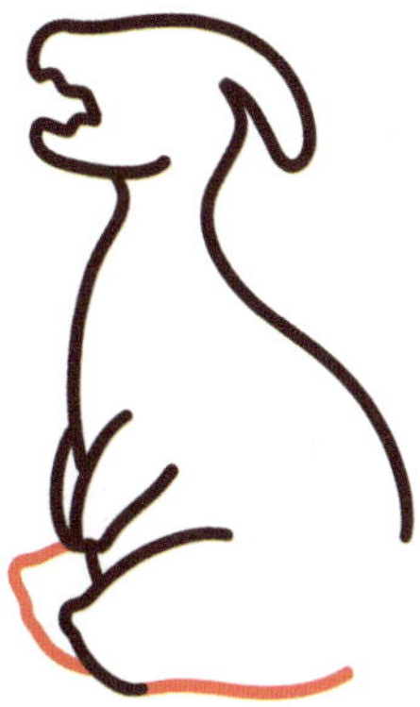

7. Add the second leg and a curved line for the bottom of the body.

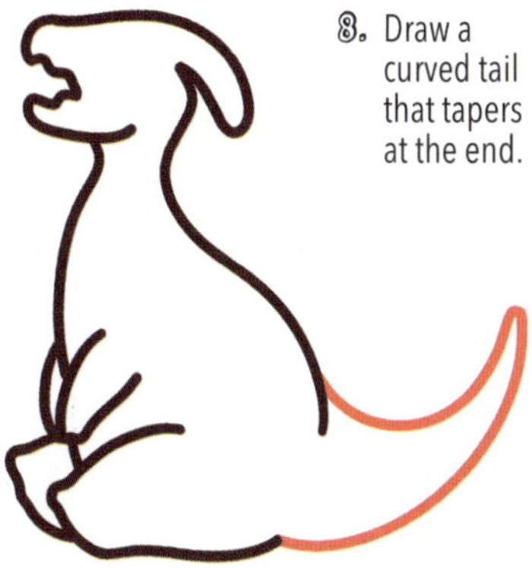

8. Draw a curved tail that tapers at the end.

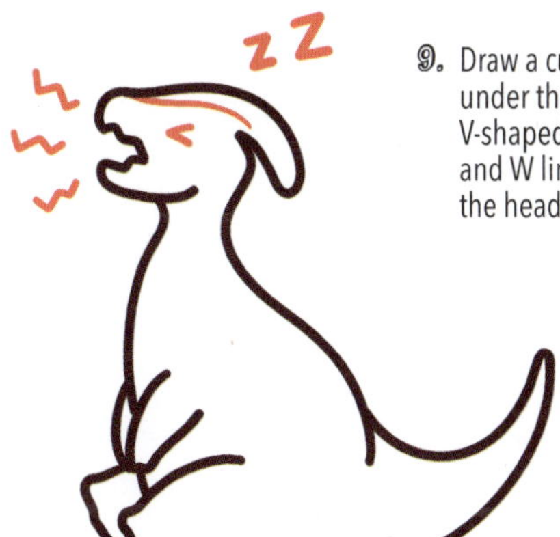

9. Draw a curved line under the crest and a V-shaped eye. Add Zs and W lines around the head.

INTRIGUED DIPLODOCUS

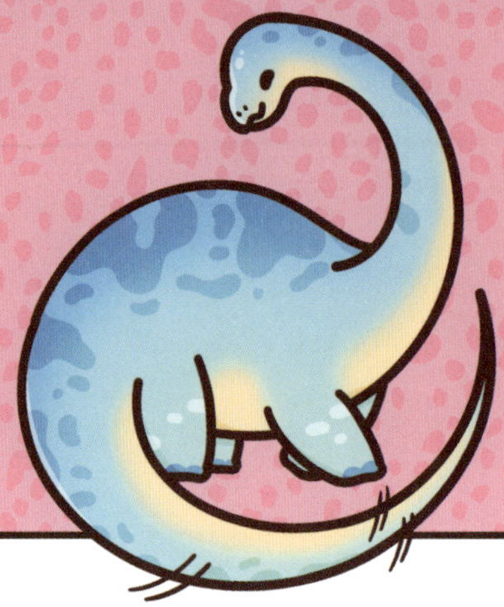

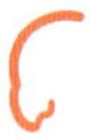

1. Draw a curved head with a bump for the snout and a W mouth.

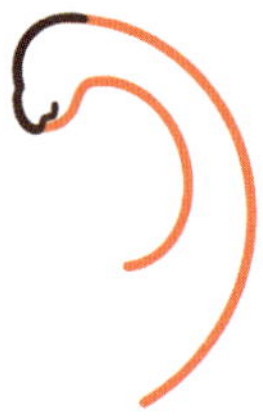

2. Add two curved lines for the neck.

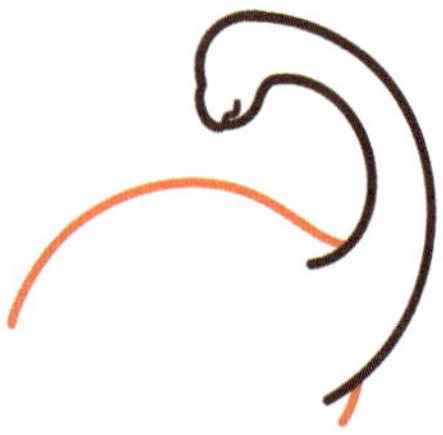

3. Add two curved lines for the body.

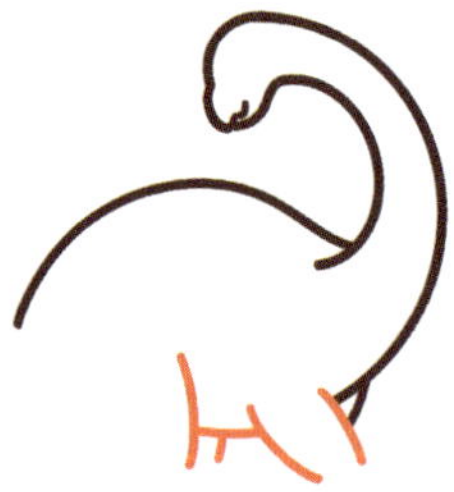

4. Add curved lines for the stomach and the legs.

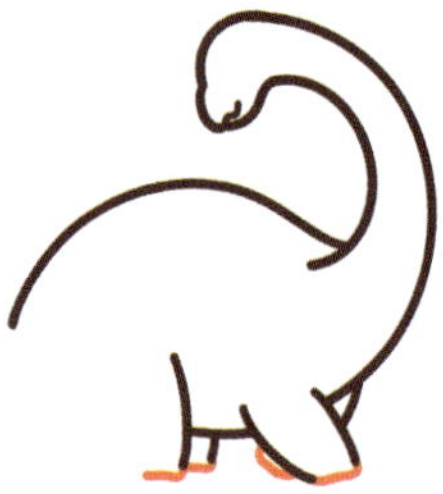

5. Draw two toes for each leg.

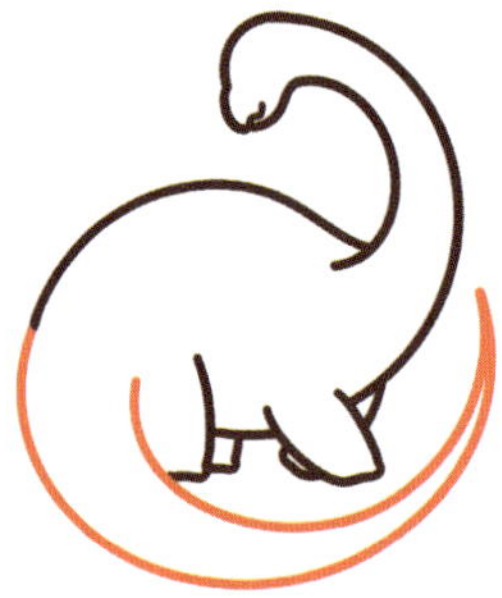

6. Draw a long, curved tail that tapers at the end.

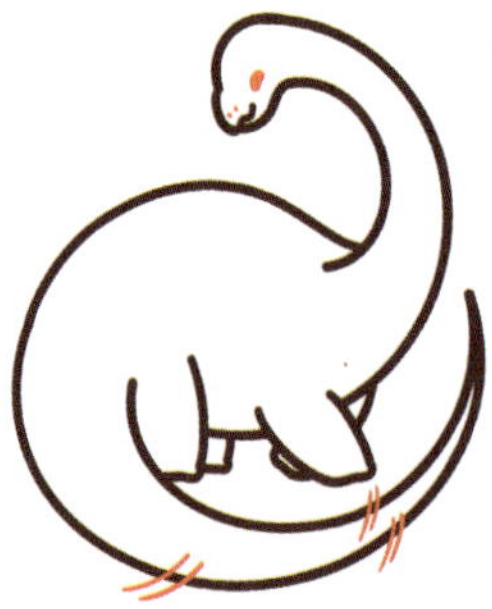

7. Add an oval eye and two dashes for the nostrils. Draw action lines around the tail.

ROARING TYRANNOSAURUS

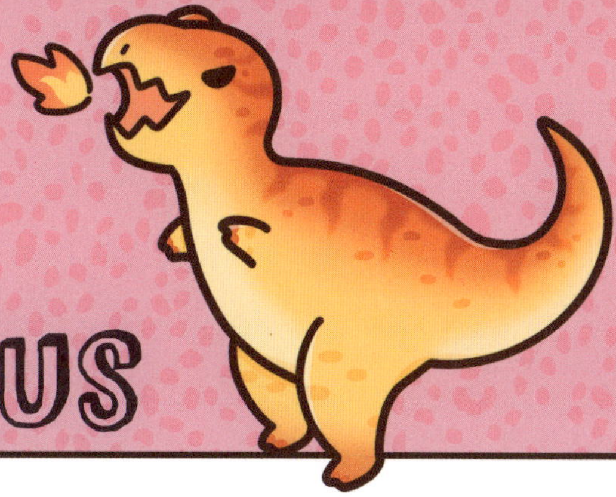

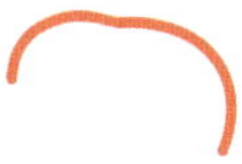

1. Draw a curved line with a bump for the head.

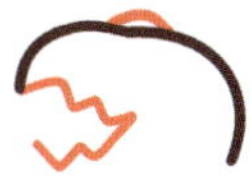

2. Draw a jagged mouth and a curve above the head.

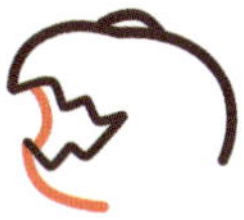

3. Add curved lines around the mouth and the chin.

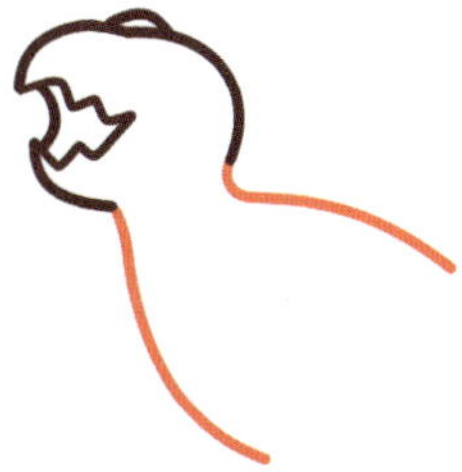

4. Add two curved lines for the body.

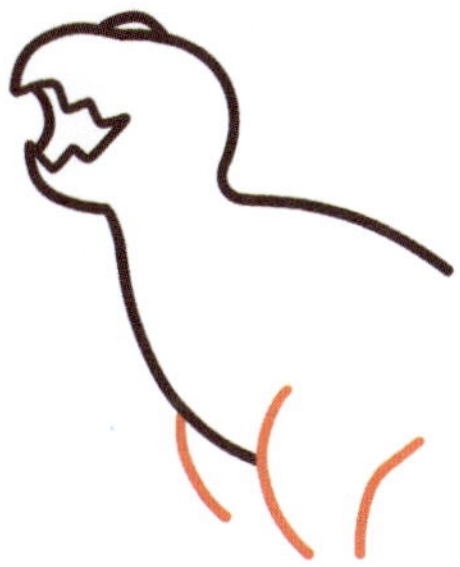

5. Draw three curved lines for the legs.

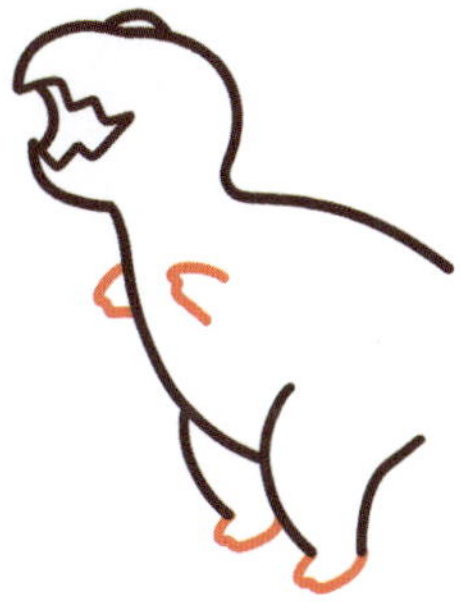

6. Add two stubby arms with two fingers each. Add two U-shaped feet with two toes each.

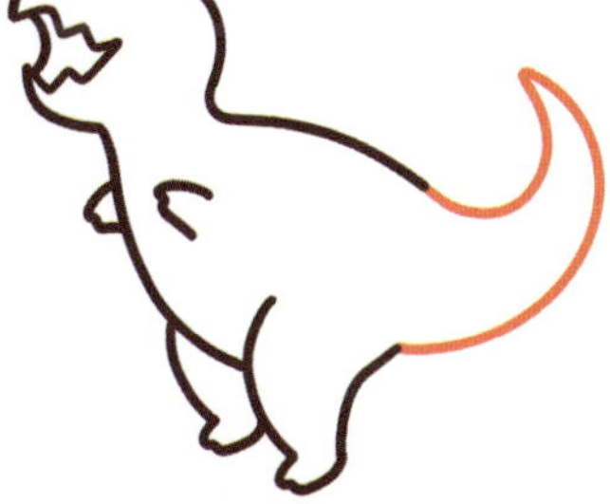

7. Draw a curved tail that tapers at the end.

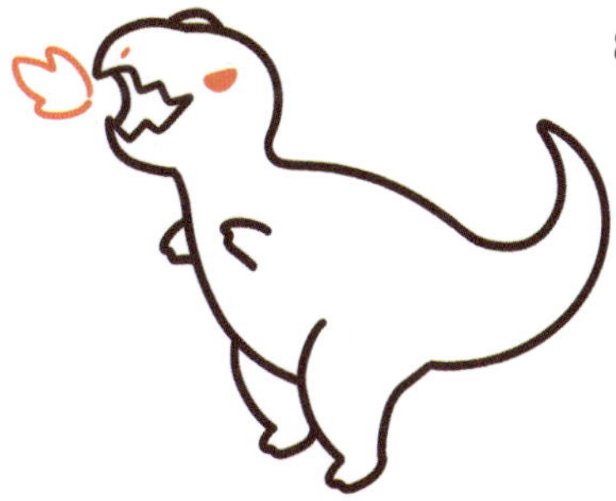

8. Add a semicircle eye and a dash for the nostril. Add a flame in front of the mouth.

DAILY ACTIVITIES

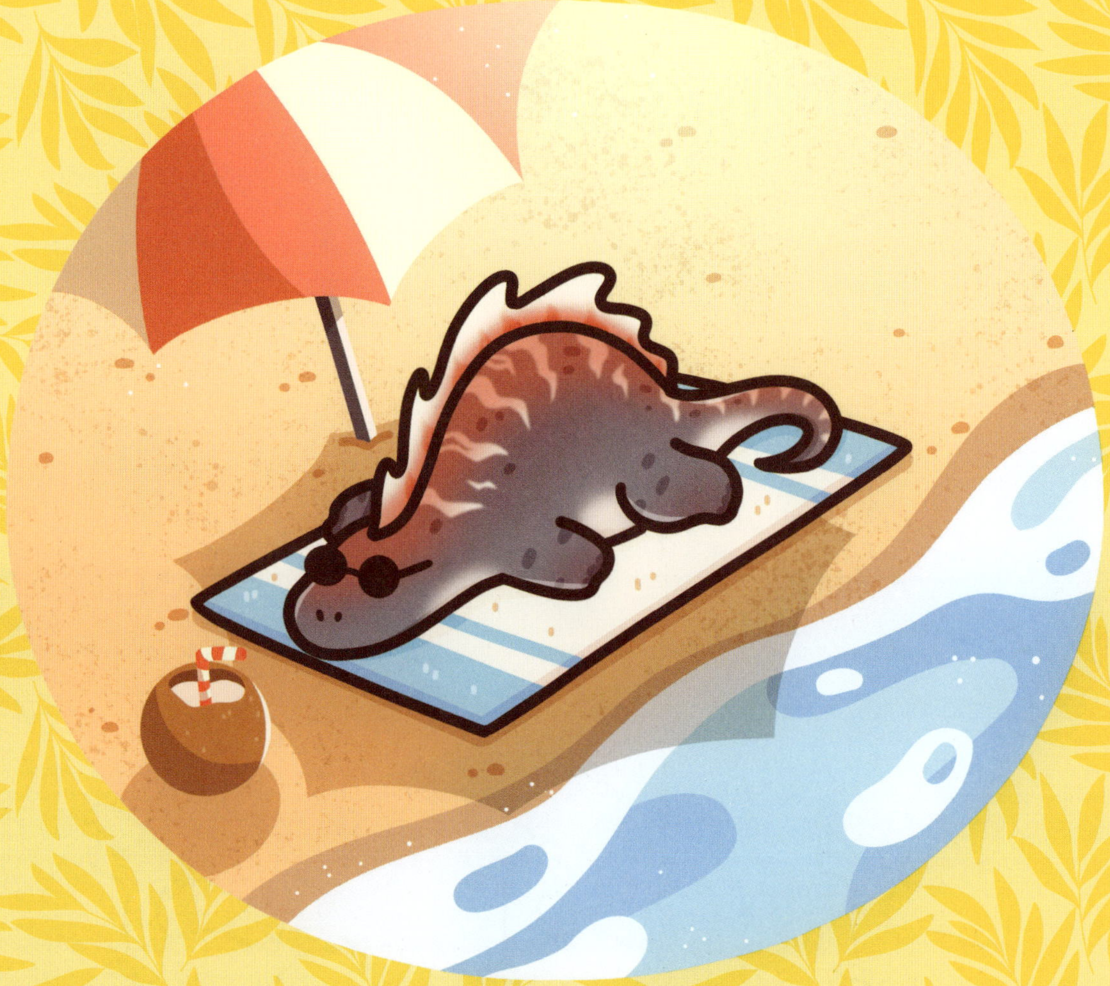

CHASING BUTTERFLIES COMPSOGNATHUS

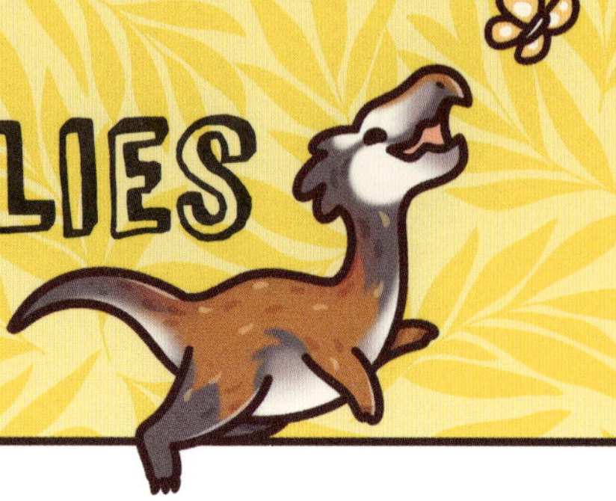

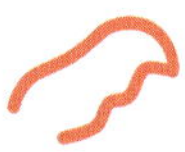

1. Draw a curved oval snout with a jagged line for the mouth.

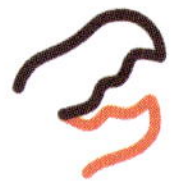

2. Add the bottom jaw with a jagged line and a curved line.

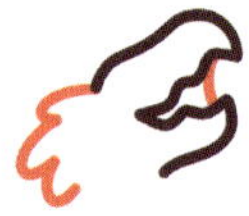

3. Add a curved line for the side of the mouth and feathers on the back of the head.

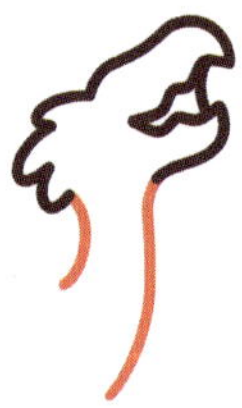

4. Draw two curved lines for the neck.

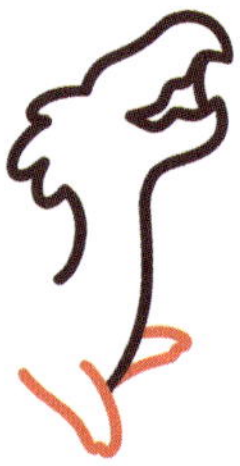

5. Add two thin arms with two fingers each.

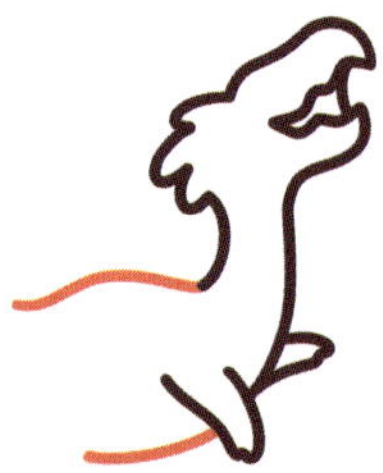

6. Add two curved lines for the body.

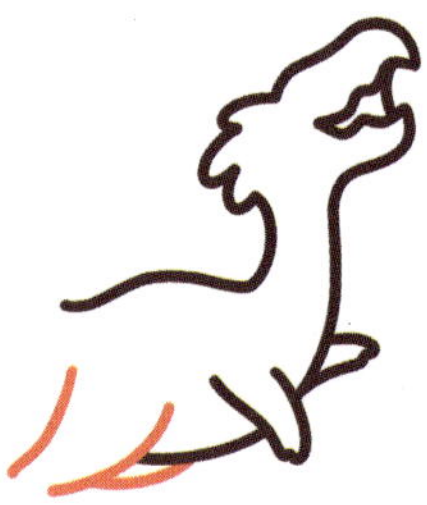

7. Draw three curved lines for the legs.

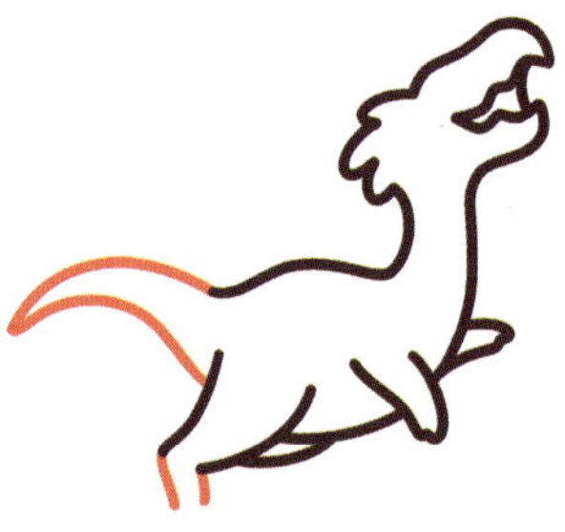

8. Add two lines for the foot. Draw a curved tail that tapers at the end.

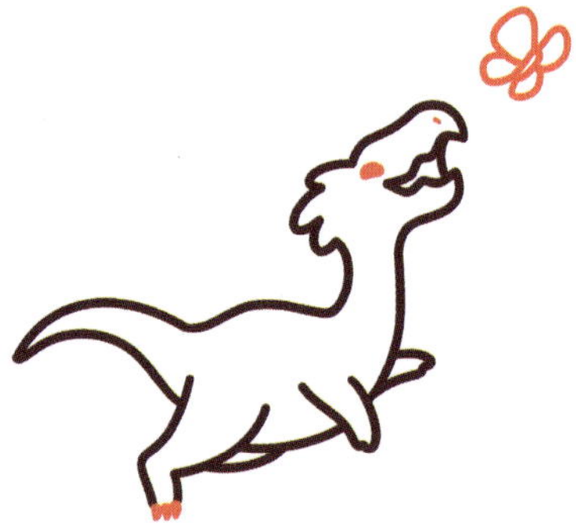

9. Add three talons to the foot. For the face, draw an oval eye and a dash for the nostril. Add a butterfly above the head with four round wings and an oval body.

MUD PUDDLE EORAPTOR

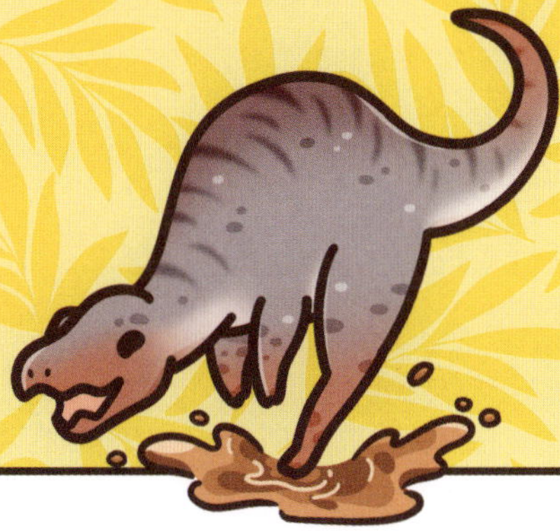

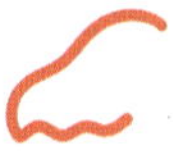

1. Draw a curved oval head with a jagged line for the mouth.

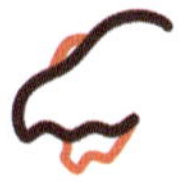

2. Add a jagged W shape for the bottom jaw. Add a curve on the side of the head.

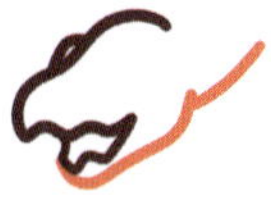

3. Add two curved lines for the chin and the neck.

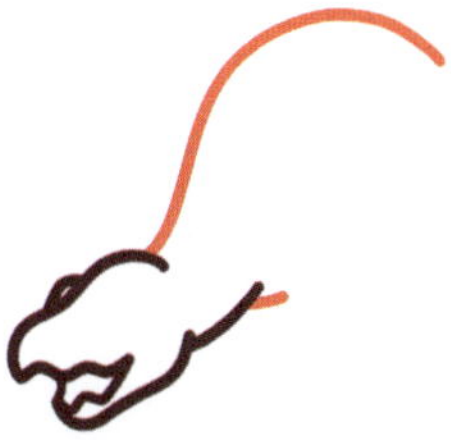

4. Draw an arch for the top of the body and a curved line under the neck.

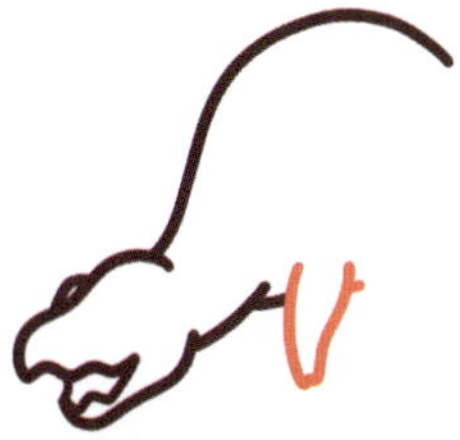

5. Add a thin arm with two fingers and a line next to it.

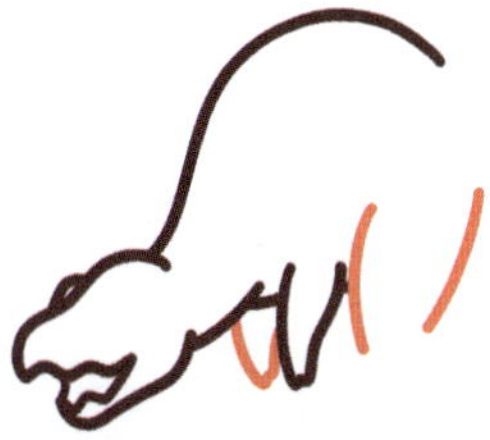

6. Draw a second arm. Add two curved lines for the leg.

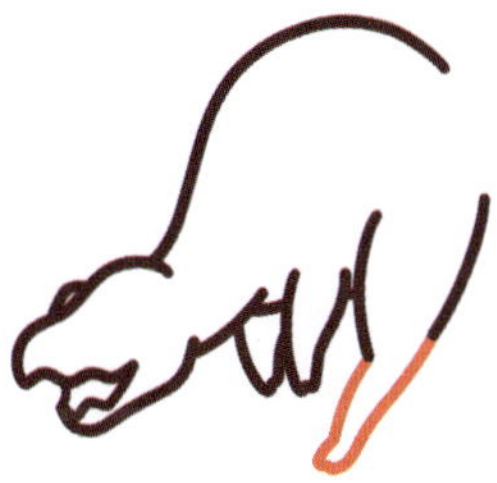

7. Add a U-shaped leg and foot, with two toes.

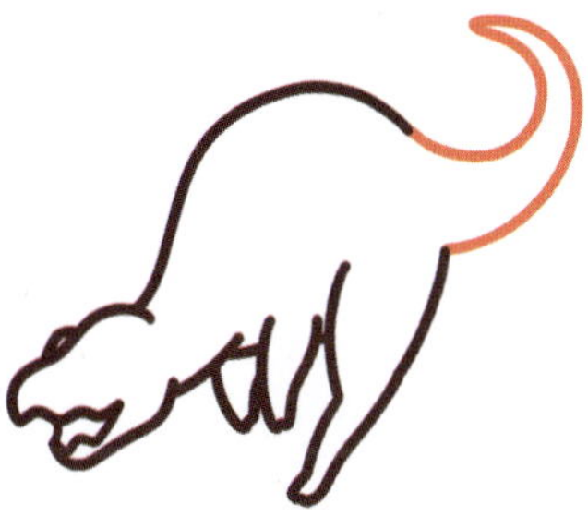

8. Draw a curved tail that tapers at the end.

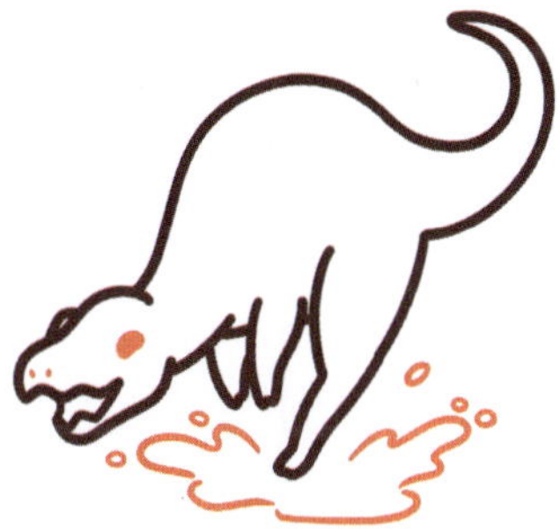

9. Add an oval eye and two dots for the nostrils. Draw a puddle under the foot with curving lines and ovals.

SINGING GIGANOTOSAURUS

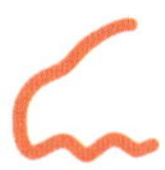

1. Draw a wavy line and a jagged line for the nose and mouth.

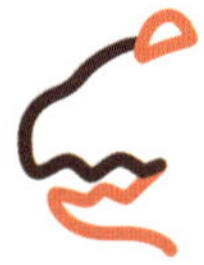

2. Add the bottom jaw with a jagged line and a curved line. Draw a semicircle on top of the head.

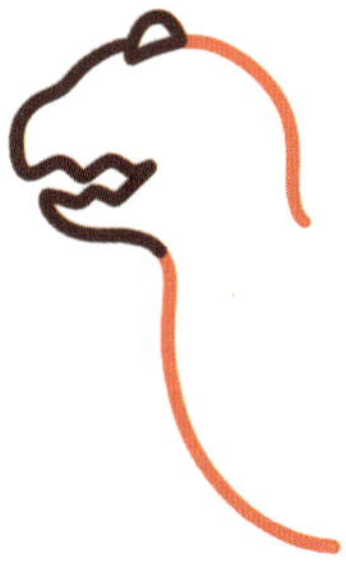

3. Add two curved lines for the head and the stomach.

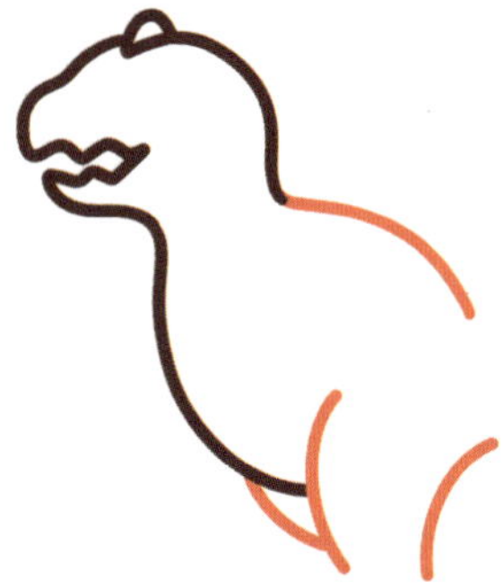

4. Draw curved lines for the top of the body and the legs.

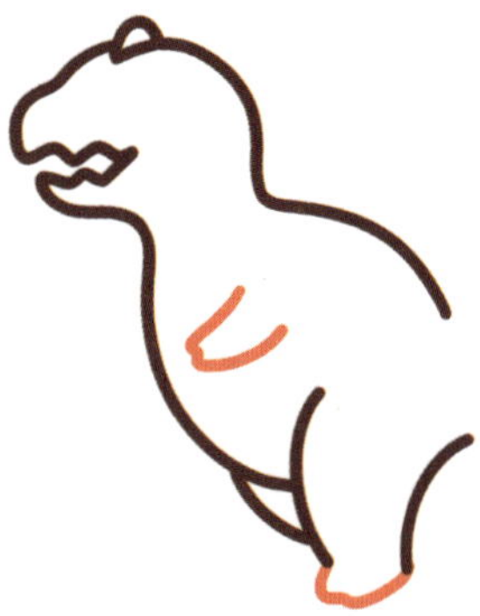

5. Add a curved arm with two fingers and a U-shaped foot with two toes.

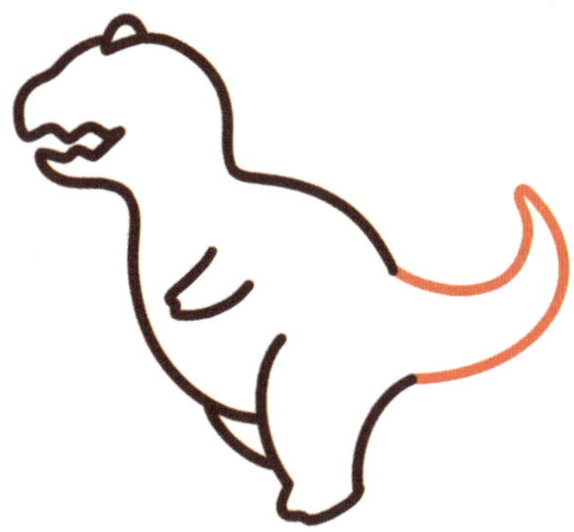

6. Add a curved tail that tapers at the end.

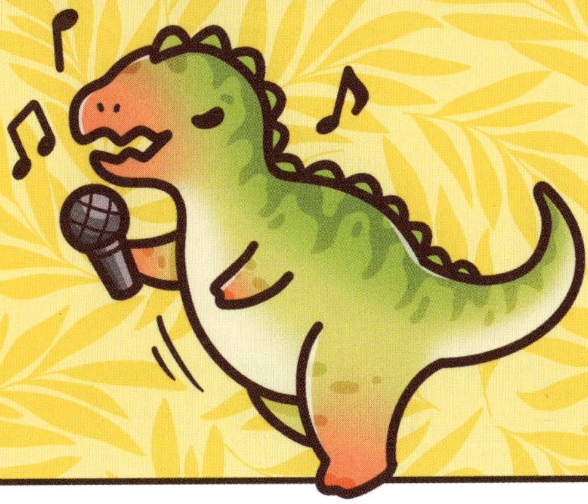

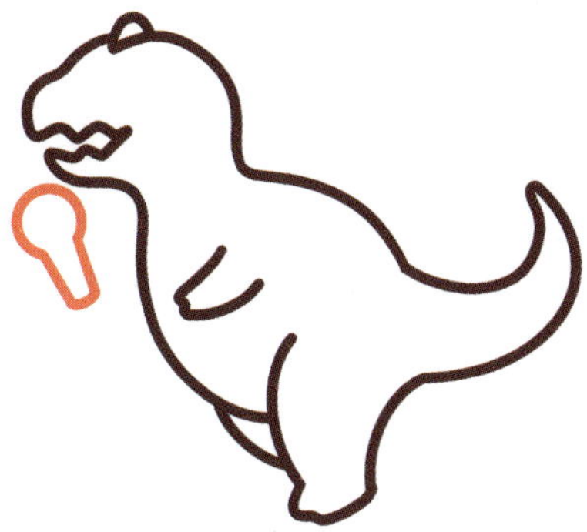

7. Draw a microphone under the mouth in the shape of an ice cream cone.

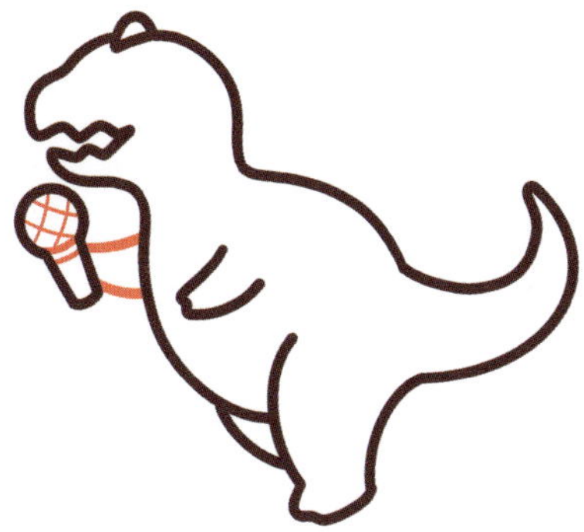

8. Add crisscrossing and horizontal lines to the microphone. Draw two curved lines for the second arm.

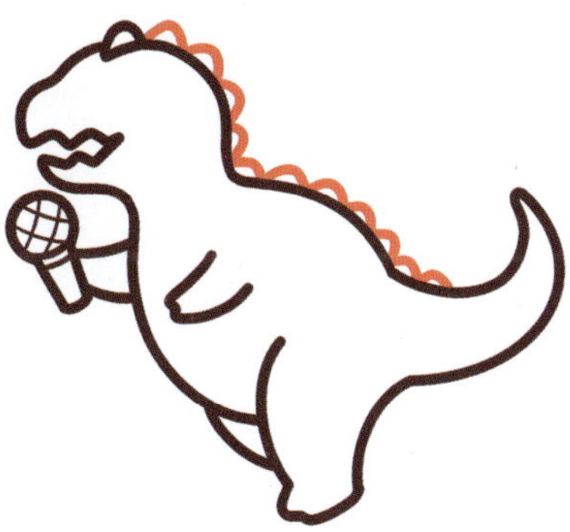

9. Add a bunch of semicircles down the head, neck, and back for the ridges.

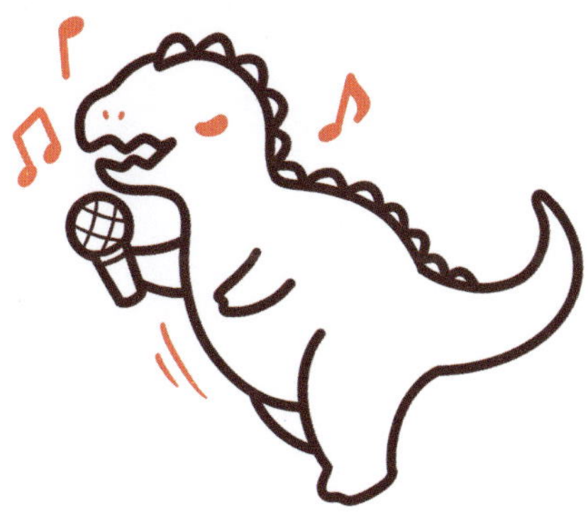

10. Draw an oval eye and two dashes for the nostrils. Add music notes and movement lines around the dino.

STRETCHING BRACHIOSAURUS

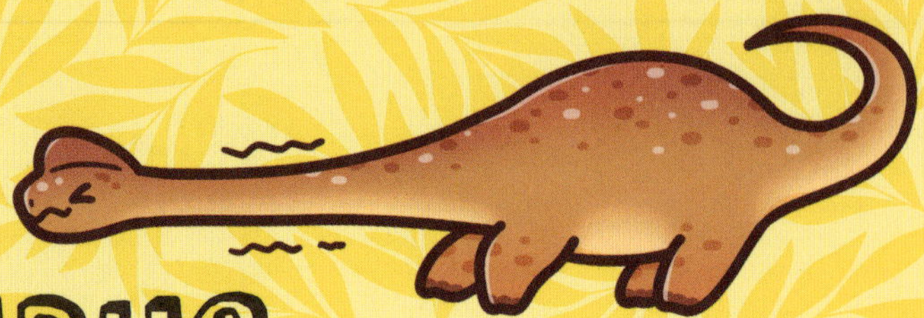

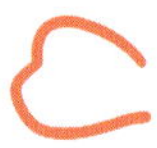

1. Draw a heart-shaped head with the end open.

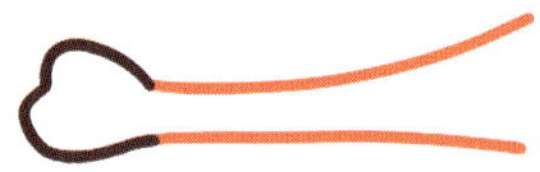

2. Add two curved lines for the neck.

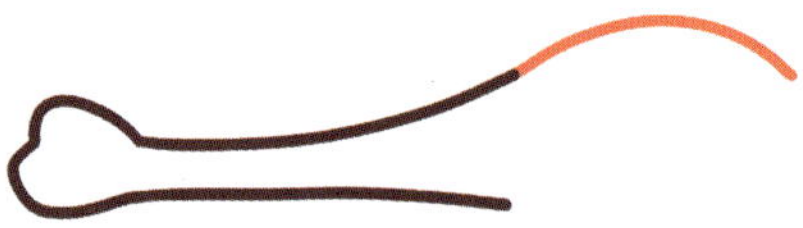

3. Draw a curve for the top of the body.

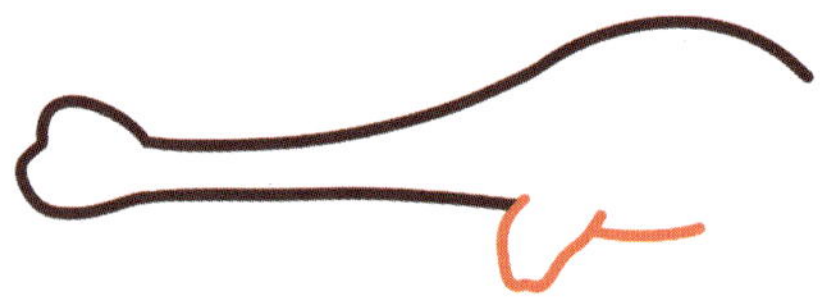

4. Add a U-shaped leg with two toes and a curve for the stomach.

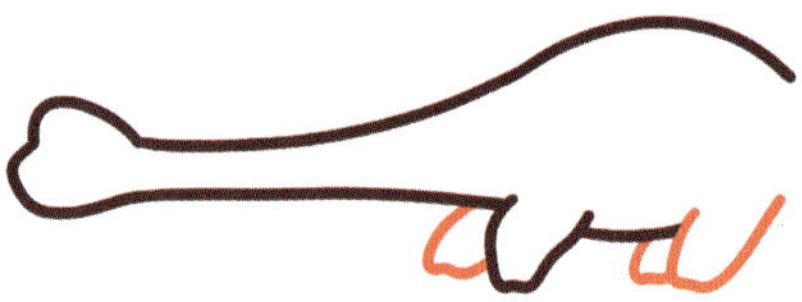

5. Add three more legs.

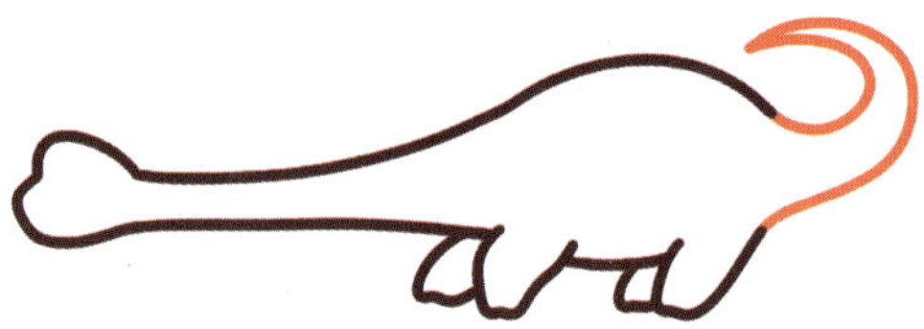

6. Draw a curved tail that tapers at the end.

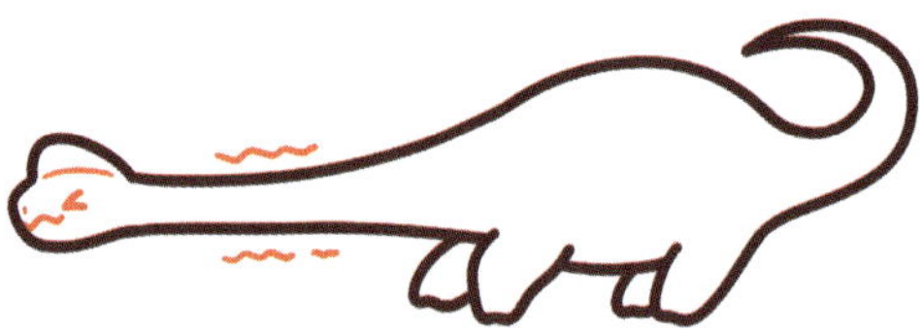

7. Add a curve on the head. For the face, add a V-shaped eye, a dot for the nostril, and a W mouth. Draw wavy lines above and below the neck.

AUTUMN FUN ATROCIRAPTOR

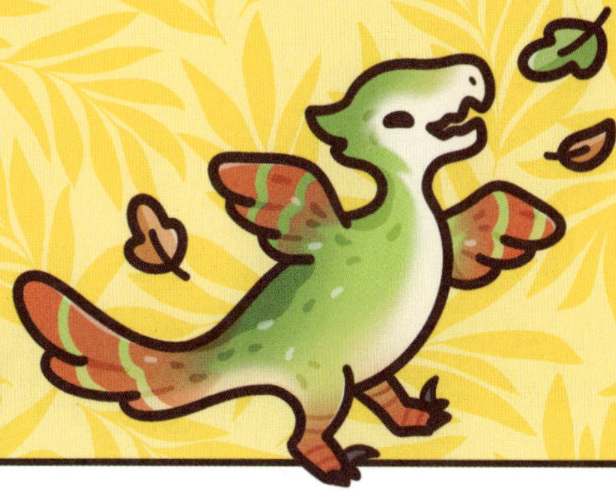

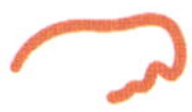

1. Draw an oval head that flattens at the nose and a jagged mouth.

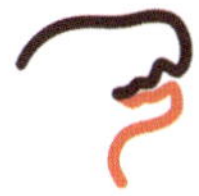

2. Add the bottom jaw with a jagged line and a curved line.

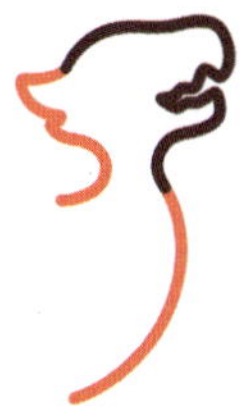

3. Add feathers on the back of the head. Draw two curved lines for the neck and the stomach.

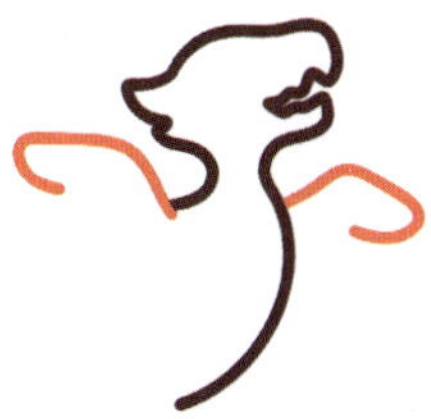

4. Add two wings with angled lines that curve in at the ends.

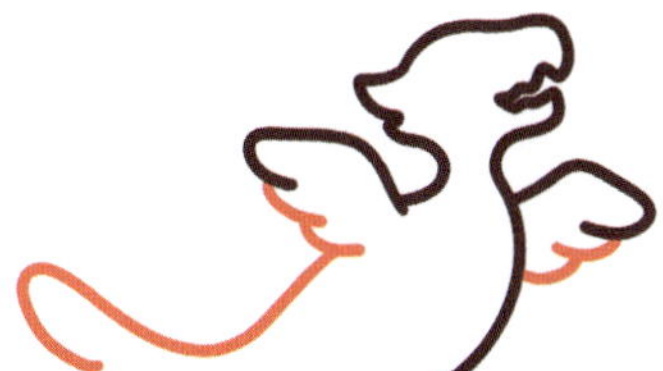

5. Draw curved feathers on the wings. Add a curved line for the back of the body and the tail.

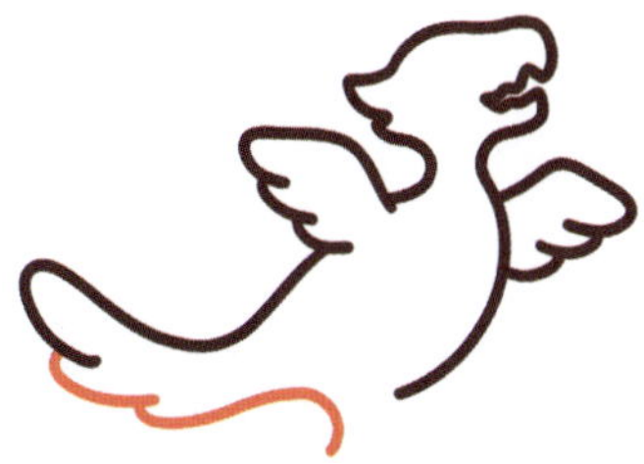

6. Add curved feathers to the tail that curl into the leg.

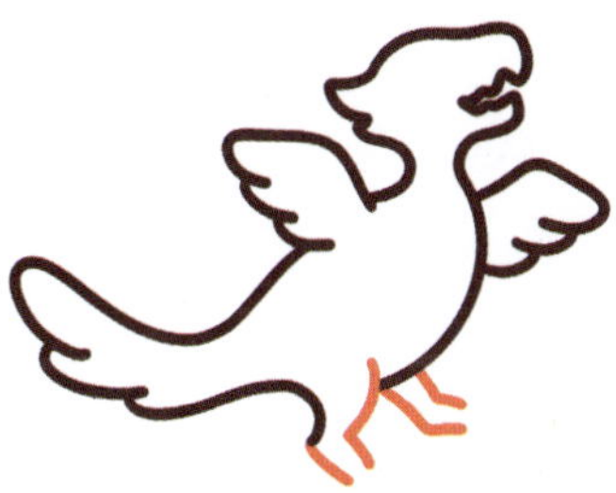

7. Add straight and V-shaped lines for the legs.

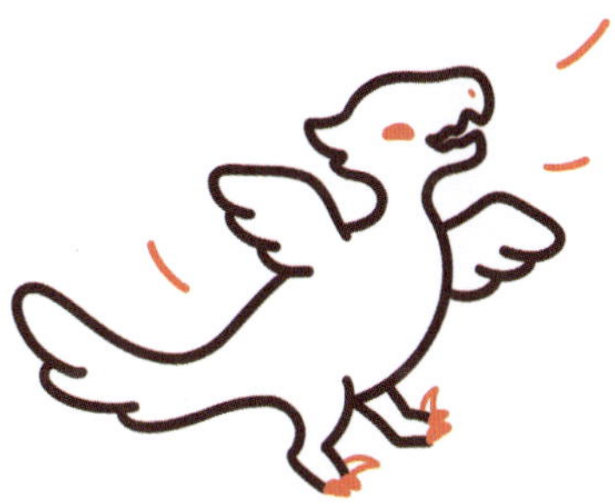

8. Draw a large triangle talon with two smaller talons on each foot. For the face, add a semicircle eye and a dash for the nostril. Draw three lines around the dino.

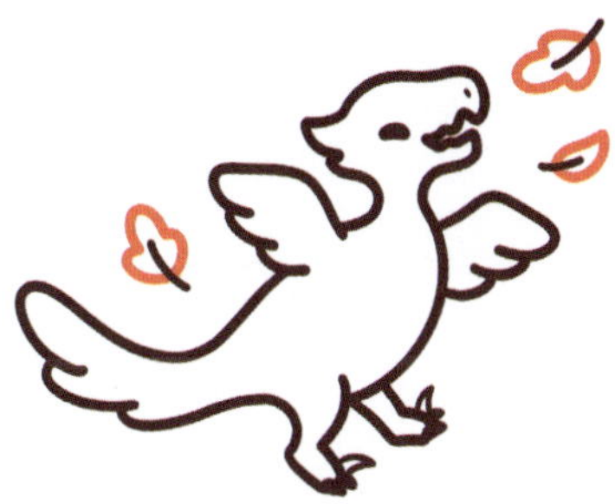

9. Turn the lines into leaves with round and teardrop shapes.

TEA PARTY MEGALOSAURUS

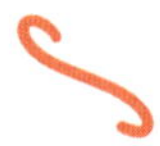

1. Draw an S-line for the hat's brim.

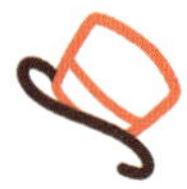

2. Add a square hat with a line inside.

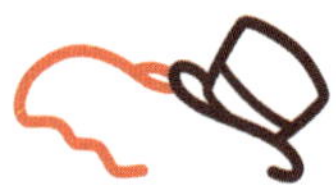

3. Draw a curved line and a jagged line for the mouth. Add a small, curved line for the eye.

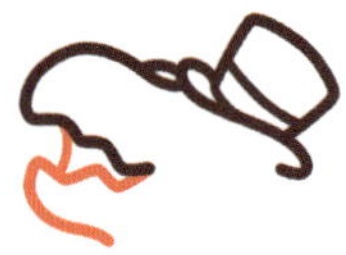

4. Add the bottom jaw with another jagged line and a curved line. Draw a curved line for the side of the mouth.

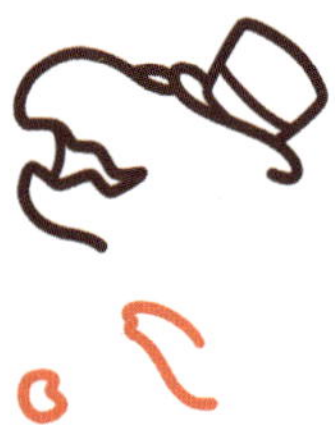

5. Draw a curved arm with two fingers. Add the second hand with a C shape with two fingers.

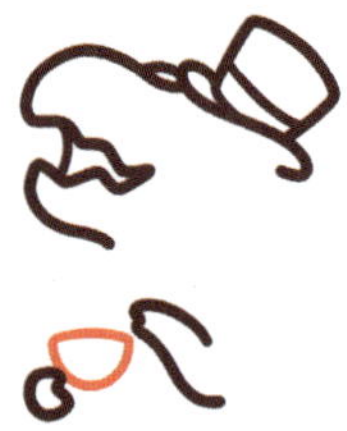

6. Add a semicircle mug between the hands.

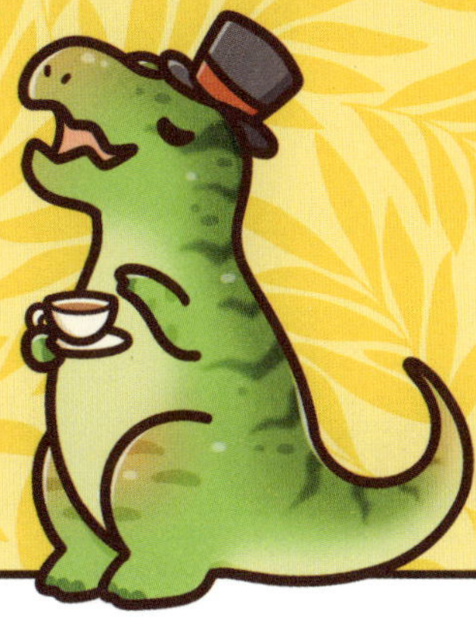

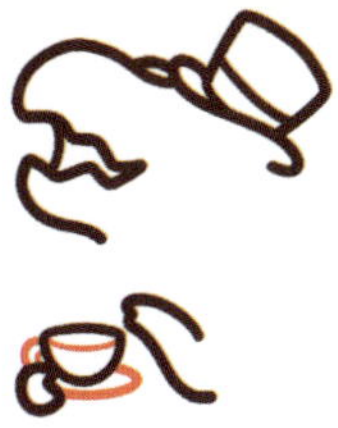

7. Draw curved lines in the mug, under the mug for a saucer, and for the handle.

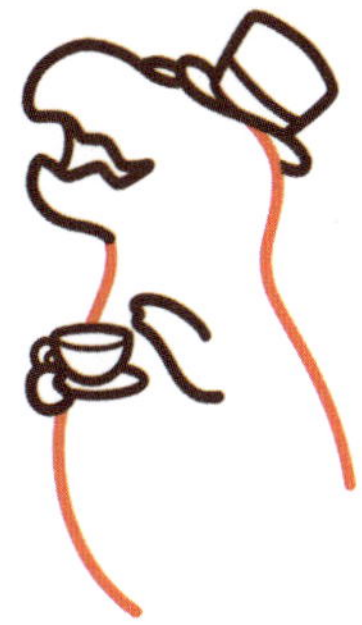

8. Draw two curved lines for the body.

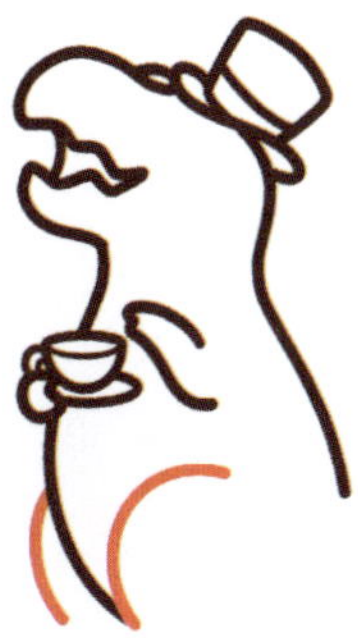

9. Add two curved lines for the legs.

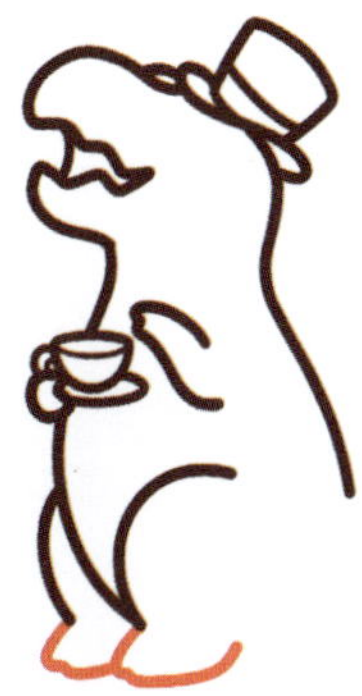

10. Add the large U-shaped feet with two toes each.

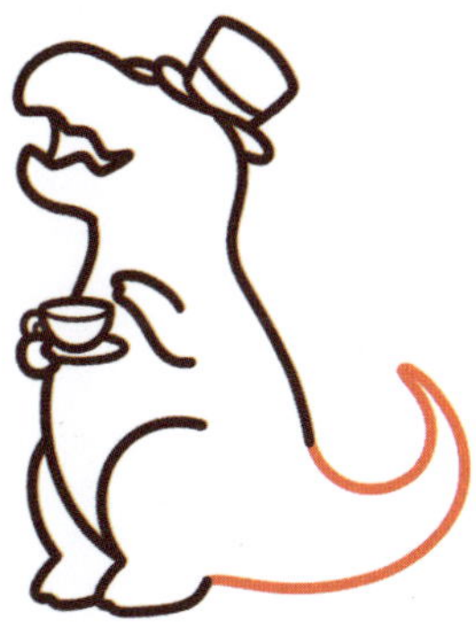

11. Draw a curved tail that tapers at the end.

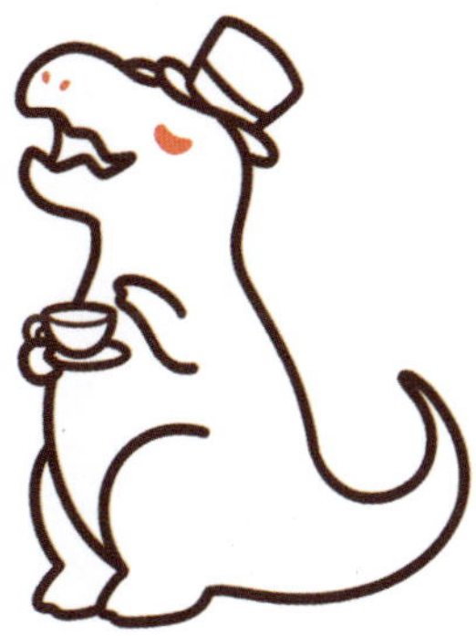

12. Add a U-shaped eye and two dashes for the nostrils.

READING OVIRAPTOR

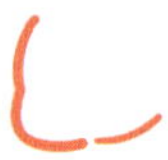

1. Draw two curved lines with a pointed beak in the center.

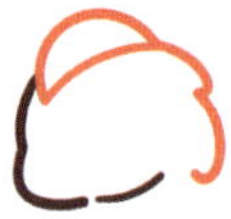

2. Add a semicircle crest on top of the head with feathers down the back of the head.

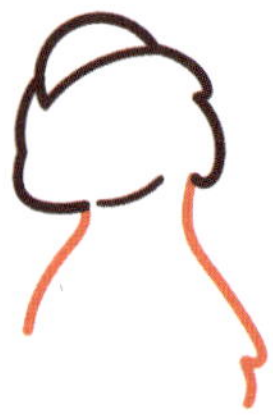

3. Draw two curved lines for the body with some feathers near the bottom.

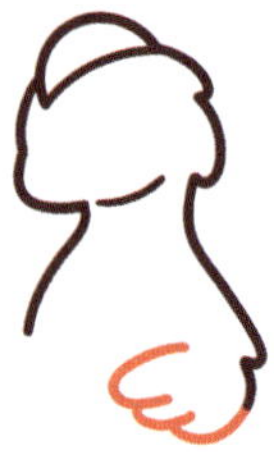

4. Add a feathered wing with three curves.

5. Draw a book with two angled rectangles. Add two oval feathers for the other wing.

6. Add two curved lines for the legs. Draw a curved line for the tail that hooks over at the end.

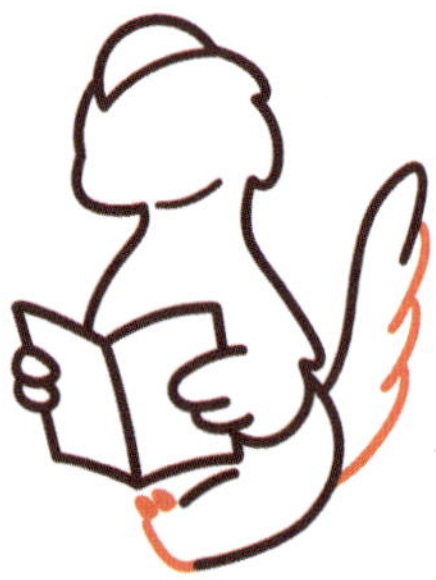

7. Add three curved feathers to the tail. Draw a curved line and two talons for the foot.

8. Add the second foot and a curved line for the stomach. For the face, add an oval eye, a curve around the beak, and a W mouth.

BATHING PARASAUROLOPHUS

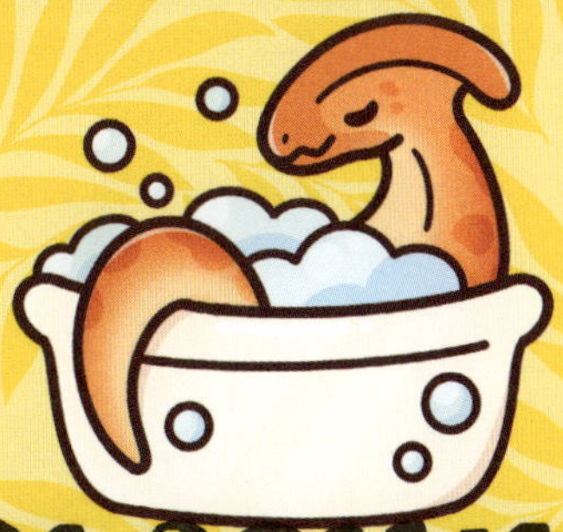

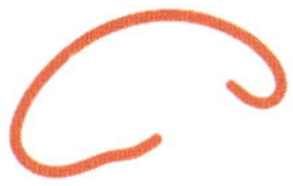

1. Draw a partial oval head with a rounded curl on the right.

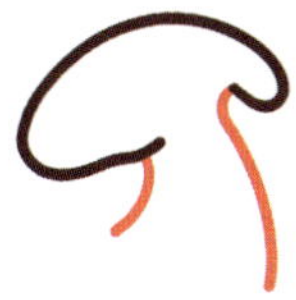

2. Add two curved lines for the neck.

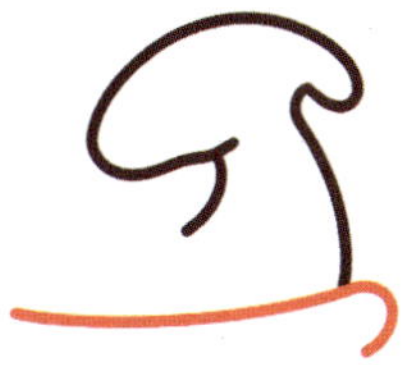

3. Draw the curved top of the tub that hooks on the right.

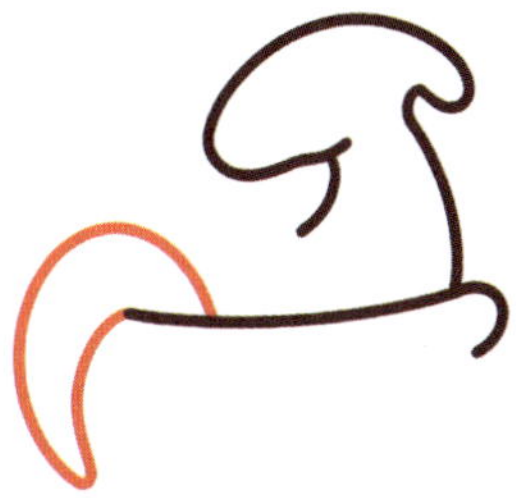

4. Add two curved lines for the tail that drapes over the lip of the tub.

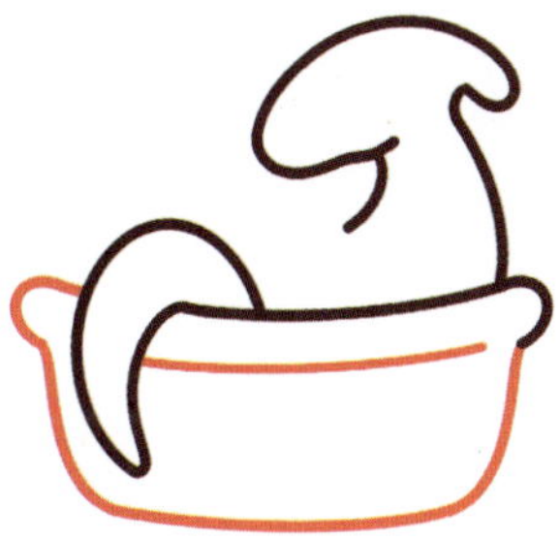

5. Add the tub in the shape of a butter dish with a curved line inside.

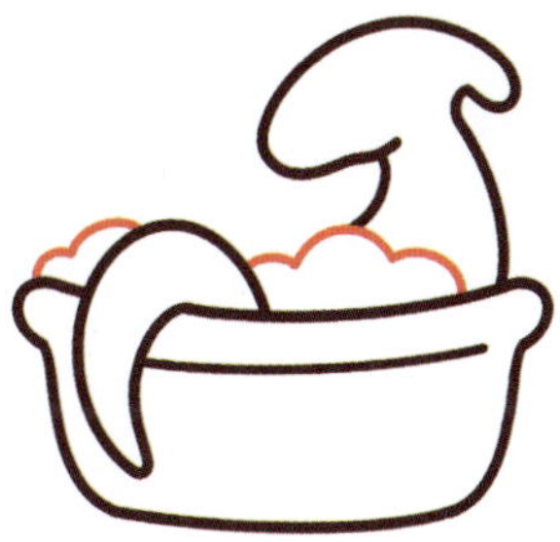

6. Draw bubbles inside the tub with scalloped shapes.

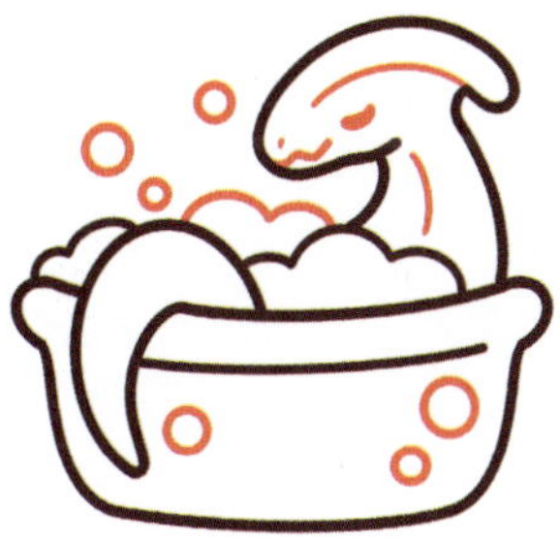

7. Add more bubbles with scallops and circles. For the face, add a curved oval eye, a dash for the nostril, and a W mouth. Draw two curved lines on the head and the neck.

KITE FLYING COELOPHYSIS

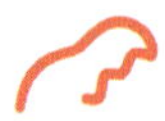

1. Draw a wavy line that curves in a jagged line for the mouth.

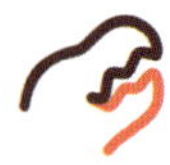

2. Add the bottom jaw with a jagged line and a curved line.

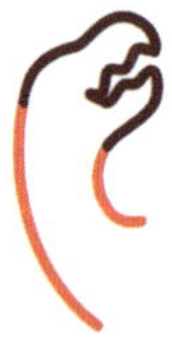

3. Add two curved lines for the neck.

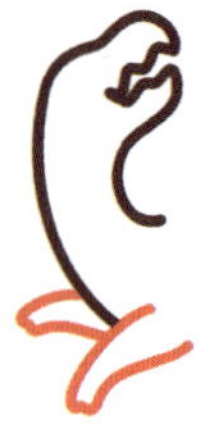

4. Draw two U-shaped arms with two fingers each.

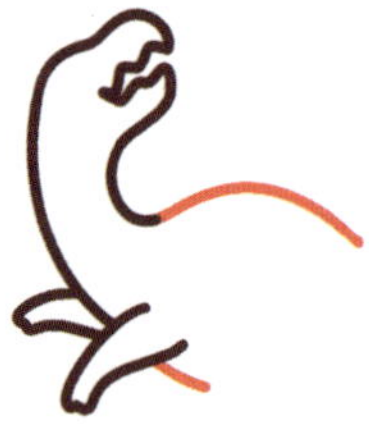

5. Draw two curved lines for the top of the body and the stomach.

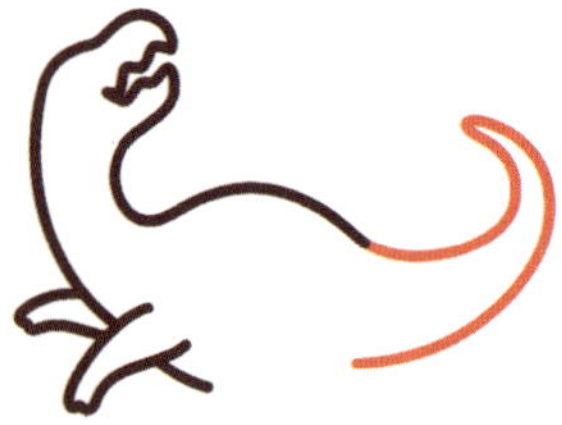

6. Add a curved tail that tapers at the end.

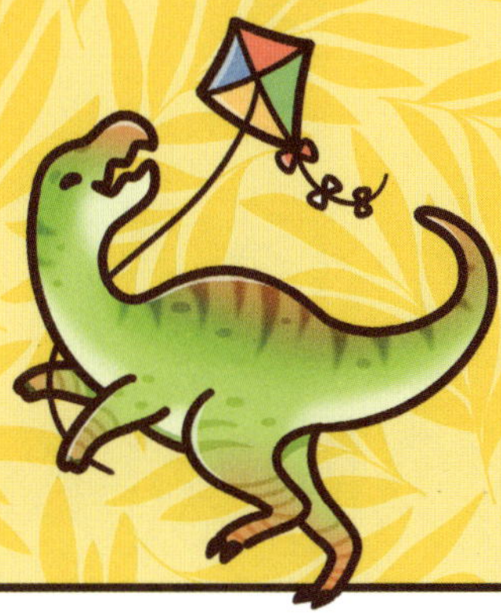

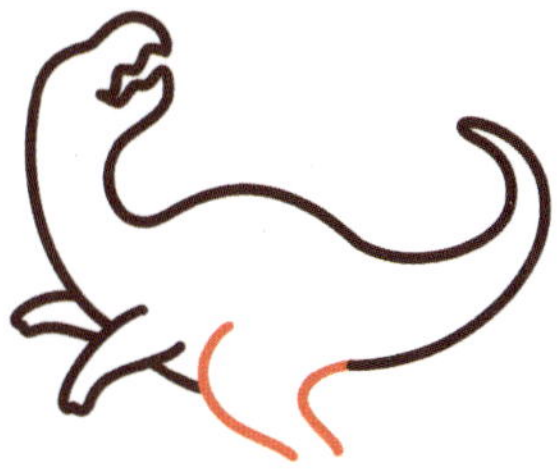

7. Add two curved lines for the leg.

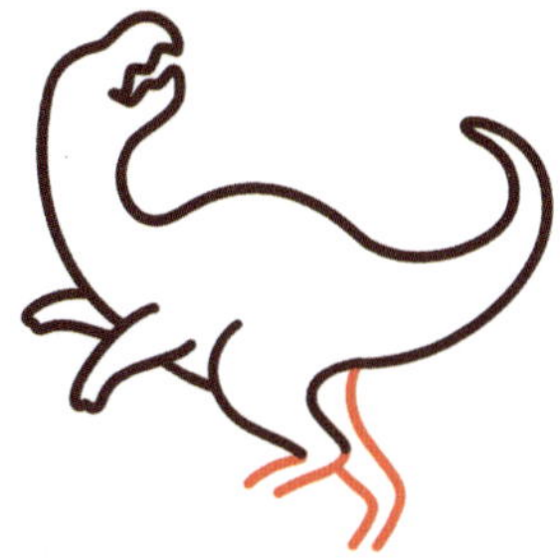

8. Draw the second leg and both feet with curved and straight lines.

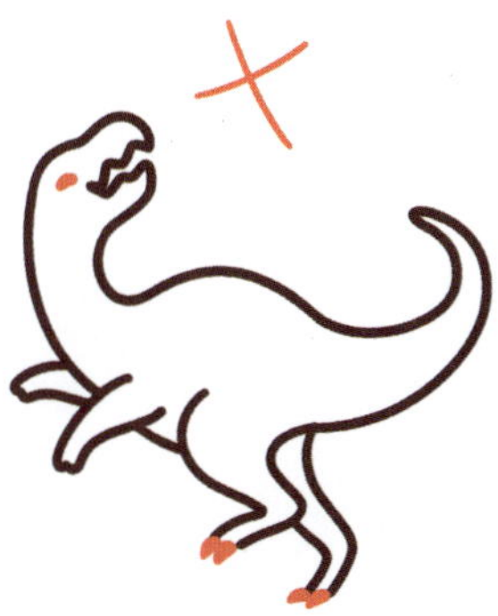

9. Add two talons to each foot and an oval eye. For the kite, draw an X above the head.

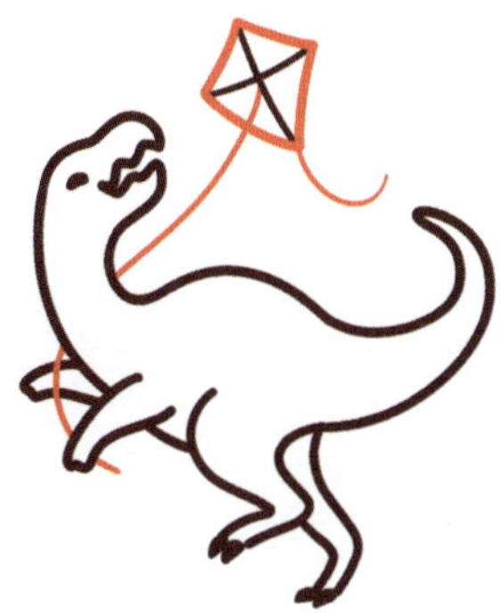

10. Draw a diamond around the X and add two curving lines of string.

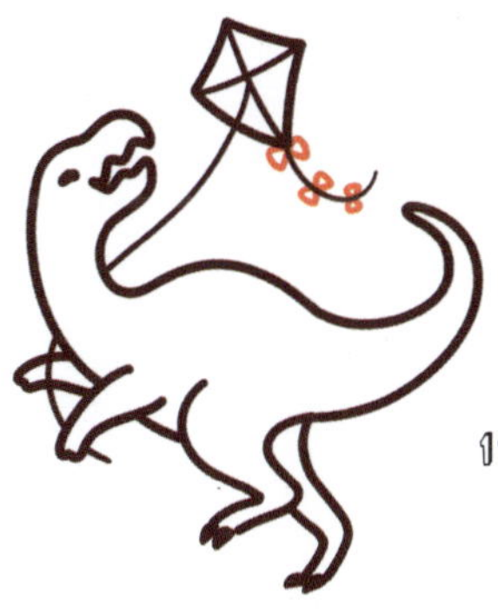

11. Add three bowties to the shorter string with triangles.

SUNBATHING AMARGASAURUS

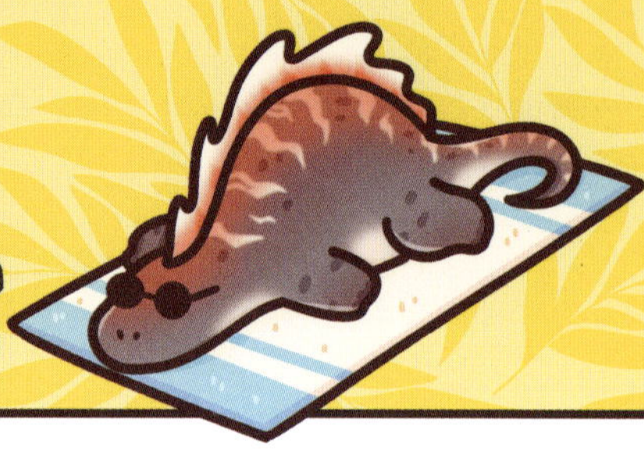

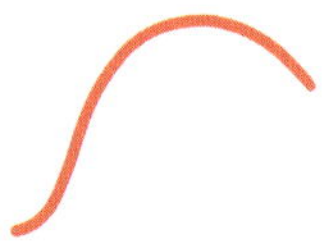

1. Draw an arched line for the top of the body.

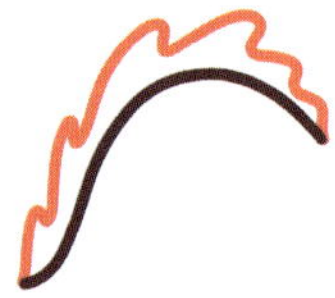

2. Add a spiked line along the spine.

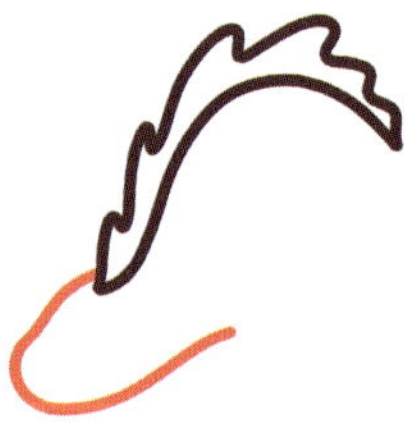

3. Add a U-shaped head.

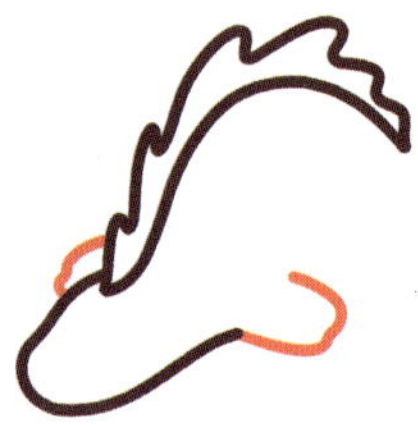

4. Add a U-shaped leg with two toes and a partial left leg with a curve and two toes.

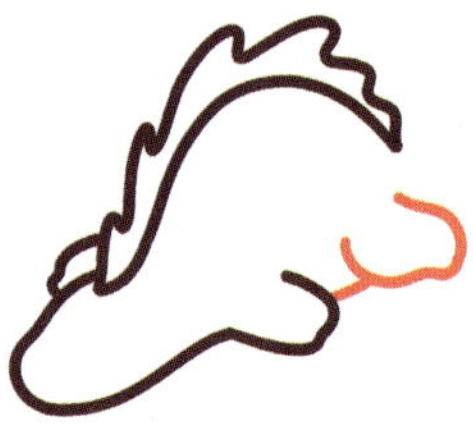

5. Draw a line for the stomach and a curved leg.

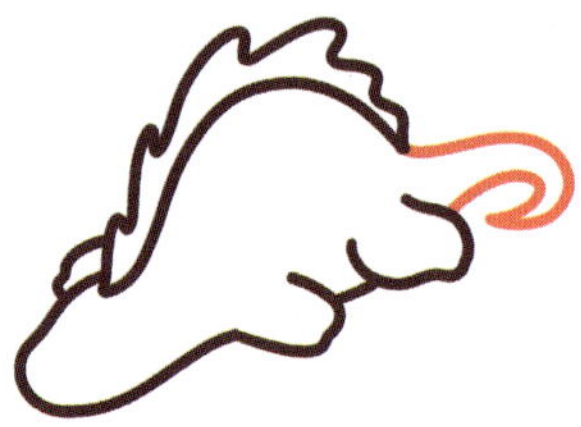

6. Add a curved tail that tapers into a point.

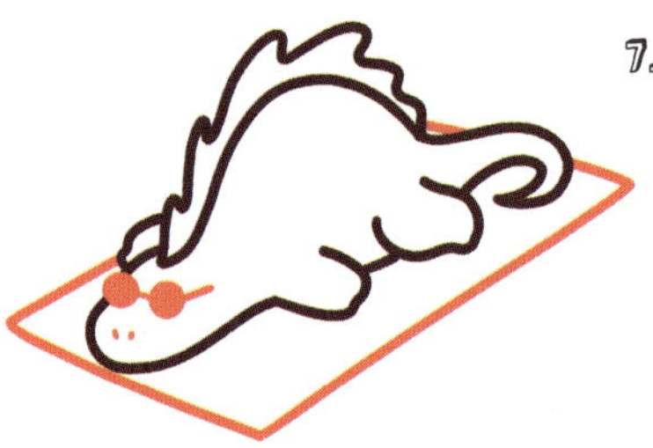

7. Give the dino sunglasses with two circles and two lines. Add two dashes for the nostrils. Draw a rectangle towel around the body.

SKIPPING ROCKS ENIGMACURSOR

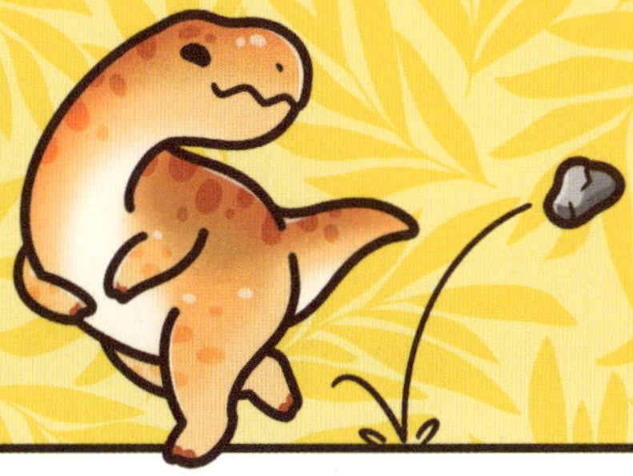

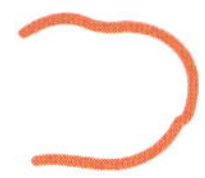

1. Draw a U-shaped line with a bumpy top and snout.

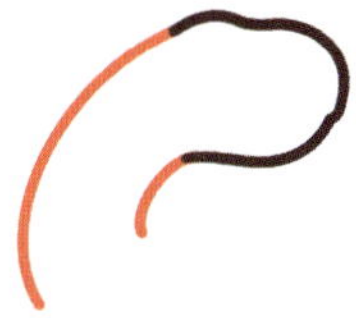

2. Add two curved lines for the neck.

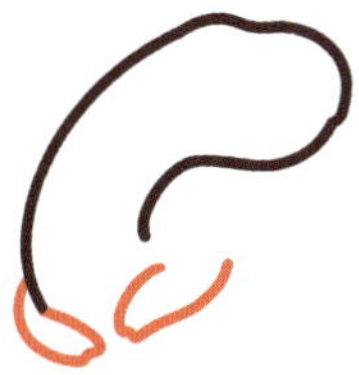

3. Add two rounded arms with two fingers each.

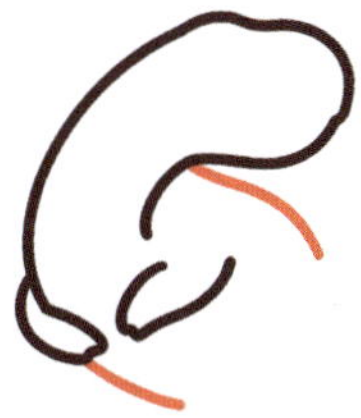

4. Draw two curved lines for the body.

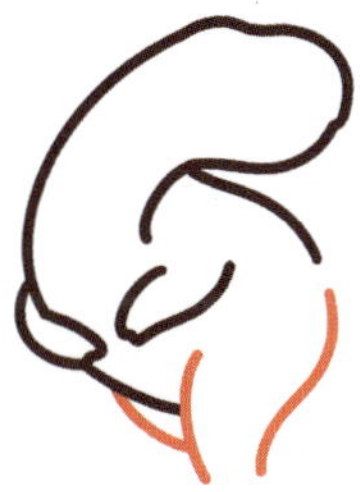

5. Draw three curved lines for the legs.

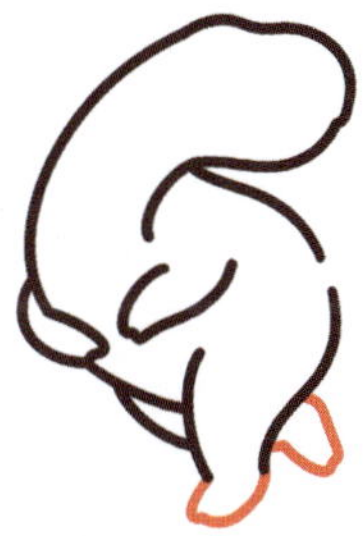

6. Add two U-shaped feet with two toes each.

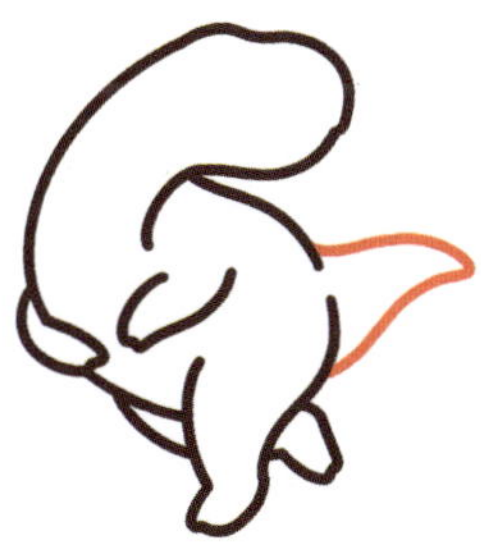

7. Add a curved, triangle tail.

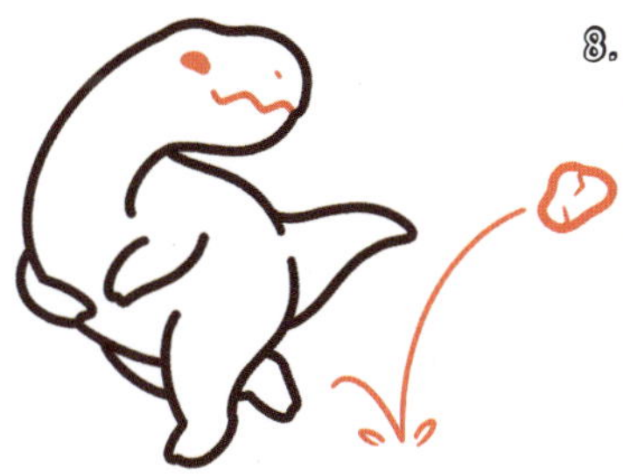

8. Add a semicircle eye, a dash for the nostril, and a jagged mouth. For the rock, draw an abstract shape with some cracks. Add a line marking the path of the rock and some rounded grass.

CELEBRATING APATOSAURUS

1. Draw a round head with a bump on top. Extend the bottom line upward.

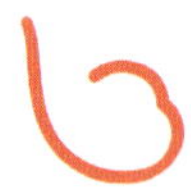

2. Add two curved lines for the long neck.

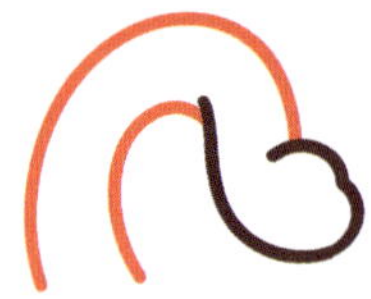

3. Add two curved lines for the body. Draw the arm with a G-line and two fingers.

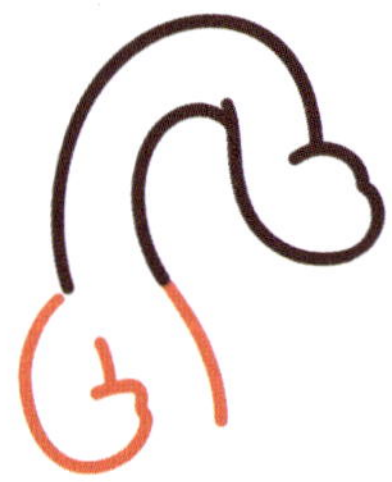

4. Draw the second arm with a J-line and bumps for the fingers. Add a curved line for the back of the body.

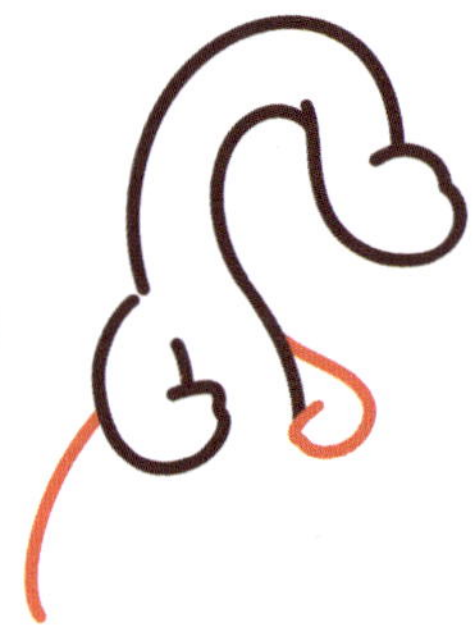

5. Draw a spoon in the left hand and a rectangle cake with a bite taken out of it.

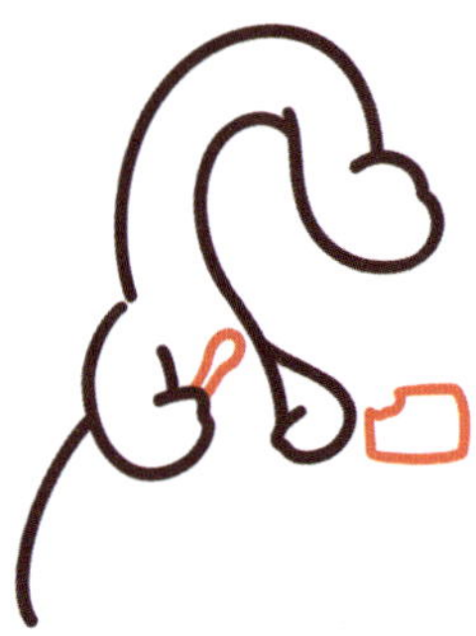

6. Add the table with an oval and a curved rectangle underneath.

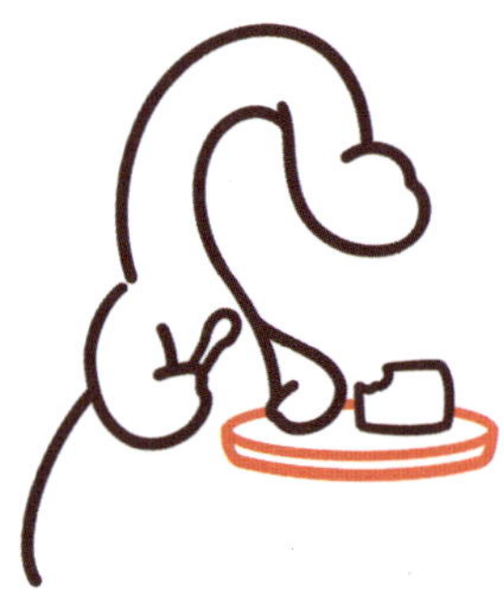

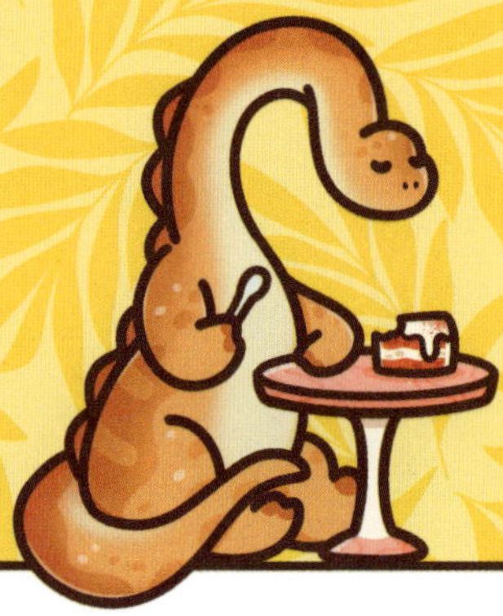

7. Draw two curved lines and an oval base for the table leg.

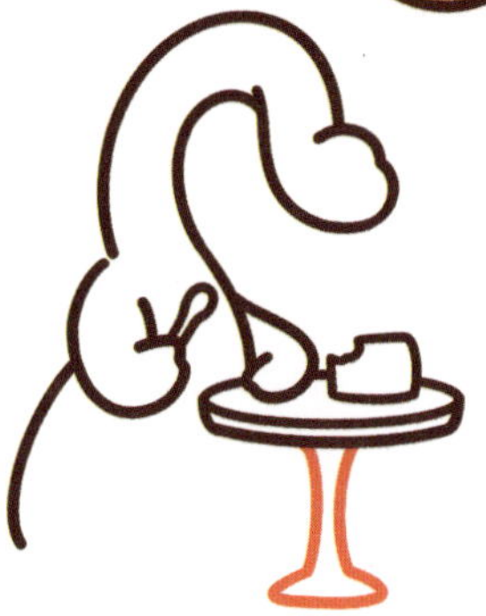

8. Add a bunch of semicircles down the dino's spine.

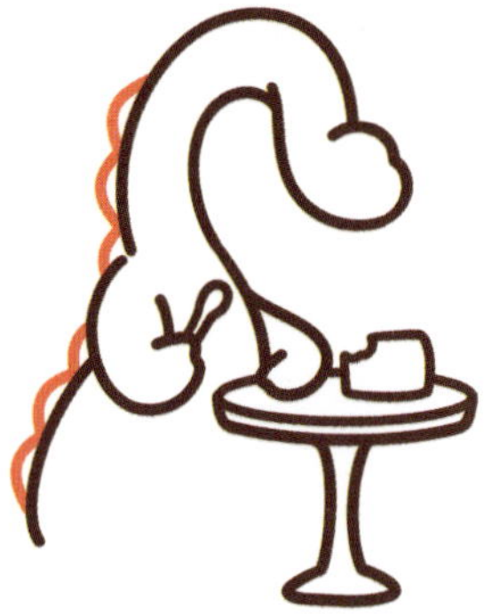

9. Draw two curved lines for the tail.

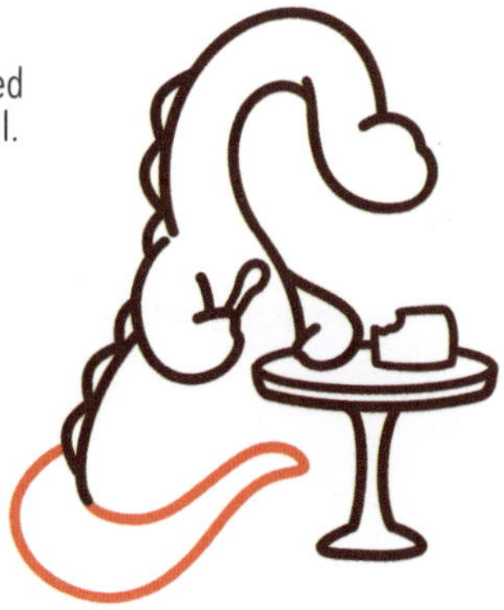

10. Add three curved lines for the stomach and the legs.

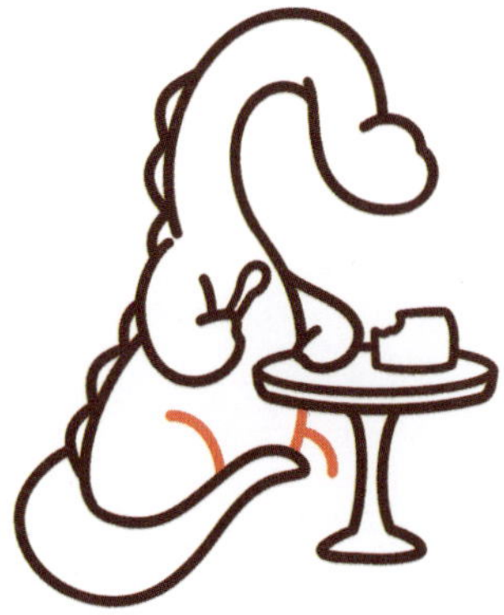

11. Draw two rounded feet with two toes each.

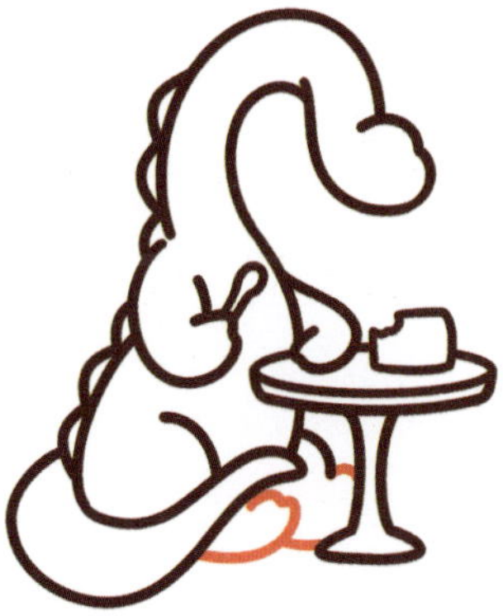

12. Add icing on the cake with a dripping line. For the face, add two U-shaped eyes and two dots for the nostrils.

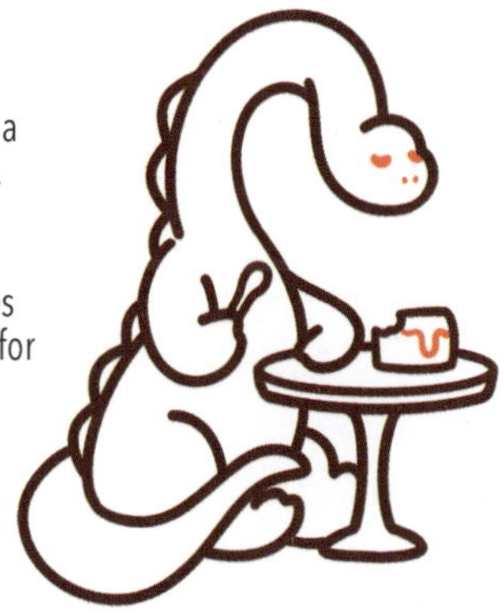

PROTECTING ANKYLOSAURUS

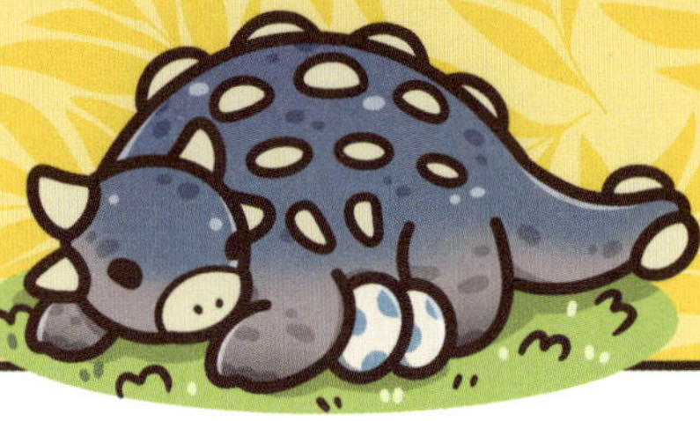

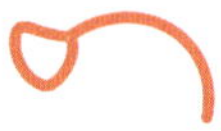

1. Draw a curved line and a triangle horn.

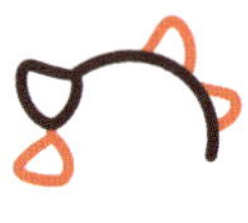

2. Add three more horns around the head.

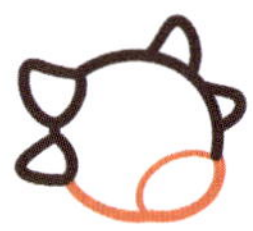

3. Complete the head with a curved line and an oval nose.

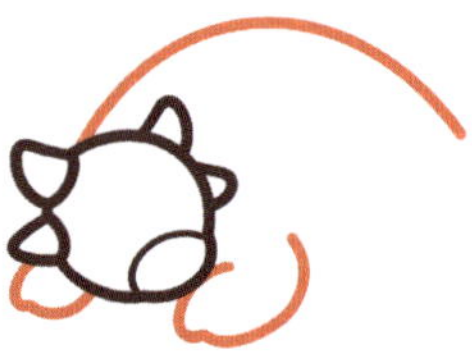

4. Draw a curved line for the top of the body. Add two rounded arms with two fingers each.

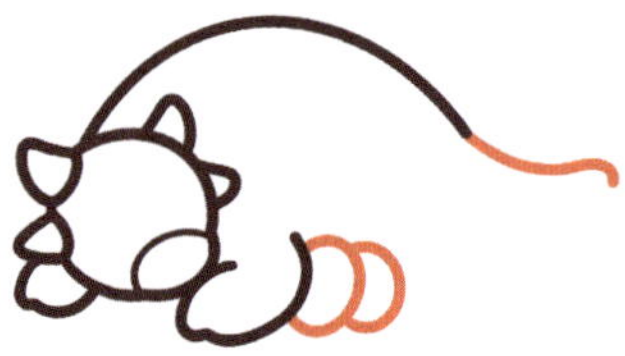

5. Add two oval eggs behind the arm and a curved line for the tail.

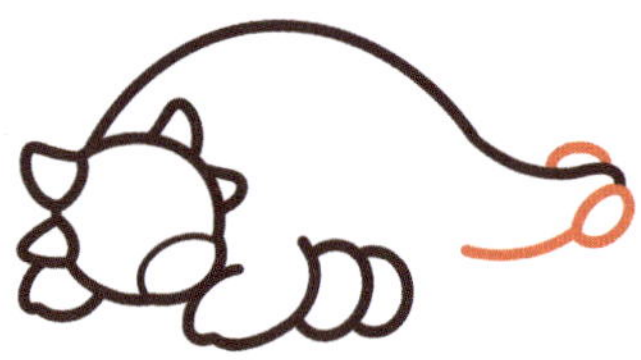

6. Complete the tail with two ovals on the end and a curved line.

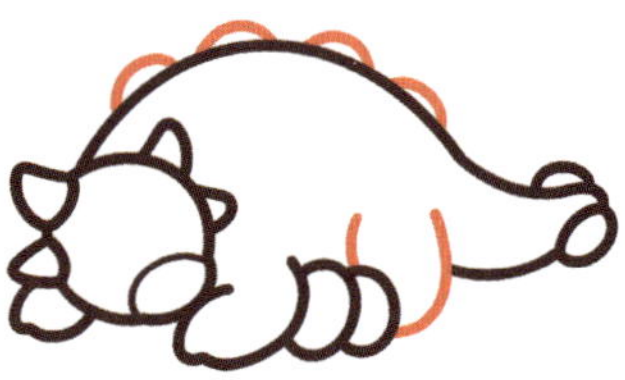

7. Add four curves on top of the body. Draw a U-shaped leg.

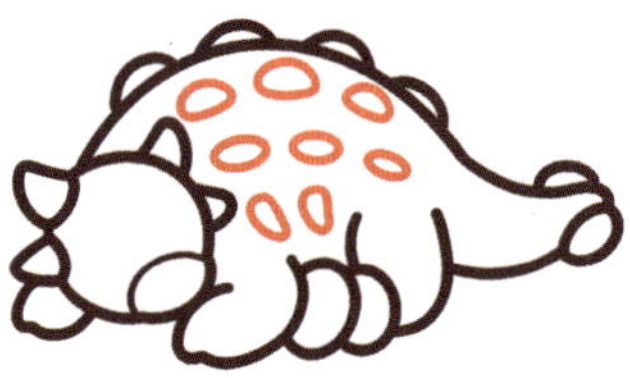

8. Add ovals and triangles on top of the body.

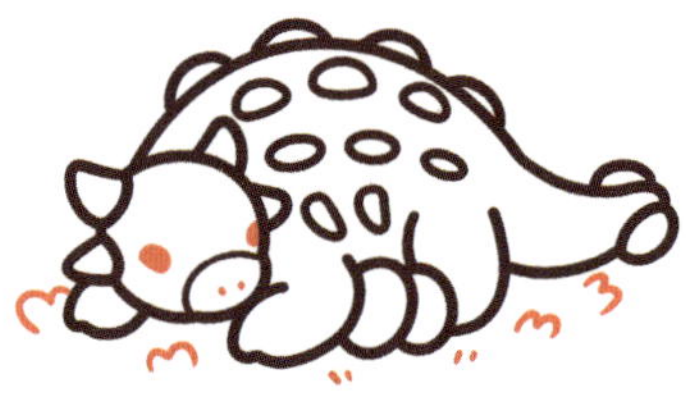

9. Add two oval eyes and two dots for the nostrils. Draw M shapes and dashes for the grass around the dino.

PAINTING DIPLODOCUS

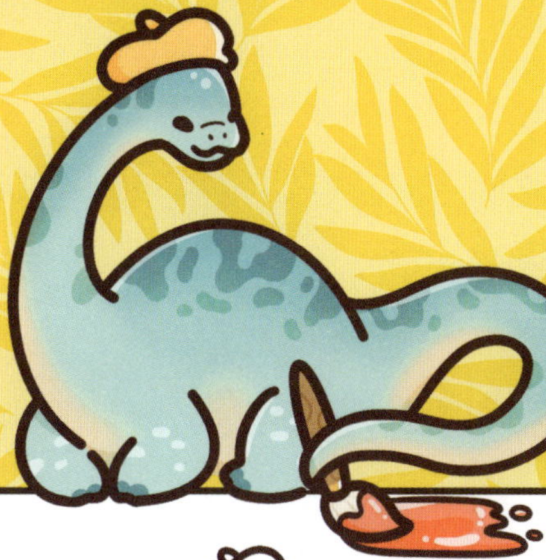

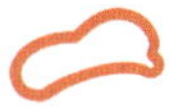

1. Draw a B-shaped beret.

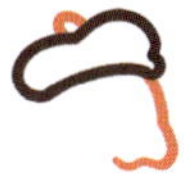

2. Add a curve on top of the beret. Draw a bumpy head and wavy line for the mouth.

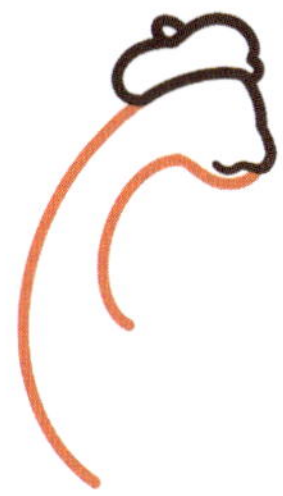

3. Add two curved lines for the neck and a curve for the bottom jaw.

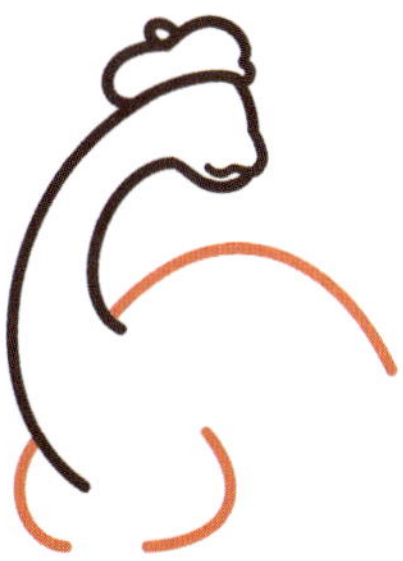

4. Draw an arch for the top of the body. Add two curved lines for the legs.

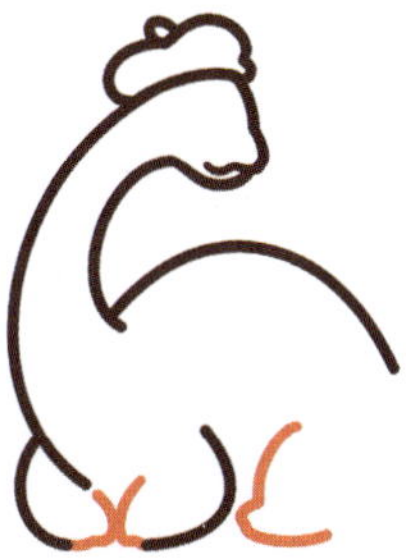

5. Add angled lines on the hands with two fingers each. Add the back leg with a curved line and two toes.

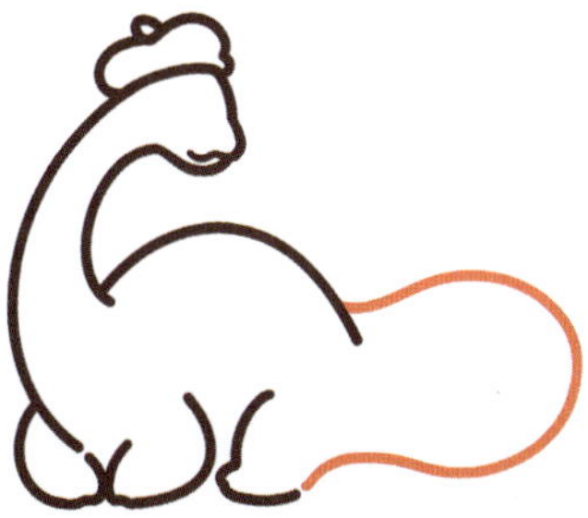

6. Draw a large U shape for the tail.

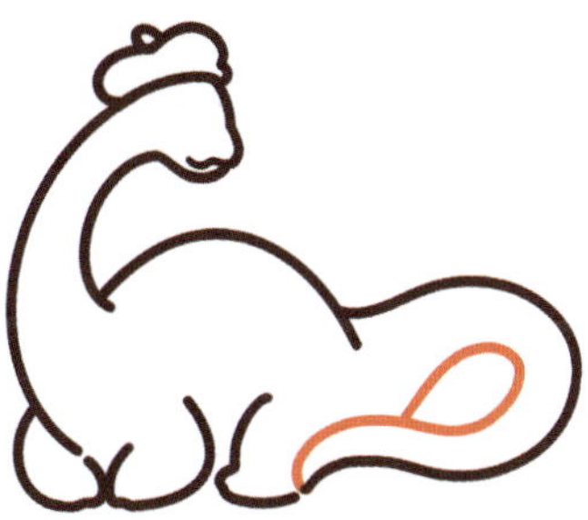

7. Add a teardrop shape inside the tail and extend the bottom line left.

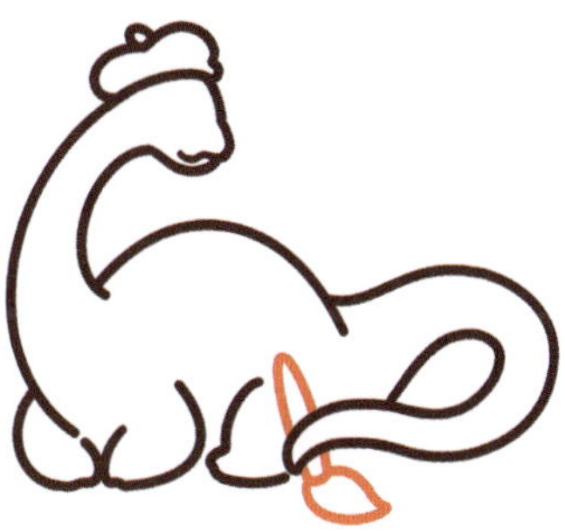

8. Add a paintbrush at the tip of the tail with an oval handle and a teardrop-shaped brush.

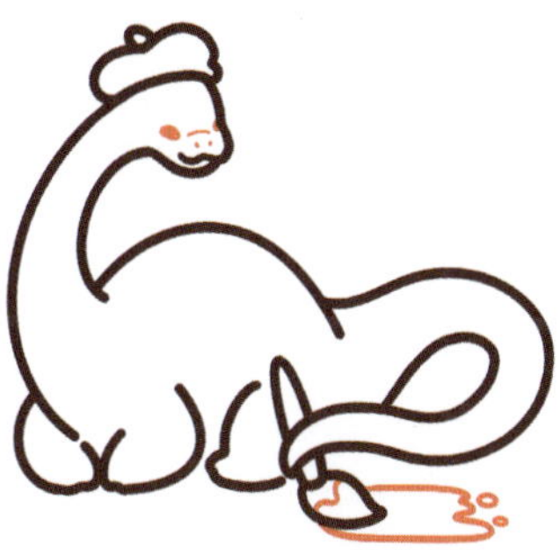

9. Add an M-line on the brush and a puddle of paint with curved lines and circles. For the face, add two oval eyes, a line for the snout, and two dashes for the nostrils.

CUDDLING MICRORAPTOR

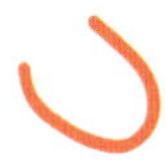

1. Draw a U for the head.

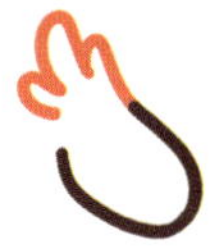

2. Add three U-shaped feathers on top of the head.

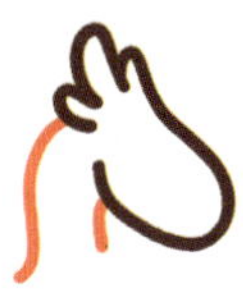

3. Add two curved lines for the neck.

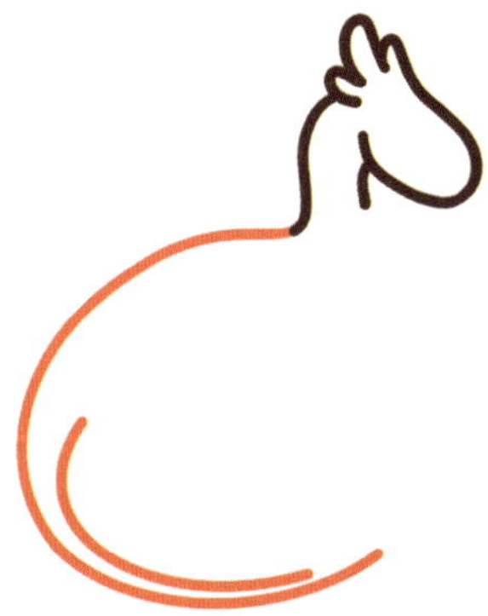

4. Draw two C-shaped lines for the body and the tail.

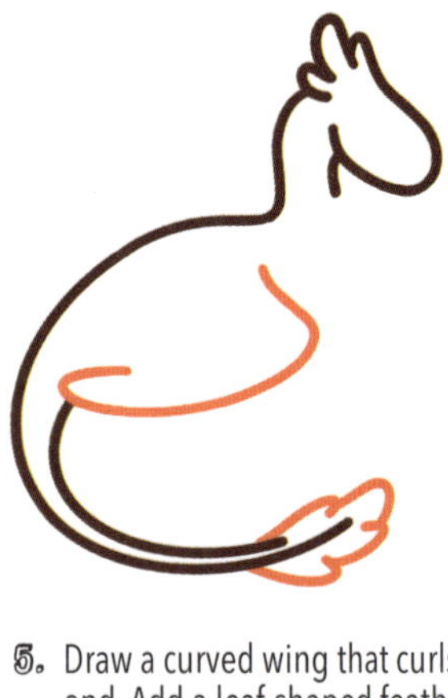

5. Draw a curved wing that curls at the end. Add a leaf-shaped feather to the tail.

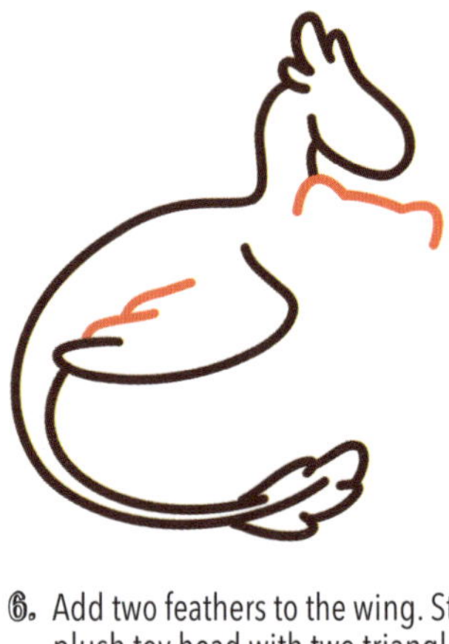

6. Add two feathers to the wing. Start the plush toy head with two triangle ears and a line connecting them.

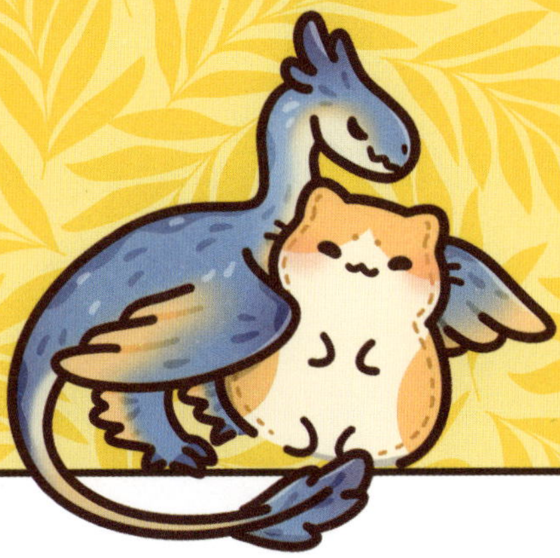

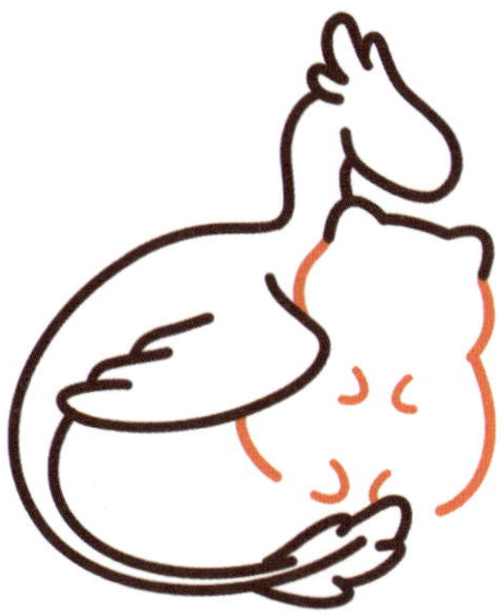

7. Draw the plush toy with curved lines for the head and body and U shapes for the hands and feet.

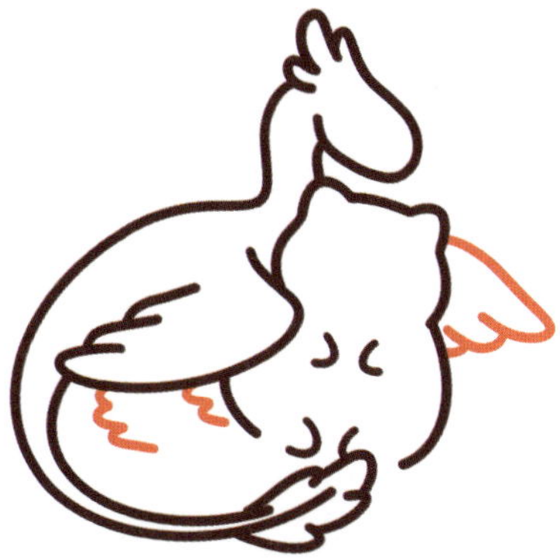

8. Add a second wing behind the plush toy with three feathers. Draw feathered legs under the left wing.

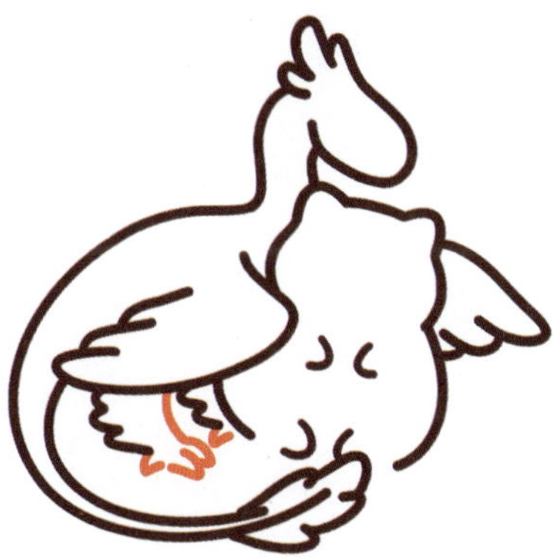

9. Add a curved line for the leg and pointed talons to each foot.

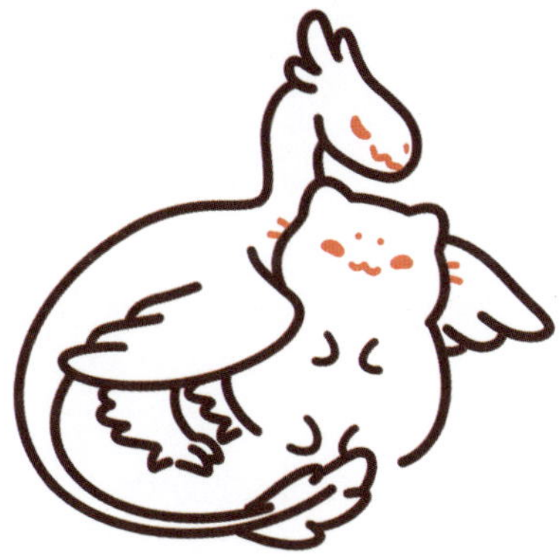

10. For the dino face, add a U-shaped eye, a dash for the nostril, and a W mouth. For the toy face, add two oval eyes, two dots above the eyes, a W mouth, and whiskers on the sides of the head.

BABY DINOS

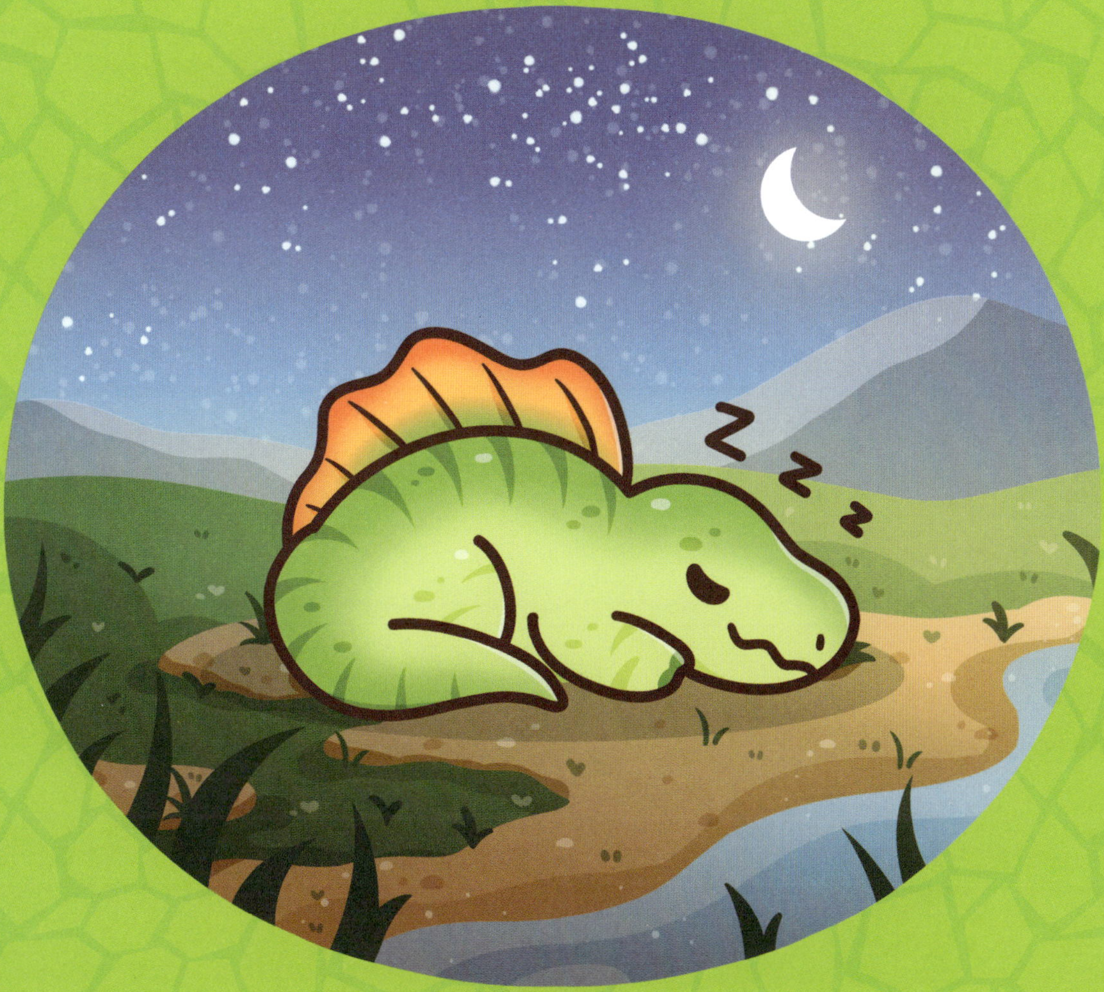

STYGIMOLOCH

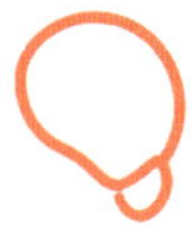

1. Draw a balloon shape with a semicircle attached to the bottom for the dome.

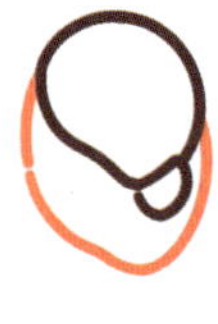

2. Draw an oval head underneath the dome.

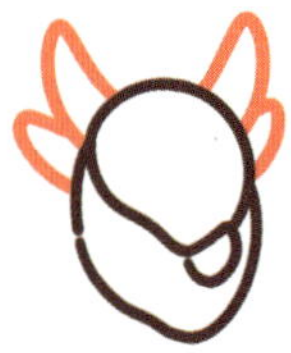

3. Add two long triangle spikes on top of the head with a smaller spike below each.

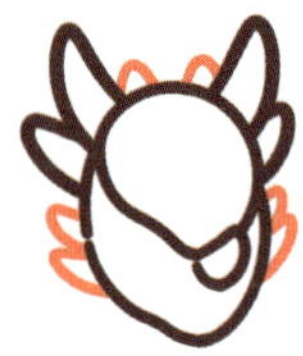

4. Add two short triangles between the long spikes. Add two more triangle spikes on each side of the head.

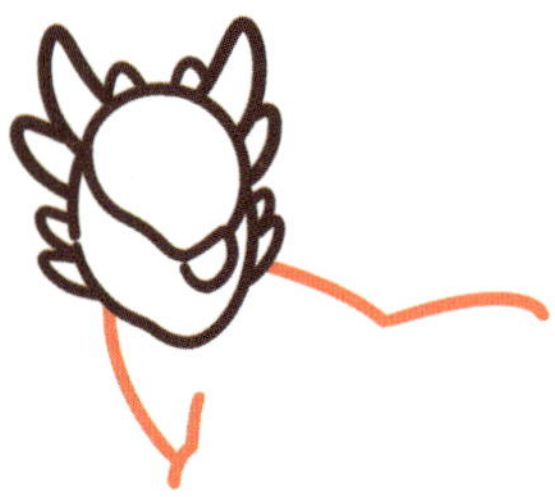

5. Draw the body with an M-line and a curved line. Draw a short M-line at the end of the curved line for the arm.

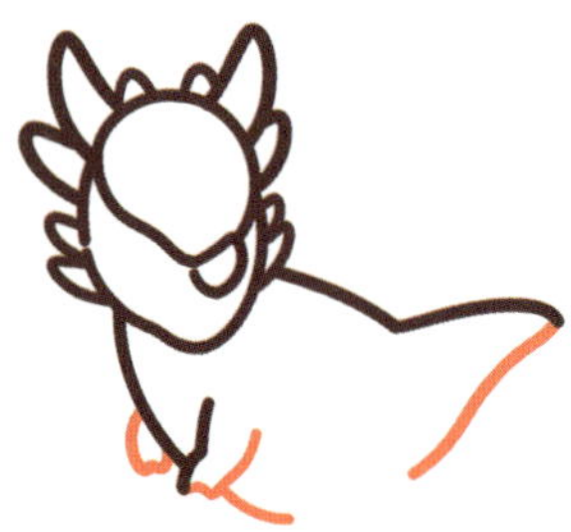

6. Make a short arm with a line and two points for the fingers. Draw a second curved arm above. Add a curved line under the arm and a diagonal line for the tail.

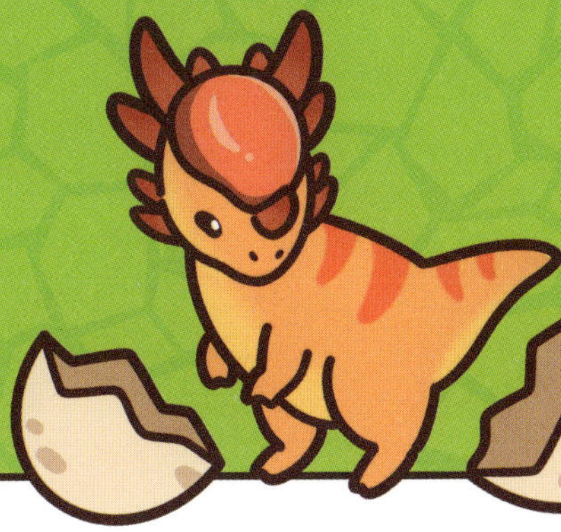

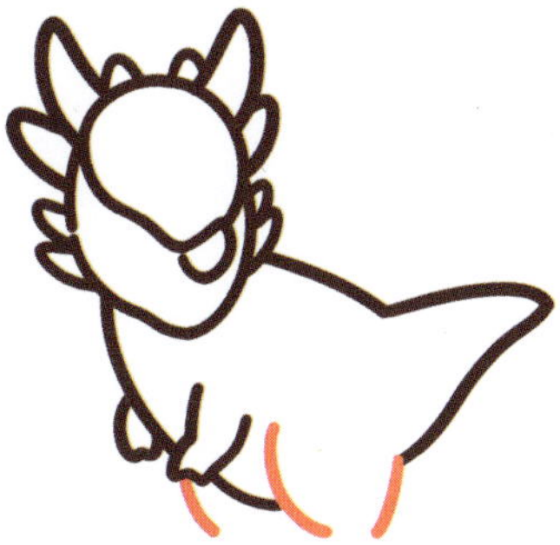

7. Add the legs with three curved lines.

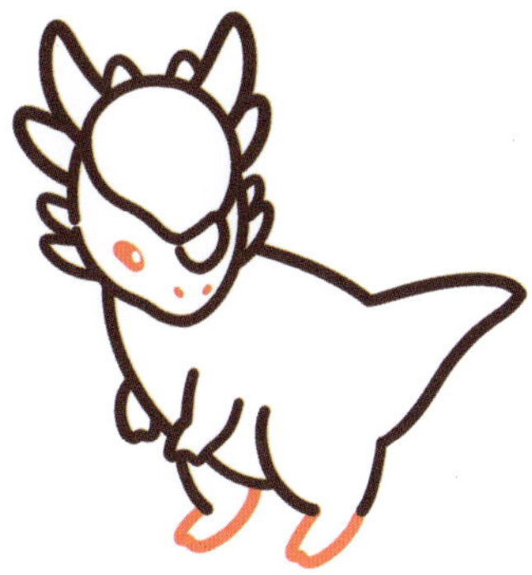

8. Add the U-shaped feet with two toes each. For the face, draw a bean-shaped eye with a circle highlight and two dashes for the nostrils.

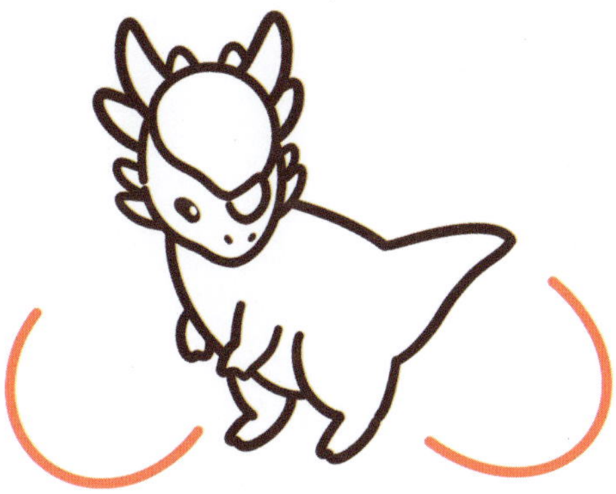

9. Draw two C-shaped lines on each side of the dinosaur for the eggshells. Angle the openings at the dinosaur.

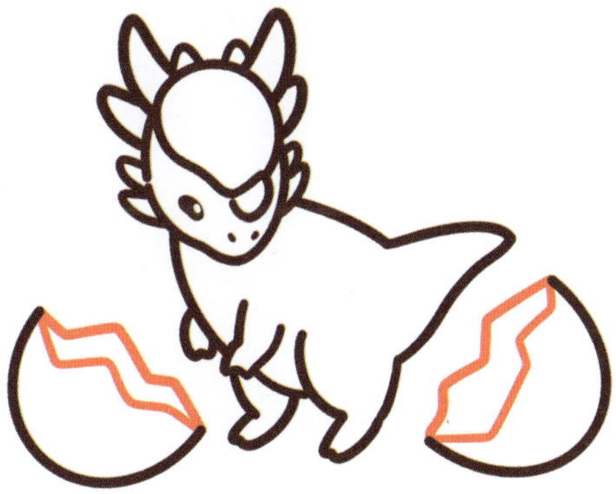

10. Draw two jagged lines on each eggshell.

DIPLODOCUS

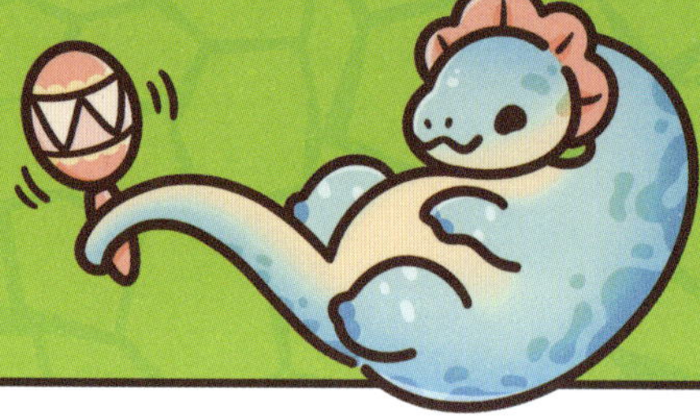

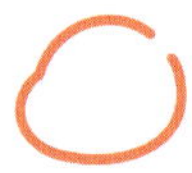

1. Draw an unfinished round head with a bump for the nose.

2. Add four scallops around the head.

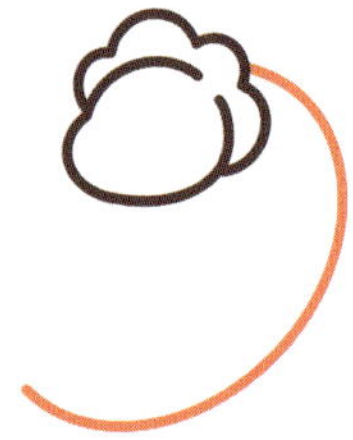

3. Draw a curved line for the body.

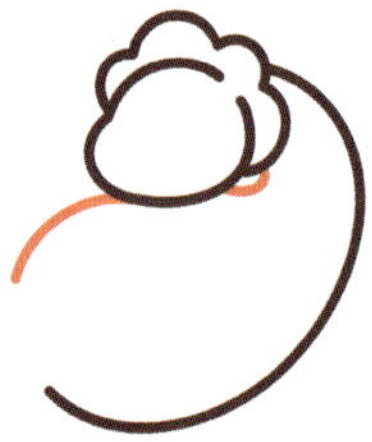

4. Add two curved lines for the neck and the stomach.

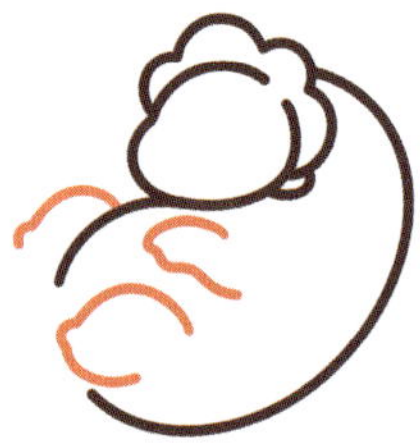

5. Draw a curved arm with two fingers. Add two rounded legs with a bump for the toe on each.

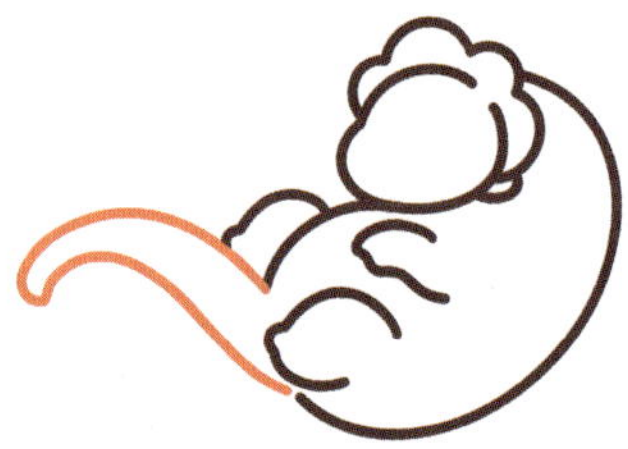

6. Add a long, curved tail.

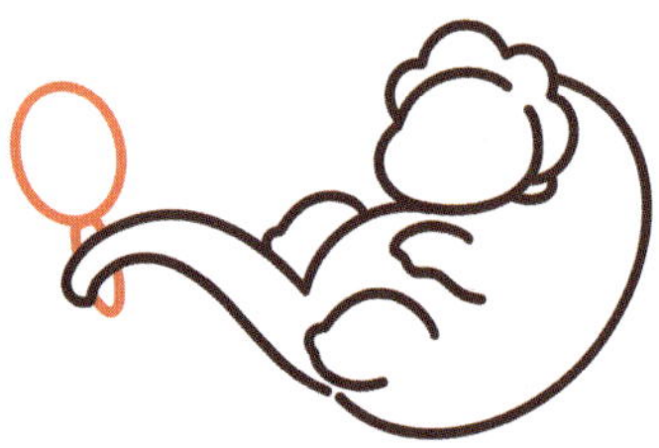

7. Draw a rattle with an oval and a thin oval handle.

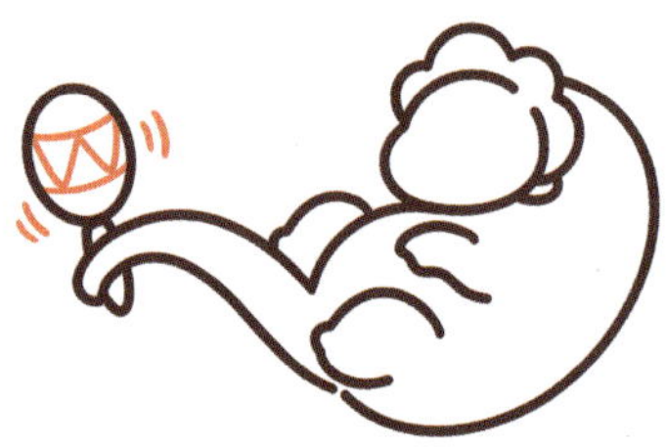

8. Decorate the rattle with two curved lines and a W. Add curved action lines around the rattle.

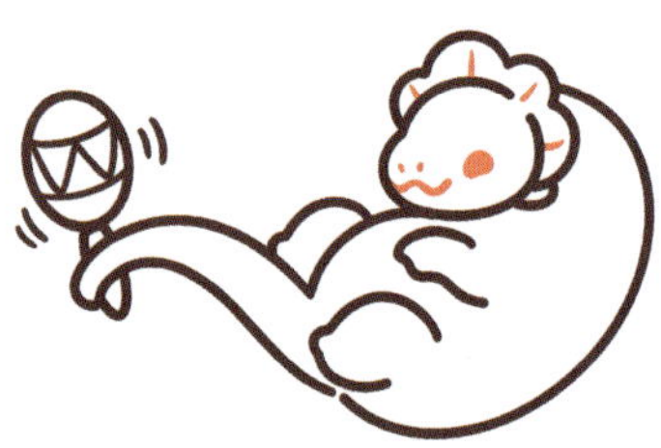

9. Add lines in the scallops. For the face, add a semicircle eye, two dashes for the nostrils, and a W mouth.

BRACHIOSAURUS

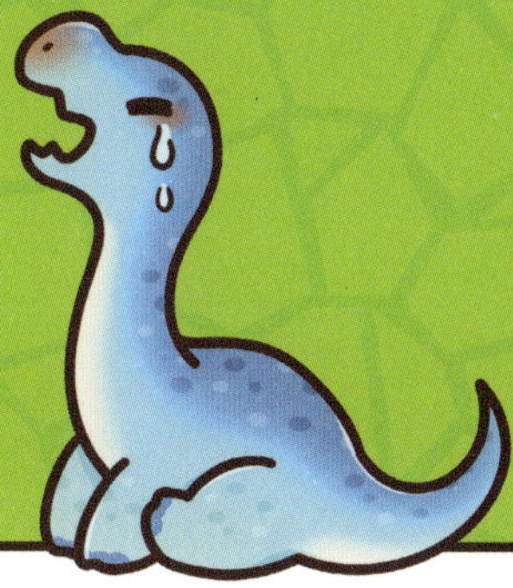

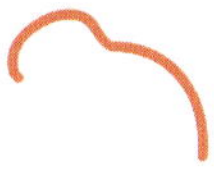

1. Draw a curved line for the snout and the head.

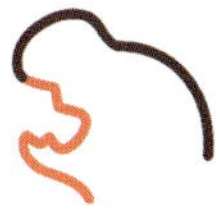

2. Add jagged lines for the mouth and a curved line for the chin.

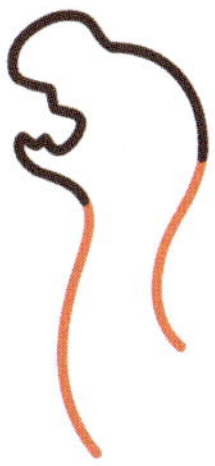

3. Add two curved lines for the neck.

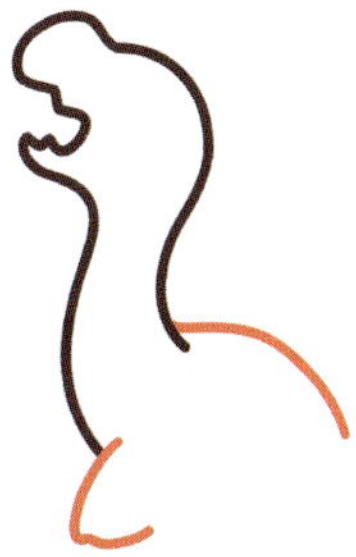

4. Draw a curved line for the top of the body. Add a short arm with two fingers.

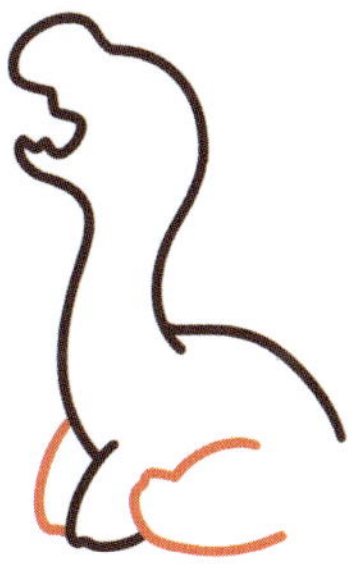

5. Draw a second arm and add a curved leg with two toes.

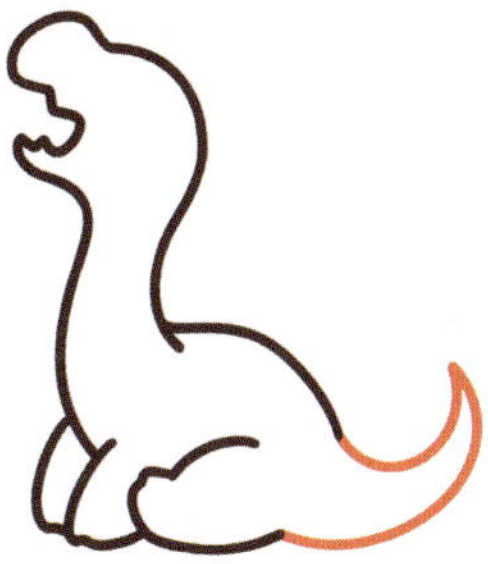

6. Add a curved tail that tapers into a point.

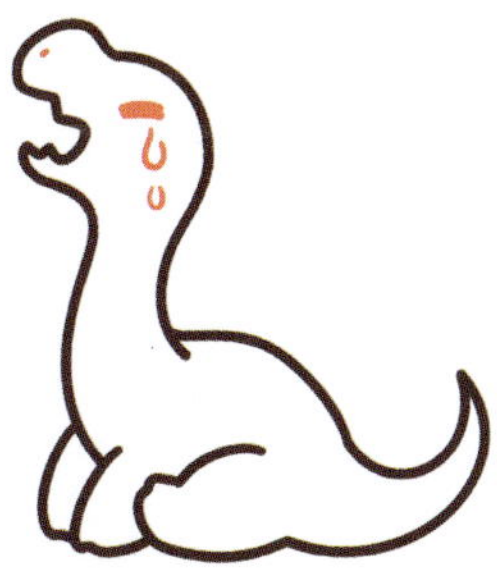

7. Draw two lines for a squinted eye, a dash for the nostril, and some teardrops below the eye.

APATOSAURUS

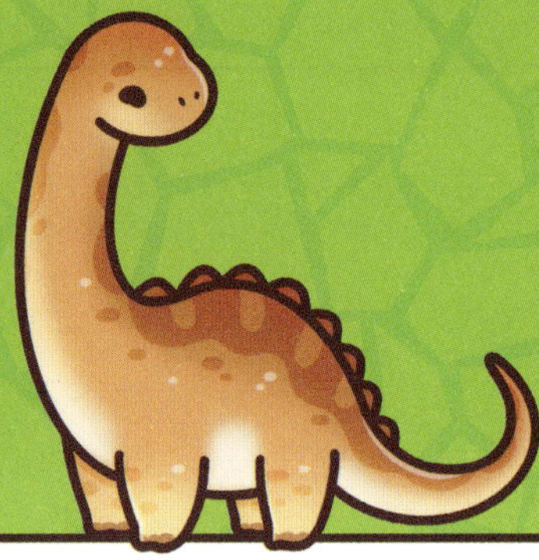

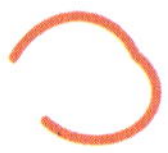

1. Draw a round head with a bump for the snout.

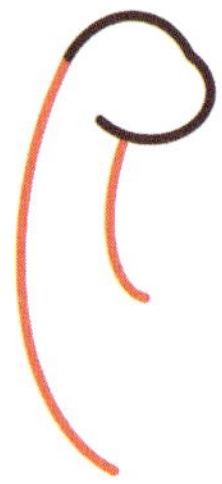

2. Add two curved lines for the neck.

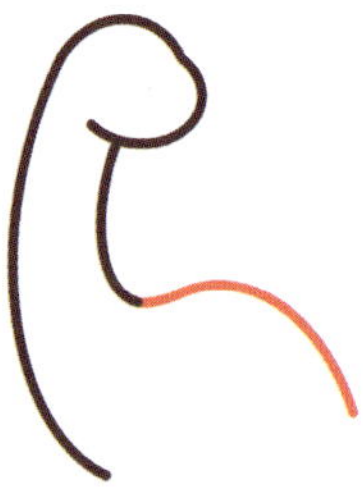

3. Add a curved line for the top of the body.

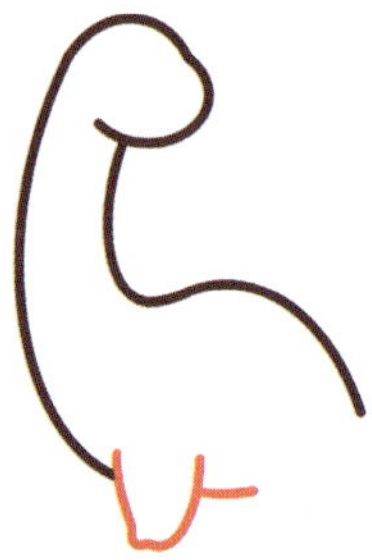

4. Draw a U-shaped leg with two toes and a curve for the stomach.

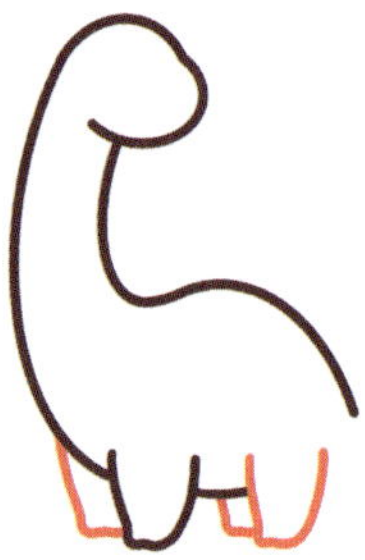

5. Add three more legs.

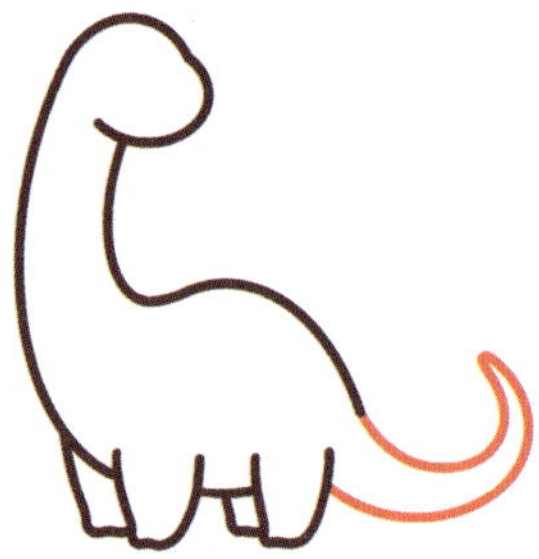

6. Add a curved tail that tapers at the end.

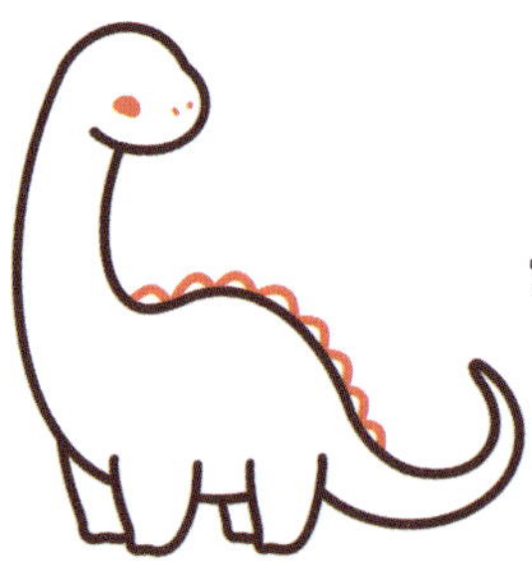

7. Draw curves along the spine. For the face, add a semicircle eye and two dashes for the nostrils.

SPINOSAURUS

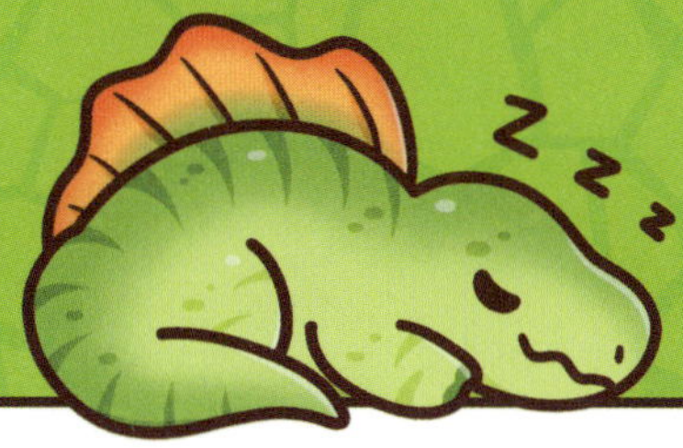

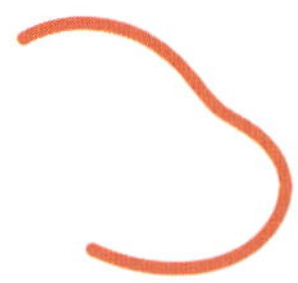

1. Draw a curved line with a bump for the snout.

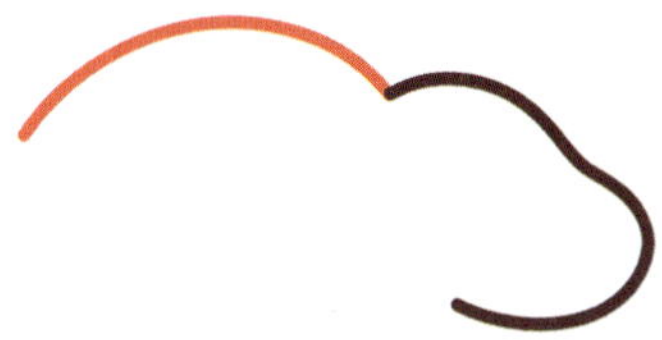

2. Add a curved line for the top of the body.

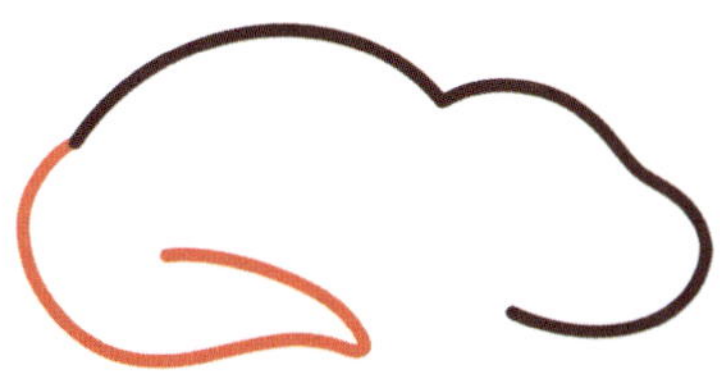

3. Add a curved tail that tapers at the end.

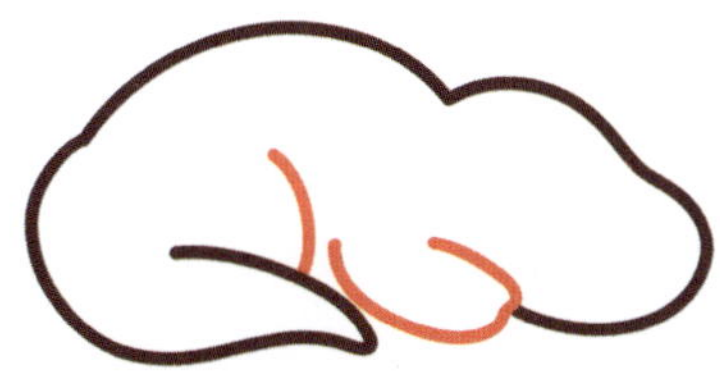

4. Draw a curved line for the back leg. Add a rounded arm with two fingers.

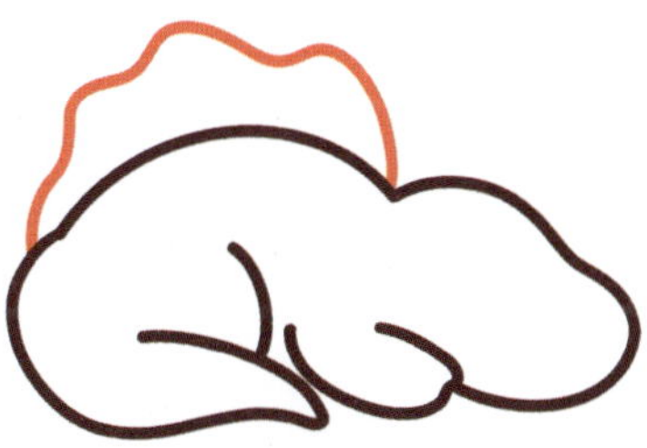

5. Add the sail with a wavy line on the back.

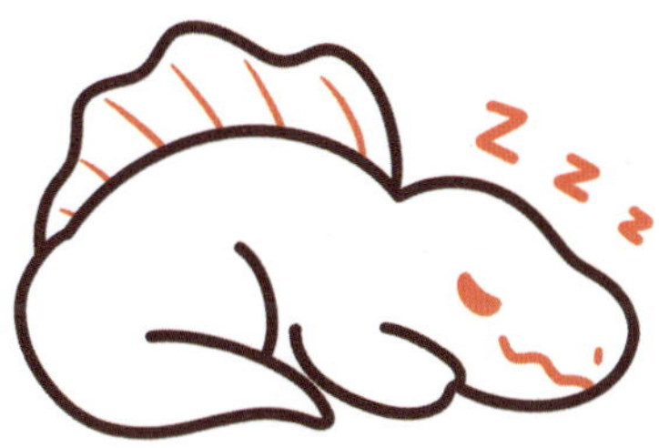

6. Draw lines in the sail. For the face, add a U-shaped eye, a dash for the nostril, and a jagged mouth. Draw Zs above the head.

STEGOSAURUS

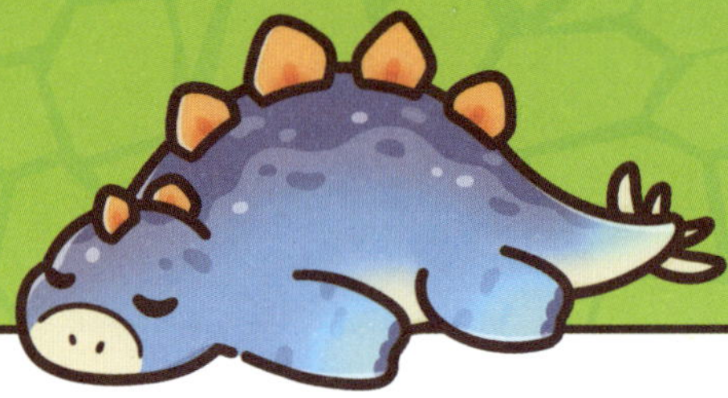

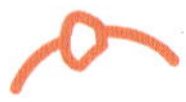

1. Draw a curved line and a triangle horn in the middle.

2. Add a curved line for the bottom of the head. Draw another triangle horn.

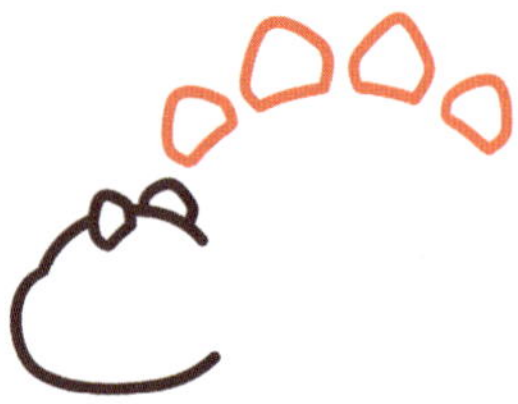

3. Draw four pentagons for the spikes on the back.

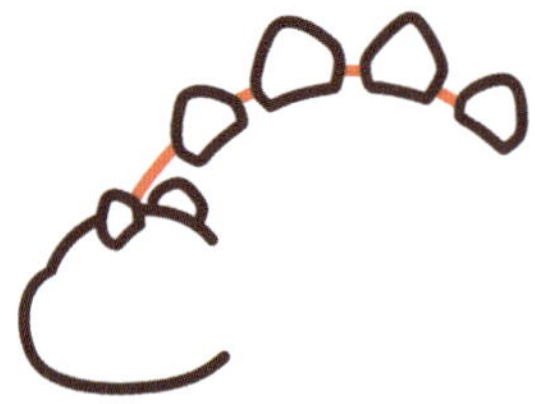

4. Add a curved line between the spikes.

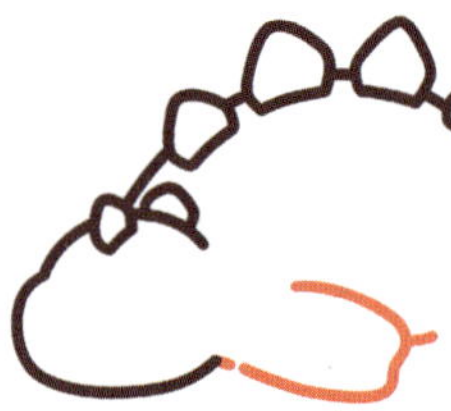

5. Add a rectangle arm with two fingers and two lines on the sides.

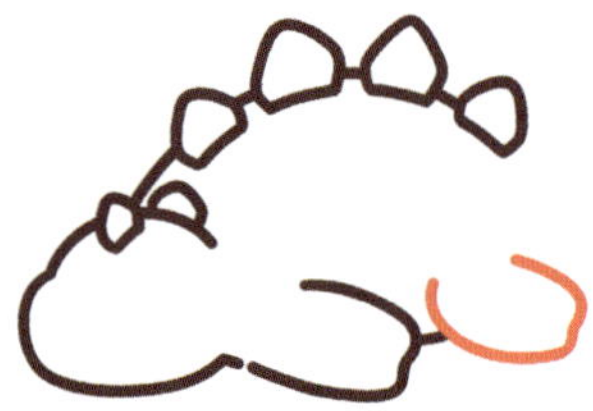

6. Add a rounded leg with two toes.

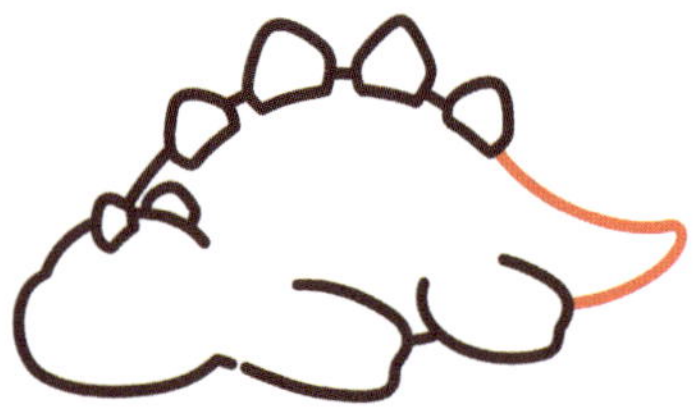

7. Draw a curved, triangle tail.

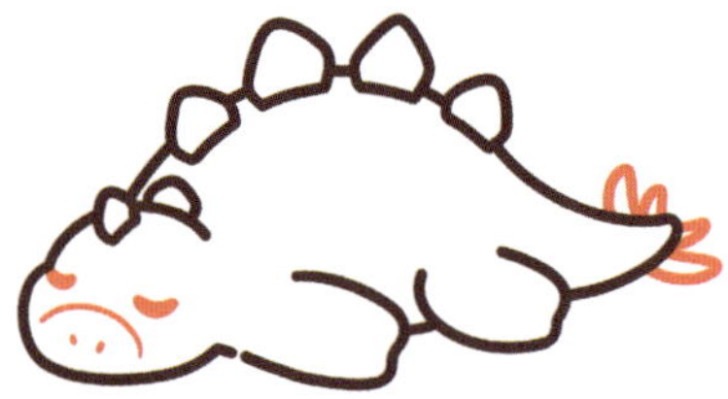

8. Add four spikes to the end of the tail. For the face, add two U-shaped eyes, a curve around the nose, and two dashes for the nostrils.

TYRANNOSAURUS

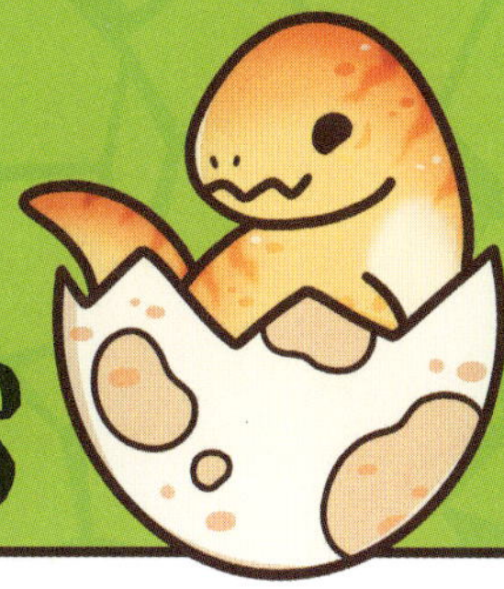

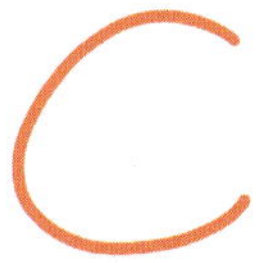

1. Draw a C-shaped head.

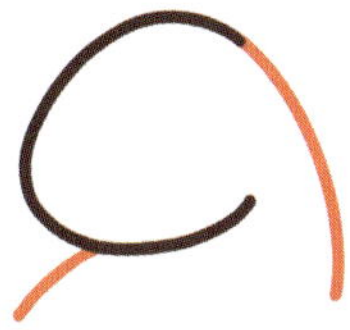

2. Add two curved lines for the back of the head and neck.

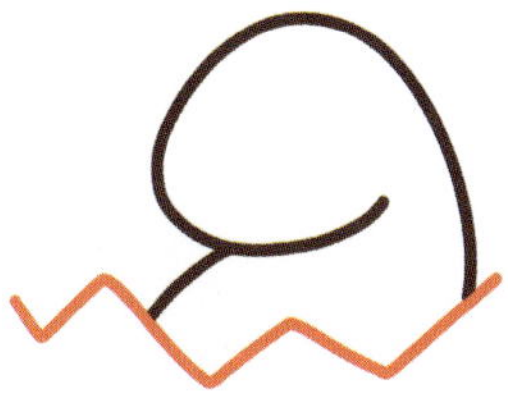

3. Draw a jagged line for the top of the shell.

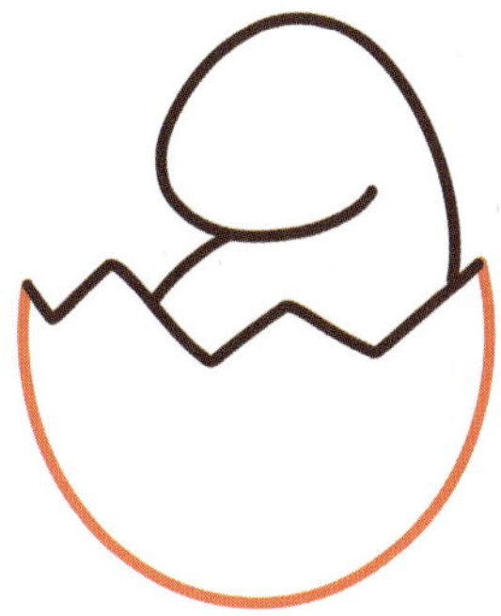

4. Add a U shape for the eggshell.

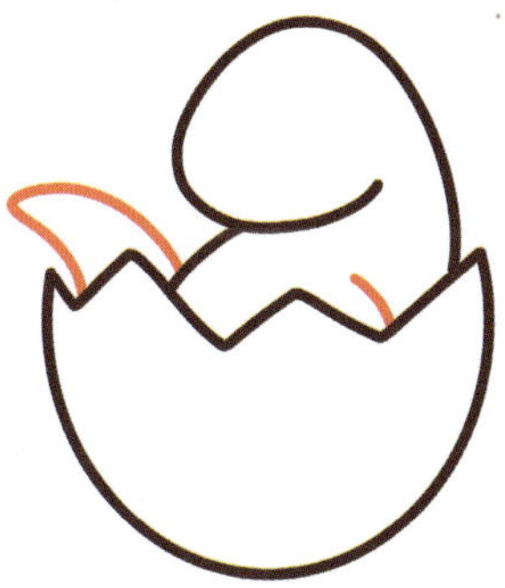

5. Add a curved tail and a curved line for the arm.

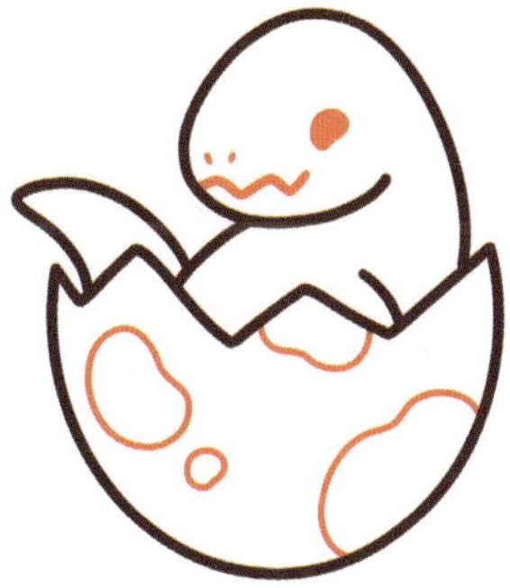

6. Decorate the shell with abstract shapes. For the face, add a semicircle eye, two dashes for the nostrils, and a jagged mouth.

CARNOTAURUS

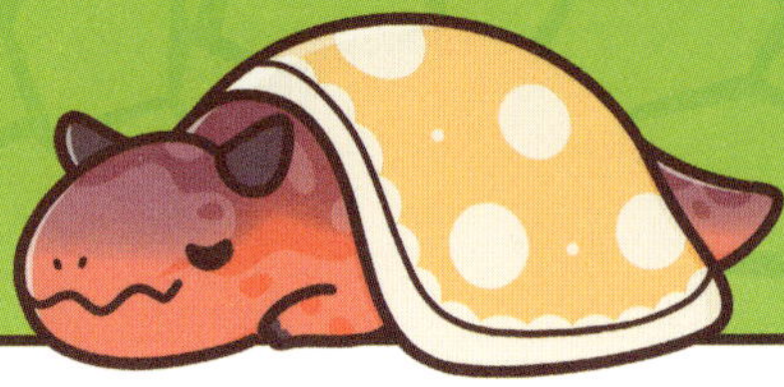

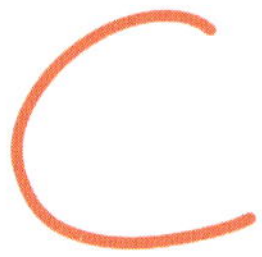

1. Draw a C-shaped head.

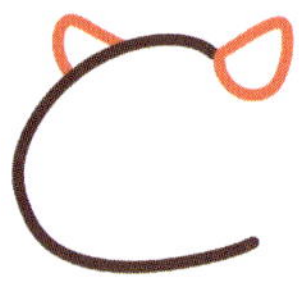

2. Add two cone-shaped ears.

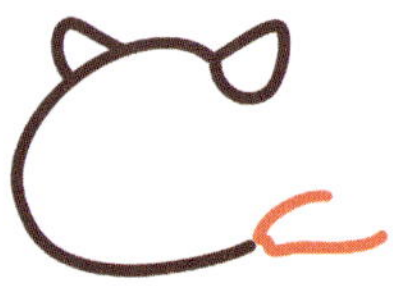

3. Add a curved arm with two fingers.

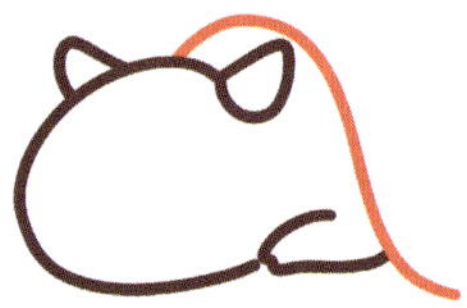

4. Draw a curved line for the edge of the blanket.

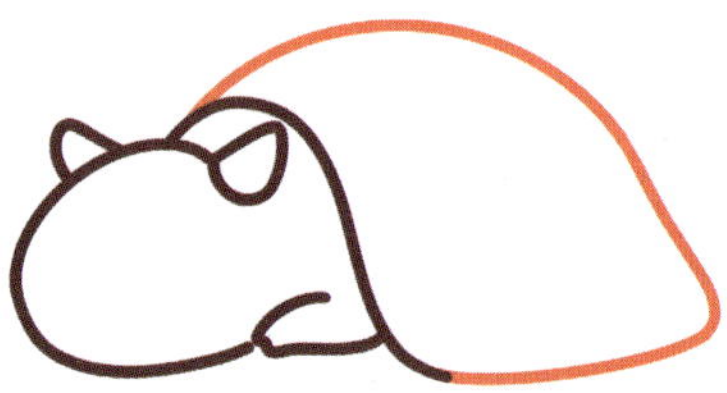

5. Draw the blanket with a curved line and a flat bottom edge.

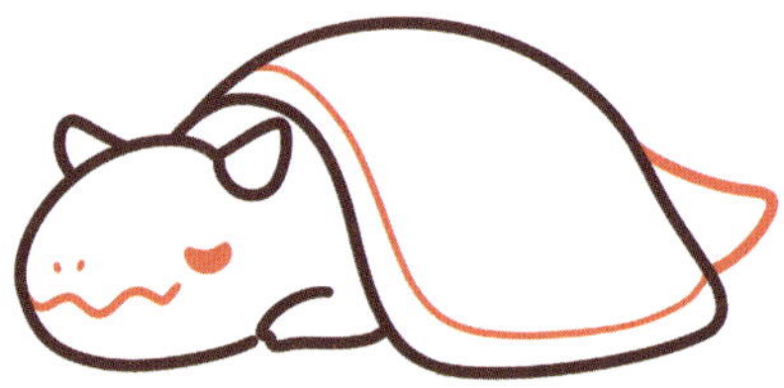

6. Add an L-shaped line along the edge of the blanket. Draw a triangle tail. For the face, add a U-shaped eye, two dashes for the nostrils, and a jagged mouth.

TRICERATOPS

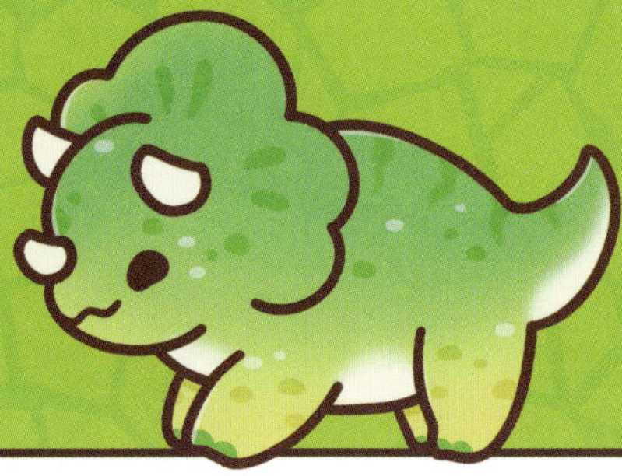

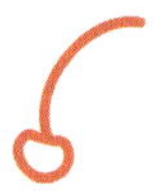

1. Draw a curved line and a triangle horn.

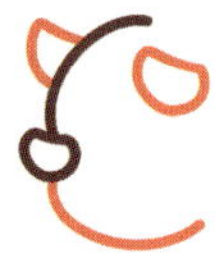

2. Add a curved line for the bottom of the head. Draw two triangle horns.

3. Add four scallops around the head, with the largest on top.

4. Draw two curved lines for the top of the body and the neck.

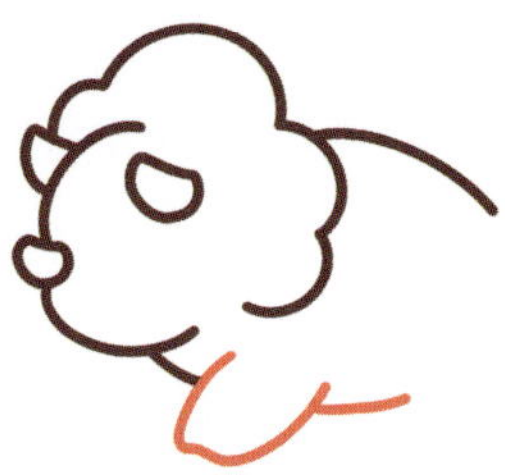

5. Add a U-shaped leg with two toes and a curved line for the stomach.

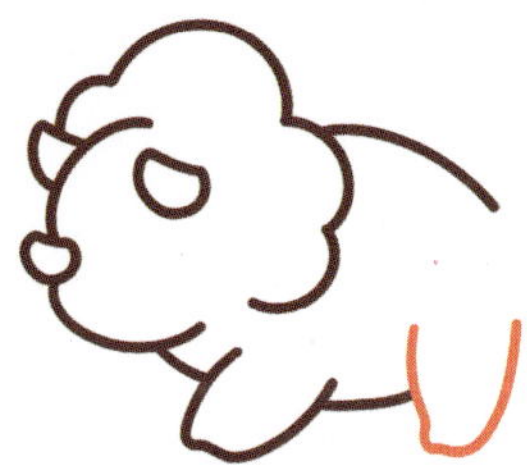

6. Add a second leg.

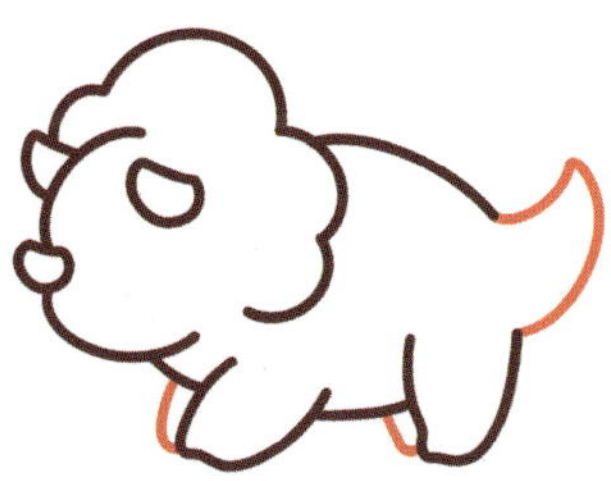

7. Draw two more legs. Add a curved, triangle tail.

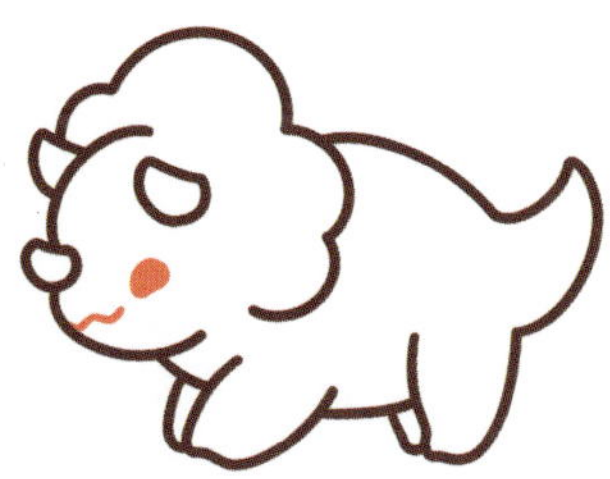

8. Add a semicircle eye and a W mouth.

VELOCIRAPTOR

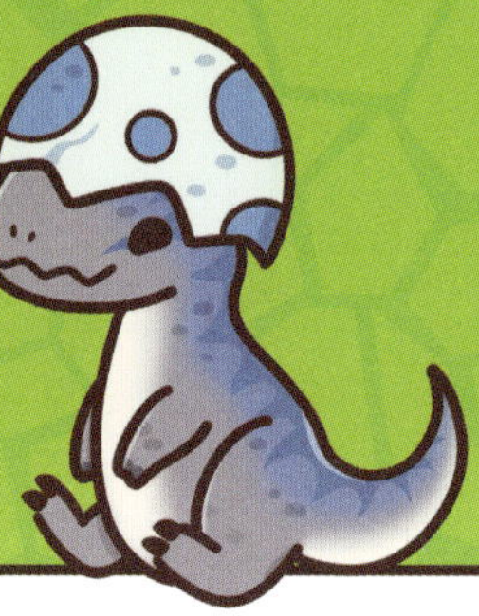

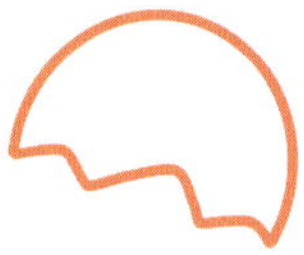

1. Draw a semicircle with a jagged bottom for the eggshell.

2. Add a C-line for the head.

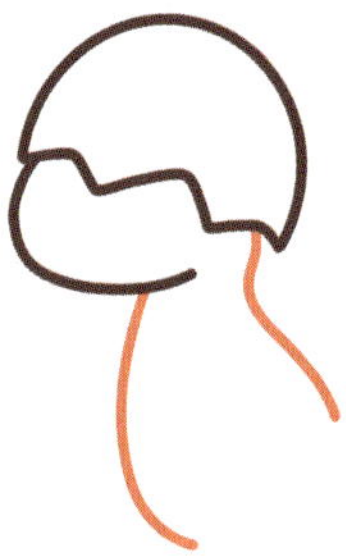

3. Add two curved lines for the body.

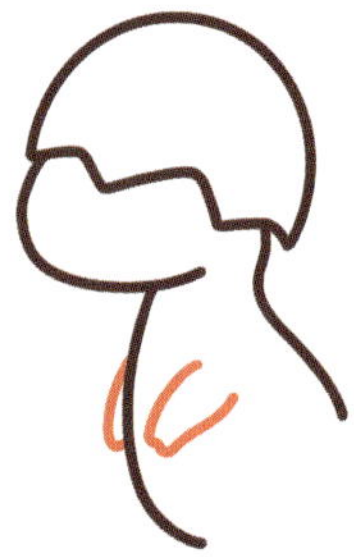

4. Draw two U-shaped arms with two fingers.

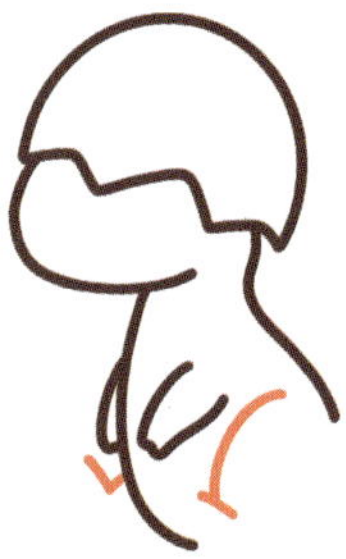

5. Draw a curved line for the leg. Add a V and a line for the feet.

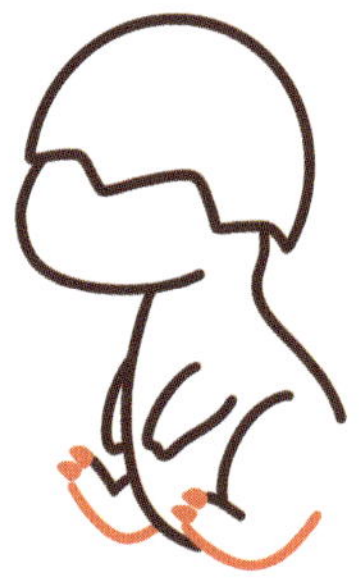

6. Complete the feet with a U and two talons each.

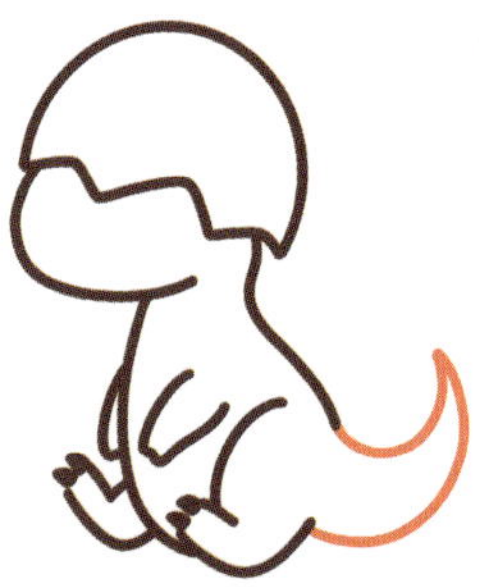

7. Draw a curved tail that tapers at the end.

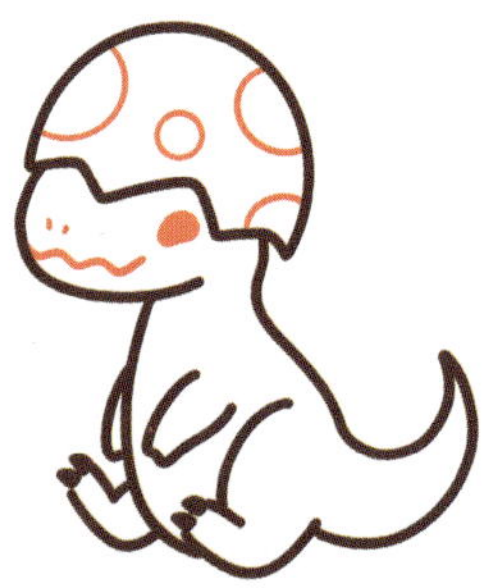

8. Decorate the shell with curved lines and circles. For the face, add a semicircle eye, two dashes for the nostrils, and a jagged mouth.

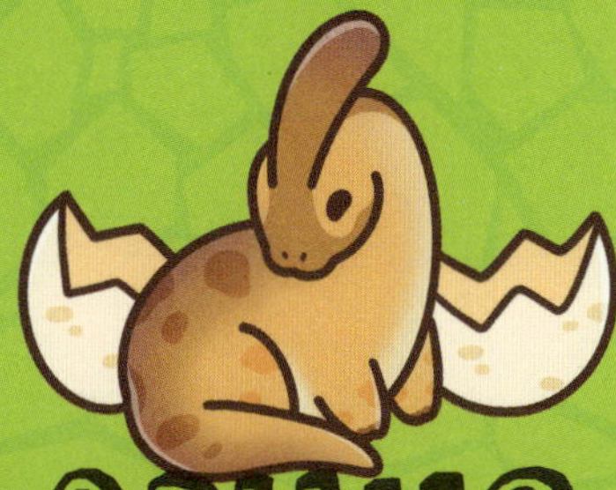

PARASAUROLOPHUS

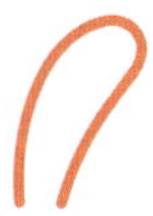

1. Draw a narrow arch for the crest.

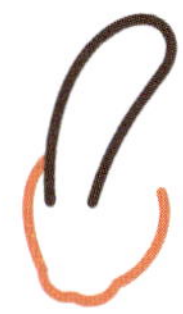

2. Add a U-shaped head with two bumps for the snout.

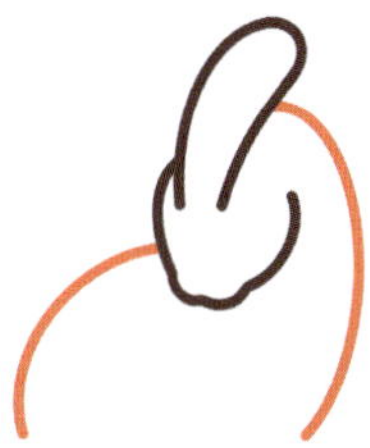

3. Draw two curved lines for the neck and the body.

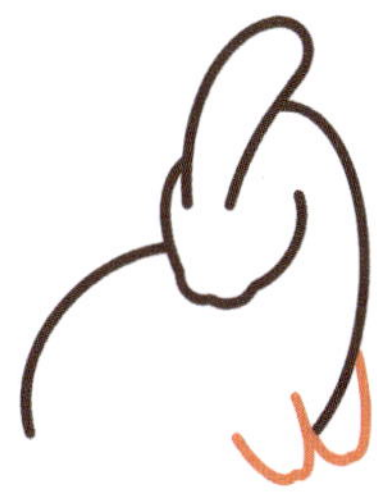

4. Add two U-shaped legs with two toes each.

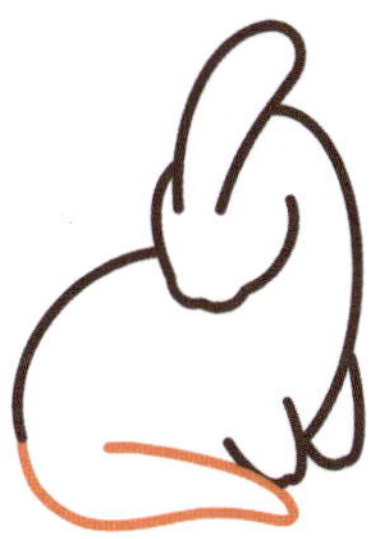

5. Draw a long, curved tail.

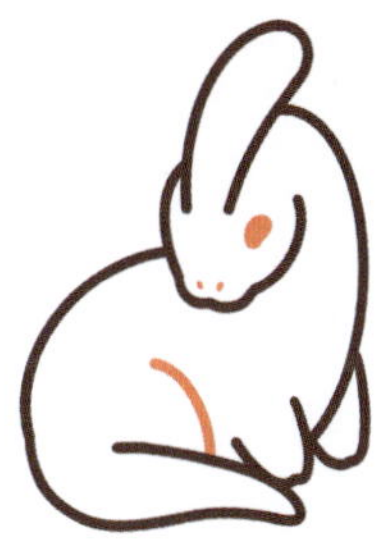

6. Draw a curved line for the leg. For the face, add an oval eye and two dashes for the nostrils.

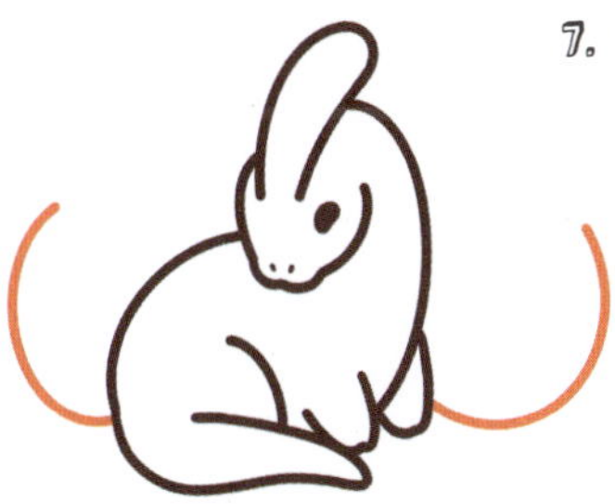

7. Add two U shapes on the sides of the dino.

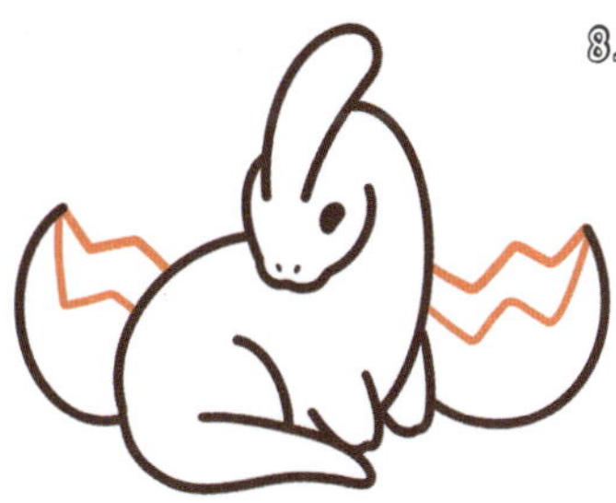

8. Draw two jagged lines on top of the U shapes to make broken eggshells.

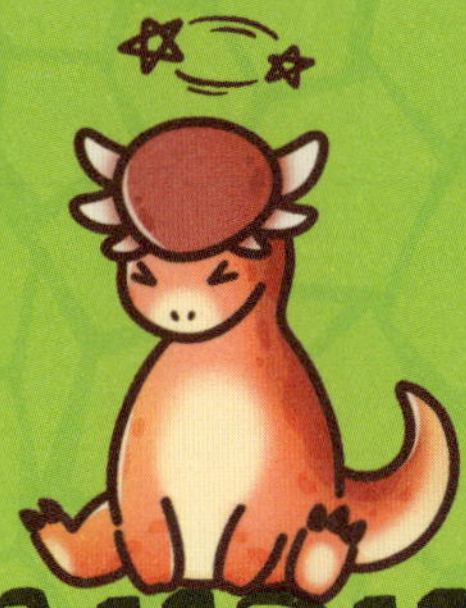

PACHYCEPHALOSAURUS

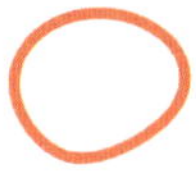

1. Draw an oval dome.

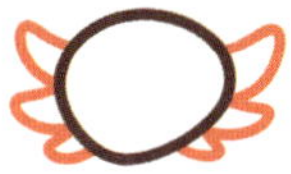

2. Add three triangle spikes on the sides of the dome.

3. Add a U for the head.

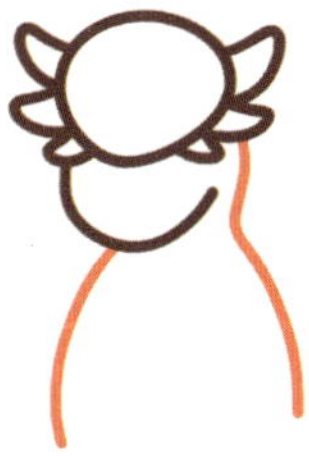

4. Draw two curved lines for the body.

5. Add two U-shaped arms with two fingers.

6. Add two curved lines around the arms. Draw a V-line for the left leg and add talons to both feet.

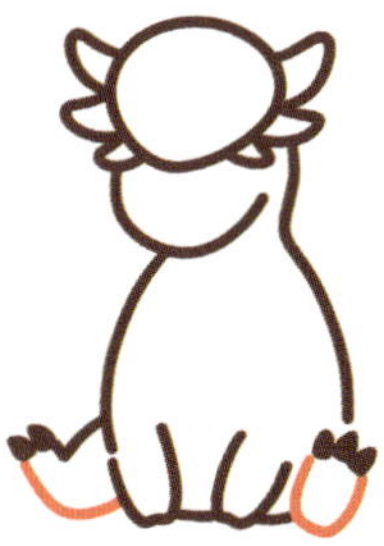

7. Draw an L-line for the left foot and a U for the right foot.

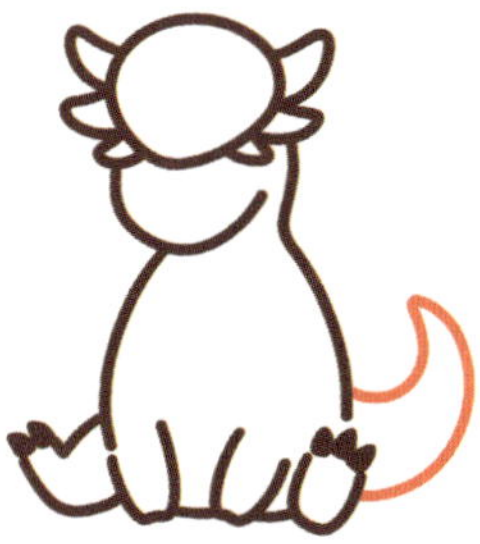

8. Add a curved tail that tapers at the end.

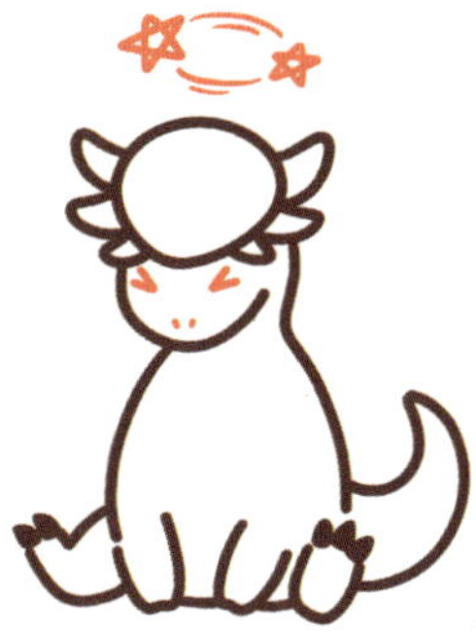

9. Add two V eyes and two dashes for the nostrils. Draw stars and curved lines above the head.

MICRORAPTOR

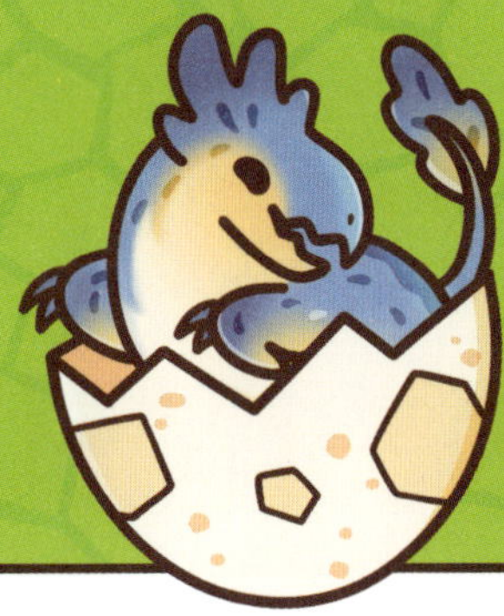

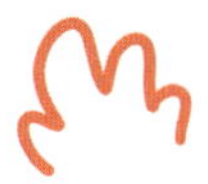

1. Draw four curved feathers.

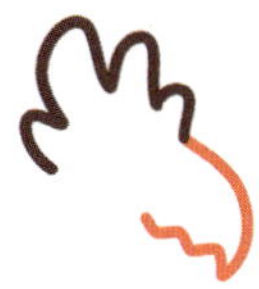

2. Add a curved beak with a jagged mouth.

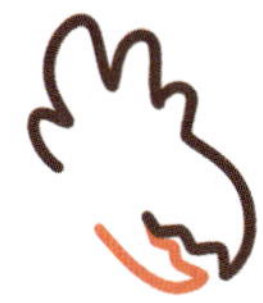

3. Draw the bottom jaw with a jagged line and a curved line.

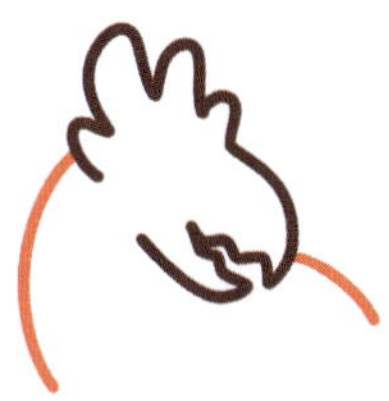

4. Add two curved lines for the neck and the body.

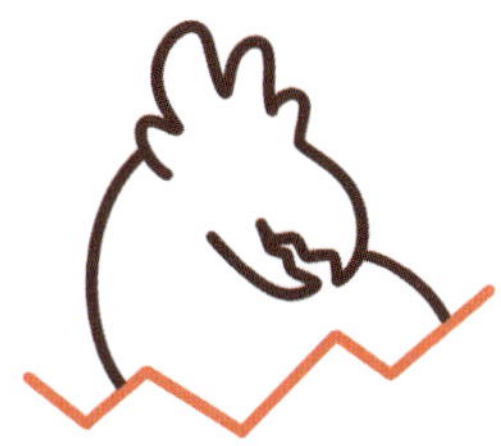

5. Draw a jagged line for the top of the eggshell.

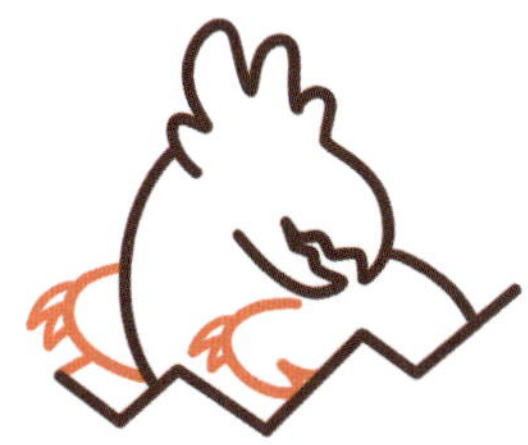

6. Add C-lines for the arms, with two triangle talons. Draw a line on the left of the eggshell and a triangle under the right arm.

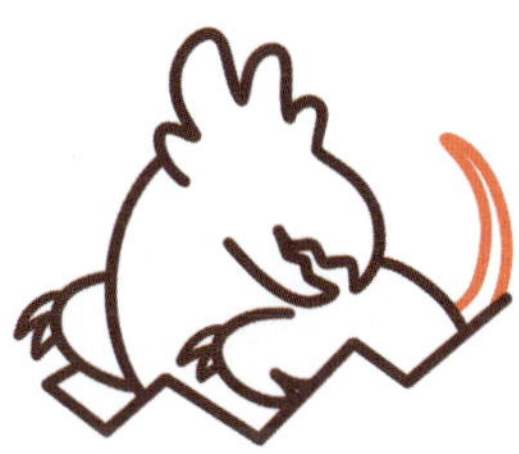

7. Draw a thin, curved tail.

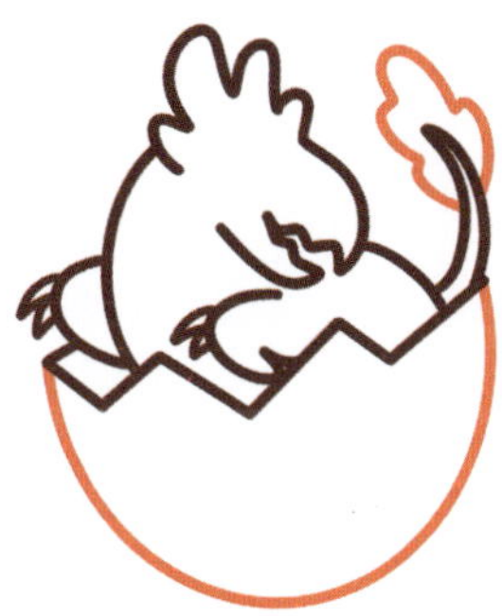

8. Add a leaf-shaped feather at the end of the tail. Draw a U for the eggshell.

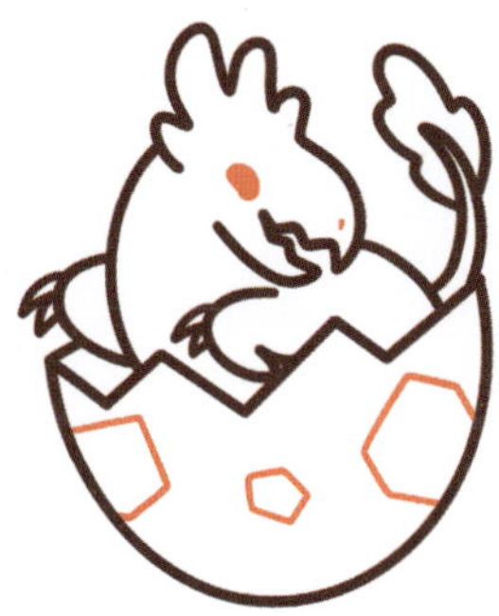

9. Decorate the shell with abstract shapes. For the face, add an oval eye and a dash for the nostril.

CORYTHOSAURUS

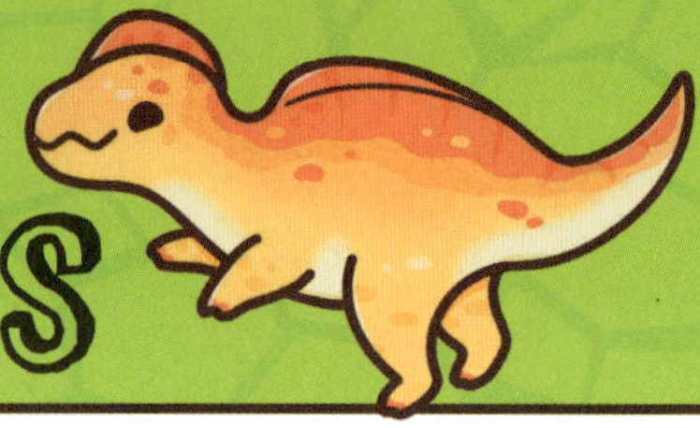

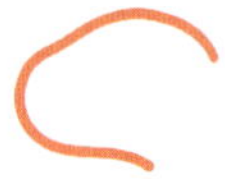

1. Draw a C-shaped head with a bump for the snout.

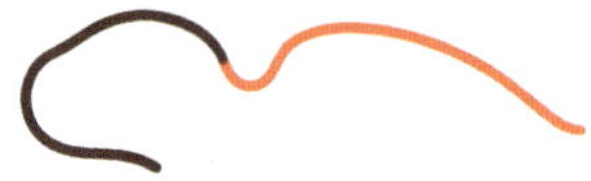

2. Add a U shape and a curved line for the top of the body.

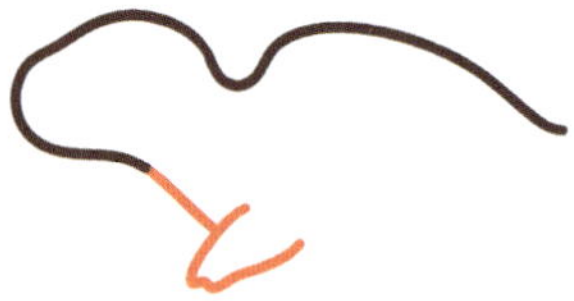

3. Add a line for the neck and a U-shaped arm with two fingers.

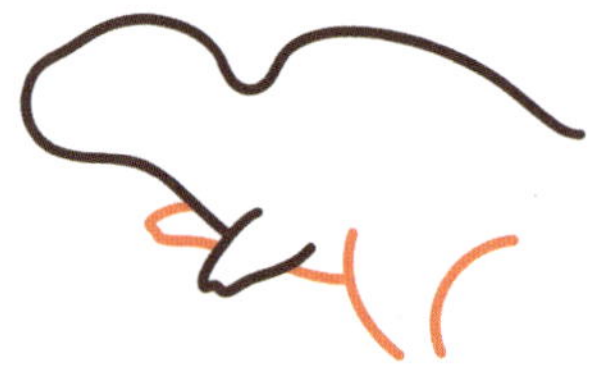

4. Draw a second arm. Add three curved lines for the stomach and the leg.

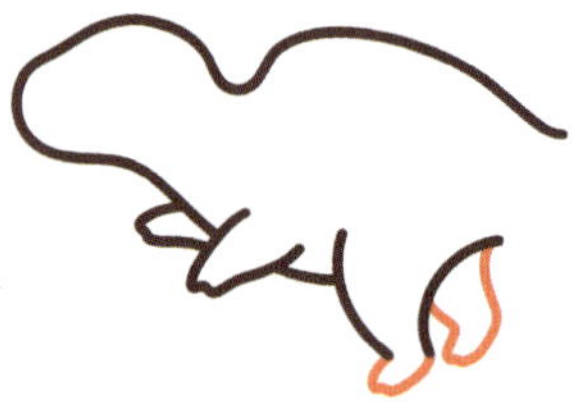

5. Add a U-shaped foot with two toes. Draw the second leg and the foot.

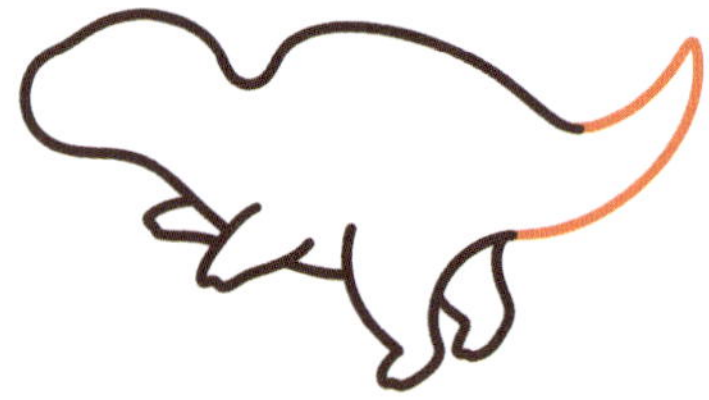

6. Draw the curved tail.

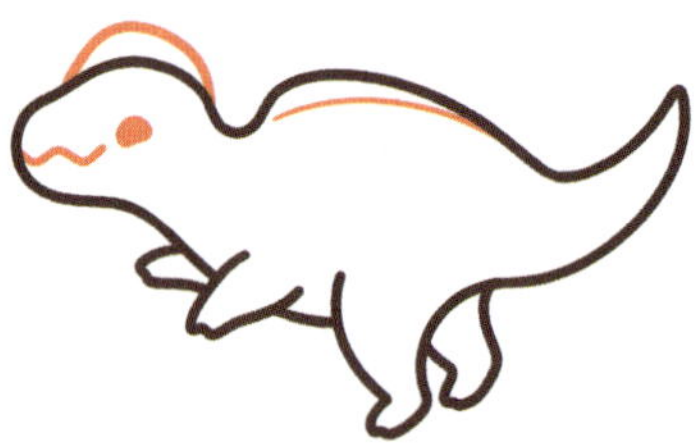

7. Add a curve along the back and on top of the head. For the face, add an oval eye and a W mouth.

ANKYLOSAURUS

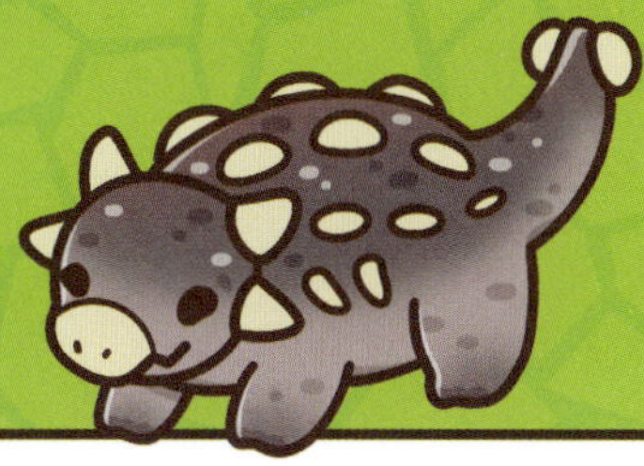

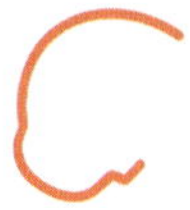

1. Draw a curved line for the head with a flat snout and a V tooth.

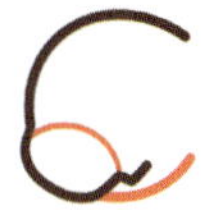

2. Add two curved lines for the snout and chin.

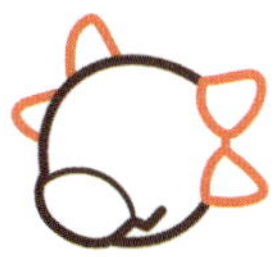

3. Add four triangle horns.

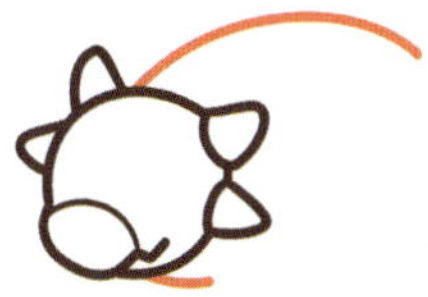

4. Draw two curved lines for the top of the body and the neck.

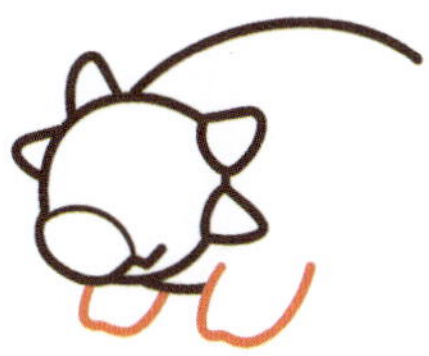

5. Add two U-shaped arms with two fingers each.

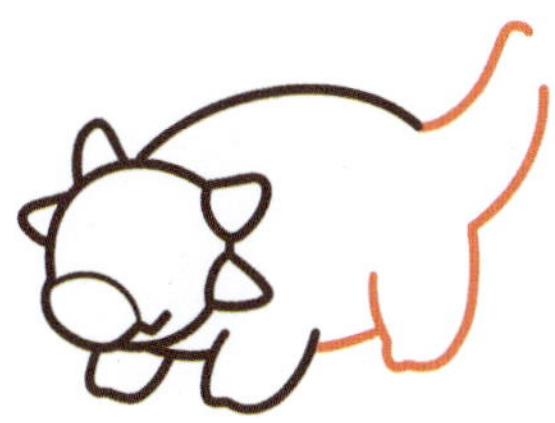

6. Draw a curved line for the stomach. Add another leg and two curved lines for the tail.

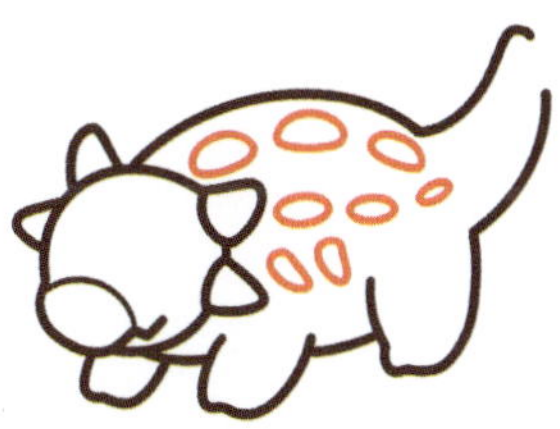

7. Add oval and triangle armor on the body.

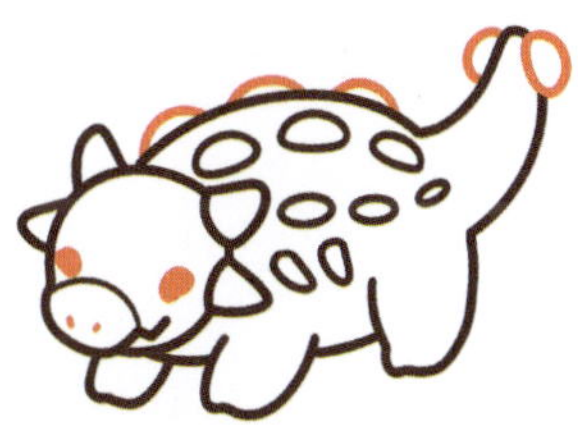

8. Add arches and ovals on top of the body and at the end of the tail. For the face, add two oval eyes and two dashes for the nostrils.

DINO DRESS-UP

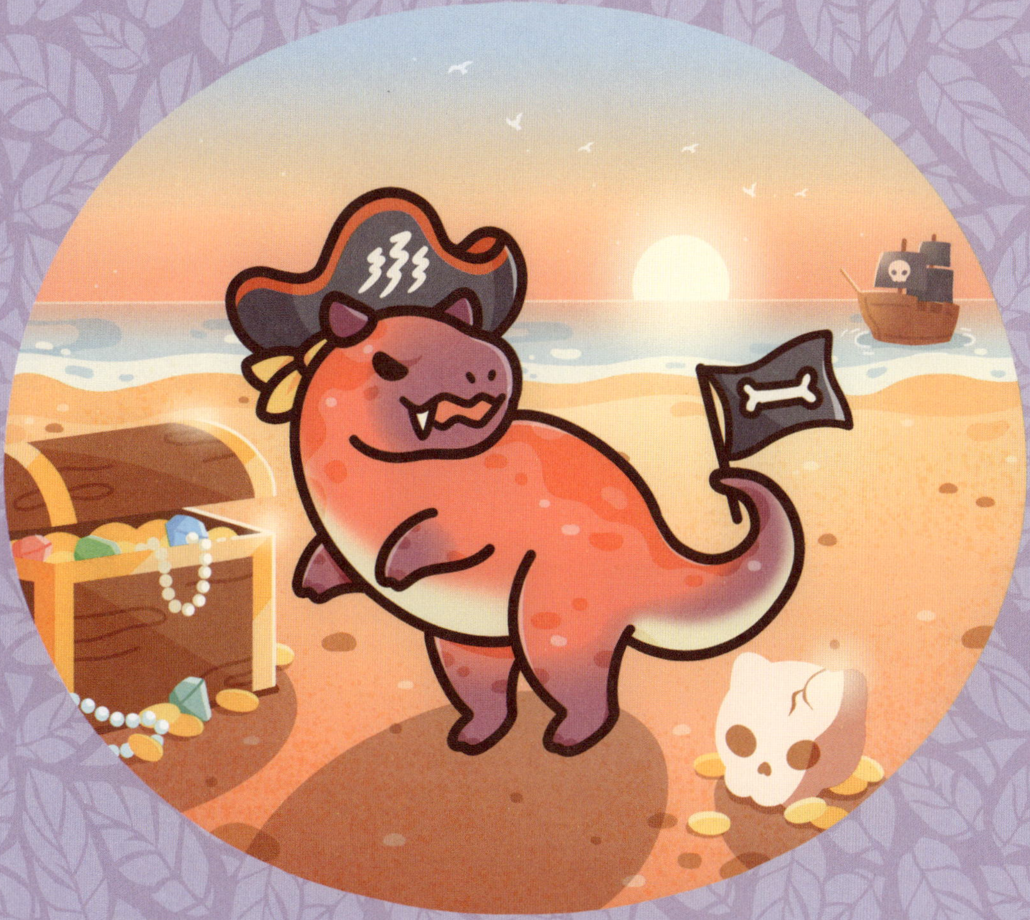

CHEF VELOCIRAPTOR

1. Draw a cloud-shaped hat with three curved sides.

2. Add a fourth curved side and attach a square underneath with a curved line inside.

3. Draw a C-shaped snout and a curved line for the back of the head.

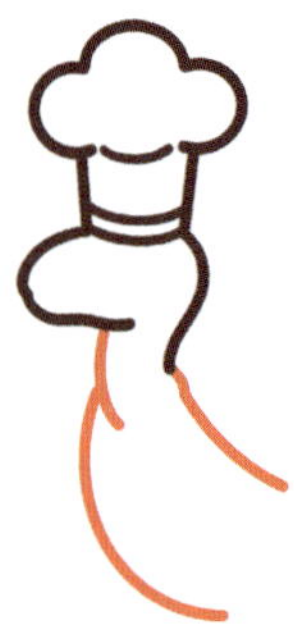

4. Draw the body and the neck with three curved lines. Add a bump where the neck meets the back.

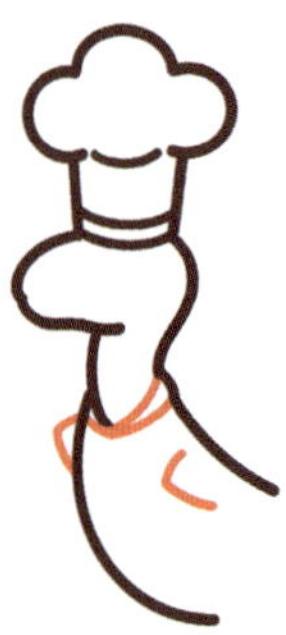

5. Add a V-shaped shirt collar. Draw the sleeves with two triangles.

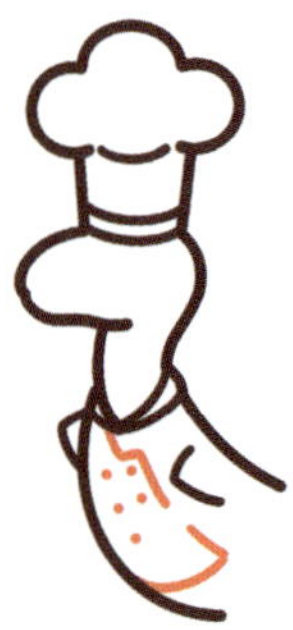

6. Draw the coat seam on the front of the body with lines and dots for the buttons.

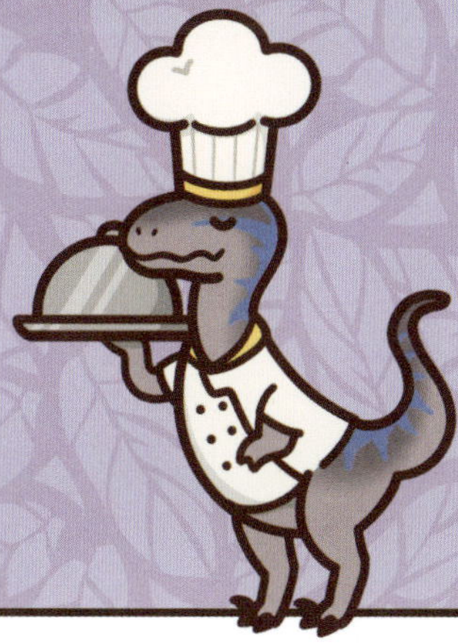

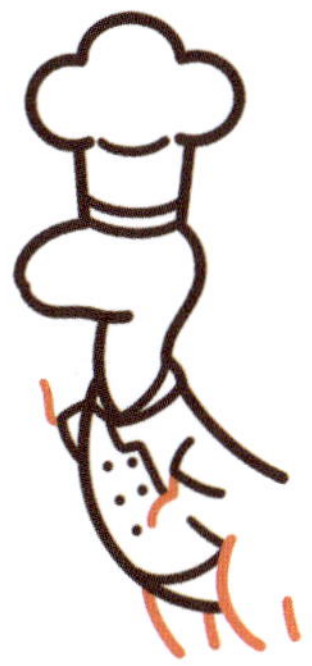

7. Start the arms with two wavy lines. Draw the legs with four curved lines.

8. Add a second wavy line to each arm and the fingers of the right hand. Add lines for the bottom of the coat and the legs. Add a pointed talon to each foot.

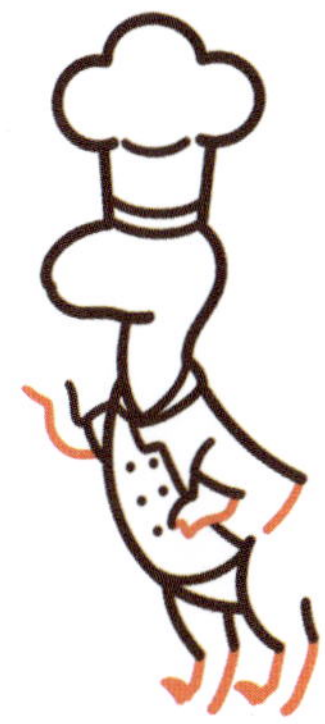

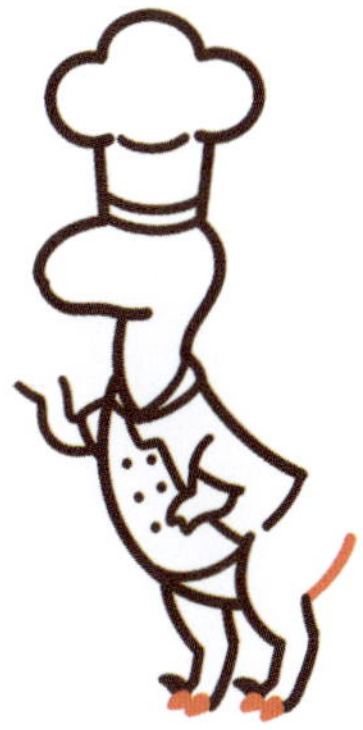

9. Add two talons to each foot and a curved line for the bottom of the body.

10. At the back of the body, draw a curved tail that tapers off at the end in the shape of an S. On top of the left hand, draw a thin rectangle.

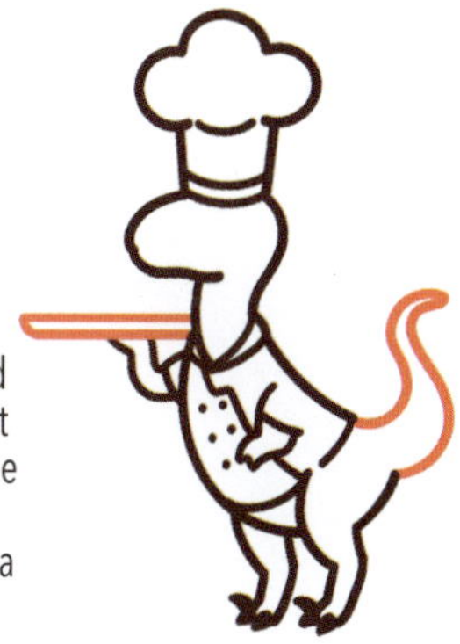

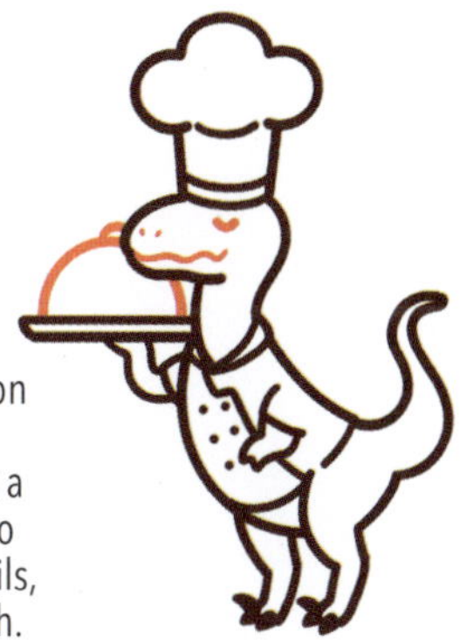

11. Draw a covered platter with a semicircle and a small semicircle on top for the knob. Add the face with a U-shaped eye, two dots for the nostrils, and a wavy mouth.

WIZARD STEGOSAURUS

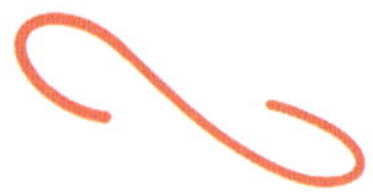

1. Draw a backward S-line for the hat's brim.

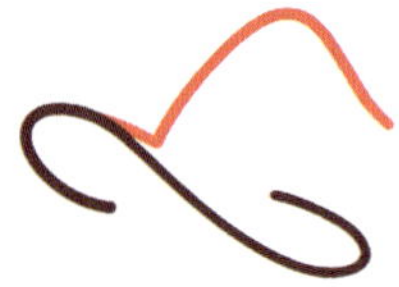

2. Add the pointed top of the hat and connect it to the left side of the brim.

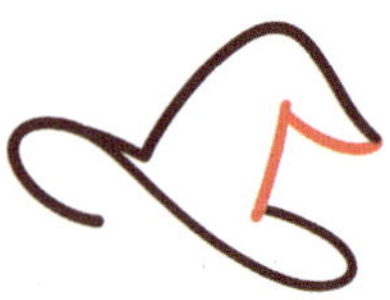

3. Draw a straight line and a curved line to complete the drooping top.

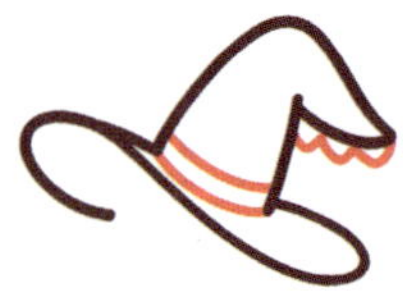

4. Add three small curves under the tip of the hat. Add two curved lines at the base of the hat.

5. Draw the head and the snout with two curved lines.

6. Draw an oval neck with a curved line that connects to the hat.

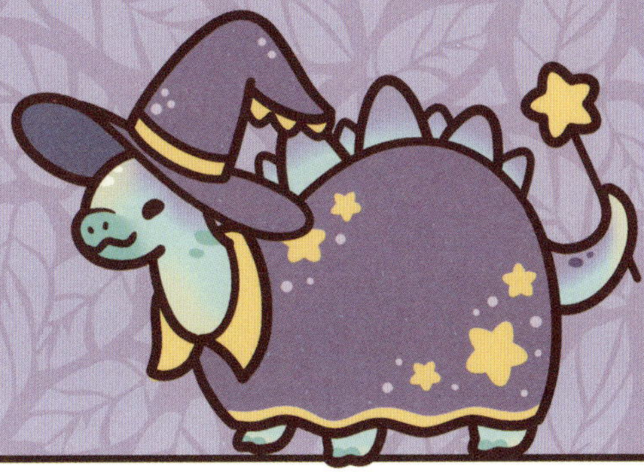

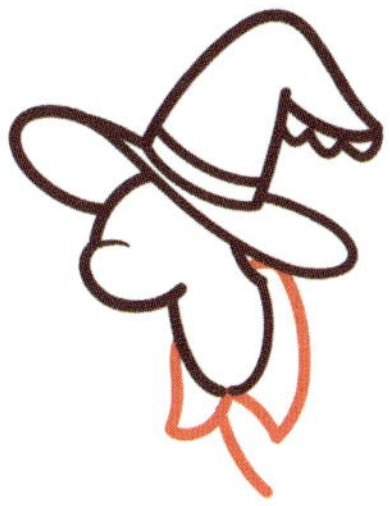

7. Add the cape's collar under the neck with two pointed ends. Add a curved line under the collar.

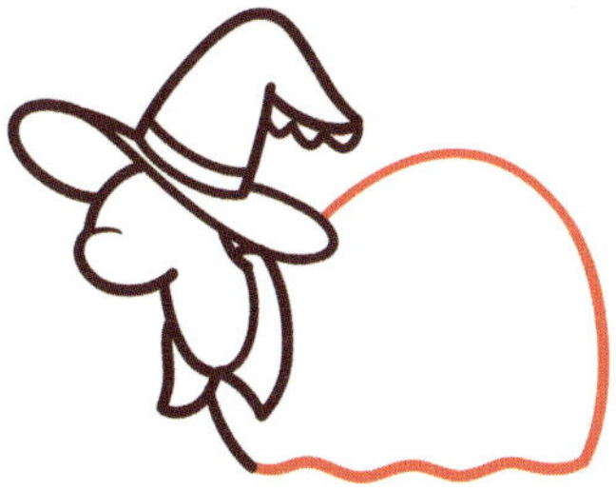

8. Draw a semicircle for the caped body with a wavy bottom.

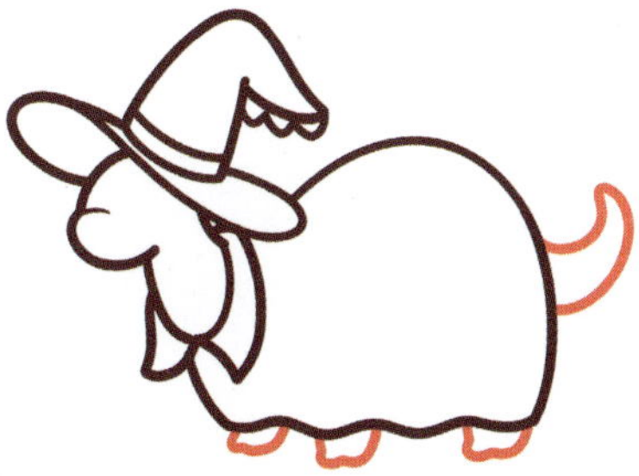

9. Add three U-shaped feet with two toes each. Add a short, curved tail that tapers at the end.

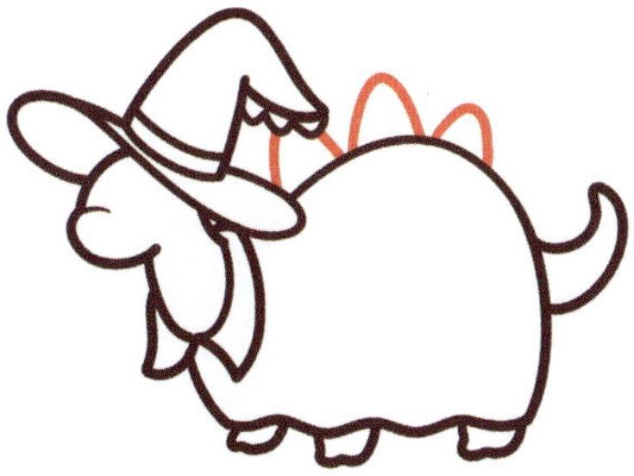

10. Draw three triangle spikes on top of the back.

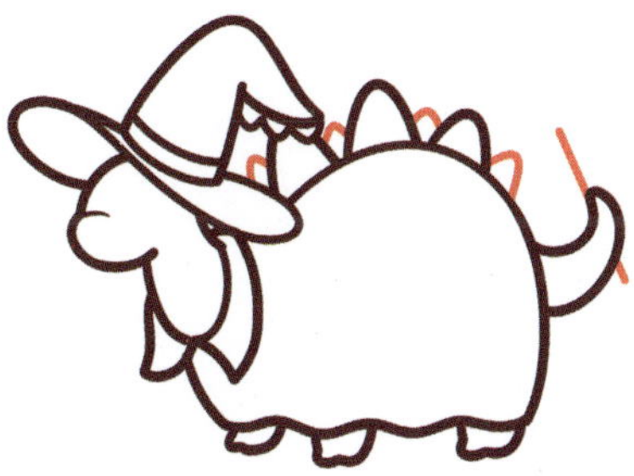

11. In between the spikes, draw four smaller spikes. Add a line for the wand at the end of the tail.

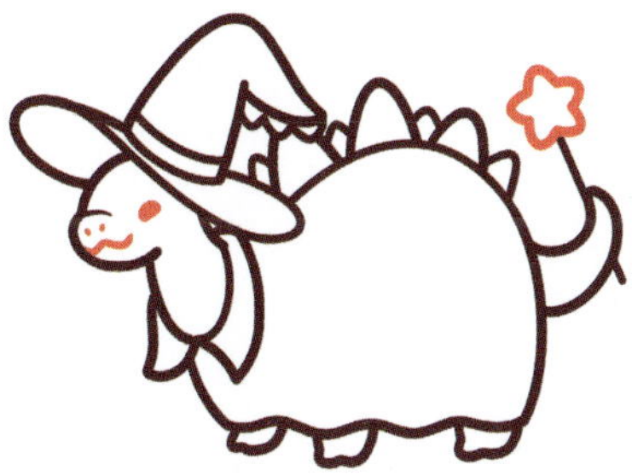

12. Draw a star at the top of the wand. For the face, add an oval eye, two dots for the nostrils, and a W mouth.

CLOWN BRACHIOSAURUS

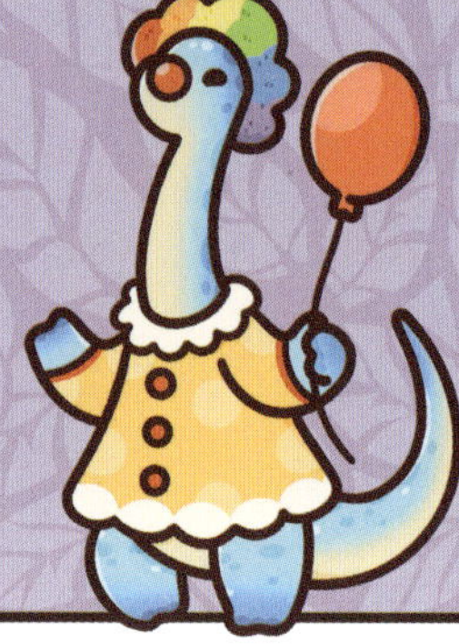

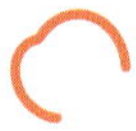

1. Draw a curve with two bumps for the snout.

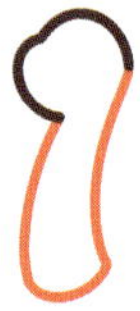

2. Add a curved rectangle neck.

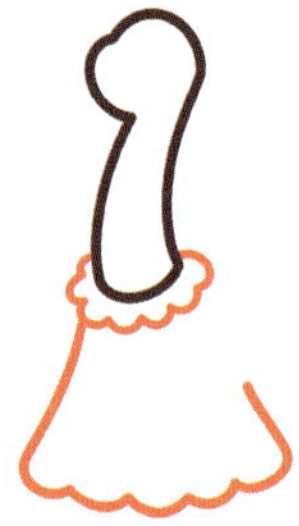

3. Draw a scalloped collar around the base of the neck. Add a triangle shirt with a scalloped bottom edge.

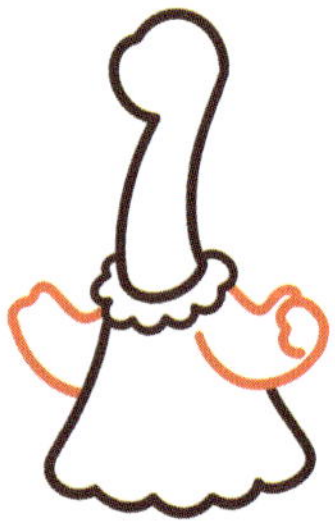

4. Add a curved left arm with two fingers. For the right arm, curl the hand in like the shape of an E.

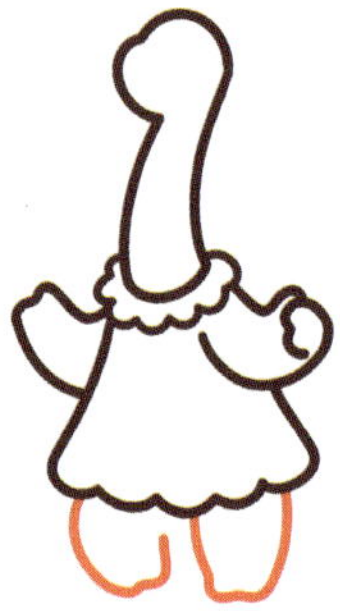

5. Add a round left leg with two toes and a rectangular right leg.

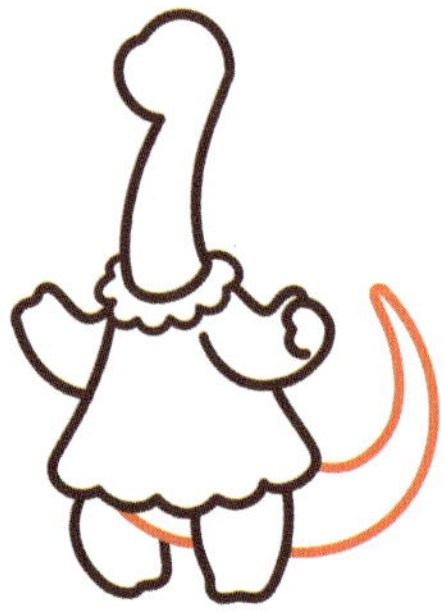

6. Draw a long, curved tail starting under the body.

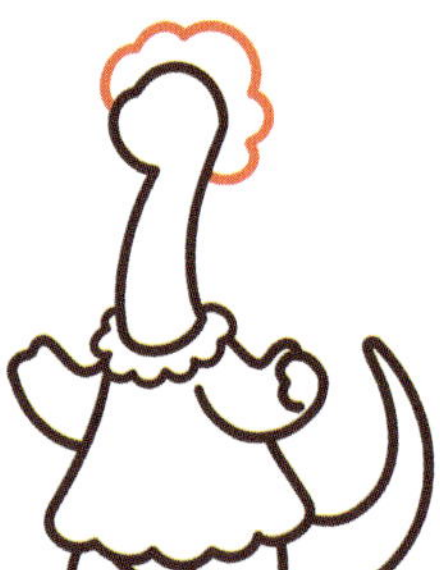

7. Add a scalloped hat on top of the head.

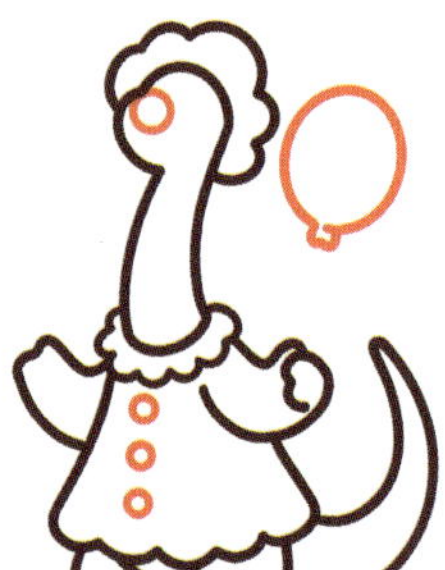

8. Draw a circle on the nose and three circles down the shirt. Add a balloon next to the head.

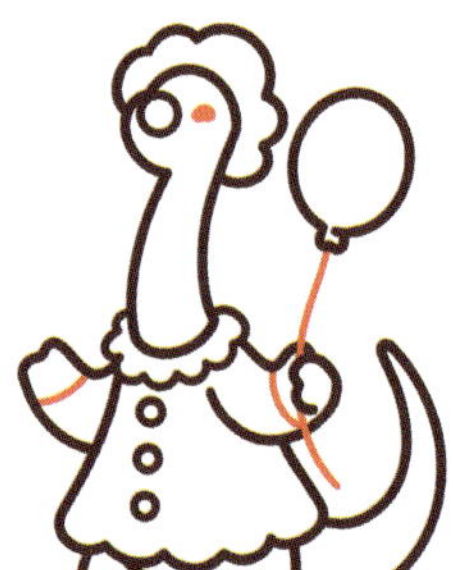

9. Add curved lines for the string of the balloon and shirt sleeves. Draw an oval eye.

FAIRY TRICERATOPS

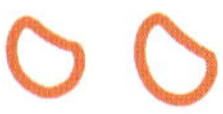

1. Draw two rounded, triangle horns.

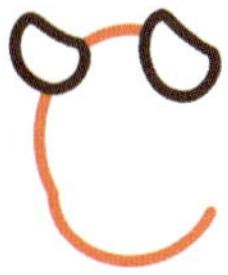

2. Add an oval head with a bump for the snout.

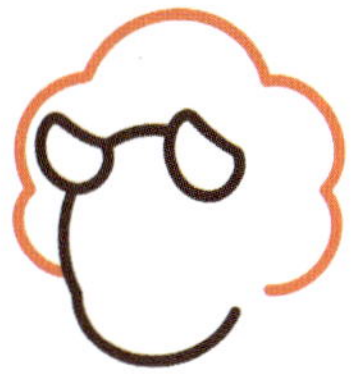

3. Add five scallops around the head, with the largest on top.

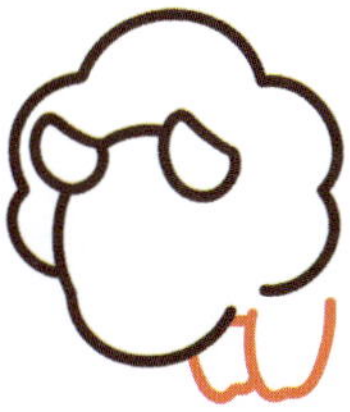

4. Draw two U-shaped legs with two toes. Draw a line for the neck.

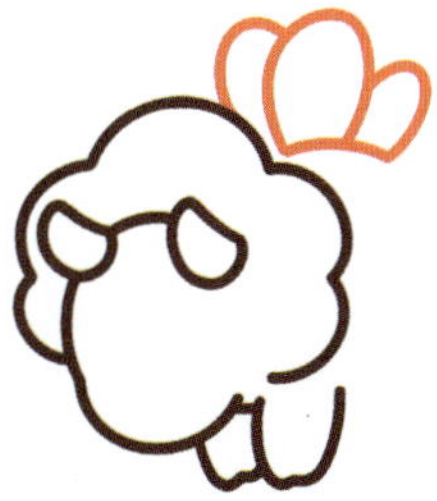

5. Add three arches for the wings with a curved line underneath.

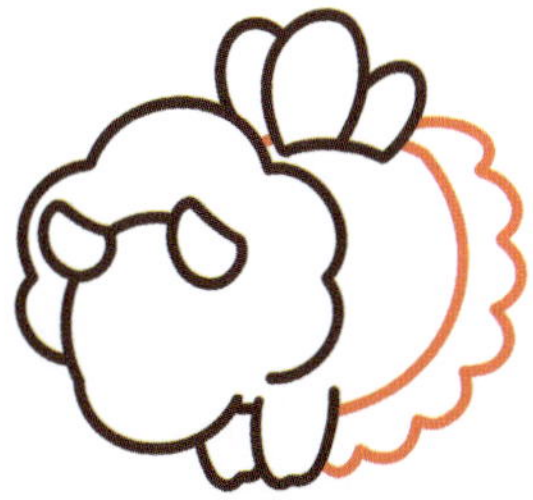

6. Draw a curved line for the body. Add a scalloped tutu around the body.

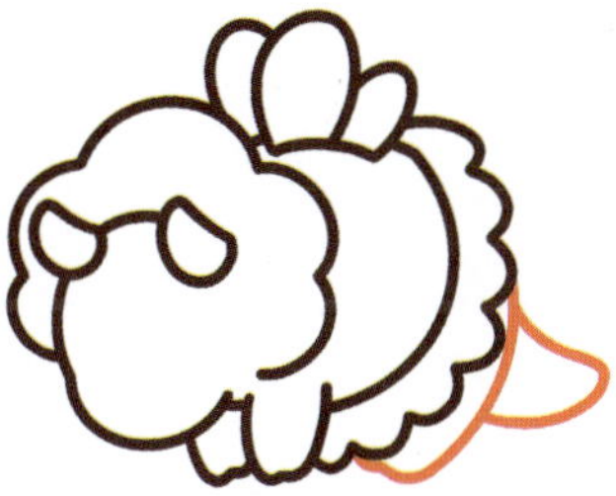

7. Add a curved line for the leg with two toes at the bottom. Draw a short triangle tail.

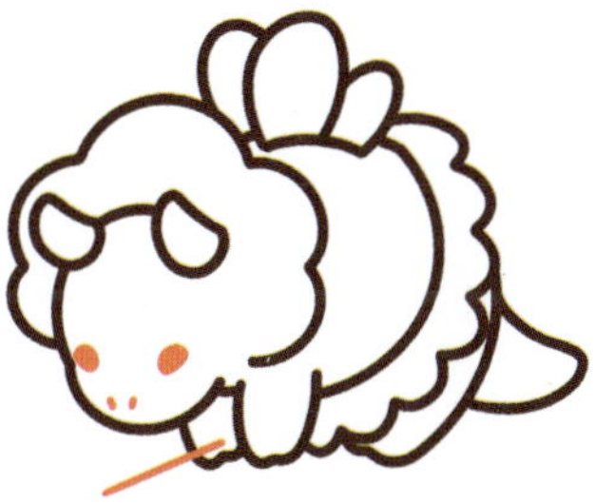

8. Add a line for the wand in front of the hand. For the face, add two oval eyes and two dashes for the nostrils.

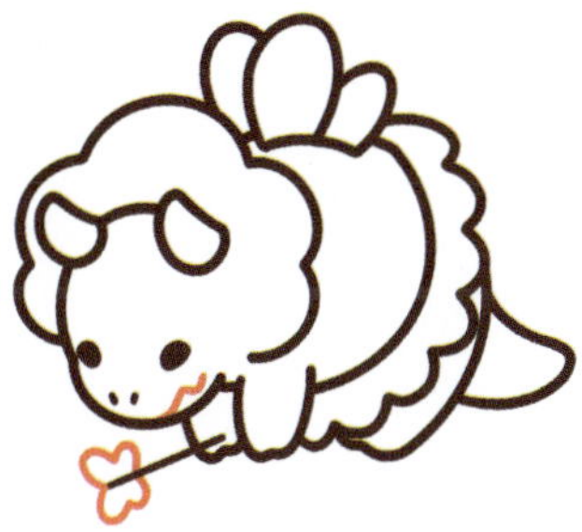

9. Draw a W mouth. Add a butterfly at the end of the wand with two M shapes.

PILOT MICRORAPTOR

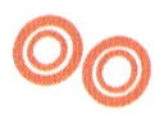

1. Draw a circle within a circle twice for the goggles.

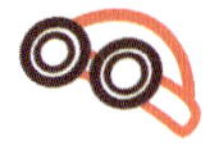

2. Add a curved line on top and a rectangle for the strap.

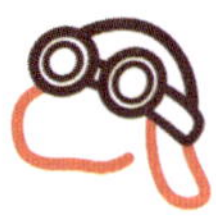

3. Draw a wavy C-line for the head and a rectangle for the ear flap.

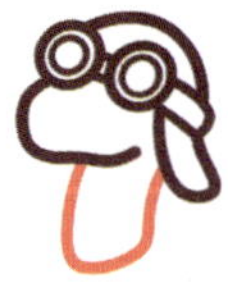

4. Add a rectangle neck.

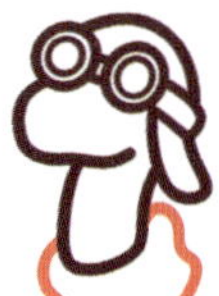

5. Draw a wavy, abstract shape for the scarf.

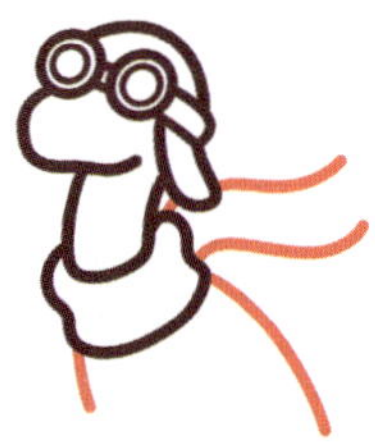

6. Draw two wavy lines for the scarf. Add two curved lines for the body.

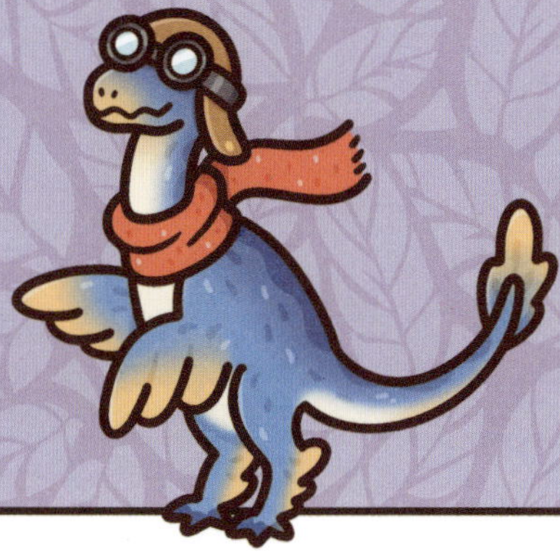

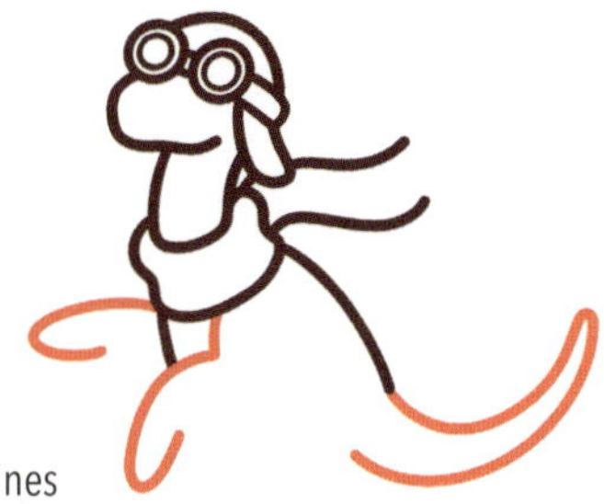

7. Add curved lines for the wings that hook at the end. Draw a long, curved tail.

8. Add two curves for feathers on each wing. Draw a leaf-shaped feather at the end of the tail.

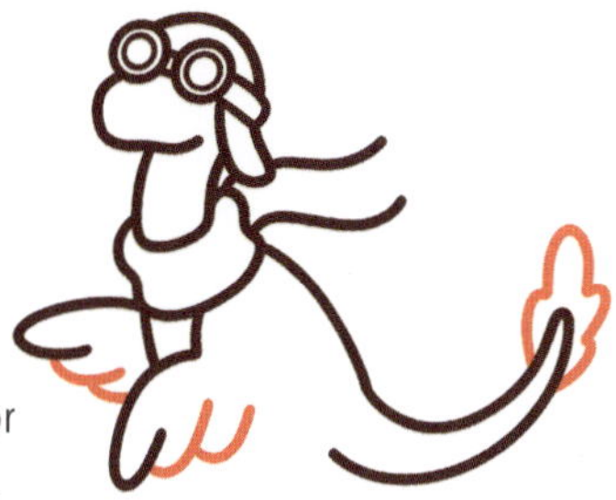

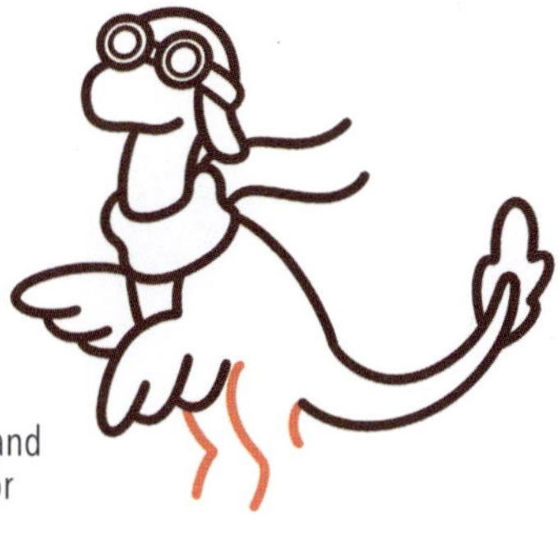

9. Draw a V-line and curved lines for the legs.

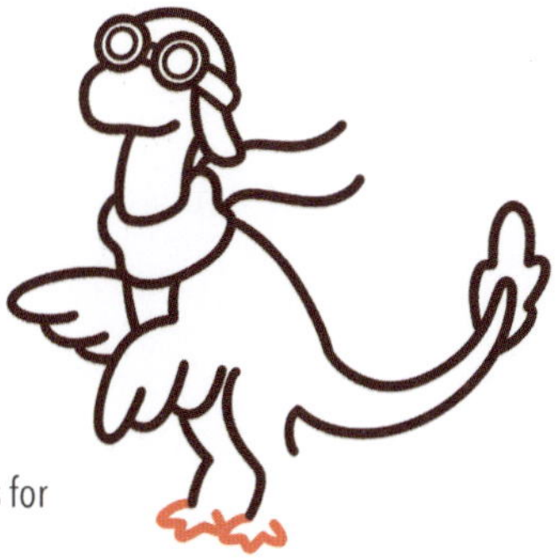

10. Add three spikes for each foot.

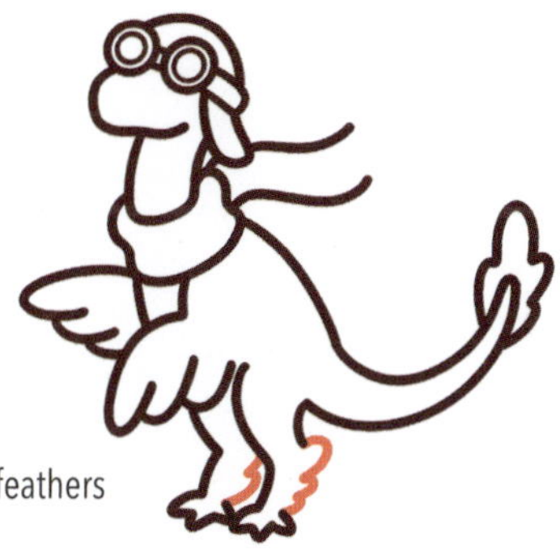

11. Add round feathers to the legs.

12. Draw lines on the scarf. Add two dashes for the nostrils and a jagged mouth.

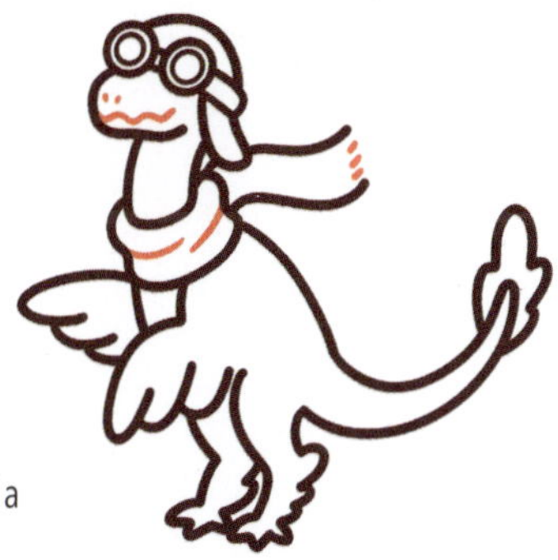

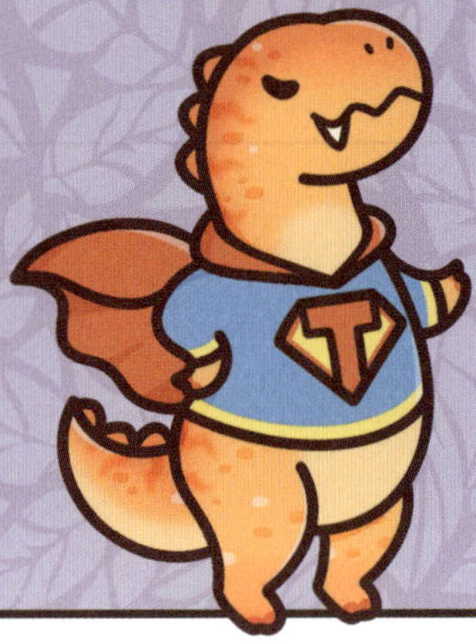

SUPER TYRANNOSAURUS

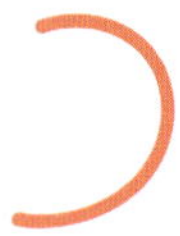

1. Draw a backward C for the head.

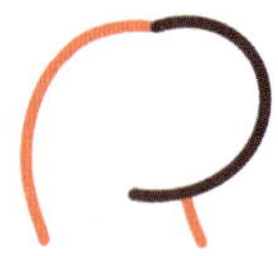

2. Add a curved line for the back of the head and a straight line for the neck.

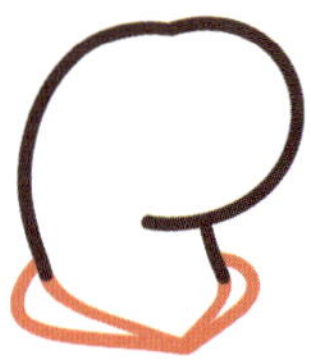

3. Draw a V for the neckline. Add two curves on the sides of the V.

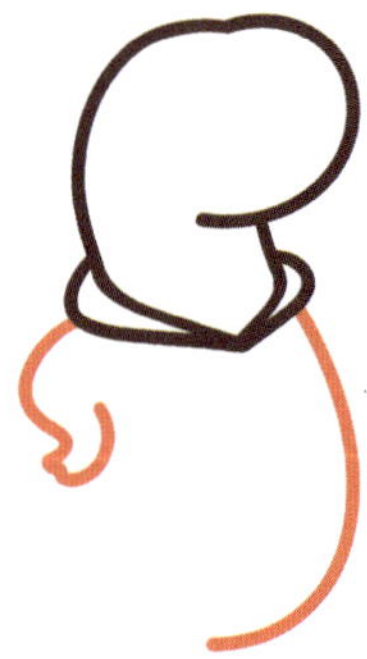

4. Add a curved line for the stomach. Draw two wavy lines for the arm with two fingers.

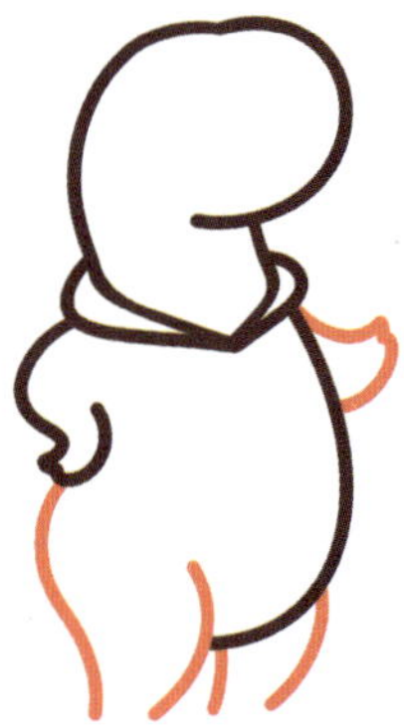

5. Add a second arm. Draw four curved lines for the legs.

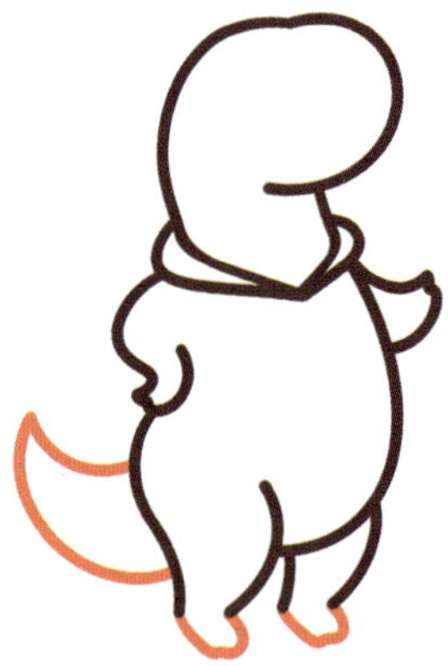

6. Add U shapes for the feet with two toes. Draw a curved tail.

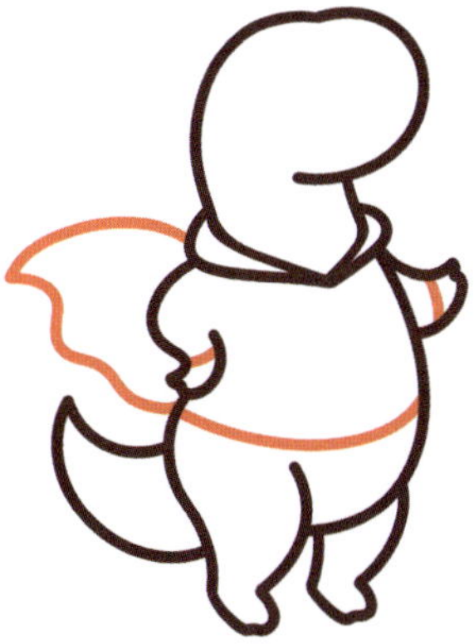

7. Draw three curved lines for the bottom of the shirt and sleeves. Add a cape with a curving shape.

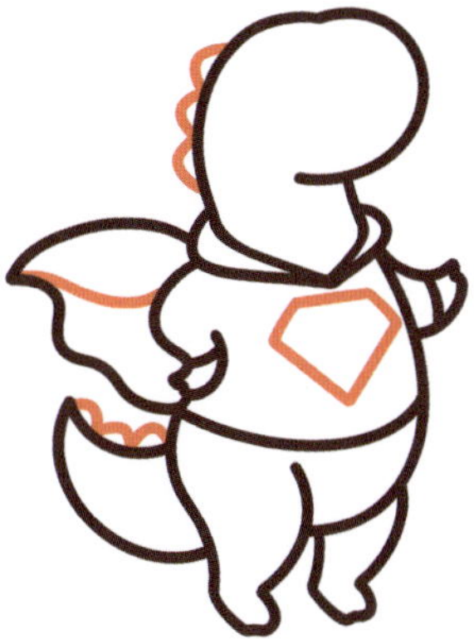

8. Add curves on the back of the head and along the tail. Draw a curved line in the cape and a pentagon on the shirt.

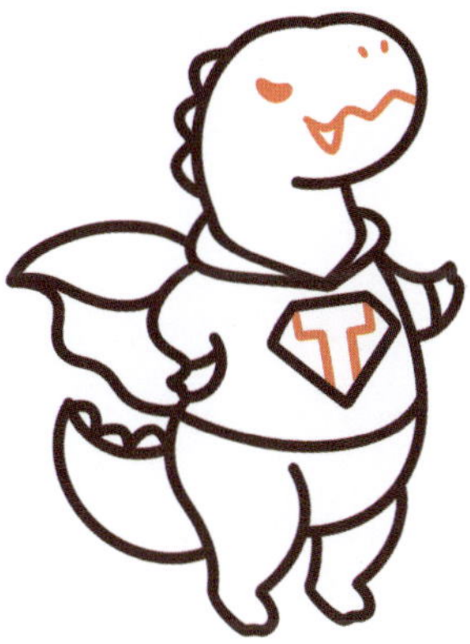

9. Draw a T in the pentagon. For the face, add a U-shaped eye, two dashes for the nostrils, and a jagged mouth with a triangle tooth.

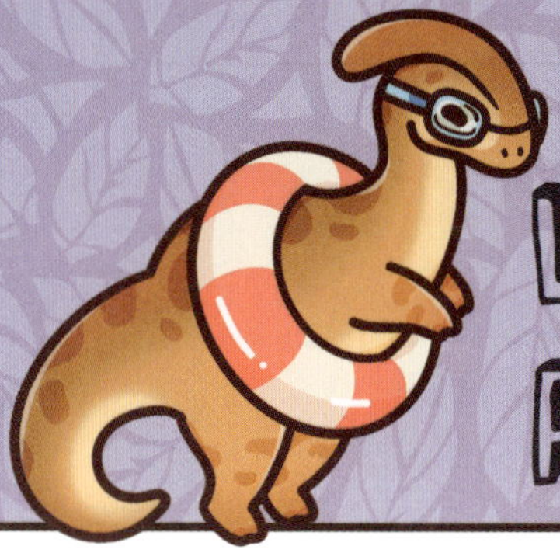

LIFEGUARD PARASAUROLOPHUS

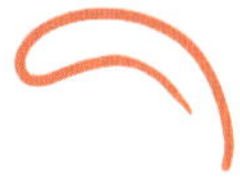

1. Draw a curved shape for the crest.

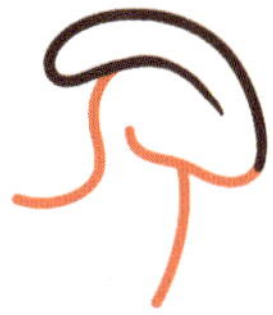

2. Add curved lines for the head and the neck.

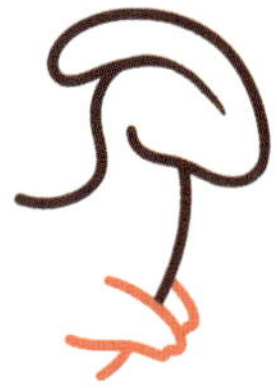

3. Draw two short arms with two fingers each. Add a curved line for the stomach.

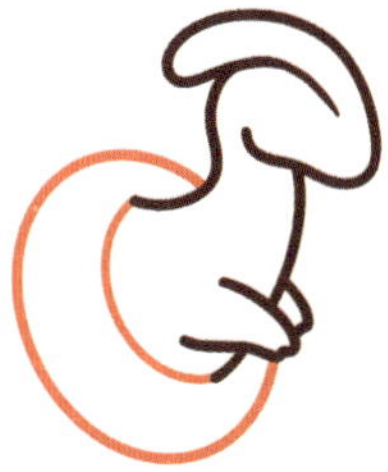

4. Draw a circle around the body for the floaty with a curved line inside.

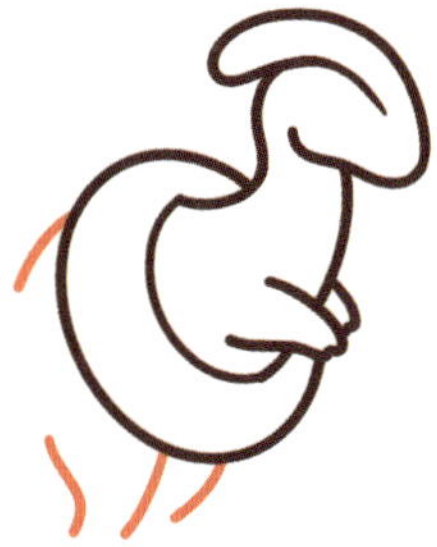

5. Add curved lines for the back of the body and the legs.

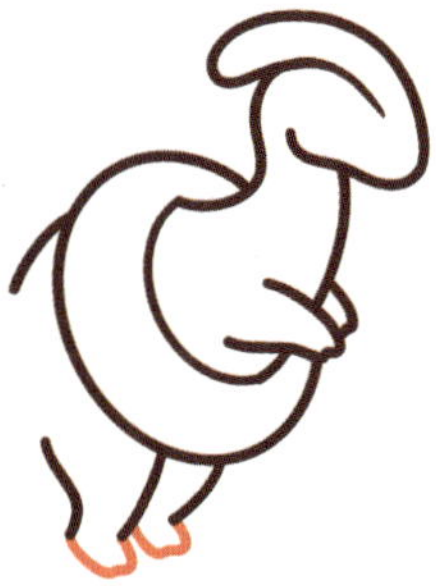

6. Draw U-shaped feet with two toes each.

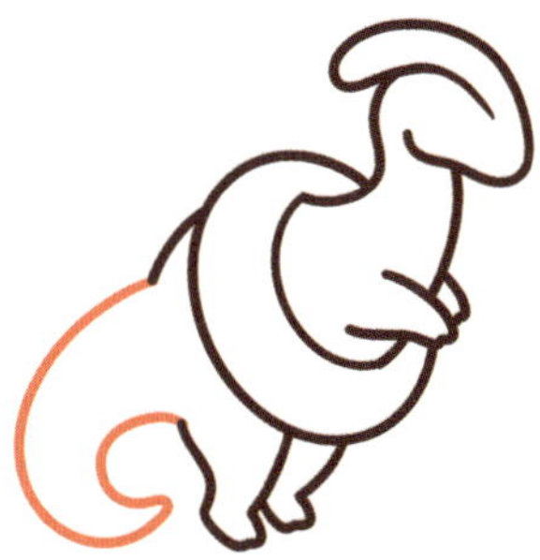

7. Add a large, curved tail.

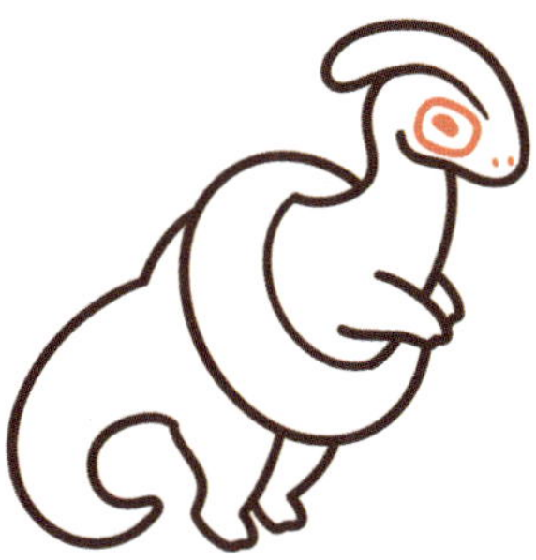

8. Add an oval eye and two dashes for the nostrils. Draw a rectangle around the eye for a goggle.

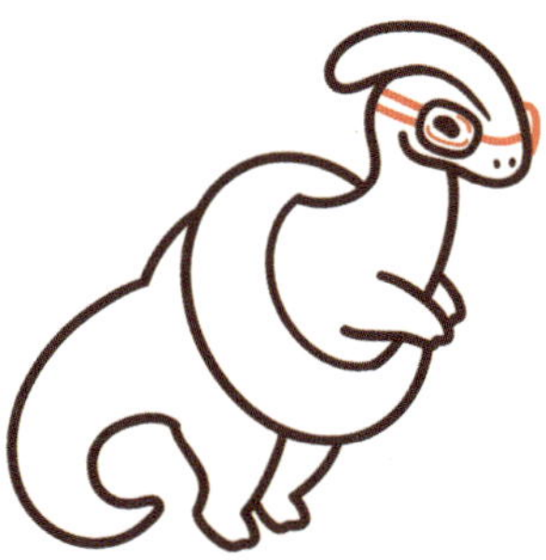

9. Draw lines for the goggle straps and curved lines for the second goggle eye and inside the rectangle.

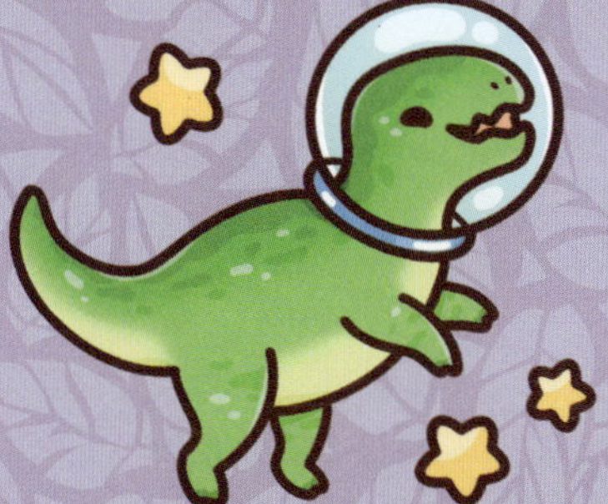

ASTRONAUT FUKUISAURUS

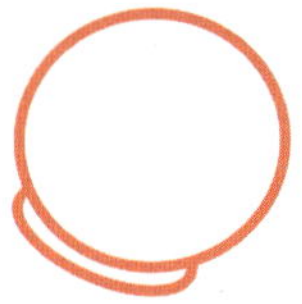

1. Draw a circle with a curved line underneath for the helmet.

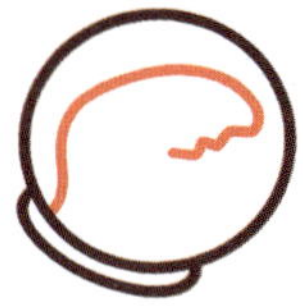

2. Add the curved head of the dino inside the circle with a jagged mouth.

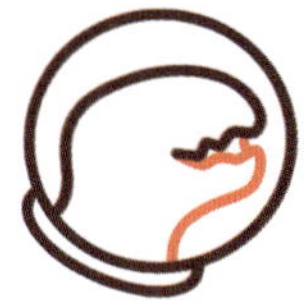

3. Add the bottom jaw with a jagged line and two curved lines.

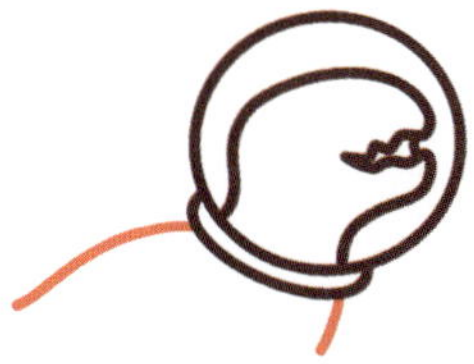

4. Draw two curved lines for the body.

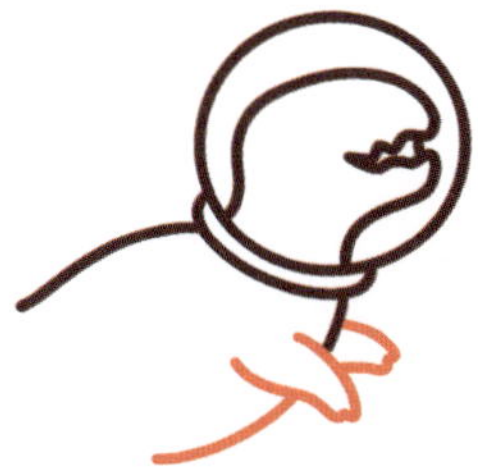

5. Add two curved arms with two fingers each. Add a curved line for the stomach.

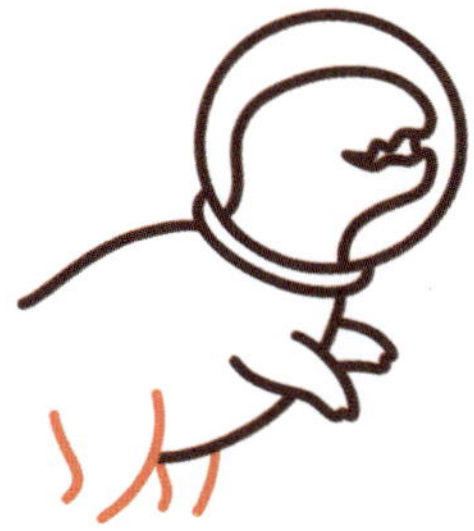

6. Draw four curved lines for the legs.

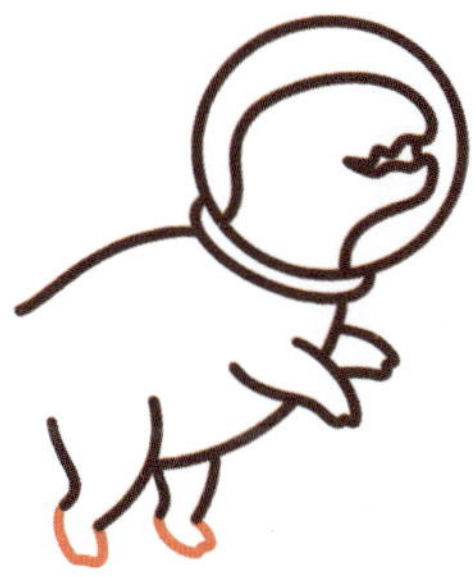

7. Add U-shaped feet with two toes each.

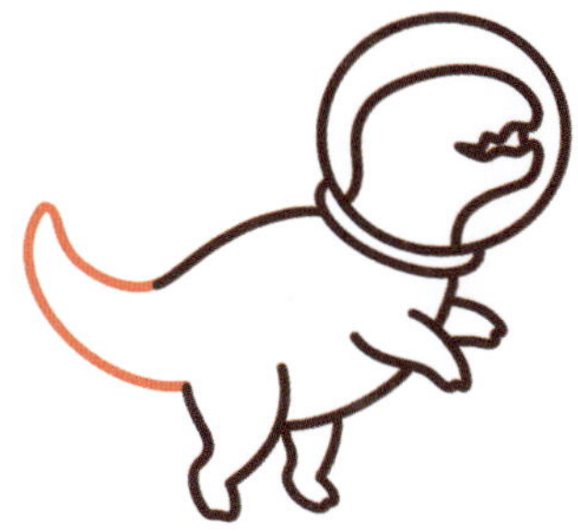

8. Add a curved tail.

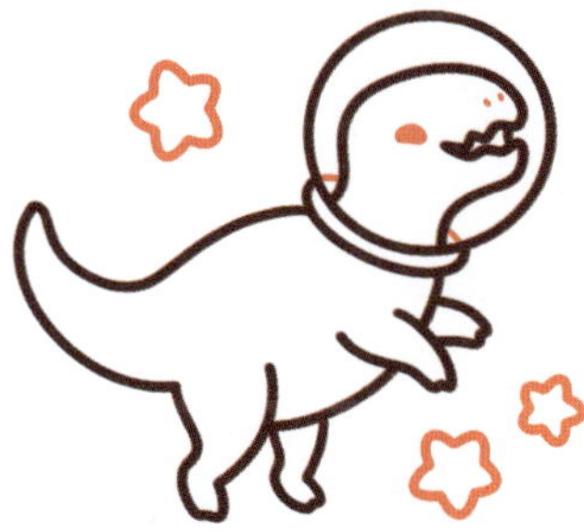

9. Draw curved lines for the bottom of the helmet. For the face, add an oval eye and two dashes for the nostrils. Draw stars around the dino.

PIRATE CARNOTAURUS

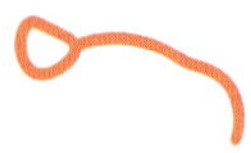

1. Draw a curved line and a triangle horn.

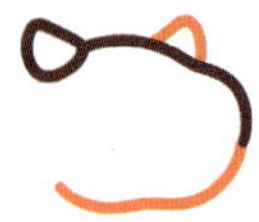

2. Add a second triangle horn. Draw a curved line for the bottom of the head.

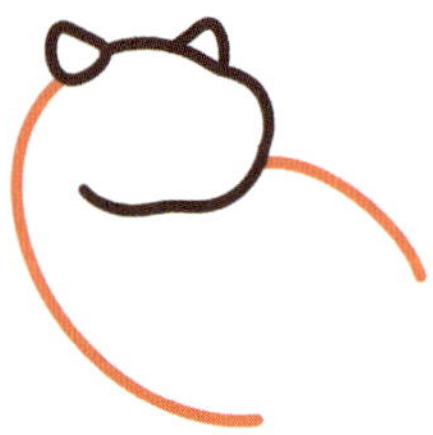

3. Draw two curved lines for the neck and the body.

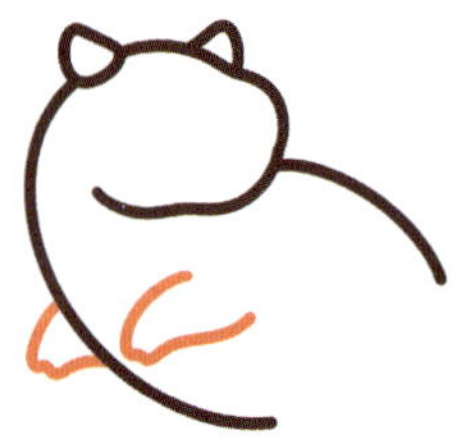

4. Add two curved arms with two fingers each.

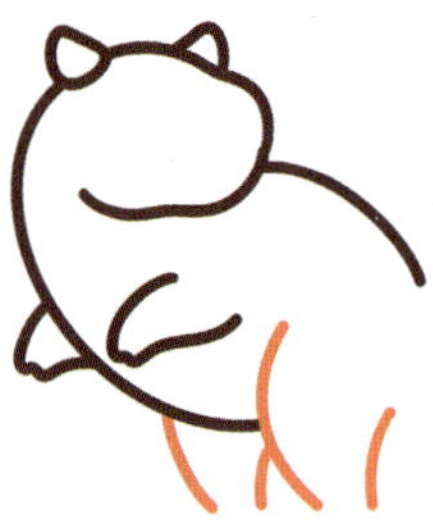

5. Draw four curved lines for the legs.

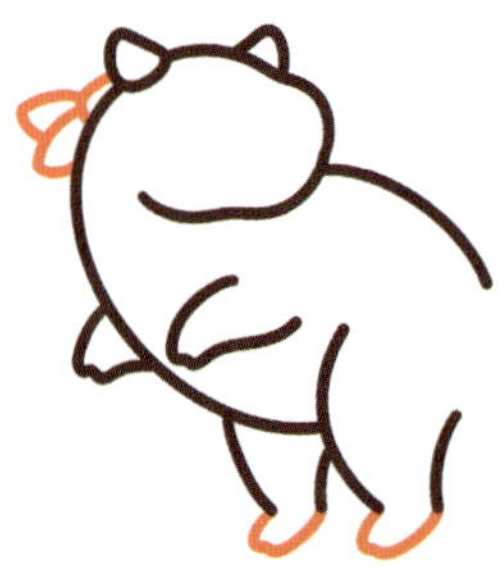

6. Add two U-shaped feet with two toes each. Draw three triangle shapes behind the head.

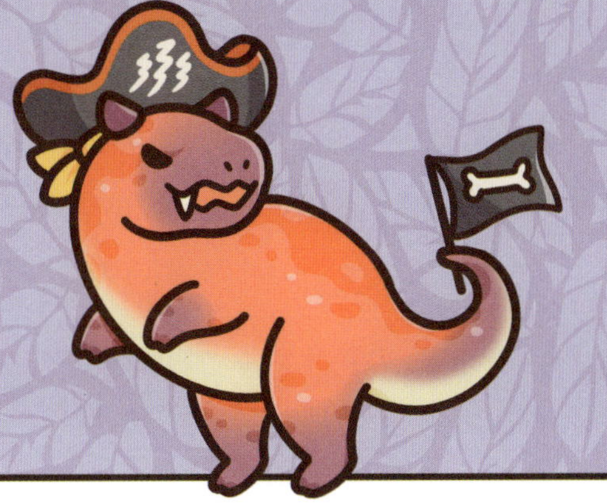

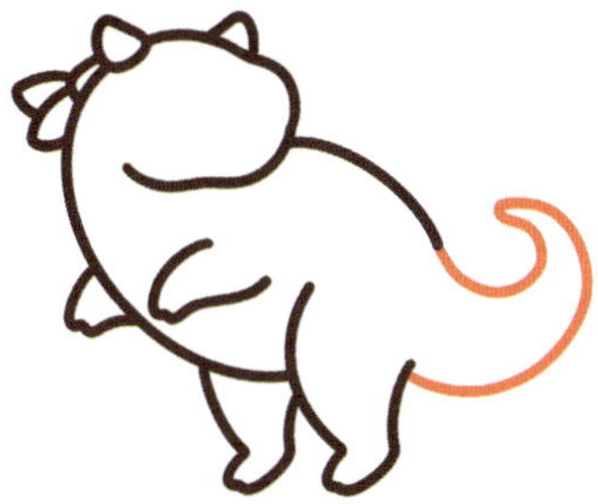

7. Draw a curved tail that tapers at the end.

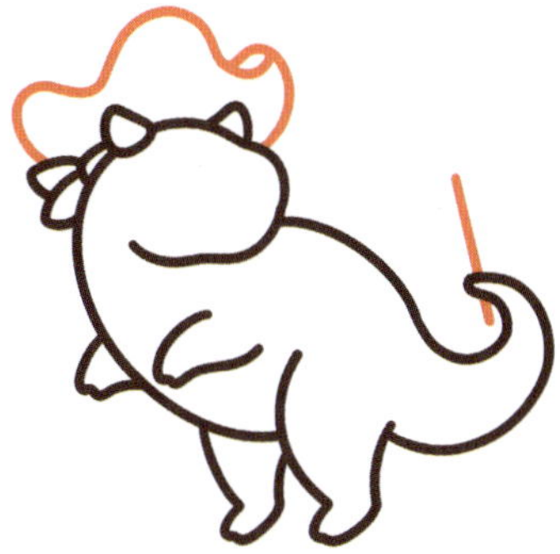

8. Draw a curved shape with three bumps for the hat. Add a curved line on the right and a stick for the flag.

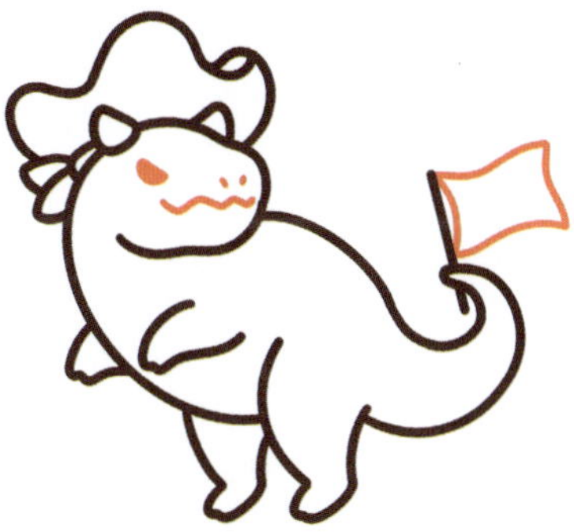

9. Add a rectangle flag with curved sides. For the face, add a semicircle eye, two dashes for the nostrils, and a jagged mouth.

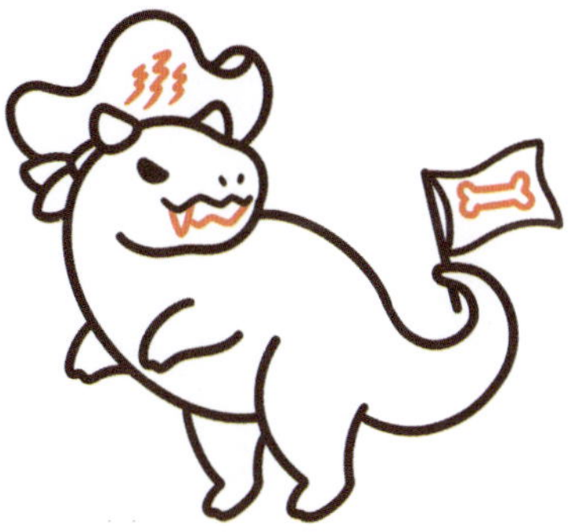

10. Add a triangle tooth and a W for the mouth. Decorate with jagged lines on the hat and a bone on the flag.

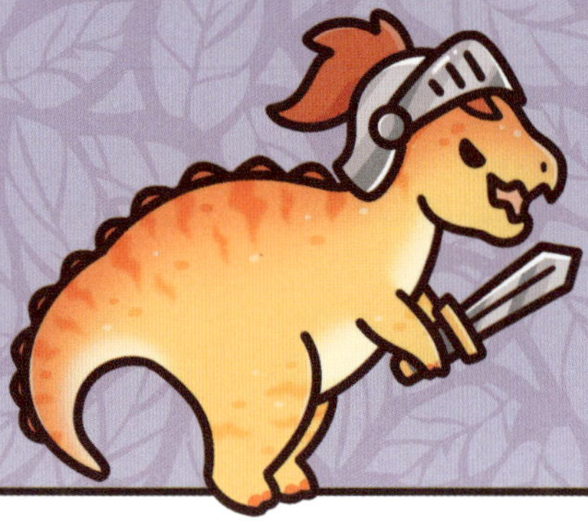

KNIGHT ALLOSAURUS

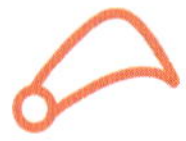

1. Draw a triangle and a circle for the helmet.

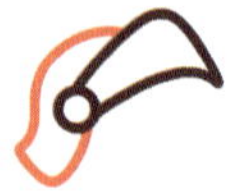

2. Add a curved rectangle for the back of the helmet.

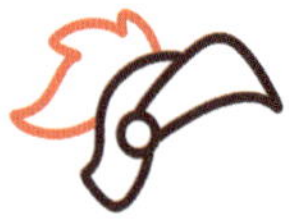

3. Add the feather plume with a spiked shape on top of the helmet.

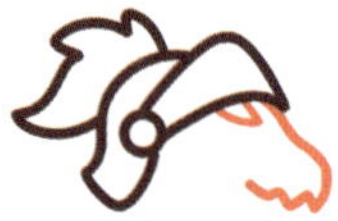

4. Draw a curved line with a jagged edge for the mouth. Add a triangle to the helmet.

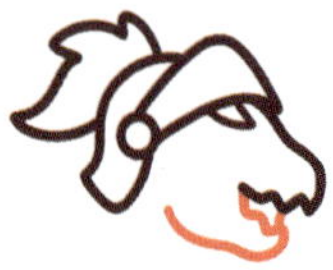

5. Add the bottom jaw with a jagged line and curved lines.

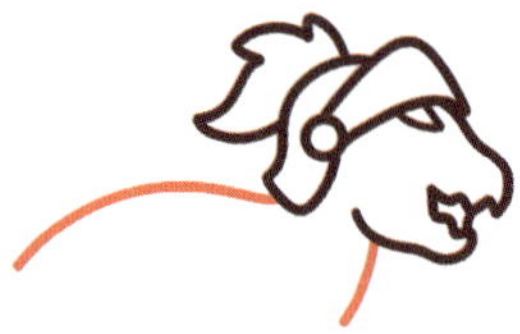

6. Draw two curved lines for the top of the body and the neck.

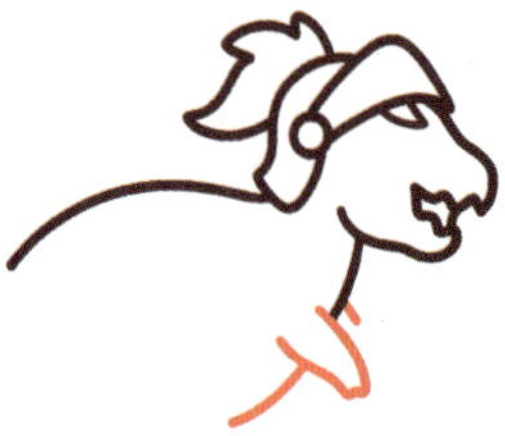

7. Draw a U-shaped arm with two fingers. Start the second arm with a short line. Add a curved line for the stomach.

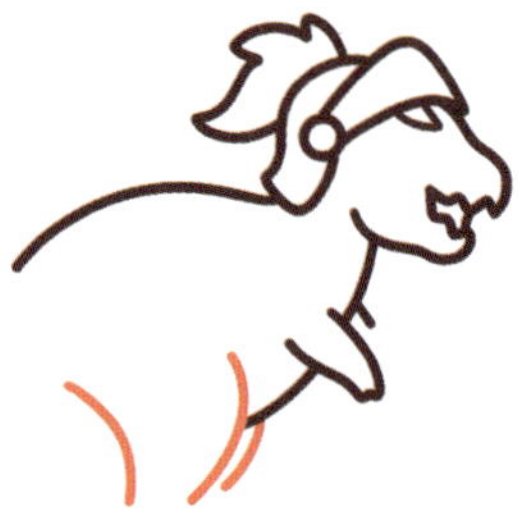

8. Add three curved lines for the legs.

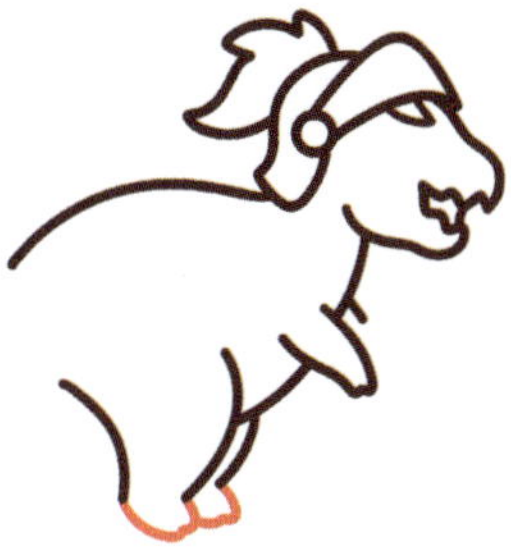

9. Draw U-shaped feet with two toes each.

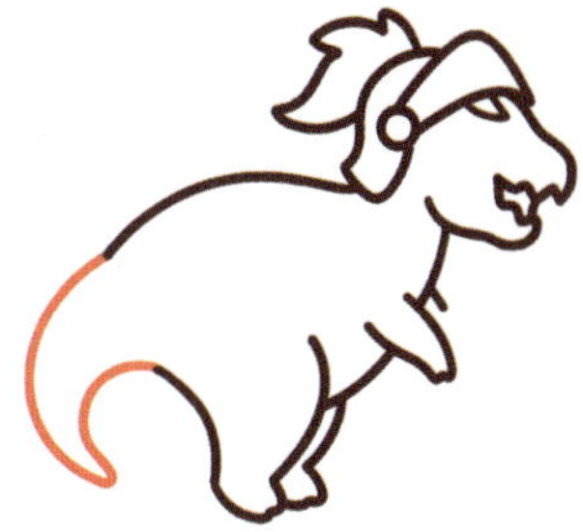

10. Add a curved tail that tapers at the end.

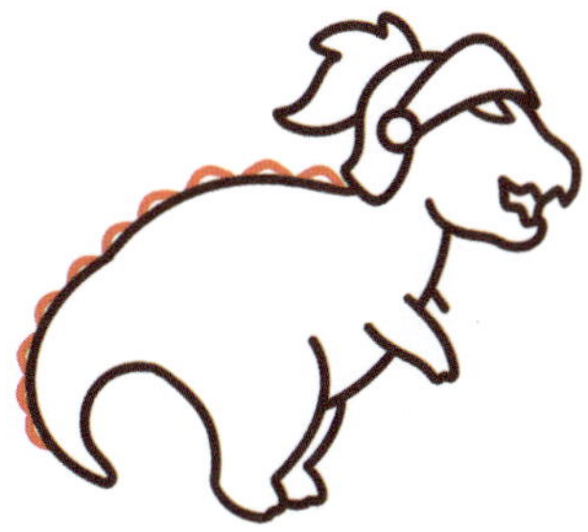

11. Draw curves along the spine and the tail.

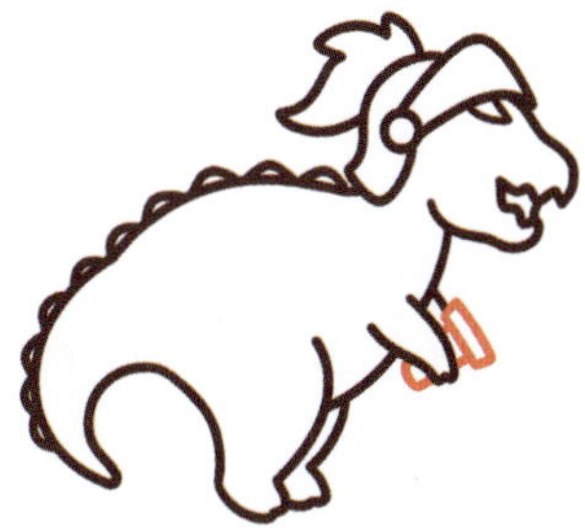

12. Draw the hilt of the sword with two rectangles.

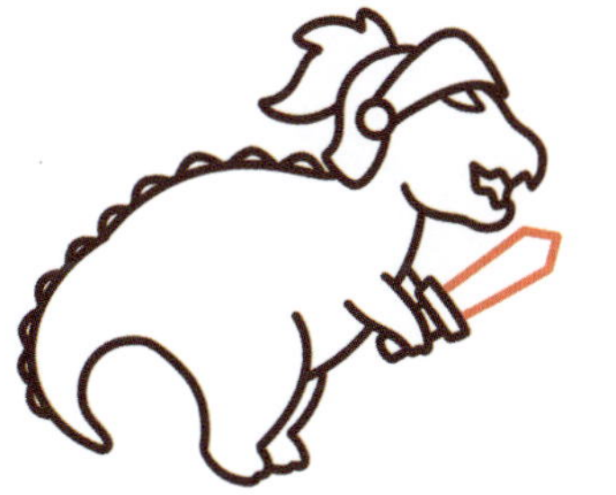

13. Add the blade with a rectangle with a pointed end.

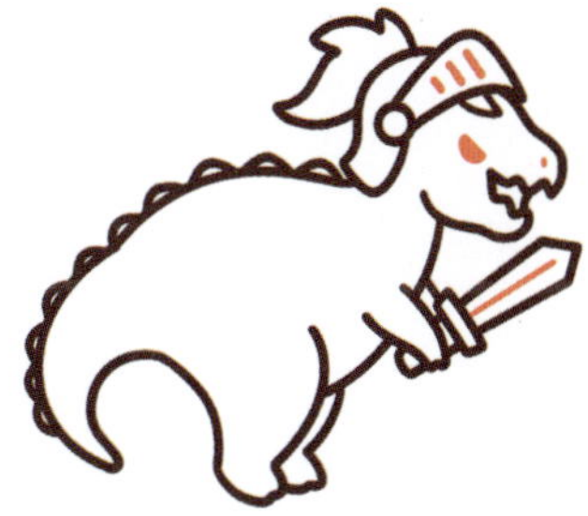

14. Add lines on the helmet visor and the blade. For the face, add a semicircle eye and a dash for the nostril.

DINO DIRECTORY

Here's a handy directory to find out which dinosaurs belong to the same order. It's organized by two orders and their suborders. Within the order of Saurischia is Theropoda (long-legged carnivores and birds) and Sauropodomorpha (long-necked herbivores).

SAURISCHIA

Theropoda

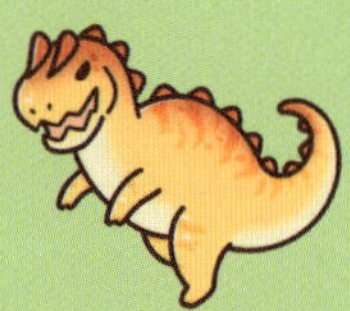
Allosaurus

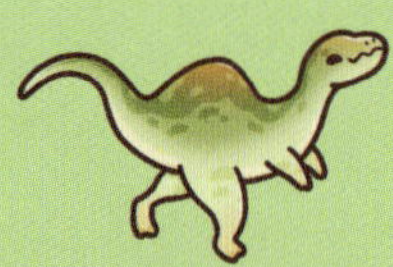
Altispinax

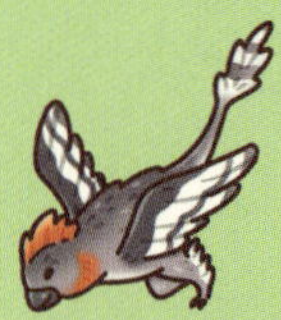
Anchiornis

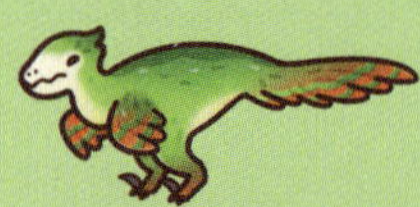
Atrociraptor

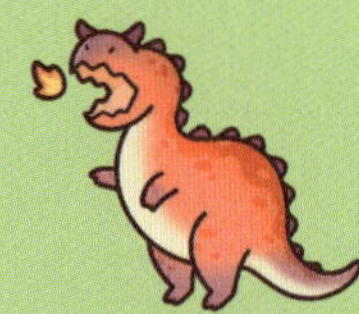
Carnotaurus

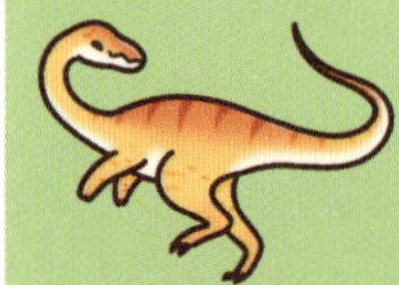
Coelophysis

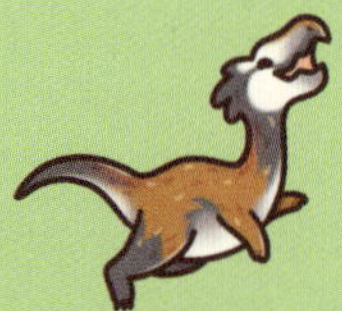
Compsognathus

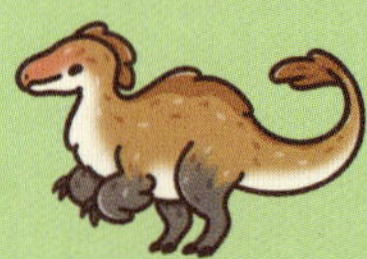
Deinocheirus

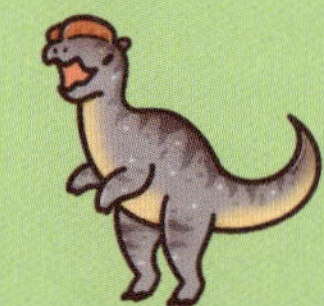
Dilophosaurus

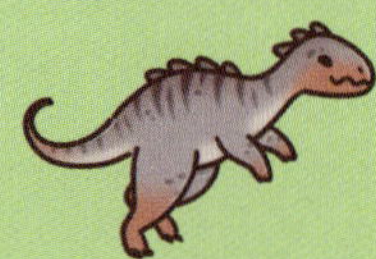
Eoraptor

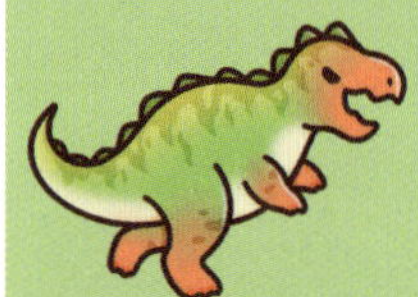
Giganotosaurus

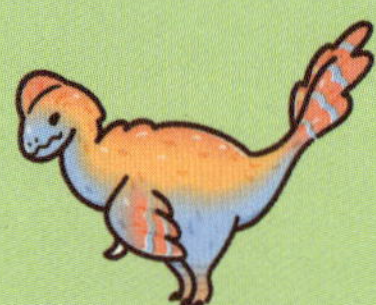
Gigantoraptor

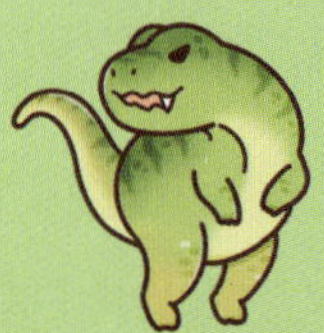
Megalosaurus

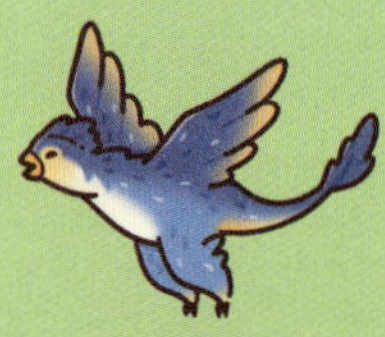
Microraptor

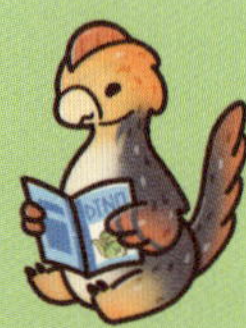
Oviraptor

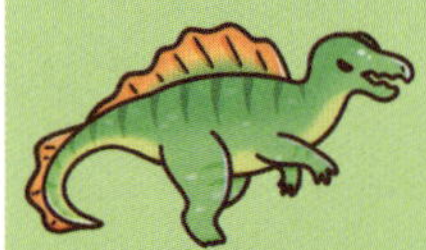
Spinosaurus

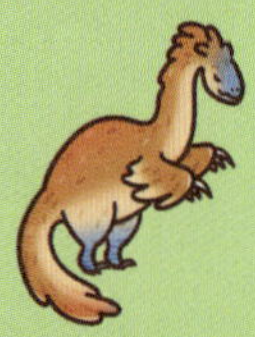
Therizinosaurus

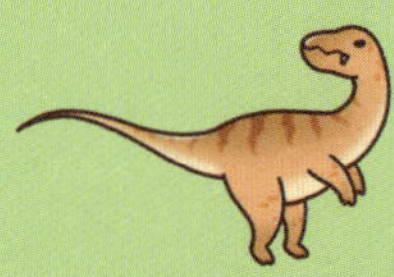
Troodon

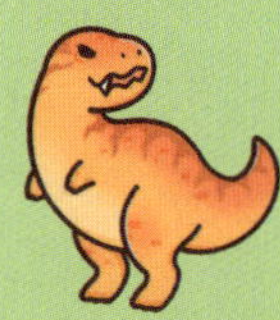
Tyrannosaurus

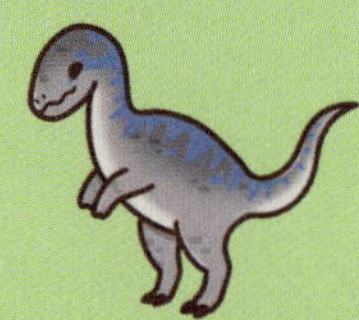
Velociraptor

Sauropodomorpha

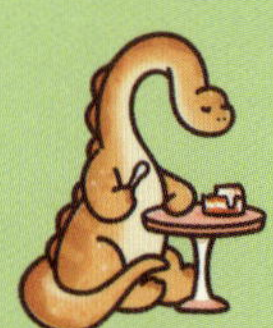
Apatosaurus

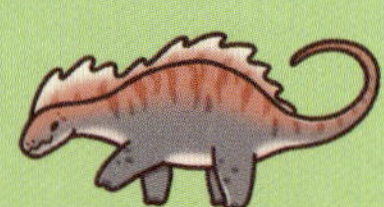
Amargasaurus

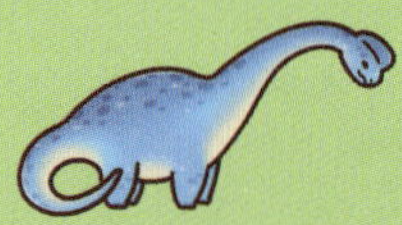
Brachiosaurus

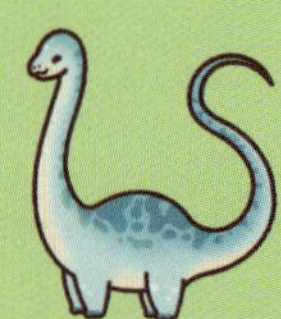
Diplodocus

Within the order of Ornithischia is Cerapoda (Iguanodon and duck-billed hadrosaurs), Thyreophorans (armored dinosaurs), Ceratopsia (horned dinosaurs), and Pachycephalosauria (bone-headed dinosaurs).

ORNITHISCHIA

Cerapoda

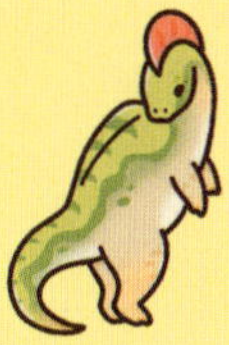
Corythosaurus

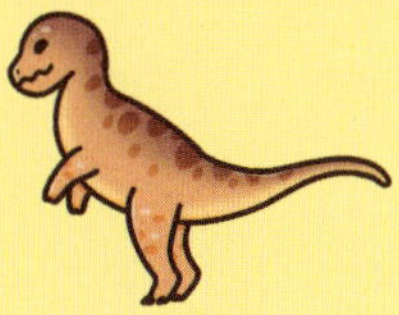
Enigmacursor

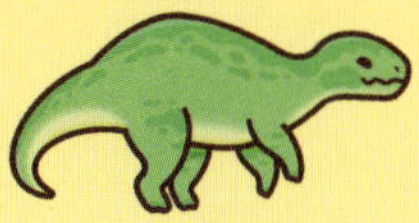
Fukuisaurus

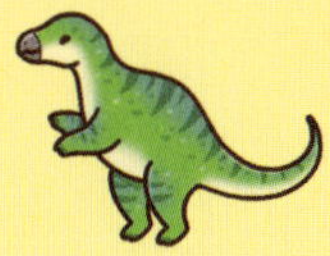
Iguanodon

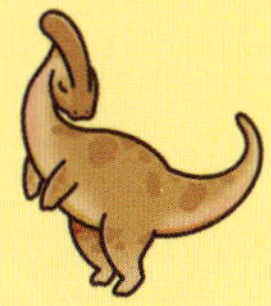
Parasaurolophus

Thyreophora

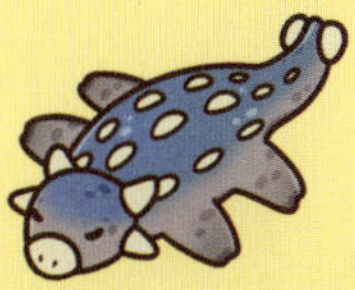
Ankylosaurus

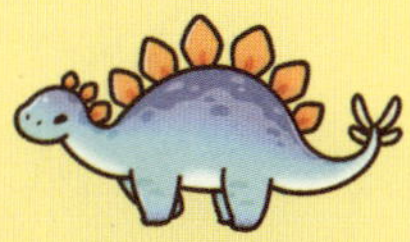
Stegosaurus

Ceratopsia

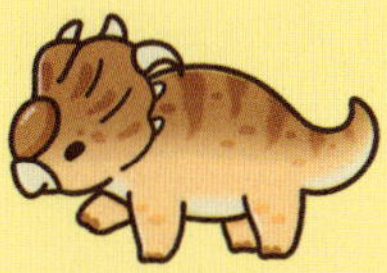
Pachyrhinosaurus

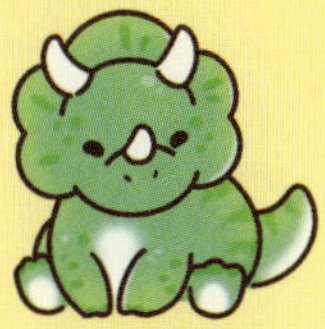
Triceratops

Pachycephalosauria

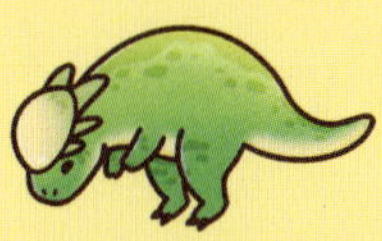
Pachycephalosaurus

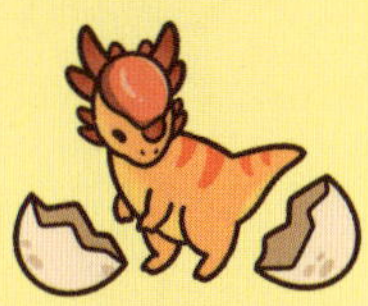
Stygimoloch

COLORING PAGES

Wait, there's more! Have fun coloring, adding patterns, decorating, or even accessorizing the dinosaurs on these pages. You can follow the color palette on pages 12-13 and pattern inspiration on page 10, or be original. It's up to you!

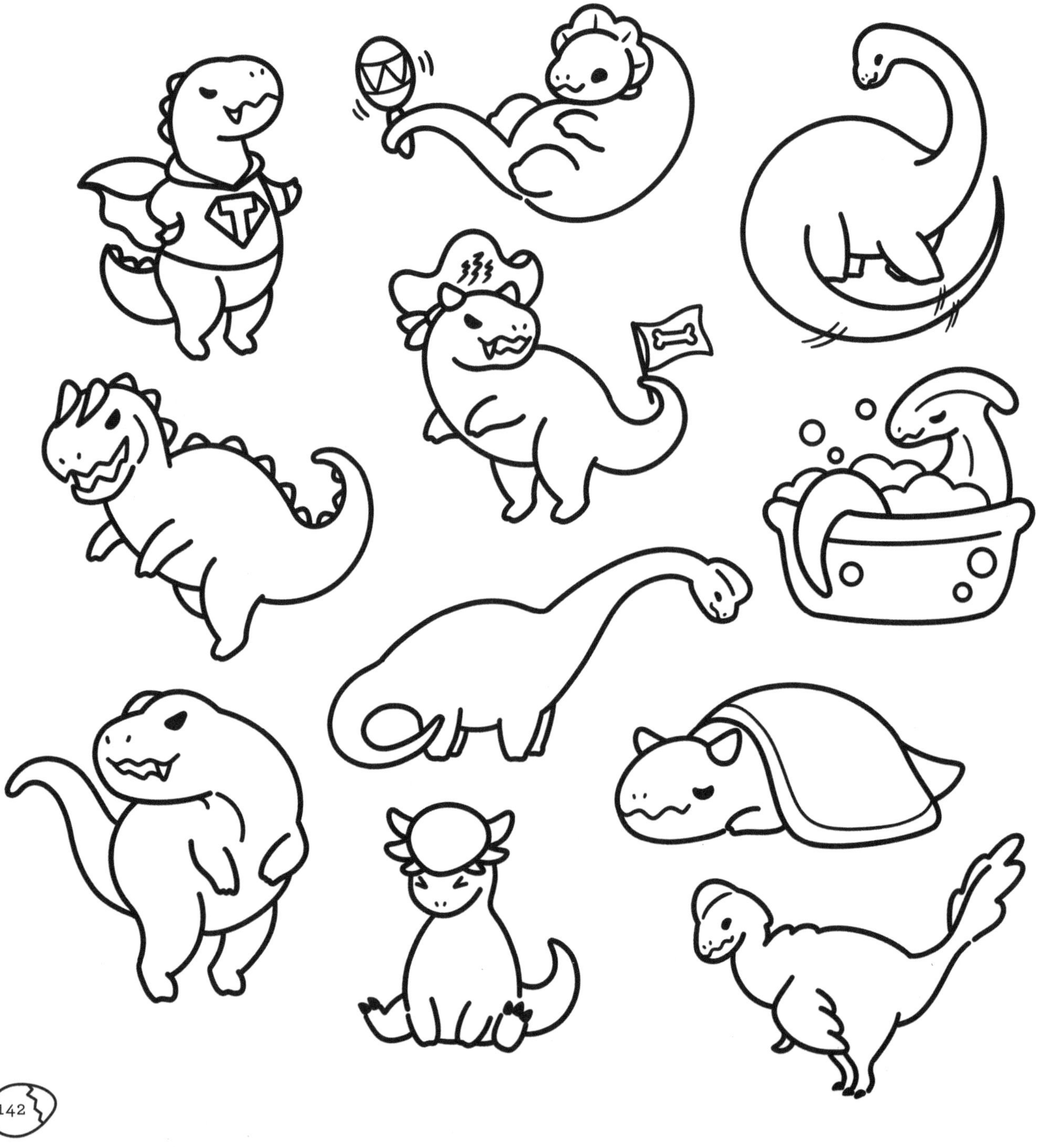

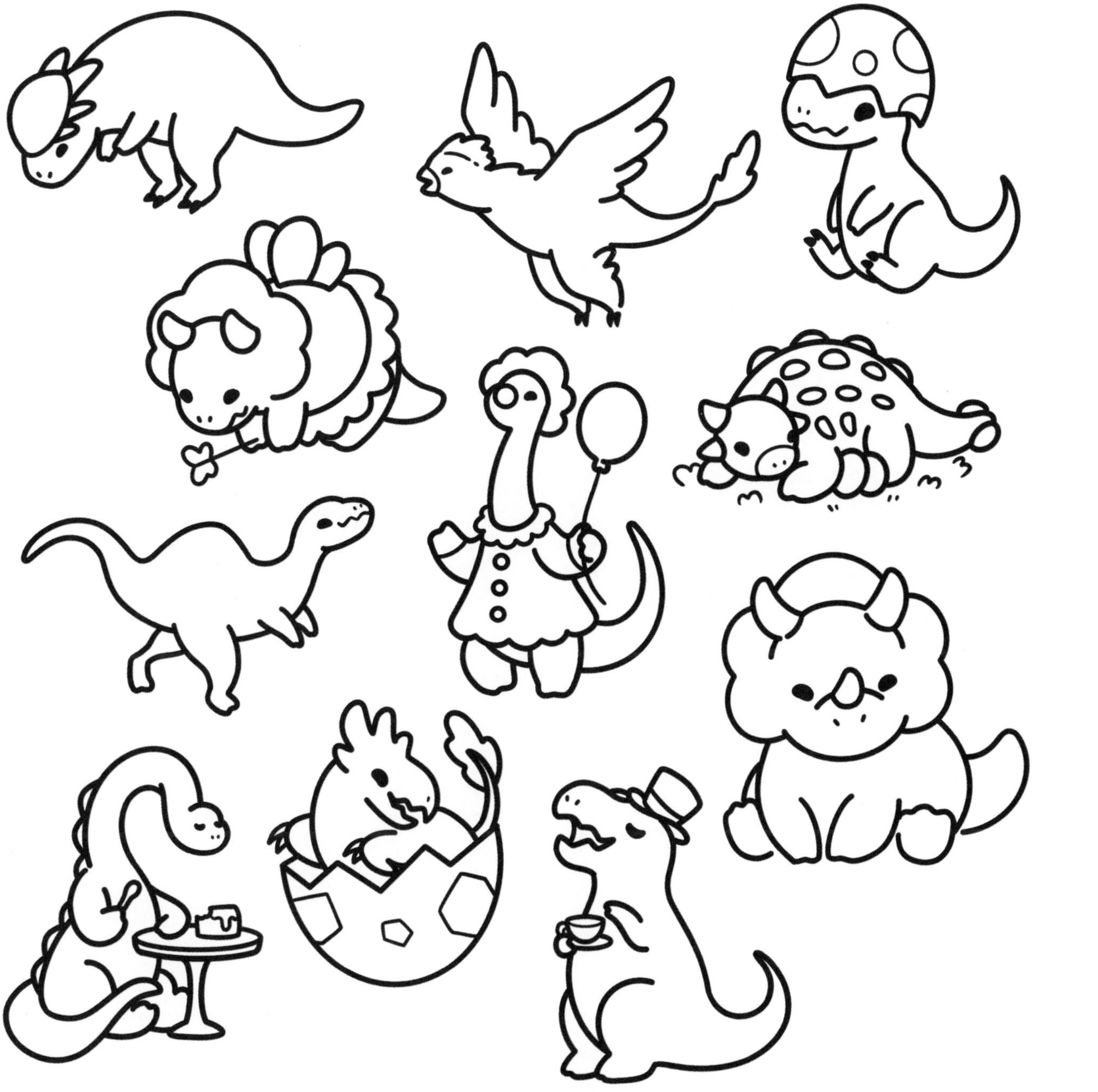

IF YOU ENJOYED KAWAII DINOS, CHECK OUT THESE OTHER LEARN-TO-DRAW BOOKS!

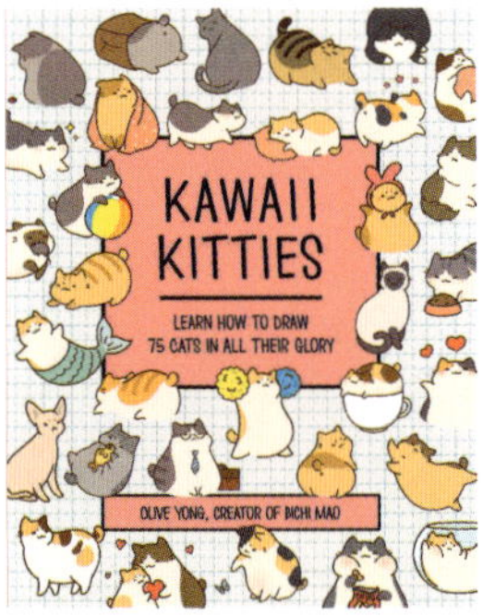

Kawaii Kitties
Learn How to Draw 75 Cats in All Their Glory
ISBN: 978-1-63106-739-6

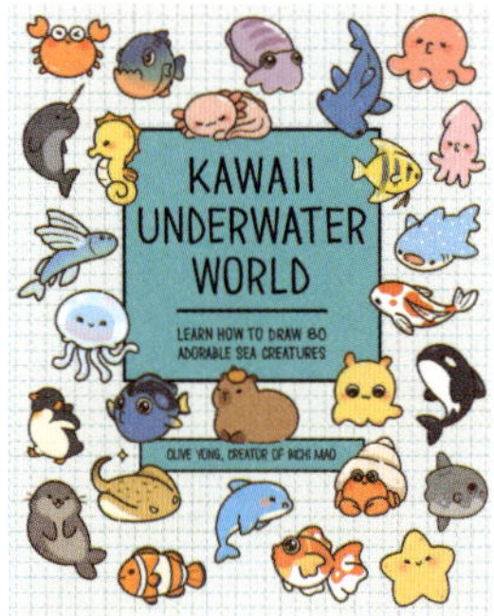

Kawaii Underwater World
Learn How to Draw Adorable Sea Creatures
ISBN: 978-1-57715-518-8

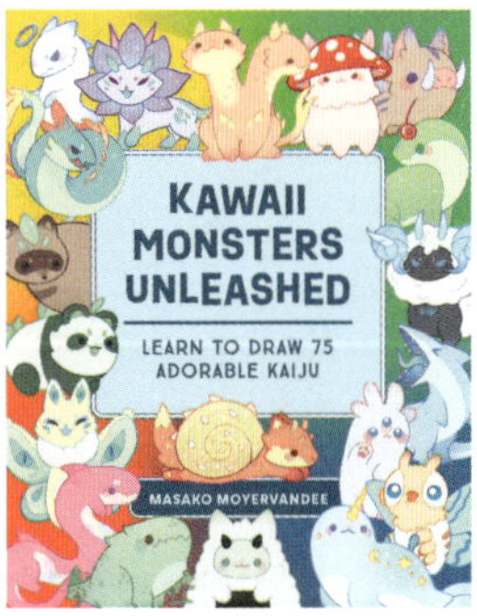

Kawaii Monsters Unleashed
Learn to Draw 75 Adorable Kaiju
ISBN: 978-1-57715-495-2

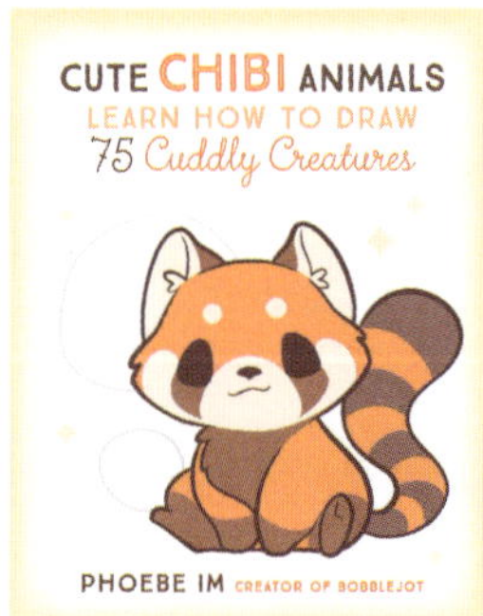

Cute Chibi Animals
Learn How to Draw 75 Cuddly Creatures
ISBN: 978-1-63106-729-7

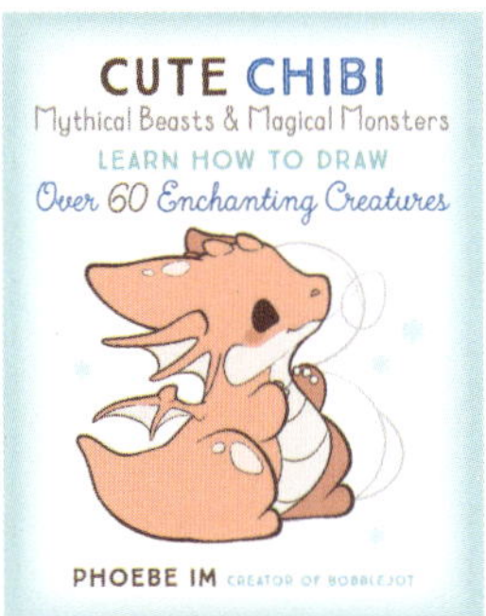

Cute Chibi Mythical Beasts & Magical Monsters
Learn How to Draw Over 60 Enchanting Creatures
ISBN: 978-1-63106-872-0

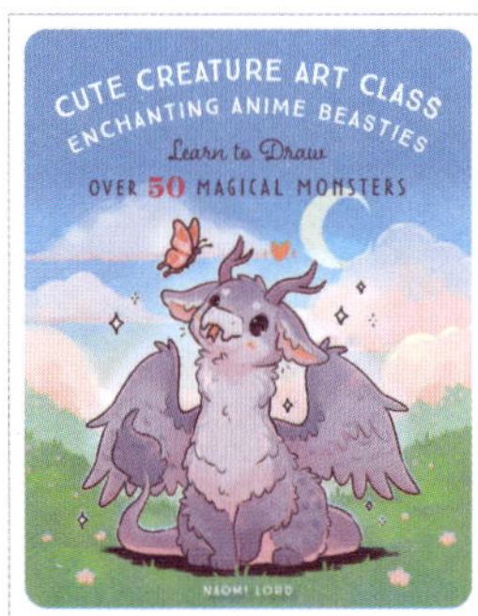

Cute Creature Art Class
Enchanting Anime Beasties—Learn to Draw over 50 Magical Monsters
ISBN: 978-1-63106-977-2